Europe's Contending Identities

Supranationalism, Ethnoregionalism, Religion, and New Nationalism

Edited by

ANDREW C. GOULD
University of Notre Dame

ANTHONY M. MESSINA
Trinity College

CAMBRIDGE
UNIVERSITY PRESS

CAMBRIDGE
UNIVERSITY PRESS

32 Avenue of the Americas, New York NY 10013-2473, USA

Cambridge University Press is part of the University of Cambridge.

It furthers the University's mission by disseminating knowledge in the pursuit of education, learning, and research at the highest international levels of excellence.

www.cambridge.org
Information on this title: www.cambridge.org/9781107036338

© Cambridge University Press 2014

First published 2014

Printed in the United States of America

A catalog record for this publication is available from the British Library.

Library of Congress Cataloging in Publication Data
Europe's Contending Identities: Supranationalism, Ethnoregionalism, Religion, and New Nationalism / edited by Andrew C. Gould, University of Notre Dame, South Bend, Indiana; Anthony M. Messina, Trinity College, Hartford, Connecticut.
    pages   cm
Includes bibliographical references and index.
ISBN 978-1-107-03633-8 (hardback)
1. Regionalism – European Union countries.   2. Nationalism – European Union countries.   3. Group identity – European Union countries.   4. Ethnicity – European Union countries.   5. Religious minorities – European Union countries.   6. National characteristics, European.   7. European Union countries – Economic integration – Social aspects.   8. European Union countries – Ethnic relations.   9. European Union countries – Religion.   I. Gould, Andrew, 1962– author, editor of compilation.   II. Messina, Anthony M.
JN34.5.E64   2014
320.54094–dc23   2013022247

ISBN 978-1-107-03633-8 Hardback

To my son, Caio, my wife, Isabel, and our Portuguese and American families abroad and at home.
Andrew C. Gould

To my extraordinary son, Michael, who is becoming increasingly sure of his identity.
Anthony M. Messina

Contents

Figures

Tables

Contributors

Marco Cinnirella is Senior Lecturer in Psychology at Royal Holloway, University of London, and obtained his Ph.D. in social psychology from the London School of Economics. His articles have appeared in *The Psychologist, European Journal of Social Psychology, British Journal of Medical Psychology, Ethnic and Racial Studies*, and *British Journal of Social Psychology*, among other journals. His recent research explores how a fear of terrorism may foster Islamophobia and, in addition, the interplay of multiple identities in the context of multicultural Britain, looking particularly at British Muslims of South Asian descent.

Jack Citrin is Professor of Political Science and Director of the Institute of Governmental Studies at the University of California at Berkeley. He is the author or coauthor of *The Politics of Disaffection among American and British Youth* (1969); *Tax Revolt* (1982, revised 1985); *California and the American Tax Revolt* (1984); and *How Race, Ethnicity, and Immigration Shape the California Electorate* (2002). Cambridge University Press will publish his next book, *American Identity and the Politics of Multiculturalism*. He is also the coeditor of *Public Opinion and Constitutional Controversies* (2008) and has published numerous articles and book chapters on trust in government, the initiative process in California, immigration and language politics, and the future of national identity in the United States and Europe.

Terri E. Givens is Associate Professor in the Government Department at the University of Texas at Austin. She is the author of *Voting Radical Right in Western Europe* (2005) and coeditor of *Immigration Policy and Security: U.S., European, and Commonwealth Perspectives* (2008) and *Immigrant Politics: Race and Representation in Western Europe* (2012). She has contributed articles to *Political Communication, Comparative Political Studies*, the *Journal of*

Common Market Studies, the *Policy Studies Journal*, *Comparative European Politics*, and other publications. She is currently working on a book on antidiscrimination policy and the politics of immigration in Europe.

Margarita Gómez-Reino is Professor of Political Science and Administration at the University of Santiago de Compostela, Spain. Her research primarily focuses on the comparative study of new political parties and movements in Europe and especially nationalist parties and parties of the new radical right, the Europeanization of political actors, and public attitudes toward the European Union. She is the author of *Ethnicity and Nationalism in Italian Politics: Inventing the Padania – Lega Nord and the Northern Question* (2002) and coeditor of the two-volume work, *Autonomist Parties in Europe: Identity Politics and the Revival of the Territorial Cleavage* (2006). Her most recent work deals with party-based Euroscepticism and party-voter links on European integration.

Andrew C. Gould is Associate Professor in the Department of Political Science at the University of Notre Dame. He is the author of *Origins of Liberal Dominance: State, Church, and Party in Nineteenth Century Europe* (1999) and coeditor of *The Rise of the Nazi Regime: Historical Reassessments* (1986). He has contributed articles to *West European Politics*, *Studies in Comparative International Development*, *Annual Review of Political Science*, and *The Review of Politics*. His current research project investigates the political regulation of religion in European states.

Saira Hamilton previously served as a Researcher in Psychology at Royal Holloway, University of London.

Asifa M. Hussain is Lecturer in Management and Deputy Director of the Durham Business School, Durham University, United Kingdom. She is the author of *Managing British Immigration Policy under the Conservative Government* (2001) and, with William L. Miller, *Multicultural Nationalism: Islamophobia, Anglophobia and Devolution* (2006). Among other journals, her articles have appeared in *International Journal of Small Business*, *International Journal of Public Sector Management*, *Defence and Security Analysis*, and *Policy Studies*.

Seth Kincaid Jolly is Assistant Professor in the Department of Political Science at the Maxwell School of Syracuse University. He has contributed three articles to *European Union Politics* and chapters to several edited volumes. His doctoral dissertation, "A Europe of Regions? Regional Integration, Sub-National Mobilization and the Optimal Size of States," won the European Union Studies Association's prize for the best dissertation in EU Studies in 2007.

Nicole Lindstrom is Lecturer in the Department of Politics at the University of York, United Kingdom. She is the coeditor of *Transnational Actors and Central* *and East European Transitions* (2008) and is completing a book that examines how domestic conflicts over European integration in new EU member-states are embedded within different post-socialist development paths. Her publications include contributions to the journals *Governance, Journal of Common Market Studies, East European Politics and Societies*, and *Journal of Peace Research*, as well several anthologies.

Bonnie M. Meguid is Associate Professor of Political Science at the University of Rochester. Her 2008 book, *Party Competition Between Unequals*, received the 2009 Riker Prize, awarded by the Political Economy Section of the American Political Science Association; the 2009 Best Book Award by the European Politics and Society Section of the APSA; and the 2010 Council for European Studies Best Book Award. She has published articles in *American Political Science Review* and *Electoral Studies*.

Anthony M. Messina, John R. Reitemeyer Professor of Politics at Trinity College in Connecticut, specializes in the politics of ethnicity and immigration in Europe. He is the author of *Race and Party Competition in Britain* (1989) and *The Logics and Politics of Post–World War II Migration to Western Europe* (2007) and is the editor or coeditor of *Ethnic and Racial Minorities in the Advanced Industrial Democracies* (1992), *West European Immigration and Immigrant Policy in the New Century* (2002), *The Migration Reader* (2006), and *The Year of the Euro: The Social and Political Import of Europe's Common Currency* (2006). His articles have appeared in numerous scholarly journals and anthologies.

William L. Miller is Professor Emeritus in the Department of Politics, University of Glasgow. He is the coauthor of *The Open Economy and Its Enemies: Public Attitudes in East Asia and Eastern Europe* (2006); *Multicultural Nationalism: Islamophobia, Anglophobia and Devolution* (2006); and *A Culture of Corruption? Coping with Government in Post Communist Europe* (2001) and the editor of *Anglo-Scottish Relations from 1900 to Devolution and Beyond – Proceedings of the British Academy 128* (2005). His interests in political behavior and public opinion in Eastern and Western Europe (including Britain) and East Asia have led him to contribute to numerous scholarly journals and anthologies.

Matthew Wright is Assistant Professor of Government at American University. Among other publications, he is the author or coauthor of articles in the *Canadian Journal of Political Science, Comparative Political Studies, Political Psychology, Perspectives on Politics, Political Research Quarterly, Psychological Science,* and *American Politics Research*.

Preface and Acknowledgments

Several lively conversations between the editors inspired the collaboration that eventually culminated in this volume. Although we initially approached the project from somewhat different intellectual starting points, we quickly became enthused about the possibility of working together to convene a group of distinguished scholars who would reflect upon and share their wisdom about the prospects for the emergence of a mass European identity against the backdrop of the persistence of ethnoregional, religious, and nationalist identities within the member-state countries of the European Union. For reasons upon which we elaborate in the Introduction, our impulse from the start was to privilege the role of politics in potentially impeding or facilitating the emergence of a robust European identity.

Other than the essay by Marco Cinnirella and Saira Hamilton, which originally appeared in the journal *Ethnic and Racial Studies* 30, 3 (2007), all of the volume's chapters were presented at a conference at the University of Notre Dame's London Center during October 17 and 18, 2008. In addition to the contributors to the book, the conference was enriched by the presence and participation of Mabel Berezin, Jytte Klausen, AbdoolKarim Vakil, Jonathan Laurence, and Juan Díez Medrano. We were especially pleased and honored to host Tariq Ramadan as the conference's keynote speaker. Thanks to the intellectual vitality of all the participants, the quality of intellectual exchange at the conference not only met but exceeded our very high expectations.

The dynamic nature of the issues raised in this volume was underscored from late 2009 forward – or approximately a year after our London conference – when several countries within the eurozone area found it impossible to refinance their sovereign debt without being rescued by third parties. This post-2009 turn of events appeared to pose a dilemma for our project: Was the festering crisis significantly eroding European political and social solidarity and thus making the question of a European identity – the central question of our volume – moot? As we note in the Introduction, the question is not moot; popular feelings of Europeanness and attachments to Europe have hitherto remained relatively steady even as Europe's governments impose austerity measures and disagree about how to move forward. Although the crisis has severely tested and continues to strain intermember-state and even intersocietal relations, there is still no empirical evidence that suggests that it has significantly or permanently reversed the established trend toward a dual mode of identification – national and European – among EU citizens. If anything, the relevance of European identity is increasing as national electorates and leaders wrestle with the challenges of whether and how to build new mechanisms and institutions to facilitate greater cross-border economic and political cooperation.

We are extremely grateful to the Nanovic Institute of European Studies for providing its generous financial and operational support for the London conference. Jim McAdams, the Institute's director, immediately embraced our proposal for the conference. Moreover, throughout the planning process he offered wise scholarly and practical advice and enthusiastically committed the Institute's necessary institutional resources. Monica Caro, Nanovic's assistant director of operations, and its associate director, Anthony Monta, drew upon their experience in planning and executing conferences in effecting a pleasant and rewarding experience for all. Greg Kucich, the London Center's director of undergraduate studies, was an especially gregarious and cooperative conference facility host. The Institute for Scholarship in the Liberal Arts at Notre Dame and the John R. Reitemeyer endowment at Trinity College generously provided the funds to create the book's index. Finally, we also wish to thank Lew Bateman of Cambridge University Press for his editorial guidance as well as two anonymous reviewers for their very helpful and insightful criticisms of the manuscript.

Introduction

Identifying with Europe?

Anthony M. Messina

The nations are not something eternal. They had their beginnings and they will end. A European confederation will probably replace them. But such is not the law of the century in which we are living.

(Renan 1882)

A united Europe is not far from becoming reality. A European identity that transcends the national identities of Europe's member states, however, is still a distant dream. But Europe's rapidly changing demographics cannot wait for this dream to come true. Identity is a crucial component of social cohesion, and the rapid influx of immigrants, mainly from the Muslim world, demands a choice: Should immigrants be encouraged to integrate into the national cultures and identities of the EU member states? Or should Europe instead pursue a multicultural model in which patriotism is discouraged in favor of a society divided by different identities, values, and historical narratives but united by abstract rights and duties under EU treatises and regulations? Is a third way available, a common European identity for all Europeans, old-timers and newcomers alike, that can transcend narrower communal loyalties to find a new common home?

(Ottolenghi 2005: 1)

More than 125 years have passed since the French intellectual Ernest Renan boldly predicted the demise of the traditional European nation-state and its displacement by a regional confederation. Although still in its infancy, European unification, in line with Renan's prediction, has irrefutably inched forward with the implementation of the Single European Act (1987) and the Treaty on European Union (1993). This said, neither of these seminal integration measures nor the subsequent Treaties of Amsterdam (1999), Nice (2003), and Lisbon (2010) has hitherto spawned a European state or a political community in the mold of the United States. Moreover, even if a European superstate were to emerge eventually, numerous detractors of the European Union (EU) insist that it would still lack the popular affect and legitimacy typically enjoyed by contemporary nation-states (Guibernau 2007; Shils 1997: 188–224; Smith 1991: 161; Smith 1995: 131). In their view, the EU's "legitimacy deficit" springs from the absence of a preexisting collective identity among its formal citizens. Lacking a "premodern past" or "prehistory" that could endow it "with emotional sustenance and historical depth" (Smith 1992: 62), the EU is thus likely to continue as an economic union and, to a lesser extent, a political confederation into the indefinite future, but *not* a political community founded on shared popular loyalties, norms, values, kinship, and/or or ethnic ties.

Whatever the merits of this critical perspective, two things are now evident. First, a few dissenters aside (Delanty 1995; Kantner 2006), integration scholars now concur that a vibrant European political community *must* be founded on some kind of mass European identity, although disagreement reigns about its precise nature (Cerutti 2003; Herrmann and Brewer 2004: 3; Kaina and Karolewski 2009; Karolewski 2010a; Laffan 1996: 83; Ottolenghi 2005; Petithomme 2008; van Hamm 2000; Weßels 2007). Castiglione (2009: 33), for example, argues that to the extent that "the European Union is or is becoming a political community … its stability and sustainability require that its members share some sense of being part of it." Menéndez-Alarcón (1995: 556) concurs, adding that the "EU will have to be rooted in a sense of common culture … and European affairs and symbols must acquire a positive importance in the lives of individuals." Gamberale (1997: 37) more specifically claims that a "common European identity is necessary to support a European citizenship."

Second, despite its obvious complexity (Caporaso and Kim 2009; Robyn 2005: 229) and ambiguities (Brubaker and Cooper 2000; Delanty and Rumford 2005: 50–1; Meinhof 2004), something approximating a European identity – although not necessarily one satisfying the high standards of the aforementioned critics – is in fact taking root among EU citizens (Bruter 2005; Green 2007; Scheuer 1999). According to Bruter, a "civic" European identity currently predominates over a "cultural" one, with the former founded on "the perception of belonging to the European Union as a relevant political system" (2005: 169). It is an identity grounded in a "civic community unified by common institutions, rules, and rights" (Bruter 2005: 168).

This said, much to the disappointment of European federalists, the propensity of EU citizens to identify exclusively with Europe has *not* increased over time, even within most of those countries with long-standing membership in the Community (Deutsch 2006); moreover, persons who primarily identify with their nation remain the great plurality (Díez Medrano 2008: 9). Nevertheless, as the public opinion data presented in this volume by Citrin and Wright demonstrate, there is a continuing, albeit an uneven, trend toward more EU citizens identifying both with their nation and with Europe. The question this trend raises for European federalists and Eurosceptics alike is whether a European identity *must* and/or *can* displace national identities in order to advance further the progress of European integration and political community. As Citrin and Wright astutely observe in Chapter 2, "what matters is whether and when these distinguishable identities are complementary or competitive, mutually reinforcing or exclusive in terms of their imperatives for behavior" (30).

EUROPEAN IDENTITY IN PERSPECTIVE

Assuming that a European identity remains a "work in progress" (Duchesne 2008: 402; Green 2007: 151; Group of Intellectuals for Intercultural Dialogue 2008: 6; Thiel 2012) and its emergence *is* vital for the prospects of European political community (Green 2007: 3; Hooghe and Marks 2004a), three questions logically follow. First, how well does the concept of identity travel beyond the borders of the traditional nation-state? Is it applicable to a supranational entity like the EU (Karolewski 2006; Lehning 2001)? Second, to what extent do EU citizens *need* to embrace a shared identity? What ultimately are the likely costs if a mass European identity does not evolve (Cerutti 2003: 30)? Finally, what are the major impediments to the emergence of a meaningful European political identity (Yiangou 2001)? Specifically, which ideational obstacles or competitors can potentially inhibit a critical number of EU citizens from embracing a European political identity?

In posing these questions, we broadly define *political identity* as a "set of social and political values and principles that we recognize as ours, or in the sharing of which we feel like 'us,' like a political group or entity" (Cerutti 2003: 27). Furthermore, it is an identity that has political consequences – that is, it inspires people "to imagine that a group deserves to enjoy substantial sovereignty … [or] ultimate decision-making authority" (Herrmann and Brewer 2004: 6).

A *European identity* can be defined as a set of values providing "shared meaning to most European citizens by making it possible for them to feel that they belong to a distinctive European culture and institutional system that appeals to them as legitimate and worthwhile" (Castells 2002: 3). Such an identity is "focused on the idea of Europe, but … can also be the basis of a personal identity" (Delanty 1995: 13).

Moreover, a *political community* can be said to exist when its members demonstrate an interest and ability to work together to resolve their mutual political problems (Easton 1965: 177). Such a community is more or less primary in that it represents "a condition in which specific groups and individuals show more loyalty to their central political institutions than to any other political authority, in a specific period of time and in a definable geographic space" (Haas 2004: 5).

Just as there is no single set of national identity values about which all or even a majority of nation-state citizens could ever agree, we do not presume that there is, should be, or could be a singular European identity. In this respect, we largely agree with Katzenstein and Checkel's perspective (2009: 213) that multiple European identities in various degrees of strength are currently in formation as well as Risse's view that these multiple identities can be and often are in tension (2010: 50–2). Nevertheless, we reject the presumptions that individual and/or collective political identities can be potentially infinite, are infinitely fluid, or can *necessarily* coexist simultaneously and harmoniously with others. In these respects, we mostly subscribe to the notion of political identity in the "strong" sense – that is, an identity that implies a robust notion of "group boundedness" (Brubaker and Cooper 2000: 10). Nevertheless, our idea of political identity also presumes that identities can and often do evolve across long-established legal and political communities. Indeed, if this were not so, there would be only but a remote probability of a mass European political identity ever emerging.

A Distinctive European Identity?

In his often-cited exegesis on nationalism, Anderson (2006: 6) characterizes nations as "imagined" because although their members will never become acquainted with most of their fellow members, all nevertheless embrace an identity founded on a common culture, history, language, and/or political traditions. He identifies them as "communities" because they are "always conceived as a deep, horizontal comradeship" (Anderson 2006: 7).

As measured against these standards, can Europe ever become an imagined community? Specifically, to what extent can a robust European identity evolve? Cerutti (2003: 30) skeptically poses the question of whether the concept of identity is appropriate to the EU thusly:

> How can something like identity, which is usually regarded as unitary and compact, fit the extremely composite European Union, an entity that is something more than a confederation, but is not on the way to becoming a federation, and in which governance is based on a continuously changing balance of vertical and/ or horizontal integration, while geopolitical borders as well as legal competences are not clearly and definitively defined?

For most European integration scholars, the answer Cerutti's query is self-evident: The traditional characteristics of political identity, forged as they are in the peculiar histories of nation-states and expressed by traditional varieties of nationalisms, *cannot* appropriately and/or *will not* be automatically transposed to the EU (Checkel and Katzenstein 2009: 24; Delanty and Rumford 2005; Karolewski 2006; Smith 1992: 75). Indeed, Duchesne (2008) is pessimistic that the concept of identity, as traditionally defined, makes sense in the context of contemporary citizen attitudes toward the EU. Menéndez-Alarcón (1995: 555) is similarly discouraging when he observes, "most people find it difficult to perceive of or to assume a European identity because there are not enough mirrors in everyday life to reflect that identity. It is [thus] easier to feel Spanish, French, German or Italian than European" Wintle (2005: 5) argues even more forcefully that "European identity, in the sense of feelings of 'Europeanness,' has existed widely for a very long time ... but such feelings are not the same as those which underpin national identity."

On the other side of the question, at least three schools of thought currently prevail among scholars who affirm that a European identity is a relevant concept, and they either explicitly or implicitly endorse it as a worthwhile goal. Constructivists, for example, generally believe that although a European identity can never be equivalent to nationalist identities, the former *could* eventually emerge as a consequence of the multiplication of intense, cross-European civic, cultural, and political exchanges (Fligstein 2008: 136). According to their view, distinctly European values and interests are inculcated through numerous personal, cross-national interactions (Fuss and Grosser 2006). As these interactions multiply, common cultural values inevitably emerge, consequently laying the foundation for a European identity. This said, in contrast to an affective national identity, a European identity is more likely than not to be "evaluational and reflective" (Kostakopoulou 2001: 36). Moreover, only under especially favorable, and thus unlikely, future circumstances will the ranks of exclusive Europe identifiers ever exceed the number of "situational Europeans" (Fligstein 2008: 140), or those who privilege their nation over Europe.

Communitarians, on the other hand, insist that any polity – including a European one – can endure only if it engenders a "thick identity," or one anchored in a shared culture and history (Scharpf 1999). For communitarians, cultural homogeneity is thus a necessary precondition for a European identity. They propose that a European identity can potentially emerge out of Europe's shared Roman political-legal tradition as well as its Christian, Greek, and Judaic cultural heritages (Smith 1991: 174). As Augenstein (2008: 1) optimistically opines, "In an era where functional integration has reached its limits, where a national ethos or a European demos is (still) unavailable, and a European public sphere of collective will-formation remains out of sight, the conjuration of a common Christian culture and traditions could ... (re)gain citizens' solidarity for the European project."

Finally, liberals and republicans see a European civic identity as potentially grounded in the values of democracy, human rights, and the rule of law as these values are exercised within the framework of a distinctively European communicative and political space (Follesdal 2002: 314; Guibernau 2007; Lehning 2001; Pinxten, Cornelis, and Rubinstein 2007). As expressed in article I-2 of the now defunct constitutional treaty, a commitment to democracy, human rights, and the rule of law is one that can facilitate intersocietal cohesion and, thus, a shared identity among EU citizens. Closely aligned with Habermas's (1995) concept of "constitutional patriotism," the liberal-republican view strenuously resists the notion that a European political identity needs to spring from a shared cultural identity. According to this perspective, it is neither realistic nor desirable to replicate the secular phenomenon of nation building on a European scale before the development of diffuse popular support for a constitutional regime at the EU level.

Is a European Identity Necessary?

Conceding for the moment that a European identity must inherently differ from a national identity, is the former nevertheless indispensable (Castiglione 2009: 36; Habermas 2007)? Simply put, is a mass European political identity critical to the success of the project of ever-closer union?

One affirmative response among some European integration scholars is that a mass European identity was largely unnecessary until the last few decades or so because the European project had not yet exceeded its "natural" history and/or territorial boundaries. Nevertheless, many now perceive that the increasing heterogeneity of the EU's population requires a heightened sense of community among Europeans and their collective embrace of a shared identity (Follesdal 2002). Specifically, because of the 2004 and 2007 enlargements and the effects of mass immigration, the contemporary EU has become exceedingly – and potentially problematically – diverse. In the first instance a politically liberal, Western-oriented, and nominally Catholic and Protestant but ultimately secular EU (Casanova 2004) is challenged to incorporate a critical number of predominantly orthodox Christian countries in Central and Eastern Europe with little or no recent experience of liberal democracy (Guibernau 2007: 99; Katzenstein and Checkel 2009: 213; Zielonka 2004: 31–2). In the second instance, the centrifugal societal pressures precipitated by third-world immigration and especially Muslim immigration (Laffan 1996: 88; Sides and Citrin 2007: 501) threaten to undermine the social cohesion necessary to propel the European integration project forward. In both instances, a European identity is purportedly necessary to avoid "fragmentation, chaos, and conflict" (Santer 1995).

A second affirmative response to the aforementioned question is that the emergence of a European political identity is vital because the project of ever-closer union has become increasingly ambitious (Karolewski 2006: 159) and "politicized" (van Hamm 2000: 8). Specifically, a European identity is necessary to facilitate the ever-increasing reach of European policy making (Karolewski 2006: 172). As Kaina and Karolewski (2009: 6) characterize the nature of the dilemma:

> The people's cognitive and emotional detachment from the EC/EU was hardly a severe problem as long as the so-called permissive consensus ... allowed the national and European elites to push the European unification on. However ... as the European community has enlarged and the integration process has reached a deeper level, the progress in European unification is increasingly susceptible to swings in public mood. The growing relevance of public opinion becomes dramatically apparent by the fact that numerous EU projects have been rejected by popular vote: the Maastricht Treaty in Denmark (1992), the accession of Norway (1972, 1994), the Nice Treaty in Ireland (2001), the introduction of the euro in Sweden (2003), the European Constitutional Treaty in France and the Netherlands (2005) and recently the Lisbon Treaty in Ireland (2008).

In largely endorsing this perspective, Kantner (2006: 4) argues that in order to realize "grand collective projects in ethically sensitive policy fields, a political community needs not only rational agreement, but also ... strong public support.... Without a 'collective identity' beyond the borders of the national communities as a common ground for common future projects, European efforts to institutionalize common political solutions, procedures, and sometimes very expensive commitments might fail." In sum, as the EU increasingly transcends its functionalist origins and its predominantly economic policy domains, it must instill within its citizens a sense of mystique (Delanty 1995: 8; van Hamm 2000: 8).

A third argument favoring a European identity speaks to its role in facilitating the EU's transition to a true political community. Along these lines, Cerutti (2003: 36) observes, "in the general theory of politics, identity is a precondition, or rather metacondition, for legitimizing a polity or a regime." According to Laffan (1996: 82), "the politics of identity have enormous salience ... for the European Union at this juncture in its development because the Union is moving from issues of instrumental problem-solving to fundamental questions about its nature as a part-formed polity." In Wallace's view (1990: 55), the very foundations of political integration are "a matter of identity and loyalty: of the emergence of a political community based upon shared values and mutual trust out of previously separate and mistrustful groups.... There is no simple or inexorable transition from contact through trade to the emergence of political community."

Related to this view is Risse's (2010: 178–9) argument that apart from lending legitimacy to the EU, a European identity matters for two practical reasons. First, it matters with regard to addressing and resolving issues concerning which policy areas should be within the jurisdiction of the EU – that is, whether a particular issue should fall within the domain of either national or supranational decision making. Second, a European identity influences the questions of citizenship and immigration or, more specifically, who *can* and *should* belong to the political community.

A fourth affirmative response is that a mass European identity is necessary to insulate European citizens from the contagion of Euroscepticism. Here the emphasis is not so much on the positive returns of a mass European identity but, rather, on how it circumscribes negative outcomes. Weßels's analysis of the public opinion record, for example, reveals that identifying with Europe acts as "a strong buffer against Euroscepticism, strongest at the level of higher generalization of attitudes (generalized support for the regime and the authorities) but not as effective against specific skepticism about the authorities" (2007: 303–4). Hooghe and Marks (2007) similarly find that the phenomenon of Euroscepticism is most corrosive to European unity when it is reinforced by a lack of European identity.

Finally, several scholars see a robust European identity as an antidote to the current apathy of the general public toward Europe and, in particular, to combating economic utilitarianism among EU citizens. As Kaina and Karolewski (2009: 6) observe, "this utilitarian kind of support is unstable inasmuch as the attitudes towards the European Union and the integration process rest on short-termed instrumental evaluations rather than on normatively embedded convictions." Although sometimes linked to Euroscepticism, utilitarianism among EU citizens is not necessarily seen as corrosive to European unity. Nevertheless, to the extent that it influences mass attitudes toward the EU and particularly the project of closer European integration, it makes both extremely vulnerable to the vicissitudes of contemporary economic and political events.

Impediments to a European Political Identity?

As the respective essays by Citrin and Wright, Messina, and Miller and Hussain in this volume underscore, individuals are disposed to embrace multiple political and social identities, or a shared representation of a collective self (Herrmann and Brewer 2004; Turner et al. 1987). Thus, most persons can and often do comfortably and simultaneously view themselves as members of several political communities (i.e., national, regional, local, and/or supranational) (Bruter 2005: 116; Díez Medrano 2003; Green 2007: 25; Smith 1991: 175). Indeed, if this were not so, it would be extremely difficult for either a new national or a supranational identity ever to become embedded within a given population. Consequently, most although not all (Carey 2002) European integration scholars have concluded that the respective relationships between European and national and regional identities are *not* zero sum (Castano 2004; Duchesne and Frognier 1995: 202; Duchesne and Frognier 2008; Green 2007: 25); that is, these relationships are "concordant" not "conflicting" (Deutsch 2006: 166). In this vein, Citrin and Sides (2004b: 175) persuasively characterize European identity as "supplementing" national identity; it is not dominated by national identity but rather it exists and is established alongside it. Delanty and Rumford (2005: 54) further suggest, "to varying degrees, all national identities in Europe contain elements of a European identity, which is not an identity that exists beyond or outside national identities."

This said, a nascent European identity *could* conflict with long-established national and/or regional identities in some circumstances (Hewstone 1986; Risse 2010: 10). If Anderson (2006) is correct about the way that nations are popularly imagined and in particular in the manner in which they are perceived as political, limited, and sovereign, we could reasonably anticipate that popular feelings of belonging to Europe will perhaps increasingly conflict with national attachments as the EU's policy competence within the realms of culture and politics expands (Duchesne 2008: 405). As Karolewski (2010b: 64) insightfully notes, a more conflicted relationship between national, European, and regional identities could evolve in those cases when especially conflictual and salient issues come to the fore or instances in which "the primary or core identity is activated, since individuals tend to reduce the cognitive complexity of social reality." In these circumstances, whether the solutions to the public policy challenges immediately confronting the EU recommend further deepening or, conversely, suspending or unwinding the process of European integration is likely to depend upon the extent to which a critical number of Europeans conclude that "a European politics will provide better solutions to their political concerns than the national politics that currently exists" (Fligstein 2008: 252). The latter, in turn, is likely to be strongly influenced by the extent to which they identify with Europe and perceive themselves as European.

Even short of this kind and degree of direct competition between national and European attachments, several contemporary developments raise doubts about the prospects of a European political community and the potential breadth and depth of its popular foundations. First, the metamorphosis of old and the expanding appeal of new varieties of nationalisms are powerful reminders of the lure of mass political ideologies founded on the premise of a "culturally bounded home" (Taras 2009: 227) or a "seamless, organic cultural unit" that objectively is better provided by traditional national polities than a supranational one (Smith 1992: 56). In this context, numerous nationalist and xenophobic political parties have surfaced not only within the former communist countries of Central and Eastern Europe (Kasekamp 2003; Mudde 2005) in recent years but also within the long-established democracies of Western Europe (Berezin 2009; Mudde 2000; Schain, Zolberg, and Hossay 2002). The ubiquitous and, often, the electoral vitality of these illiberal parties provides abundant evidence of the resilience of nationalism at a juncture in European history when the foundations of the traditional nation-state are purported to be crumbling (Jenkins and Sofos 1996). Despite the undeniable progress of European economic and political integration in recent decades, "the national idea seems to be as powerful and inexplicable today as it was to Lenin at the outbreak of the Great War in 1914" (Laitin 2003: 227–8).

Second, the possible unbundling of a critical number of contemporary European nation-states into "ethnic" or "micro" states (De Winter, Gómez-Reino, and Lynch 2006a) vividly underscores the fragility of a European integration project founded on the premise its member-state countries will incrementally dissolve into a "transnational polity ... which will, in the end, take over all of their essential functions" (Laffan, O'Donnell, and Smith 2000: 15). As Hoppe (2007: 68) points out, although most contemporary ethnoregionalists "see the future of their nations firmly placed within the EU," they do so "either as an independent state or as an autonomous political unit." As the essay in this volume by Gómez-Reino observes, although broadly pro-EU, empirical analyses of regionalist political party manifestoes reveal this party family to be only the fourth-most pro-European party family. In short, whatever the respective political futures of Brittany, Catalonia, Flanders, Padania, Scotland, and other imagined regional communities across Europe, it is improbable that the ethnoregionalists who currently insist that the aforementioned regions be liberated from the shackles of the nation-state will soon embrace a

European polity to which their ethnic "homeland" unit is administratively and politically subordinate (Elias 2008; Laible 2000: 240).

Finally, the expanding number of non-Christian, religious ethnics within the EU, a trend fueled by the post–World War II influx of millions of Muslim immigrants, could potentially impede the emergence of a mass European identity that, in turn, would foster a European citizenship (Gamberale 1997) and political community (Katzenstein 2006: 13). As seen in the following essays by Messina and Cinnirella and Hamilton, it is not that Europe's new ethnic and racial minorities are particularly averse to embracing a European identity – although this eventual outcome cannot be summarily dismissed – but rather because mass immigrant settlement and the dissolution of national borders may be inhibiting many so-called native EU citizens from further embracing Europe. Specifically, domestic conditions of "super diversity" (Goodhart 2004; Vertovec 2007) are currently fueling a nativist backlash that, in turn, may be suppressing popular support for European integration and offering succor to anti-European political actors (Castiglione 2009: 37).

European Identity in a Climate of an Economic and a National Welfare Crisis

As Lindstrom emphasizes in her essay in Part IV of this volume, one of Europe's defining historical features has been its comprehensive social support system, often referred to as the European welfare state or European Social Model (ESM). Indeed, the state's cradle-to-grave commitment to the social welfare of its citizens has contributed to a shared European political culture, particularly among many of the so-called Euro 15 member-state countries. Demertzis (2008: 125) has gone so far as to suggest that the ESM is largely a political construct that has been "promoted by the EU institutions (mainly the Commission and the Council) trying to define a European supranational social policy."

Against this backdrop, it is pertinent ask if the emergence of a robust European political identity remains relevant in the context of the lingering financial and economic crisis within the EU. Has the festering crisis significantly eroded European political and social solidarity, thus making this question moot (Fligstein, Polyakova, and Sandholtz 2012: 120)? In circumscribing the ability of the EU's member countries to meet their traditional welfare state obligations, is the crisis also undermining popular identification with Europe?

Somewhat surprisingly, popular feelings of Europeanness have remained relatively steady during the crisis. Although those EU citizens who see themselves as exclusively "nationals" increased from 42 percent to 46 percent, those who primarily identify with Europe declined only slightly from 12 percent to 10 percent between 2007 and 2010 (Figure 1.1). When asked whether they feel that they are a "citizen of the European Union," 62 percent of respondents

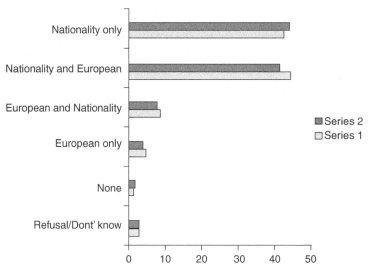

FIGURE 1.1. Percentage of persons who self-identify as national and European, 2007–10. Series 1: 2007; Series 2: 2010.
Sources: Eurobarometers 2008 and 2010.

answered affirmatively in 2010. When asked about the importance of being European, 58 percent of respondents offered that it "mattered" to them, the same percentage as in 2009 (Eurobarometer 2011b: 99).

To be sure, the rise in the number of self-declared "nationalists" during the crisis is hardly a positive development for the torchbearers for an ever-closer European Union. Nevertheless, the pertinent fact is that even in the midst of economic crisis, there were still fewer "nationalists" in 2010 (87 percent) than when the euro was formally launched as a common currency in 1999 (91 percent).

Moreover, when we rank order the ten member-state countries for which we have complete data by how badly the economic crisis has affected them, as measured by the variable of "lost economic time," and juxtapose this order against national trends in the public's attachment to and image of the EU from 2007 to 2010, three things are evident (Table 1.1). First, the public of the countries especially hard hit by the crisis (Greece, Portugal, Latvia, and Ireland) *did not* become less attached to the EU; indeed, a higher percentage of their respective nationals were *more* attached to the EU in 2010 than in 2007. Second, there is a weak association between the depth of a country's economic slump and trends in popular attachment to the EU. For example, despite experiencing one of the least-afflicted national economies, French citizens were paradoxically the only Europeans who became less attached to the EU between 2007 and 2010.

TABLE 1.1. *Economic Time and Popular Image of/and Attachment to EU*

Member State	Approximate Economic Time in 2012*	Change in Image of EU, 2011–07 (%)	Change in Attachment toward EU, 2010–07 (%)
Greece	1999	−29	8
Portugal	2002	−30	2
Latvia	2002	−15	4
Ireland	2002	−32	4
Spain	2004	−32	8
Hungary	2004	−7	8
UK	2004	−11	2
Italy	2005	−11	16
France	2006	−21	−2
Germany	2009	−19	3

* Employs seven indicators of economic health that are composed of three broad categories: (1) household wealth and its main components, financial-asset prices, and property prices; (2) measures of annual output and private consumption; and (3) real wages and unemployment. An average of how much time has been lost in each of these categories produces the overall measure.

Sources: *Economist* 2012: 83. Eurobarometer 2008: annex; and Eurobarometer 2011b; and Eurobarometer 2011c: 49.

Finally, a sharp downturn in the public's image of the EU – an obvious product of the current economic crisis – is not exclusive to those countries whose economic performances rank amongst the worst. On this score, the public's image of the EU has slumped less in Hungary, Latvia, the United Kingdom, and Italy than in France and Germany, despite the comparatively better economic performance of the latter two countries. This said, the EU's image among the public in the four countries that have been hardest hit or pushed back in economic time the farthest (Greece, Portugal, Latvia, and Ireland) did slump most: 27 percent on average versus 17 percent in the other six countries that have suffered less. The public in the four hardest-hit countries also showed a more modest change in their attachment to the EU, just a 4.5-percentage-point gain on average against a 5.8- percentage-point gain in the remaining six countries.

VARIABLES THAT CANNOT UNDERGIRD A EUROPEAN IDENTITY

Before proceeding to the essays, we wish to identify the variables upon which a robust European political identity – if it ever emerges – is *unlikely* to be anchored, irrespective of when the EU's current economic crisis is resolved. The purpose of this brush-clearing exercise is to facilitate a fuller and more productive discussion of the future prospects for European political community and a European political identity in the concluding chapter of the volume.

Shared Understanding of European Political History

Despite the persistence of the European Commission and other EU institutions in embedding the project of ever-closer union within an official narrative that emphasizes its deep historical roots and, hence, the inevitability of European unity (Shore 2000: 40–65), the history of Europe in fact has been too divergent and riddled by too many conflicts to serve as the foundation of a mass European identity (Guibernau 2011: 32; Risse 2010: 86). As Delanty (1995: 7) observes, "Europe has tended to be a divisive phenomenon; it is not inherently connected with peace and unity. It has been a fact of European history that every attempt made to unite the continent occurred after a period of major division." Habermas (2007: 81) similarly argues, "the divisive force of divergent national histories and historical experiences that traverse European territory like geographic fault lines remains potent." In sum, the history of Europe, like that of the EU and European identity (Bańkowski and Christodoulidis 1998), has been and continues to be politically and socially contested. It thus offers little guidance about who are "we," and perhaps just as if not more importantly, who are "the others" (Castiglione 2009: 36).

A Common Culture

If a shared history cannot usefully serve, what are the prospects of a European political identity grounded in a shared European culture and, specifically, a common language, religion, and/or ethnicity?

Language. As Citrin and Wright usefully point out in their essay, speaking a country's dominant language is commonly cited as an important feature of national identity and a key to, if not the foundation of, a majority group's culture. If so, what role might language play in the evolution of a mass European identity?

Unfortunately, for supranationalists, there is no European *lingua franca* or common linguistic experience (Shore 2000: 229) that could potentially anchor a mass European identity. The EU, which currently excludes Norway, Switzerland, and many East European countries, recognized twenty-four official languages in 2012, a number that will only grow further as the EU continues to enlarge. Moreover, hyperdiversity not only characterizes the EU's official languages, it is also reflected in the numerous regional and minority languages spoken by numerous fragments of its population (Barni and Extra 2008): More than sixty indigenous regional or minority language communities currently exist within the EU. Perhaps even more problematically for the cause of linguistic unity, several of Europe's linguistic minorities are currently lobbying to have their languages officially recognized. Among the more aggressive of these groups are Catalans, "on the grounds that they alone make up nearly 10 million Europeans, practically twice as many as the Danes and Finns, four times more than the Slovenes and 25 times more than the Maltese" (Archibugi 2009: 1). The Basques and the Corsicans are making similar demands. In an agreement signed in 2009 with the European Court of Justice, EU's highest court, the Spanish government secured the right for its citizens to use any one of the country's official languages (Catalan, valenciano, Basque, or gallego) in representations to the Court.

In addition to the aforementioned official and regional languages, immigrant communities have introduced numerous extra-European languages into the EU, hundreds of which are now spoken in Berlin, Brussels, London, Paris, and other "global" European cities that are magnets for immigrants (Sassen 2001); among these, Arabic and Turkish are the predominant languages of the EU's post–World War II immigrant communities. To the chagrin of many persons within these communities, the right of immigrants to maintain their native language has not been recognized in any of the affected member-state countries; although some measures have been adopted, none has been systematic. Measures for protecting immigrant minorities' languages are often implemented through bilateral agreements with the countries of origin – that is, through relationships among states. As a result, immigrant minorities' languages have not been considered part of the cultural and linguistic heritage of the receiving country. Moreover, immigrant languages are excluded from the protection that the EU and the Council of Europe grant to "regional and minority languages."

Perhaps even more problematically for the prospects of European political community and identity, only half of all EU citizens report they can speak a foreign language (European Commission 2006). English (34%) is the most popular foreign language in sixteen member-state countries and the one most often used by Europeans to communicate across national borders, with a super majority (68%) identifying it as the most useful language to know. Although most EU documents are drafted in English, French, German, and the language pertinent to the issue at hand, English overtook French during the 1990s as the language in which most European Commission texts are initially drafted.

However, while there is evidence that the acceleration of economic and political integration will foster the greater use of English across the EU and public acceptance of Anglo-Saxon culture, these outcomes are *not* goals to which the EU officially aspires (Group of Intellectuals for Intercultural Dialogue 2008). Moreover, although language diversity is considered a key feature of Europe's identity and "promoting language learning and pluralism belongs to the main activities of European institutions in the domain of language policies ... the EU does not have even the beginnings of a common language policy" (Extra and Gorter 2008: 38).

Religion. Apropos of Laitin's (2002: 77) observation that a EU-wide consensus exists "in support of a secular Christianity, a respect for national churches that do not meddle in political life, and a recognition as well of minority religious groups as long as the religious expression of these groups is contained within that community," it is highly improbable that a European political identity could be even partly based on religiosity or a shared set of formal religious beliefs. In contrast to Americans, most Europeans generally avoid public expressions of religiosity (Berger, Davie, and Fokas 2008: 130). With less than a quarter of the population in ten member-state countries on average attending religious services on a weekly basis, official church attendance is extremely low across the European Union: Three quarters of Maltese and two thirds of Poles go to church once a week, while more than 60 percent of Czechs report that they never attend religious services (*Economist* 2010). Indeed, Europeans are deeply divided on spiritual matters and, specifically, on the belief in a supreme being (European Commission 2005: 9). Moreover, the formal constitutions of most EU member-state countries are not grounded on religious principles. Most significantly, there is no singular model of relations between the state and formal religion within the EU, as heterogeneity rather than homogeneity prevails among the member-state countries (Madeley 2009).

If anything, the recent politicization of religion at the national and European levels, a development precipitated by the 2004 and 2007 enlargements and the increasing political claims by the EU's large Muslim population (approximately twenty million) for public accommodation of Islamic civil and religious practices (Risse 2010: 204–25), has only further diminished the prospect that religion could ever play a central role in facilitating the emergence of a European identity. As Katzenstein (2006: 1) observes, these trends have interjected into European political and social discourse a subject that many had long assumed to be peripheral – the role of religion in European integration and community:

> Europe, arguably the most secular part of the world, is increasingly forced to grapple with religious issues .... Focusing exclusively on the Europeanization of secular politics – of who gets what, when, and how – misses two central aspects of European politics. First ... European identity has remained largely untouched by legal and cultural processes of Europeanization, leaving the core of the emerging European polity hollow. Second, as Europe enlarges, transnational religious communities ... run up against the secular European polity.

Both of the aforementioned trends have divisively injected religiosity (i.e., Catholicism, Eastern Orthodoxy, Protestantism, and Islam) into public debates about the core values that are inherently European and, thus, compatible with the project of ever-closer union. As Figure 1.2 indicates, European Muslims are much more inclined than other Europeans to report that religion is important to their daily life and that most faiths make a positive contribution to society (Gallup 2009: 16). The increase in religiosity in a previously much more secular Europe and the religious hyper pluralism that post–WWII mass immigration has infused into contemporary Europe are indeed two of the most contested aspects of Europe's contemporary diversity.

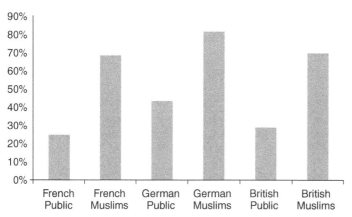

FIGURE 1.2. Role of religion is an important part of daily life, 2008.
Source: Gallup 2009: 16.

Ethnicity. There is little doubt that ethnic diversity has significantly increased within Europe since World War II. Indeed, every EU member-state is home to several or more so-called traditional ethnic and national minorities; as Table 1.2 demonstrates, there are currently more than 300 different ethnic and national minorities within the EU. With respect to traditional ethnicities, Pan and Pfeil (2003: 11–12) have identified eight-seven distinct "peoples of Europe," of which thirty-three constitute the majority population in at least one sovereign state, while the remaining fifty-four are ethnic minorities. With more than 50 ethnic groups of 10,000 persons or greater communicating in more than 300 different languages, contemporary London has become the most diverse city in the history of world (Benedictus 2005).

Ethnic super diversity, with its peculiar national historical origins, legacies, and conflicts, potentially constitutes a significant challenge for social cohesion within the EU. Along these lines, it is hardly surprising that whenever people from significantly dissimilar backgrounds inhabit and interact within the same economic, social, and political space, interpersonal and intergroup frictions ensue. This said, students of the advanced industrial democracies have typically expected that social stratification grounded in ethnic or racial differences will erode over time as immigrants are gradually incorporated into their respective host societies and/or the cultures of these societies change to accommodate new ethnic diversity (Messina and Fraga 1992). Yet, in fact, there is recent evidence that social heterogeneity, in part the product of accelerating mass immigration from an increasingly diverse set of source countries, is eroding social solidarity within the advanced countries. As Putnam (2007) sums up the problem, a spike in ethnic diversity has motivated their populations to "hunker down." Although optimistic that these societies can overcome social fragmentation in the end, in the short term, Putnam predicts the major countries

TABLE 1.2. *National Minorities of Europe, 2003*

States	Population (1,000s)	% Titular Nations/ Ethnic Community	Number	Minorities (1,000s)
Albania	3.087	97.2	5	86.000
Austria	8.033	89.0	6	172.000
Belgium	10.310	91.3	1	22.000
Bulgaria	7.933	78.8	12	1.620
Czech Rep.	10.293	93.8	8	323.000
Denmark	5.330	95.1	4	123.000
Finland	5.181	92.1	6	332.000
France	58.519	86.1	7	8.133
Germany	82.260	91.0	4	172.000
Greece	10.260	97.4	7	229.000
Hungary	10.162	89.2	13	1.096
Ireland	3.917	99.4	1	74.000
Italy	56.306	93.3	12	2.794
Latvia	2.340	58.3	11	955.000
Lithuania	3.653	82.1	10	653.000
Netherlands	15.987	92.6	3	520.000
Poland	38.644	96.7	14	1.657
Portugal	10.356	97.5	3	147.000
Romania	21.698	88.3	19	2.513
Slovakia	5.380	85.8	10	703.000
Slovenia	1.948	88.7	4	15.000
Spain	40.847	75.9	6	8.936
Sweden	8.883	86.5	4	606.000
United Kingdom	58.789	98.6	6	837.000
TOTAL	756.991	88.6	329	86.674

Source: Based on Pan and Pfeil 2003: 10.

of immigration will continue to suffer from comparatively low interpersonal trust, general altruism, and community cooperation.

Whatever the merits of Putnam's perspective, two things are evident. First, because of continuing mass immigration, the EU is becoming ever more ethnically and racially heterogeneous. Second, conditions of super diversity currently pose and will likely continue to pose challenges for intra-EU solidarity.

Intra-European Migration

The free movement of labor is one of the founding principles of the European Union. Indeed, the diffusion of workers' skills because of occupational and geographic mobility is widely perceived as the key to enhancing the productive capacity of European firms and putting Europe's national economies on a higher path of economic growth. Spatial mobility is also viewed as potentially fostering social-cultural integration within the European Union, thus strengthening European identity and intercultural networks (Recchi 2008).

Yet, in fact, relatively few Europeans live and work in another country. Approximately five million Europeans – or about 2.2 percent of the total labor force – currently work in an EU country other than their own (European Commission 2011); including volunteering and traineeships, only 13 percent of Europeans have worked in another country for at least three consecutive months (Eurobarometer 2011c: 13). Instead, Europeans are more likely to migrate from one region to another within their country of origin than to another EU member-state. Moreover, in most member-states, the majority of nonnationals are citizens of nonmember countries. The total number of nonnationals living on the territory of an EU Member State on January 1, 2010, was 32.5 million persons, representing 6.5 percent of the EU population. More than one third (12.3 million persons) of all nonnationals living in the EU in 2010 were citizens of another EU Member State (Eurostat 2011).

According to recent research, the main obstacle inhibiting EU citizens from moving to another European country is concern about possessing the necessary language skills. More than half of EU citizens report that the lack of adequate language skills was a barrier to mobility (European Commission 2010: 117). Other major concerns are finding employment in another member-state country, adapting to a different culture in the destination country, and securing adequate housing. Although significant, administrative barriers such as access to health care and social security transfer of pension rights, obtaining residency or work permits, and recognition of professional qualifications were of lesser concern. Whatever the causes of low intra–European migration, it is highly unlikely that, given current intra-EU mobility trends, a European identity will be soon constructed that results in "more Europeans" (Fligstein 2009).

Moreover, even if greater labor mobility within the EU were to accelerate in the future – as it undoubtedly will whatever the resolution of the current economic crisis – Favell's research (2008) on the social experiences of the Eurostars, the symbolically important population who have voluntarily left their "nation-state society" to reap the rewards of denizenship in big, rich Eurocities in northwest Europe, suggests that a European identity cannot be constructed exclusively on the foundation of intra-European migration. Although the greater circulation of workers and citizens in general around the EU may be a necessary condition for the emergence of a mass European identity, it is hardly a sufficient one.

European Political Space

As numerous studies have extensively documented (Kaiser and Starie 2005; Risse 2010: 127–56), the contemporary EU is an increasingly dense transnational political space. Whether at the level of civil-society organizations (Ruzza and Bozzini 2008), transgovernmental networks (Thurner and Binder 2008),

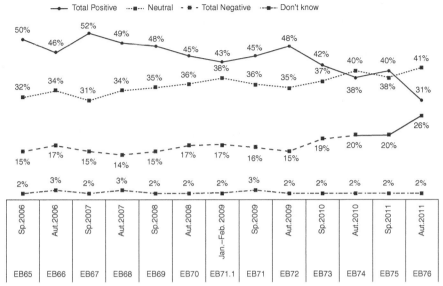

FIGURE 1.3. Public image of the EU.
Source: Eurobarometer 2011b: 20.

the structure of citizen attitudes (Gabel and Anderson 2002), political party policy positions (Gabel and Hix 2002), transnational interparty cooperation (Johansson 2005), and/or other political dimensions, there is little doubt that the emergence of a European identity could *potentially* be facilitated by the further evolution of a bounded European political space. Nevertheless, numerous obstacles are inhibiting and will likely continue to impede this outcome.

First, a large minority of EU citizens either has a neutral or negative image of the EU and/or is indifferent to or ignorant of the EU's affairs and its core institutions (Figure 1.3), a percentage that has swelled since the beginning of the current economic crisis. Therefore, the EU is persistently confronted with the problem that a low public awareness of its political tasks and activities results in reflexive mistrust and withdrawal of loyalty. A special 2008 Eurobarometer report (European Commission 2008), for example, revealed that only 16 percent of EU citizens were aware that there would be European elections the following year. Even within a few months of the election, only 44 percent of EU citizens expressed interest in it, as opposed to 53 percent who were uninterested.

Second, and perhaps most problematically, elections to the European Parliament (EP), an arena in which a European politics and a distinctively European political space could perhaps best be realized (Zielonka 2004: 33), are marred by low voter turnout and dominated by national and nationalist issues and concerns. In this context, EP elections are very much second-order elections (Reif and Schmitt 1980) during which the average voter turnout has consistently been more than 20 percentage points lower than the average turnout in corresponding prior national parliamentary elections. Although reforms in the Amsterdam and Nice Treaties enhanced the decision-making role of the EP, voter turnout for the 2009 EP elections descended to a new low of 43 percent.

Finally, the emergence of a nascent European political space has paradoxically created a new common arena for extremist politics whose impact on national electorates is only comprehensible by taking into consideration the structuring of European political competitions around the "populist-Eurosceptical" versus "democratic" cleavage. Austria's three Eurosceptical movements, including two extreme-right parties, for example, together secured 36 percent of the vote for the EP in 2009. In the Netherlands, a combination of robust Euroscepticism and strident anti–Islamic rhetoric inspired 17 percent of voters to support the Freedom Party, giving it four seats in the EP or only one fewer than the Christian Democrats. Eurosceptical political parties, including the Socialists and a pair of small Calvinist parties, took nearly a third of Dutch seats. In Hungary, three seats were won by the xenophobic Movement for a Better Hungary (*Jobbik*), which has a "civil defense" militia, the Hungarian Guard.

ORGANIZATION OF VOLUME

Given that the aforementioned challenges are unlikely to recede any time soon, this volume asks what the implications are of the persistence of ethnoregionalism, religion, and new nationalism for the emergence of a robust European identity. In addressing this question, the following essays intersect and are informed by three streams of scholarship: research on contemporary *ethnoregionalism* or *ethnonationalism* (Swenden and Maddens 2009); work on the challenges potentially posed by *immigrant* and particularly *Muslim immigrant incorporation* (Alsayyad and Castells 2002; Klausen 2005); and scholarship on the so-called *new nationalism*, including the illiberal ideas and policies promoted by extreme-right political parties and groups (Mudde 2000; 2005). In this context, we consciously chose to avoid conflating regional nationalism with the new nationalism because, as several of the authors underscore in their respective chapter contributions, regional nationalists tend to be either ambivalent or positive about the project for greater European union, while new nationalists are unambiguously and unanimously opposed to it. Therefore, regional nationalists are far more likely to embrace a European identity.

Why bring these three streams of scholarship together within a single volume? As the European Union continues along the paths of ever-deeper economic integration and broader geographical reach, two powerful and potentially troublesome countervailing trends seem to be stubbornly persisting: the cultural, political, and social fragmentation of its population within the borders of nation-states and the growing insularity of their respective languages, sub-cultures, "national" territories, and/or political identities. These trends are manifest, for example, in the percolating societal and political pressures for an autonomous state for the Basque region, Catalonia, Corsica, Flanders, "Padania," Scotland, and elsewhere and the extraordinary lengths to which ethnoregionalists are sometimes willing to travel (including resorting to violence in some cases) to protect their traditional customs, languages, values, and so forth from the "foreign." They are also evident in the disturbing rise of popular support for anti-immigrant groups and the proliferation of "nativist" opponents of multiculturalism, as well the aversion of nativists to the infusion of Islamic cultural and religious values by settled Muslim populations into European societies. Moreover, and perhaps most problematically for the prospects for European integration and the emergence of a mass European political identity, is the fact that the ongoing march of supranational decision making and the pooling of interdependence sovereignty among the member-state governments of the European Union may be fueling the very nationalist expressions that the project of ever-closer European integration was originally designed to suppress.

On other side of the so-called multicultural divide, Muslim and other immigrant populations are oftentimes conflicted about the degree to which they wish to be incorporated into Europe's predominantly secular societies. Many confessional Muslims seek to preserve their religious identity as a bulwark against their being fully incorporated into the dominant sociocultural order. What all three groups – ethnoregionalists, religious ethnics, and new nationalists – share in common is their reflexive defense of their respective traditional "communities" against homogenizing and/or centralizing pressures and trends. Moreover, each of their core interests sometimes conflict with the receptivity of their respective communities to European, centralizing, and/or globalizing influences. Although not formally allied and, indeed, sometimes in ideological and/or political conflict with one another, the aforementioned groups nevertheless occupy common ground in resisting real or perceived threats to their respective imagined communities.

In line with the fact that most of its contributors are political scientists, this volume primarily approaches the subject of European identity from a political perspective. In doing so, our intention is not to ignore or denigrate the contributions that have been and continue to be made to its study by nonpolitical science disciplines and perspectives (Checkel and Katzenstein 2009) but rather to underscore that to the degree that Europeans can develop and have developed a sense of "we-ness," that is, to the extent that the citizens of the member-state countries see themselves as Europeans in a meaningful sense for politics and particularly for European political community, it is likely to occur and have occurred through the prism of European political citizenship. Our efforts indirectly follow from and expand upon the experience of one of the editors in constructing a similar volume on the noneconomic implications of the euro, Europe's common currency (Fishman and Messina 2006). Like the latter project, this volume emphasizes the importance of contemporary political events in either facilitating or obfuscating the emergence of a European political identity.

The question of whether and to what degree a mass European political identity is possible is therefore our starting point. Our objective is not to arrive at a definitive answer to this question but rather to gain insight into the extent to which ethnoregionalism, ethnic religiosity, and the new nationalism currently or potentially impede the emergence of a meaningful European identity. By "meaningful" we mean a European identity that can underpin a *robust* European polity. It is our view that such a polity does not now exist. Thus, our dependent variable, European political identity, relatively new and perhaps in formation (Bruter 2005: 15), is one that is far from being consciously or enthusiastically embraced by a majority of EU citizens (Green 2007: 112).

Although opinion survey data inform several of its chapters (Cinnirella and Hamilton; Citrin and Wright; Jolly; Messina; Miller and Hussain), most of the essays in this volume are not exclusively founded on or informed by these data. On the other side of the coin, they refrain from offering normative judgments about whether a European identity is desirable. Rather, we have deliberately collected an eclectic set of essays that speak, albeit sometimes indirectly, to what we consider two neglected challenges (ethnoregionalism and religious ethnicity) and one understudied potential challenge (new nationalism) to the emergence of a robust European identity. In so doing, the essays cut across methodological lines.

Four parts organize the volume. The first two chapters in Part I, respectively authored by Citrin and Wright and Messina, frame the volume by establishing the broad parameters within which the subsequent essays explore the possible emergence of a robust European identity. Specifically, they underscore the trends in public opinion that suggest that something approximating a European identity is indeed evolving.

This said, both are circumspect about the depth and trajectory of this trend. Based upon their analysis of the public opinion data Citrin and Wright caution that "mass publics are ready to draw the line on EU authority when this touches on sacred elements of national myths and policies" (51). They pessimistically conclude that the goal of achieving "e pluribus Europa, a circumstance in which a European identity dominates national attachments and EU institutions preempt the power of national governments, is not on the horizon" (52). Messina concurs, arguing that as the European integration project has progressed from the economic arena to the realms of community and culture, pockets of Europeans have become alarmed that their closed and exclusive notions of national identity are being incrementally undermined. Both essays also emphasize the new nationalist threat to the emergence of a European identity.

Although generally in agreement, the aforementioned essays conspicuously part company on at least two scores. First, in a preview of the differences evident in several of the subsequent essays, Citrin and Wright and Messina's chapters diverge with respect to their conceptualization of how popular attachments feed into a European identity and, by extension, the project of ever-closer political union. While the former chapter primarily treats nonelite attitudes and attachments as independent variables, seeing them as soil from which a European identity will or will not ultimately spring, the latter mostly casts them as dependent variables that can be influenced or acted upon by either regional or national political actors. As a result, while Citrin and Wright's cautiousness about the future prospects of a European identity is primarily founded on their perception of the staying power of popular nationalist attachments, Messina, while also guarded on this score, represents these attachments as variable *and* subject to the manipulation of ethnoregionalist and/or new nationalist political parties.

From this platform, the essays in Part II assess the significance of the ethnoregionalist challenge to an attachment to Europe and the emergence of a European identity. Along these lines, Jolly's lead essay asks whether substate nationalists are pro–EU and "whether respondents' public attitudes match their party elites' cues" (86). Based on his analysis of data derived from longitudinal Eurobarometer and expert surveys, he discovers that both regionalist partisans and political parties formally support the European project to a very high degree. Nevertheless, in closely scrutinizing the Scottish case, he also finds that the EU's very existence feeds popular support for Scottish nationalism by making the prospect of an independent Scotland more economically feasible and Scottish independence less risky and, hence, facilitates the decision of many ethnic Scots to cast a vote for the Scottish National Party (SNP). As a consequence, substate nationalists and supranationalist supporters find themselves in a "strange bedfellows" coalition.

Meguid's essay specifically asks what effect domestic political decentralization has had on electoral support for ethnoregionalist political parties in EP elections. Her main finding – that high levels of decentralization are associated with higher electoral support for ethnoregionalist parties in EP elections – indirectly reinforces Jolly's conclusion that a substate nationalist-supranationalist "strange bedfellows" coalition is much in evidence across Europe and, more specifically, that multiple levels of governance can reinforce each other.

Somewhat contradicting Jolly and Meguid, Gómez-Reino is skeptical about the nature and, especially, the long-term stability of the aforementioned sub–nationalist-supranationalist coalition. Her analysis of the positions of regionalist parties on European integration finds that the contemporary map of the regionalist party family is a family with pro-EU centers and Eurosceptical extremes. Although the mean position of regionalist parties is generally favorable on European integration, it is less so than liberal, socialist, Christian democratic, and conservative political parties. Moreover, the salience of the EU for ethnoregionalist parties is remarkably low. Gómez-Reino therefore concludes that support for European integration among regionalist political parties is more conditional and ambiguous than unqualified. Rather than steadfastly supportive of Europe over time, the positions of these parties are either cyclical or evolving toward increasing skepticism.

The respective contributions by Miller and Hussain, Cinnirella and Hamilton, and Gould in Part III consider the implications of post–World War II immigration and/or the growing influence of Islam within the EU for the emergence of a robust European identity. They explicitly or implicitly raise three pertinent questions. First, do regional identities and attachments inevitably foster xenophobia and/or feelings of social exclusiveness? Second, are the EU's ethnic minorities differently or less pro–Europe than nonethnic citizens? Finally, are the views of the proper relationship between religion and politics of Muslim elites compatible with a politically liberal Europe?

With regard to the first question, Miller and Hussain conclude that a Scottish nationalist identity is "remarkably uncorrelated with anti-minority phobias" (164). Although Scottish Nationalist Party (SNP) voters are the most Anglophobic among ethnic Scots, Scottish nationalism does not make them significantly more Islamophobic. Rather, the English – and not Muslims and presumably not other Europeans – remain the "historic enemy, the 'significant other' that helps define Scottish identity" (163).

On the second question, Cinnirella and Hamilton find that that Asian Britons do view Europe differently from their white British counterparts. However, contrary to conventional wisdom, most Asians simultaneously and positively self-identify as British, ethnic, *and* European, although among these an ethnic identity is the most preferred. Unlike many white Britons, for whom a British identity impedes the embrace of a European identity, a national and a European identity are "consonant" for most British Asians. Moreover, for Asians, a British identity positively correlates with pro-European attitudes, leading Cinnirella and Hamilton to speculate that British Asians may base their "loyalties more on a sense of civic national identity that is less entrenched in emotional ties to national culture and symbols" (183).

Finally, in addressing the third question in his survey of Muslim elites in Ireland, Portugal, and Spain, Gould discovers that Muslim officeholders in civic and political organizations are as likely to cite European as non-European writers, thinkers, and political figures as sources of influence about their ideas about faith and political life, with liberalism, universalism, and political Islamism the most widely acknowledged inspirations. As a group, they demonstrate "distinctive signs of adopting and elaborating European worldviews and identities, yet … in ways that redefine what it means to be European" (185).

The essays by Givens and Lindstrom in Part IV broadly assess the relevance of the new nationalist challenges to European political community and identity. Givens's examination of the rising political support for and influence of radical right political parties (RRPs) in Europe and particularly in Austria and France leads her to the insight that this phenomenon has precipitated a mainstream political elite reaction that, paradoxically, has created a window of opportunity for these elites to forge policies that are supportive of the interests of immigrants and ethnic minorities at the European level. More specifically, she claims that the rising influence of the radical right precipitated the passage of the European Union's racial equality directive (RED), a milestone of European cooperation in the field of immigrant policy. The RED, in turn, has indirectly facilitated a deeper nation-state commitment to a European citizenship and political identity.

Lindstrom's essay considers the effects of the EU's recent enlargements on European solidarity – and particularly the future of the European Social Model – through the prism of Estonia and Slovenia's respective paths and political reactions to full EU membership. Although not universally embraced, many if not most EU citizens and elites consider the ESM as one of the linchpins of a European political identity (Demertzis 2008: 138). Lindstrom's analysis of the political debates over European integration within Estonia and Slovenia in recent years suggests that "longstanding divisions among advocates of further economic liberalization and proponents of social cohesion" among the original fifteen member-state countries are largely mirrored in the following ten member-states. Thus, neither advocates of the Single Market nor those of the ESM have gained a decisive upper hand because of the post–2004 enlargements. This said, Lindstrom's two most different cases appear to suggest at least one similar outcome that is ultimately detrimental to European political solidarity and community: a rise in popular and elite Euroscepticism in Estonia and Slovenia that is grounded in a shared concern "about the threat of EU membership to national interests" (227).

PART I

FRAMING THE PROSPECTS FOR A EUROPEAN IDENTITY

2

E Pluribus Europa?

Jack Citrin and Matthew Wright

The search for the Holy Grail of a collective European identity goes on. Electoral defeats at the hands of French, Dutch, and Irish heretics still in the thrall of nationalism have stalled the faith-based project of political integration; forward movement may require a coordinated crusade for new converts.

The remarkable achievement of a European "market-state" rested on a permissive public consensus that increasing the purview of EU jurisdiction did not threaten core principles of national identity (Risse 2005). In the public mind, the dominant pattern of feelings was the "Nation First, but Europe Too" configuration of peacefully coexisting attachments (Citrin and Sides 2004a). Recent studies, however, show that with political rather than economic union their focus, the integrative efforts of political and economic leaders no longer are unconstrained by quiescent mass publics (Green 2007; Hooghe and Marks 2007; Lubbers and Scheepers 2005; and McLaren 2002). The powers and policies of the European Union now are a salient and politicized issue, and this means that voters as well as governments will determine the future trajectory of integration. With pro–European elites no longer insulated from party competition and media scrutiny, how people prioritize and frame their identities has grown in political significance (Díez Medrano 2003; Hooghe and Marks 2005).

The emergence of a legitimate European nation-state resembling the American federal system may depend on a paradigmatic shift in which the people of Europe adopt a common collective identity and *favor* it over their national identity. A united crusade by the governments of member-states to coordinate education policies and shared communications through media and culture arguably could create a new generation of European loyalists, as in the state first, nation second model of British and French nationalism (Fabbrini 2007; Gellner 1983). Yet the constraints of democratic politics might make it difficult to impose these Europeanizing policies without the prior development of a bloc of supporters, as in the nation first, state second model of German and French nationalism (Fligstein 2008; Hooghe and Marks 2005).

This chapter's modest aim is to look again at the current landscape of public attachments to Europe and nation, focusing on how ordinary citizens negotiate and prioritize their dual identities as Europeans and nationals. We take it as axiomatic that people have multiple political identities. What matters is whether and when these distinguishable identities are complementary or competitive, mutually reinforcing or exclusive in terms of their imperatives for behavior. Moreover, this may depend on the meaning or content of specific group identities – that is, whether national identities are framed in exclusive terms, rather than just the strength of national attachments, seems to be a determinant of the individual's level of opposition to European integration (Hooghe and Marks 2005).

To further explore these ideas, this chapter proceeds as follows. The next section proposes a conceptualization of collective identities. A synthesis of Eurobarometer and International Social Survey Program (ISSP) data then considers trends in public attitudes and cross-national differences in the relative strength of European and national identities. This review of survey evidence focuses on two main questions: the significance of differences in how citizens define what it means to be a Briton, Frenchman, German, and so forth for their opinions about what Europe is and should become and how the individual's patterning of collective identities influences his or her for preferences about the balance of power in the European Union's multilevel system of governance. From a theoretical vantage point, throughout the analysis we apply conceptual distinctions developed in the scholarly literature on nationalism to the idea of a common political identity in an emerging European polity (Green 2007).

DEFINING COLLECTIVE IDENTITY

The voluminous academic literature on "identity" resembles a quagmire rather than a tunnel ending in conceptual clarity. Because the term is used to mean both sameness and difference, both commonality and individuality, this should not be surprising. Still, the drawing power of "identity" makes it unlikely that the suggestion to consign it to the dustbin of scientific history will take hold (Brubaker and Cooper 2000), so the best one can do is to stipulate a definition that helps address the dominant theoretical and empirical issues concerning "identity politics." And although definitions of "identity" abound, there is a surprising consensus about the nature of these questions. Here are five main points of agreement.

First, supranational, national, and ethnic identities are *social* identities. They have *relational content* in the sense that they refer to dimensions of one's self-concept defined by perceptions of similarity with some and difference from others. Social identities develop because people perceive themselves as belonging to groups and pursue their goals through membership in these groups. Social identities arise from a process of social comparison, and their formation inevitably requires drawing boundaries between "us" and "them." Visible markers may define the relational content of identity, the aspect of one's self shared with a specified set of others. But group boundaries also may be socially constructed. Sometimes "we" draw the boundaries, sometimes "they." In Sartre's famous comment: anti-Semitism assures that Jews (and a Jewish identity) will endure. So one important question with implications for group conflict is whether there is agreement about the boundaries of group membership. The assimilated German Jews thought of themselves in national rather than ethnic terms; the Nazis viewed things differently. A European identity thus entails distinguishing an expansive set of "ins" from others – like Americans – whose defining attributes are visibly different.

Second, in defining social identities, it is critical to distinguish between their cognitive aspects and dimensions of their normative content (Brewer 2000; Brubaker and Cooper 2000; Citrin, Wong, and Duff 2001). The act of self-categorization answers the cognitive "who am I" question, but the *strength* of one's identification with a particular membership group – the emotional significance of a social identity – varies. One can support the existence and policies of the EU without a strong emotional attachment to Europe or a sense of solidarity with citizens of other member-states. Identifying *as* is not the same as identifying *with*.

Third, the content of a social identity gives concrete meaning to membership in a particular group. Identities may be defined by their purposes, but typically there are constitutive norms that define full membership in a group. The normative content of an idea spells out the physical features, values, and conduct represented by the prototypical member of the group. A standard expectation is that strong psychological identification with the group will engender conformity to the group's constitutive norms. The bases on which collective judgments of sameness or difference rest can vary across time and space (Horowitz 1985). In other words, the content of national identity can be contested as well as constructed. A common contrast in the European context is between the civic conception of French national identity, which rejects ethnic or religious criteria in favor of the norm of citizens as individuals committed to universal values of democracy and secularism, and an ethnic conception of German national identity as based on common descent (Brubaker 1992). Since Europe is by definition a multicultural entity, building a common identity on the idea of shared ancestry is a nonstarter. Moreover, the presence of so many Muslims makes it difficult to sustain an image of Europe as fundamentally Christian. Hence, those seeking to build a collective European identity take the idea of "constitutional patriotism" as a starting point, founding the idea of a European "nation" on shared political values and policies that somehow are distinct from those of the American "other."

Similarly, whether the normative content of national and European identities conflict will depend on how each is conceived and framed. For example, Díez

Medrano (2003) argues that the Spanish tend to support European integration as a proxy for modernization and democratization that are crucial features of that country's post-Franco self-image, while the Euroscepticism of the English is rooted in Britain's history of empire and the Channel's reinforcement of the separation of the island "us" from the collection of continental "thems." More generally, Hooghe and Marks (2005) propose that national identities defined in exclusive ethnic or territorial terms are less compatible with attachment to a multicultural European Union.

Fourth, politics can be critical in the "social construction" of group identities. Members of the group are connected by common goals such as attaining political independence, securing representation, or obtaining symbolic recognition for prior achievements. Nation building is a process of inclusion and exclusion, and political decisions help determine the boundaries of the group and their permeability. The same processes clearly apply to defining the geographic and ideological boundaries of Europe, and the dominant answer to the question "Who is a European?" may change over time, much as the answer to questions about the boundaries of particular nations has changed. Identities are politicized by cues from political elites, and these cues sometimes are consensual, sometimes conflictual (Zaller 1992). Electoral considerations and party competition have shattered the earlier permissive consensus of the pre-Maastricht era. Radical-right parties attack the idea of European political integration as a threat to the nation's sovereignty and cultural unity, and when this argument resonates, the center of political gravity shifts (Hooghe and Marks 2009; Kitschelt 2007).

Fifth, social identities have political relevance because they channel feelings of mutuality, obligation, and antagonism, delineating the contours of one's willingness to help other people and the boundaries of support for policies allocating resources based on group membership. Indeed, the intimate connection between the personal and the social bases of self-regard becomes clear when one recalls how quickly an insult to the dignity of one's group can trigger ethnic violence (Horowitz 1985). Identities can be a matter of life and death. In the name of the nation, ethnic group, or religion, people are willing both to die for "our people" and to commit unspeakable crimes against the dehumanized "others." More generally, identity politics refers to the mobilization of group pride to advance perceived collective group interests, calling on people to judge events, policies, and candidates primarily in terms of how they would affect the standing and heritage of one's group. Since people have multiple identities, belonging to Europe, to nations, and to subnational units, they sometimes have to decide, when confronting a political choice such as whether to give up the nation's veto when the European Union makes policy, which identity has priority. Social identities are more likely to influence behavior, even overriding instrumental considerations, as they acquire emotional significance (Tajfel 1981). Whether a strong sense of European identity is necessary to advance integrative policies thus depends on what the citizens of member nations are required to do for each other. One indicator of European identity is the willingness to make personal sacrifices such as paying taxes or even fighting for member states other than one's own (Green 2007).

THE PROBLEM OF IDENTITY CHOICE

Nationalists insist on the priority of identity with the nation over all other foci of affiliation. If this is true, then nationalism is a threat to the emergence of a predominant European identity, much as the persistence of strong loyalties to the states was an obstacle to the emergence of an overarching American identity after the founding of that new nation in the late eighteenth century. Along these lines, the British politician Norman Tebbitt proposed the oft-cited "fan's test" for national identity. He proclaimed that the failure of British citizens of South Asian or West Indian origin to cheer for the English cricket team when it played India, Pakistan, or Jamaica meant that their strongest identification was with their country of origin and not their physical and political home.

In rebuttal, Amartya Sen (2000) argued that the "fan's test," does not prove that nationality and ethnicity were competing identities; one could root for the Pakistani cricket team and still fulfill all the responsibilities of citizenship. If Sen is correct, then nationality and ethnicity do not always compete. Put another way, context helps determine the salience of group identities and their relevance for behavior. In England's Premier League, the relevant identities are local, so fans of Manchester United embraced Christiano Ronaldo as "ours" when the team played Liverpool. In the European Cup competition, national identities are dominant, and Ronaldo was condemned by English fans for provoking his United teammate, Wayne Rooney.

In some critical circumstances, political identities do tug in opposite directions. After Pearl Harbor, Japanese Americans faced a choice between loyalty to their new country and support for their country of origin. Overwhelmingly, and despite internment by their own government, they demonstrated the primacy of their American national identity. Identity choice matters for how Muslim Britons would react to the terrorist attacks by their coreligionists and whether distant EU countries would send troops to protect Estonia from a Russian invasion.

To summarize, European and national identities overlap but are not identical; national citizens share membership in a more encompassing group of Europeans with people from national "out-groups." There are several important psychological models for reconciling the tensions that may emanate from this circumstance. Of particular significance is what each mode of ordering one's multiple identities implies for deciding who belong to "us" and who to "them."

Dominance is the strategy of subordinating all potential group identities to one primary attachment. Nationalists insist that one's national loyalties always should take precedence over the claims of Europe when one is forced to choose. "*Europa über alles*" reverses this ordering of identities and, if achieved in the public's mind, would signal the successful creation of the continental nation-state.

Compartmentalization is a solution in which the particular collective identity activated depends on the situation. Another way of characterizing this approach is that the individual's primary identity is heavily contextual, as in the example of football contests. Sometimes only one social identity is evoked by a situation; for example, local elections and environmental policies rarely activate nationalist sentiments. Of course, even in contexts with both national and European self-categorizations, as say in reactions to asylum seekers, the preferences dictated by group identities may not conflict. Indeed, a third model of managing multiple group identities, *merger*, widens the boundaries of the in-group of imagined community (Anderson 2006) to include people who share any of one's important memberships. This merged collective identity is highly inclusive and diverse as in the maximalist case when ethnic, national, and European identities are subordinated to the norms and values of a cosmopolitan, humanitarian ideology held by individuals who see themselves as "world citizens."

It is, of course, misleading to conceive of identity choices in purely individualistic terms. As noted, how to integrate national and European identities is a collective problem for which there are competing ideological and institutional solutions. Hence social norms, party positions, and official policies coping with national diversity within Europe are likely to influence the distribution of identity choices, much as national policies differ in their approaches to integrating immigrants from different cultures.

TRENDS IN ATTACHMENT TO NATION AND EUROPE

The Eurobarometer surveys include a potpourri of questions asking people whether they see themselves as European, whether they feel close to Europe (and their nationality), and whether they support their country's membership in the European Union. This chapter extends an earlier analysis (Citrin and Sides 2004a) by incorporating data from 1999 – the year before the Treaty of Nice proposed changes in the decision-making procedures of the Council of Ministers, reducing the veto powers of individual countries – to 2007. In addition, we concentrate here on indicators of affective rather than utilitarian attachments. The set of countries surveyed in the later period includes Sweden, Austria, and Finland as well as France, the Benelux countries, Germany, Italy, Denmark, the United Kingdom, Ireland, Greece, Spain, and Portugal but omits the Eastern European countries from the last wave of enlargement.

The question "In the future do you see yourself as (Nationality) only, as (Nationality) and European, as European and (Nationality) or as European only?" is primarily an indicator of self-categorization and has the advantage of assessing both the extent of multiple identifications and identity choice or

TABLE 2.1. *Percentage Who Self-Identify as National and European, 1999–2005*

	Nation Only		Nation and Then Europe		Europe and Then Nation		Europe Only	
	1999	2005	1999	2005	1999	2005	1999	2005
France	38	33	50	51	7	10	5	6
Belgium	42	30	43	51	9	10	7	6
Netherlands	45	29	48	55	6	12	1	3
Germany	51	35	39	49	7	11	3	6
Italy	26	52	59	38	10	8	6	2
Luxembourg	24	24	43	46	13	17	20	12
Denmark	55	38	38	51	3	8	3	2
Ireland	52	59	40	34	5	4	3	3
United Kingdom	67	59	25	32	5	6	3	4
Greece	59	51	39	44	2	4	1	1
Spain	33	37	57	52	7	6	4	6
Portugal	54	52	42	41	2	4	2	3
Finland	60	52	36	44	3	3	1	1
Sweden	60	45	34	49	4	5	1	2
Austria	46	45	44	47	6	7	4	1
Total	49	43	42	45	6	8	4	4

Notes: Question wording is "In the near future, do you see yourself as (nationality) only, (nationality) and European, European and (nationality), or European only?"
Source: Eurobarometer Surveys 2000 and 2005b. Downloadable from GESIS Data Archive, http://www.gesis.org/eurobarometer-data-service/survey-series/standard-special-eb/.

prioritization. Table 2.1 presents the responses of people in each of the fifteen countries surveyed. In the pooled sample, there is relatively little overall change. Those identifying solely as Europeans or thinking of themselves as Europeans first remain a small minority, but there is a 6 percent drop in the proportion thinking of themselves solely in terms of their nationality. Belgium, the Netherlands, Germany, and Denmark register the largest declines in a purely national self-identification, while Italy is the only country in which attitudes moved in the opposite direction, with the proportion saying they saw themselves only as nationals doubling from 26 to 52 percent.

Figures 2.1 and 2.2 present this information in a slightly different manner, showing the changes between 1999 and 2005 in the proportions expressing dual identifications and prioritizing their national identities, respectively. The aggregate levels of change are small, but on balance there is some growth in the segment of European societies thinking of themselves as Europeans as well as nationals and slight erosion in the number choosing to prioritize their nationality.

One disadvantage of the identification variable described above is that it limits the opportunity of respondents to express an equally strong sense of

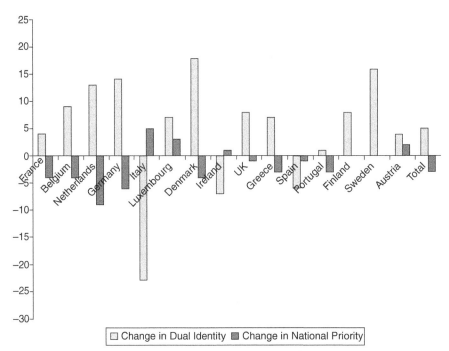

FIGURE 2.1. Change in multiple identities and priority of national identity.

Notes: Question wording is "In the near future, do you see yourself as (nationality) only, (nationality) and European, European and (nationality), or European only?" Cell entries represent (1) changes in dual identity (sum of those who agreed "nation and then Europe" and "Europe and then nation" for 2005 minus that sum for 1999); and (2) changes in national priority (sum of those who agreed "nation only" and "nation and then Europe" for 2005 minus that sum for 1999).

Source: Eurobarometer Surveys 2000 and 2005b. Downloadable from GESIS Data Archive, http://www.gesis.org/eurobarometer-data-service/survey-series/standard-special-eb/.

attachment to multiple territorial foci, including both nation and Europe. To overcome this problem, Citrin and Sides (2004a) developed a measure based on a dichotomized cross-tabulation of answers to separate questions about how attached (very, fairly, not very, or not at all) people felt to their country and to Europe.

Table 2.2 presents the distributions for the 1999 and 2005 surveys with respondents grouped into four categories: those closely attached to neither nation or Europe, those closely attached just to the nation, those closely attached to Europe alone, and those attached to both country and Europe.

The first and third categories are tiny and will be ignored. Table 2.2 does show a continued, albeit slowing, trend toward a dual sense of attachment.

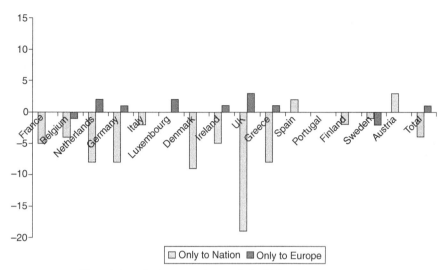

FIGURE 2.2. Change in priority to nation and dual identities, 1999–2005.

Notes: The attachment measure is constructed from responses to two separate items asking respondents to characterize their degree of "attachment" to their country and to Europe, respectively, on a four-point scale (very, fairly, not very, not at all). Respondents are considered attached "only to nation" if they are very or fairly attached to the nation but not very or not at all to Europe (they are considered attached "only to Europe" if the opposite holds). Respondents are considered "attached to both" if they are very or fairly attached to both their country and to Europe. Figures show simple differences between 2007 and 1999.

Source: Eurobarometer Surveys 1999 and 2005a. Downloadable from GESIS Data Archive, http://www.gesis.org/eurobarometer-data-service/survey-series/standard-special-eb/.

Between 1991 and 1999, this outlook grew from 46 to 59 percent; in 2005 the dual mode of attachment had reached 64 percent, with the largest shifts occurring in Belgium, the Netherlands, Germany, Denmark, the United Kingdom, and Greece (see Figure 2.2). In 2005, Greece was the only country surveyed with a majority saying they were attached only to their country; in Italy, where a majority in 2007 said that in the future they expected to see themselves solely in terms of their nationality, fully 69 percent were very or fairly attached to both Europe and their country.

Another way of looking at responses about attachment is to order responses in numerical form from those with the weakest to the strongest degree of closeness and then to "subtract" the European from the national answer. This yields three groups: those who feel closer to Europe, those who feel closer to their country, and those who feel equally close to both. Between 1991 and 1999, those feeling equally close rose from 26 to 42 percent of the pooled sample and those feeling closer to their country dropped from 70 to 53 percent. Between

TABLE 2.2. *Emotional Attachment to Nation and Europe, 1999–2005 (in percent)*

	Attached to Neither		Attached Only to Nation		Attached Only to Europe		Attached to Both	
	1999	2005	1999	2005	1999	2005	1999	2005
France	10	6	36	31	2	2	53	61
Belgium	14	8	21	17	9	8	57	68
Netherlands	10	11	38	30	4	6	39	53
Germany	11	8	30	22	3	4	56	65
Italy	7	7	25	23	2	2	66	69
Luxembourg	5	4	14	14	2	4	79	79
Denmark	2	2	25	16	1	1	72	81
Ireland	2	3	38	33	0	1	60	63
United Kingdom	6	12	55	36	2	5	37	47
Greece	2	2	59	51	0	1	39	47
Spain	7	6	22	24	3	3	69	67
Portugal	3	3	34	34	1	1	62	62
Finland	2	2	30	28	2	2	66	69
Sweden	7	3	19	18	4	2	70	77
Austria	5	5	32	35	1	1	62	60
Total	7	6	32	28	2	3	59	64

Notes: The four-category attachment measure is constructed from responses to two separate items asking respondents to characterize their degree of "attachment" to their country and to Europe, respectively, on a four-point scale (very, fairly, not very, not at all). Respondents are considered attached to neither if they answer not very or not at all to both items. They are considered attached to only to nation if they are very or fairly attached to the nation but not very or not at all to Europe (they are considered attached only to Europe if the opposite holds). Finally, they are considered attached to both if they are very or fairly attached to both their country and to Europe.

Source: Eurobarometer Surveys 1999 and 2005a. Downloadable from GESIS Data Archive, http://www.gesis.org/eurobarometer-data-service/survey-series/standard-special-eb/.

1999 and 2005, there was almost no aggregate change. There is, of course, variation across countries, including the somewhat unintuitive rise in the proportion of those saying that they felt equally close to Europe and their country in such Eurosceptical nations as the United Kingdom (23 percent to 35 percent) and Denmark (39 percent to 48 percent). These changes seem largely due to declining feelings of attachment and pride in their national governments during this period (Risse 2005).

Overall, then, a variety of subjective indicators shows a continuing but relatively slow trend toward a dual mode of identification among Europeans. Increasingly they categorize themselves in both national and continental terms and feel equally close to both political units. When it comes to prioritization or identity choice, however, very few people put Europe first. When push comes to shove, the dominant view remains "Nation First and Europe Too." A comprehensive analysis of these and additional survey data by Green (2007)

TABLE 2.3. *Relationship between Affective and Utilitarian Support for Europe*

	Feeling European vs. Nationality	National Pride – European Pride	Attachment to Nation – Attachment to Europe	Membership: Good/Bad	Benefit: Yes/No
Feeling European vs. Nationality	1.00				
National Pride – European Pride	0.41	1.00			
Attachment to Nation – Attachment to Europe	0.39	0.54	1.00		
Membership: Good/Bad	0.27	0.30	0.27	1.00	
Benefit: Yes/No	0.23	0.25	0.22	0.63	1.00

Notes: All correlations are significant at the .01 level, two-tailed.
Source: Eurobarometer Surveys 2003 and 2004, pooled. Downloadable from GESIS Data Archive, http://www.gesis.org/eurobarometer-data-service/survey-series/standard-special-eb/.

reaches a similar conclusion. He writes (147) that a European identity clearly exists but that in the sense of our term "dominance," it clearly is a minority sentiment. Green also confirms previous research showing that identification with Europe is associated with elite status and cosmopolitanism. It also is well known (Citrin and Sides 2004a; Fligstein 2008) that age is correlated with feelings of European identity, with younger citizens more likely to adopt a dual mode of attachment. Indeed, a recent paper by Lutz, Kritzinger, and Skirbekk (2006) predicts that cohort replacement will continue to increase the proportion of EU citizens with multiple identities. Using the identification variable discussed here in Table 2.1, they calculate that over the period from 1996 to 2004, for cohorts born one year later, the proportion with some mention of a European identity is on average a half percentage point higher. Aging does reduce the tendency to have a dual mode of attachment beginning after one turns fifty, but this effect is less robust than the cohort effect. The implication is that cohort replacement will continue to reduce the number of Europeans with strictly national identities, assuming that socialization patterns sustain the current relationship between age and patterns of identification. The graying of European societies may slow the trend, but, even so, as of now death remains as inevitable as taxes.

To provide a more detailed look at the structure of attitudes toward Europe, Table 2.3 presents the intercorrelations (Pearson's *r*) among five indicators: the self-identification variable, indicators of relative attachment to and pride in Europe and one's nation, and questions asking whether membership in the European Union is good for one's country or not and has been beneficial or

TABLE 2.4. *Country Scores on Affective and Utilitarian Support Scales*

	Affective Support		Utilitarian Support	
	Score	Rank	Score	Rank
France	0.62	6	0.37	5
Belgium	0.59	9	0.34	6
Netherlands	0.64	5	0.32	8
Germany	0.59	9	0.41	4
Italy	0.60	8	0.35	7
Luxembourg	0.58	10	0.27	11
Denmark	0.64	5	0.30	9
Ireland	0.66	4	0.20	13
United Kingdom	0.68	2	0.44	2
Greece	0.72	1	0.23	12
Spain	0.61	7	0.27	11
Portugal	0.66	4	0.28	10
Finland	0.67	3	0.43	3
Sweden	0.62	6	0.47	1
Austria	0.62	6	0.43	3

Notes: Both "Affective Support" and "Utilitarian Support" factor scores are scored from 0 = least in favor of Europe/most in favor of nation to 1 = most in favor of Europe/least in favor of nation.
Source: Eurobarometer Surveys 2003 and 2004, pooled. Downloadable from GESIS Data Archive, http://www.gesis.org/eurobarometer-data-service/survey-series/standard-special-eb/.

not. As Table 2.3 shows, all five questions are significantly related, with pro–European responses going together. Table 2.3 also shows that the affective items more closely correlate with each other than with the two utilitarian items. An exploratory factor analysis with an oblimin rotation extracts two underlying dimensions. The Self-Identification, Net Attachment, and Net Pride measures comprise one factor, labeled Affective Identification, and the Good Thing and Benefits item comprise a second factor, labeled Utilitarian Identification. The factor scores based on the oblimin rotation have a correlation of .35.

To array respondents from each country on these two dimensions, scales based on the factor loadings for the defining items of each dimension were constructed, with scores ranging from −1 (most pro-European) to +1 (most nationalist). Table 2.4 gives the mean score on each scale for each of the fifteen countries as well as its rank from most nationalist to most pro-European. The correlation between the two rank orders (Spearman's rho) is −0.043, indicating at the aggregate rather than individual level, the two dimensions are unrelated. The mean scores do clearly show that the balance of affective attachments continues to tilt in the nationalist direction, even as the mean score of utilitarian evaluations of membership in the EU indicates that favorable assessments prevail in all countries. Looking at the place of individual countries in the two rank orders, the Euroscepticism of the United Kingdom stands out: Britain has the second-highest nationalist score on both affective and utilitarian measures. By contrast, the Greeks and Irish are strongly nationalist when it comes to identity choice (affective attachment) but among the most fervent believers in the benefits of EU membership in their country, an interesting fact given the rejection of the Lisbon Treaty by Irish voters. Table 2.4 also shows a high level of European identification among Germans despite their relatively lower enthusiasm about the concrete benefits of EU membership for their country. Taken as a whole, these data underscore the value of distinguishing between affective and utilitarian support for Europe and are another confirmation of Hooghe and Marks's (2009) warning that arguments based on economic rationality alone are insufficient to push publics further down the road to political integration.

THE POLITICAL MEANING OF IDENTITY CHOICE

The political relevance of multiple identities and how they are ordered at the psychological level depends on whether and how identity choices reflect people's hopes for and fears about the increased power of European institutions. Several Eurobarometer surveys addressed this issue by asking respondents whether they personally were currently afraid of a list of specific concerns sometimes associated with "the building of the European Union." Table 2.5 compares the answers of respondents who say they only feel attached to their country, those with a dual attachment to country and Europe, and the smaller group with a sense of closeness to Europe alone (Citrin and Sides 2004a).

The potential problems listed are an amalgam of economic and cultural concerns, and it is striking that in every specific potential outcome, those attached to the nation alone express the highest level of fear, followed by the group of respondents with a dual sense of attachment, with the European loyalists consistently the most sanguine group. Fear of increased crime, presumably due to more permeable borders, and economic losses sparked the highest levels on anxiety, but cultural threats such as the national language being used less, the loss of the nation's unique culture, and the loss of a country's distinctive pattern of social benefits all were mentioned by a majority of those whose attachment was to the nation alone. About 40 percent of those with dual attachments also worried about the loss of their national culture and language. Because it is likely that the growing group of people who see themselves as both nationals and Europeans will cast the deciding vote on the future of political integration, this level of cultural threat is a cautionary note. Indeed, a sense of cultural threat is a powerful determinant of opposition to immigration (Sides and Citrin 2007) and multiculturalism (Sniderman, Hagendoorn, and Prior 2004) as well as to European immigration (Hooghe and Marks 2005).

European attitudes about shared sovereignty reinforce these findings. For many years the Eurobarometer recorded beliefs about whether authority over particular policy domains should be shared jointly by the national government

TABLE 2.5. *Identity Choice and Fears about the European Union (in percent)*

Currently Afraid of ...	Attached to Nation Only	Attached to Europe Only	Attached to Both
Smaller EU States Losing Power	60	39	49
Increased Drug Trafficking/Organized Crime	73	50	65
National Language Being Used Less	50	29	41
Loss of Social Benefits	67	47	53
Loss of National Culture	58	27	41
End of National Currency	47	20	33
Transfer of Jobs Outside Country	80	64	74
More Difficulty for Nation's Farmers	76	59	67
Economic Crisis	57	36	42
Country Paying More and More to EU	73	49	60

Notes: Question wording is "Some people may have fears about the building of the European Union. Here is a list of things which some people say they are afraid of. For each one, please tell me if you, personally, are currently afraid of it, or not?"

Source: Eurobarometer Surveys 1999, 2000a, 2004, 2005a, and 2006, pooled. Downloadable from GESIS Data Archive, http://www.gesis.org/eurobarometer-data-service/survey-series/standard-special-eb/.

and the EU or controlled by the national government alone. Table 2.6 compares the preferences of Europeans in 1992 and 2004 for the allocation of jurisdiction in defense, currency, immigration, education, foreign, and cultural policies. Respondents are classified by the identification variable (see Table 2.1).

These data indicate clearly and consistently: (1) that whatever the policy domain one considers, prioritizing one's national identity reduces the willingness to share political authority with the European Union; (2) that those with a dual attachment, even if they place their national identity first, generally are closer in their policy preferences to the small group of "Europe-firsters" than to those with a purely national identification in their willingness to accept shared sovereignty; and (3) that whatever their self-identification or mode of attachment, all respondents are less willing to cede authority to Europe in the domains of education and cultural policy (areas that touch directly on the distinctive identity or soul of a nation) than in the foreign, defense, immigration and currency policies (areas in which the European role can readily be framed as helping to protect the nation's safety and welfare).

Worth noting also is that the trend between the early 1990s and 2004 is in the direction of diminished support for sharing political authority with Europe when it comes to education and cultural policy. This shift in outlook holds true among all four groups of identifiers, though it clearly is strongest among those who prioritize their national identity. For example, in 1992, 48 percent of the pooled sample was prepared to share control of cultural policy with

TABLE 2.6. *Willing to Allow Joint National and European Authority in Selected Domains, by Identity Choice (in percent)*

	Defense		Currency		Immigration		Education		Foreign Policy		Cultural Policy	
	1992	2004	1992	2004	1992	2004	1992	2004	1992	2004	1992	2004
Nation (N) Only	43	36	45	54	45	41	29	24	66	62	41	26
N + EU	65	59	70	77	64	59	45	34	79	78	52	34
EU + N	73	72	80	87	72	69	50	46	83	81	56	43
EU Only	75	67	83	83	74	72	56	49	82	81	62	51
Total	57	50	61	68	57	53	39	31	74	72	48	32

Notes: Question wording is "Should each of these areas be handled by national governments only or jointly with the European Union?"

Source: Eurobarometer Surveys 1992 and 2004. Downloadable from GESIS Data Archive, http://www.gesis.org/eurobarometer-data-service/survey-series/standard-special-eb/.

the European Union; in 2004, the comparable figure was 32 percent, and only 26 percent among those who said they saw themselves only in terms of their nationality. One interpretation of the overall trend toward more reluctance about ceding power to European institutions, of course, is that the status quo in 2004 is one in which the authority of European institutions is substantially greater than a decade earlier. In other words, in 1992, people were willing for the EU to become stronger; now they are saying "enough" as the policy makers in Brussels turn their attention to more sensitive domains and may be less constrained by the unanimity rule. Again, the political implication of current public opinion is the evidence that as many as two thirds of those who identify themselves as *both* nationals and Europeans are unwilling to cede more authority over education and cultural (and welfare) policy to the Union.

THE IMAGINED COMMUNITY: NATION AND EUROPE

Collective identities are by necessity exclusive; they divide "us" from "them," so there is always an "other," whose contrasting qualities help to define our own distinctiveness. This familiar point draws attention to what previously was termed the normative content of an identity, that is, the criteria or attributes that make a group regard its members as unique. Viewed as "imagined community" (Anderson 2006), the nation refers to a body of individuals "who believe themselves to be united by some set of characteristics that differentiate them from 'outsiders' and who are striving to create or maintain their own state" (Haas 1964: 465). The nature of the criteria defining a nation's identity may vary over time or space. In a successful or stable nation, beliefs about its unique identity acquire the status of a collective myth; they are taken for granted and transmitted from one generation to the next as unexamined truths. The normative content of a nation's identity sets the boundaries for membership that usually are enforced by in-group policing (Laitin 2008). Minority group challenges to the dominant rules for inclusion and exclusion can become the bases of movements for secession. The problem of multiple identities, as in the case of nationality versus Europeanness, is the compatibility of their defining norms and rules for inclusion and exclusion. One difficulty of establishing the degree of such compatibility is the fluidity of these self-definitions and the absence of consensus on the thematic content of an European identity (Green 2007).

Again, the most familiar and resonant distinction among nationalisms is the contrast between civic and ethnic conceptions of national identity. Civic nations – often characterized as liberal, voluntarist, and inclusive – base membership on common citizenship; ethnic nations – labeled as illiberal, ascriptive, and exclusive – decide who belongs on the basis of common ethnicity (Brubaker 2004). The civic and ethnic conceptions of nationhood are analytical ideal-types, not accurate descriptions of historical cases. Brubaker (2004) points out that both categories rest on a conception of separate peoplehood, so whatever the contemporary normative prestige of the seemingly tolerant underpinnings of the civic nation, the dividing line between citizen and alien powerfully affects life chances. More to the point, in all cases, common myths, memories, values, and symbols are involved in defining national identities. So in the end, the ethnic-civic distinction rests on how to code and classify these features of a shared and inherited "culture" (Brubaker 2004: 138–9).

If the European Union is treated as a nation-state, what is the content of its collective identity? The controversy concerning the admission of Turkey into the EU illustrates that the meaning of Europe's geographic, religious, and ideological boundaries is not a settled matter. To be sure, if Europe is to be the first twenty-first-century multinational state, it cannot define itself in purely ethnic or linguistic terms. Laitin (2008) argues that the European "nation" will combine the use of English as the principal means of international communication while national and regional languages remain the principal media of instruction and daily interaction. Habermas (1995) insists that given the cultural diversity of its member states, a collective European identity must rest on "constitutional patriotism," a thin form of civic nationhood in which people value peace, democratic political principles, and welfare state policies above more primordial bases of loyalty. Indeed, one conception of the EU is a league of democracies with a stringent list of institutional and political rules for entry.

The continuity of nation-states rests in part on the popular acceptance of symbols of nationhood such as flags and anthems and agreement about the laws governing full membership in the community such as language and education policies and access to citizenship. Accordingly, do governments and citizens agree about what it means to be truly European over and above one's particular nationality? Unfortunately, the Eurobarometer provides no evidence of public opinion on this matter. There are, however, data from other cross-national surveys about how people define their national identities, and these can be studied to explore whether a strong sense of attachment to Europe is related to a more civic than ethnic conception of nationhood – how people balance their European and national identifications with their beliefs about multiculturalism, defined as support for immigration, and the policies that sustain cultural differences within nation-states.

A common European identity might well resemble what hopeful North American scholars have called "multiculturalist nationalism" (Aleinikoff 1998; Hollinger 2006). Hollinger, for example, yearns for a "postethnic" America, in which group identities would be fluid. People may opt to link to their ethnic ancestry or not as they please, and others would respect either the emphasizing or discounting of one's ethnicity in response. A sense of national solidarity, in other words, would rest on mutual tolerance rather than a common culture. Aleinikoff (1998) also tries to find a formula for nationalism congenial to multiculturalism. His conception of an American identity is one that "fosters a nation at peace with its constituent groups and groups that identify with the nation." He accepts that there must be a common allegiance to the nation as a whole in the context of persisting group identities and that this must be "paramount," just as a European identity would have to trump national loyalties. Commenting on the Canadian, Australian, and British efforts to redefine their national identities as multicultural, Joppke (2004), agrees that these amount to no more than acknowledging that the ethnic composition of society had changed and that democracy required acceptance of pluralism. What makes multicultural Britain, Canada, Australia, and the United States distinguishable from each other (or a united Europe) vanishes in this formulation, which admittedly resonates well with Habermas's (1995) idea of "constitutional patriotism."

In measuring the content of collective identities, one should distinguish between classifications built on the study of laws, speeches, rituals, literature, and song, on the one hand, and the prevailing beliefs and attitudes of living people on the other. For example, "ethnic" doctrine may coexist with "civic" public opinion or vice versa. When models derived from analyses of the historical record conflict with the predispositions of mass publics, even path-dependent nationalizing policies may have to give way.

Concerns about the social and political integration of immigrants existed before but received new emphasis in the aftermath of 9/11. In the wake of these worries, the policy pendulum throughout much of Europe has swung back from multiculturalism to assimilation (Brubaker 2001; Joppke 2004). The official outlook in Britain, the Netherlands, France, Germany, Denmark, and Norway now emphasizes the need for minority groups to learn the national language and adapt to national values and customs. The implication is that there is a renewed emphasis on a common culture as the appropriate foundation for membership in the imagined national community.

The 2003 International Social Survey Program (ISSP) conducted by the National Opinion Research Center (NORC) explores mass conceptions of mass conceptions of national identity. Respondents in national samples from most of the countries included in the Eurobarometer surveys were asked this question: "Some people say the following things are important for being truly British (German, Spanish, etc.). Others say they are not important. How important to you think each of the following is for making someone truly." The list of traits included: being born in a country, having citizenship, having lived in a country most of one's life, being able to speak the country's language, being a Christian, respecting a country's political institutions and laws, and "feeling" like a member of the country. Attributes like nativity and Christian faith are on their face ethnic criteria, whereas respecting a country's laws and simply feeling like a member of a country are inclusive and putatively civic norms.[1]

The 2003 ISSP also asked respondents separate questions about their sense of closeness to their country and to Europe, enabling replication of the Eurobarometer classification of respondents as feeling close only to their nation, close to both their nation and Europe, and close to Europe alone. Table 2.7 compares the answers of these three groups of identities to the question about the foundations of nationality in their country.

An earlier analysis (Citrin and Wright 2008) concluded that ordinary citizens retain features of a traditional, ethnic outlook about national identity despite official endorsements of cultural pluralism. It is true that there is a tendency for "civic" traits such as feeling like a national, respecting a country's laws, and being a citizen to be named more frequently than the ascriptive traits of religion or place of birth. Still, speaking the country's language is, on balance, most commonly cited as a very important component of a nation's identity. Language clearly is central to any group's culture, though languages can be learned, so one might regard this trait as exclusive only in the short or medium term. (Interestingly, Ireland, Spain, and Japan give less importance to language than the other countries surveyed. The Irish case is explained by the fact that in daily life, English rather than Gaelic is the country's common language; the Spanish case may reflect the public's recognition that several important linguistic minorities are conationals). Citrin and Wright (2008) also found that between 1995 and 2003, there was an across-the-board shift in favor of ascriptive characteristics (such as being born in the country and being a member of the predominant national religion) and a fairly pronounced shift toward discounting the importance of some of the more civic items, such as respect for institutions and laws as well as "feeling" like a national. An interesting sidebar that highlights the possible discrepancy between traditional characterizations

---

[1] Underlying the use of this measure is the assumption, admittedly incompletely tested, that people are not simply identifying a negative cultural stereotype when they say how important something is to making one a "true" national. Rather, they are assumed to view the "true" national, the ideal-typical fellow citizens, in positive terms.

TABLE 2.7. *Identity Choice and Conceptions of National Identity (in percent)*

Answering "very important" to ...	More Attached to Europe	Equally Attached to Both	More Attached to Nation	Total
Be born in the country	14	33	43	38
Have the country's citizenship	25	45	55	50
Have lived in the country for most of one's life	15	31	35	33
Speak the country's main language	49	53	57	55
Be Christian	8	18	16	17
Respect country's political institutions and norms	47	49	56	53
Feel like a national	33	46	55	50

Notes: Identity choice is constructed by subtracting responses to the question about closeness to Europe from responses to the question about closeness to one's nation. The normative content of national identity is measured by the percentages of respondents in the 2003 ISSP saying that a particular quality is *very important* for making one truly a national (International Social Survey Program 2003).

of historians and current public opinion is that in Germany, supposedly an ethnic nation, ascriptive traits are mentioned less often than in the United Kingdom or in Ireland as very important for defining a "true" national.

Table 2.7 reports the connections between identity choice and conceptions of national identity for the pooled sample of respondents, but the pattern that emerges here repeats itself in every individual country. Those who feel closer to their own country than to Europe generally are most likely to name the listed traits as very important for making one a true exemplar of his or her nation's identity. This holds whether the specific attribute is an "ethnic" trait like nativity or a "civic" quality such as respect for the country's laws. Differences between those who prioritize their national identity and those with a dual sense of attachment in how national identities are framed are not large, although they are statistically significant. The large gap in outlook is between the Europhiles (those who put their European identity first) and everyone else. For example, only 14 percent of those prioritizing Europe compared to 43 percent of those prioritizing their national identity think it is very important to have been born in their country to be a "true" national. Only when it comes to speaking the national language and respecting the country's laws are the Europhiles close to the remaining group of citizens. There also is a consensus that national identities in contemporary Europe are defined in secular terms; in no country does the proportion of those saying that being a Christian is very important for nationhood reach the level of 30 percent. This indifference to religious identity may partially explain the widespread resentment in Europe for demands that

Muslim law and traditions receive official recognition. The main interest of Table 2.7, though, is that identity choices that prioritize Europe seem to imply the loss of the very idea of national boundaries or uniqueness.

In Europe as a whole, enlargement has created new forms of cultural and linguistic diversity. Within individual member states, immigration, from both inside and outside the EU, is the main source of demographic multiculturalism. Economists argue that an aging Europe needs immigrants, but the public's response tends to be hostile, in part because the largely Muslim and non-European immigrant streams are viewed as a cultural threat (Crepaz 2006; Sides and Citrin 2007; Sniderman, Hagendoorn, and Prior 2004). There is a heated debate about whether policies that endorse multiculturalism in the sense of giving minority cultures official support and recognition diminish the integration of newcomers and erode national cohesion and solidarity. Critics call for policies to speed assimilation – actively through language training and civic education and passively by denying multiculturalist demands.

Previous research indicates that only a small minority in all European countries favors accepting many more immigrants; the modal view is to support admitting just "some" more, an ambiguous position without precise limits (Sides and Citrin 2007). Crepaz (2006: 98) reports that in the 2000 World Values Survey, an average of two thirds of the public in eleven countries (Austria, Belgium, Denmark, Finland, France, Germany, Ireland, Italy, Netherlands, Sweden, and the United Kingdom) said that immigrants should "take over the customs of their new country" rather than maintain their distinct customs and traditions. Similarly, the 2002 European Social Survey found that majorities in every country except Sweden said "it would be better for a country if almost everyone shares the same customs and traditions" (Crepaz 2006; Citrin and Sides 2008). Majorities everywhere also felt that knowing the receiving country's language should be a criterion in deciding which immigrants to admit (Citrin and Sides 2008).

The 2003 ISSP survey allows a look at several aspects of immigration and multiculturalism. One question asks whether immigration levels should be increased or decreased, which is measured by a single item.[2] Another battery of four items attempts to measure the respondent's opinion of the consequences of immigration on the economy, jobs, crime, and culture.[3] Generally speaking, these items tend to be highly intercorrelated, and we find similar results here. As a result, a single index based on all four items was created.

A third policy dimension could be loosely called "access to citizenship" and includes three items tapping agreement/disagreement with the following

---

[2] Question wording: "The number of immigrants coming to [country] should: (Increase a lot, increase a little, stay the same, decrease a little, or decrease a lot)."

[3] These are measured by agreement/disagreement with the following: (1) immigrants are generally good for the [country's] economy; (2) immigrants take jobs away from people born in [country]; (3) immigrants improve [country nationality] society by bringing in new ideas and cultures; (4) immigrants increase crime rates.

notions: that legal immigrants who are not citizens should be granted equal rights as those born in the country; that children born in the country should have citizenship even if their parents are not citizens; and that children born abroad should have citizenship if at least one parent does. Yet again, these items are quite strongly intercorrelated, so we use a single index that averages them together into one "citizenship" index.

Finally, the ISSP includes several items meant to ascertain respondent attitudes on multiculturalism. The first of these is an item asking respondents whether they agree or disagree that "it is impossible for people who do not share [Country's] customs and traditions to become fully [Country's nationality]." Another item asks respondents whether they agree or disagree that "ethnic minorities should be given government assistance to preserve their customs and traditions." The third item asks respondents whether cultural minorities should maintain their own separate traditions or try to blend into the larger culture. Taken together, these questions assess the extent of tolerance for subnational identities within one's nation-state. This tolerant outlook is a criterion that elites have made a hallmark of European identity and is a featured criterion when applications for accession to the EU are considered.

What is the effect of prioritizing a national over a European identity on public attitudes toward immigration and multiculturalism? Table 2.8 presents the results of a multiple-regression analysis in which the standard measure of identity choice (the subtraction of closeness to Europe scores from closeness to the nation scores) is a predictor along with measures of a respondent's left-right orientation, religiosity, gender, age, level of education, employment status, and urban-rural residence. The results are straightforward and consistent. Identity choice matters for policy preferences in a predictable way. Those who prioritize their national identity are more hostile to immigration, more willing to restrict access to citizenship, and more insistent that cultural minorities adapt to the mainstream national culture. The relatively small group who prioritize their European identity are more willing to adopt an inclusive definition of national identity and to accept the maintenance of cultural diversity as acceptable policy at both the national and European levels. Multiple identifications have implications for domestic policy.

Table 2.8 shows the familiar pattern of greater support for immigration and multiculturalism among the political left, the relatively young, the better educated, women, and city dwellers. Not unexpectedly, people with some history of immigration in their family also are more in favor of liberal immigration and citizenship policies. To the extent that these groups become a larger segment of European populations, a more permissive outlook toward internal multiculturalism may grow.

CONCLUSION

In Mark Twain's words, news of the death of the nation-state in Europe has been greatly exaggerated. Europeans continue to prioritize their national

TABLE 2.8. *Identity Choice as a Predictor of Immigration and Multiculturalism Preferences*

	Desired Immig. Level	Immig. Conseq.	Citizenship Rights	Impossible to Be Nat. w/out Sharing Trad.	Gov't Support for Minority Culture	Maintain or Adapt?
National-European Attachment	.10***	.10***	.06***	.08***	.06***	.08***
Party ID/Ideology	.17***	.15***	.12***	.18***	.19***	.23***
Gender	.01	-.01*	-.02**	-.02***	-.01	-.01
Age	.04***	.04***	.02*	.10***	.06***	.15***
Education	-.17***	-.17***	-.08***	-.15***	-.07***	-.08***
Rural/Urban	.02*	.03***	.01*	.03**	.01	-.01
Unemployed	.02	.04***	.01	.00	.00	.03
Religiosity	-.04***	-.03***	-.03***	.00	-.04***	-.04*
History of Immigration in Fam.	-.09***	-.07***	-.05***	-.05***	-.05***	.00
r²	.18	.17	.15	.10	.23	.09
n	7,341	7,036	7,327	7,620	7,499	6,628

Notes: Each column is a separate OLS regression with the column variable as the dependent variable. *** $p < .001$, ** $p < .01$, * $p < .05$. Unstandardized regression coefficients are reported. In addition to variables listed above, country-dummies were also included in the equation although their coefficients are not reported. National-European Attachment is coded in the pro-nation direction and constructed by subtracting the closeness to Europe score from the closeness to country score.

"Immigration Level" refers to a single five-category item asking respondents whether the country's immigration level should be increased or decreased.

"Immigration Consequences" represents the respondents' factor scores on a factor analysis of four items on the effects of immigration; the items themselves concern immigrants' effect on the country's economy, jobs for nationals, crime rates, and their contribution of new ideas into national culture.

"Citizenship Access" refers to respondents' factor scores on three items tapping willingness to grant equal rights to citizens not born in the country and nationals, willingness to extend citizenship to children born in the country even if parents are not citizens, and willingness to extend citizenship to children born abroad if at least one parent is a citizen. All variables and indices are scored from 0 = most favorable to immigrants/immigration to 1 = least favorable to immigration and immigrants.

"Cultures and Traditions" refers to a single item asking respondents if they agree or disagree with the notion that someone who does not share the nation's culture and traditions can never truly be considered a national, scored from 0 = strongly disagree to 1 = strongly agree.

"Government Aid for Minority Culture" refers to a single item tapping whether respondents agree or disagree that the government should provide aid to help minorities preserve their culture, scored from 0 = strongly agree to 1 = strongly disagree.

"Minorities Should Maintain or Adapt" is a single item asking respondents whether minority groups should maintain their own separate cultures or try to adapt to the predominant national one, scored 0 = Maintain and 1 = Adapt.

"Gender" is a dummy variable coded 0 = male and 1 = female. "Age" is a five-category variable coded from 0 = youngest to 1 = oldest. "Education" is a five-category variable coded from 0 = least educated to 1 = most educated. "Rural/urban" is coded 1 = Urban, 2 = Suburban, 3 = Rural.

"Unemployed" is a dummy variable coded 0=other and 1=currently unemployed, looking for work. "Religiosity" is a 6-category variable coded from 0=least religious to 1=most religious.

"Some History of Immigration in Family" is a dummy variable coded 0=citizen, both parents citizens and 1=non-citizen or at least one parent is a non-citizen.

Source: 2003 ISSP Survey Countries included are Germany, UK, Austria, Ireland, Spain, France, Portugal, Denmark, and Finland.

identity over their attachment to the European mega-state. At the same time, a dual sense of attachment – a sense of closeness to Europe as well as one's nation – has been growing. This is likely to continue with the replacement of older cohorts by more pro-European younger citizens, by increased travel within Europe, and by more people learning a second language, usually English. Moreover, the data presented here show that the way people accommodate their two identities matters for public policy. Those for whom a European identity has a positive emotional value are more likely than those with a purely nationalist outlook to trust European institutions, to accept sharing sovereignty in significant policy domains, and to acquiesce in liberal immigration and asylum policies. A strong sense of European identity also is associated with greater tolerance for cultural minorities within one's own country.

From the nationalist's perspective, the problem of multiple identities is Janus-faced. On the one hand, a supranational European government may threaten the essence of a nation state's sense of uniqueness by forcing conformity to continentwide symbols, rules, and policies. On the other hand, most European nations are becoming more internally heterogeneous due to immigration. In addition, some nation-states such as Britain and Spain have acceded to regional demands for self-determination and facilitated the development of quasi-autonomous subnations in Scotland and Catalonia. Ironically, the existence of the EU umbrella may make it easier for separatism to succeed. Czechoslovakia split up and both parts are in the European Union; it is not difficult to imagine Flanders, Wallonia, and Scotland as members should Belgium and the United Kingdom break apart.

The staying power of national identity thus has obvious political relevance, and it is fair to say that the European project is the single greatest challenge to Rupert Emerson's (1960: 95–6) statement in his magisterial *From Empire to Nation* that the nation is "the largest community which, when, the chips are down, effectively commands men's loyalty, overriding the claims both of the lesser communities within it and those which cut across it or potentially enfold it within a still greater society." To the extent, then, that the nation legitimates the state, continuing the creep toward European statehood requires the growth of a more intense sense of European identity. The unresolved question is whether a stronger Europe comes to be perceived as a threat to the cultural identities of its member nations. The data reported here suggest that mass publics are ready to draw the line on EU authority when this touches on sacred elements of national myths and policies.

The financial crisis of the late 2000s points to the limits of Europe's supranational institutions, despite decades of effort aimed at creating a united political policy. In response to the Eurozone financial crisis of 2008, national governments have moved swiftly to protect the finances of their own citizens and have proved unwilling to take steps to support banks in other countries. Governments ignored the bloc's rules for a collective line of defense to take care of their own. And this example points to the crux of the problem of multiple identities.

When push came to shove this time, national allegiance took precedence. What might one expect, therefore, if the EU ordered Britain to go to war to rescue French and Italian tourists kidnapped somewhere in Africa? At the psychological level, choices like these define how multiple identities are balanced. At the political level, the stubborn defense of national economic interests suggests that European governments recognize the reluctance of citizens to yield control over fundamental decisions. A referendum on giving up the unanimity rule in EU decision making in favor of more qualified majority voting is a step fraught with political risks.

In a recent book, *Compound Democracies,* Sergio Fabbrini (2007) argues that governance in Europe and the United States is converging. The EU is "nationalizing" and the United States is moving toward a looser set of rules that recognize limits on federal power and sovereignty. However, is the American achievement of *e pluribus unum* a realistic prospect for Europe? In the American case, the creation of a dominant national identity first involved a century-long struggle against state interests and identities, a struggle that was decided by a bloody civil war. The emergence of an inclusive American identity also involved both the absorption of waves of immigrants who shed, not always voluntarily, their native languages and customs and the belated shattering of the racial barrier to full citizenship.

If the United States is taken as a model, achieving *e pluribus Europa,* a circumstance in which a European identity dominates national attachments and EU institutions preempt the power of national governments, is not on the horizon. The supranational European state will continue to exercise important powers because the costs of exit for member-states are too great and because the demands placed on most individual citizens to sacrifice on behalf of their fellow Europeans are not great. As to the future status of minority cultures within nation-states, much depends on how immigrants and their children negotiate their own multiple identities as ethnics, nationals, and Europeans.

This study of mass publics replicates many of the findings and reinforces the conclusions of Fligstein (2008), Green (2007), and Hooghe and Marks (2008) regarding the new relevance of public opinion for European integration. How identities are constructed and framed matters. The current landscape as seen from a distant satellite has changed little over the past decade. In most countries, the Europhiles are a small minority. The majority of the public feel themselves attached both to the nation and to Europe. Identity choice as a political imperative may not arise often, but it is relevant for public choices when another big step toward European political integration is proposed. However, the mobilization of political identities does not occur in a vacuum. Elites – party leaders and interest-group activists – make arguments and appeals that promise benefits or elicit a sense of threat. European integration is a line of political cleavage in a number of countries, creating opportunities for oppositions on both the left and right, albeit for different reasons (Hooghe and Marks 2008: 120–2). In a contest for mass support, context matters, too, and an important if somewhat neglected factor is the decline of political trust in European democracies (Dalton 2008). With internal political cohesion and respect for the established, largely pro–European elites fragile, winning a popular referendum for Jean Monnet's dream of One Europe would be challenging indeed.

3

European Disunion?

The Implications of "Super" Diversity for European Identity and Political Community

Anthony M. Messina

> One needs to distinguish between people's identification with a political community or sense of citizenship and their sense of communal identity. The latter might enhance the former but the two concepts are not identical.
>
> (Thomassen 2006: 4)

> The way identity bears on European integration depends on how it is framed, and it is framed in domestic political conflict.
>
> (Hooghe and Marks 2008: 120)

> Giving up one's loyalty to the nation is not required for a European demos. But we know little about those social and political contexts in which European and national identities might actually clash.
>
> (Risse 2004: 271)

As the above quotes suggest, issues of identity and political community are increasingly coming to the fore across contemporary Europe. *Why so* and *why now* are not difficult to fathom. As the center of gravity of the project of "ever-greater European union" has migrated from the economic realm to that of citizenship and political community during the past three decades (Duchesne 2008: 405), numerous Europeans have become alarmed that their hitherto exclusive notion of national or subnational identity is increasingly at risk. Indeed, for many Europeans, the quickening pace of European integration has raised the disquieting specter that their terminal identity is being redefined and the membership of their political community uncomfortably and undesirably expanded (Laffan 1996: 89).

Compounding the popularly held perception that terminal identities are under threat are the societal aftershocks resulting from the permanent settlement in Europe of hundreds of thousands of immigrants during the past several decades – most from developing countries – who have introduced a plethora of

TABLE 3.1. *Foreigners in Spain's Autonomous Communities, 2009*

Community	% of Community Population	% Distribution in Country	Incidence*
Andalucía	8.1	12.0	.68
Aragón	12.7	3.0	1.1
Asturias	4.3	.84	.36
Islas Baleares	21.7	4.2	1.8
País Vasco	6.1	2.4	.51
Islas Canarias	11.5	5.4	.96
Cantabria	6.5	.68	.54
Castilla-La Mancha	10.8	4.0	.90
Castilla y León	6.5	2.9	.54
Cataluña	15.9	21.2	1.3
Extremadura	3.3	.65	.28
Galicia	3.8	1.9	.32
La Rioja	14.5	.83	1.2
Madrid	16.4	18.7	1.4
Murcia	16.3	4.2	1.4
Navarra	11.1	1.3	.93
Comunidad Valenciana	17.4	15.8	1.5
Spain	12.0	100	1.0

* Represents the ratio between the numbers of foreigners/immigrants living in the region (percentage of total regional population) to the total number of foreigners in the country (percentage of the total national population).

Source: Instituto Nacional Estadística 2009.

new cultures, ethnicities, languages, and religious practices into the European Union. Along these lines, the number of Muslims currently resident within the European Union is estimated at greater than 20 million, including 5 million in France, 3.3 million in Germany, and 1.6 million in the UK (Vaisse 2008: 3). The presence of Muslim immigrants in Europe's major cities is especially high, and as much as 25 percent of the total population in Rotterdam, 24 percent in Amsterdam, 20 percent in Marseille, 17 percent in Brussels, and 16 percent in Bradford (Wikipedia 2010). More broadly, as of January 1, 2008, the second-biggest share of foreigners in the EU consisted of 6 million people from non-EU European countries, followed by 4.7 million from African countries and 3.7 million from countries on the Asian continent (Vasileva 2009: 1-2). In once homogeneous, labor-exporting countries like Ireland, Germany, and Spain, the number of foreign-born persons is now between 11 and 14 percent of the total population.

A similar pattern of increasing population diversity obtains in many of Europe's once fairly homogeneous regions. In ten of seventeen of Spain's autonomous communities, for example, the foreigner population now exceeds 10 percent (Table 3.1); in the traditional region of Valencia, foreigners outnumber

TABLE 3.2. *Immigrants in France's Regions, 2009*

Region	% Regional Population	% Distribution in Country	Incidence
Alsace	7.6	3.8	1.3
Aquitaine	4.2	3.6	.71
Auvergne	3.3	1.1	.56
Bourgogne	3.9	1.7	.66
Bretagne	1.9	1.7	.32
Centre	4.1	2.8	.70
Champagne-Ardennes	3.8	1.4	.64
Corse	8.3	0.7	1.4
Franche-Comté	4.5	1.4	.76
Ile-de-France	12.5	40.0	2.1
Languedoc-Roussillon	5.6	4.0	.95
Limousin	4.2	0.9	.75
Lorraine	5.1	3.5	.86
Midi-Pyrénées	4.5	3.5	.76
Nord-Pas-de-Calais	3.2	3.5	.54
Basse-Normandie	1.9	0.8	.32
Haute-Normandie	2.8	1.4	.47
Pays de la Loire	2.0	1.9	.34
Picardie	3.3	1.7	.56
Poitou-Charentes	2.7	1.3	.46
Provence-Alpes-Côte d'Azur	6.3	8.3	1.1
Rhône-Alpes	6.4	10.7	1.1
Metropolitan France	5.9	*100*	1.0

Source: Institut national de la statistique et des études économiques 2009.

Spanish citizens in no fewer than fifteen towns (News from Spain 2007). In eight of nine regions in Austria, foreigners comprise more than 5 percent of the total population, including Vienna, which has a foreign-born population of 19 percent (Statistics Austria 2007). In seven of twenty-two of France's administrative regions, the immigrant population exceeds 5 percent of the population, with Ile-de-France having an immigrant population of greater than 12 percent (Table 3.2). Although Denmark has fewer immigrants than either Austria or France, each of its five regions has an immigrant population of 5 percent or greater, including Copenhagen, which has one of the highest immigrant populations of any European region (Table 3.3). Moreover, although foreign-born persons do not exceed 4 percent of the total population in either Scotland or Wales, both of these traditional UK regions are under considerable pressure to accommodate the needs and interests of their burgeoning new ethnic and religious minority populations (Lewis 2006; Williams, Evans, and O'Leary 2003).

TABLE 3.3. *Immigrants and Descendants in Denmark's Regions, 2010*

Region	% of Regional Population	% Distribution in Country	Incidence
Copenhagen	15.4	47.9	1.6
Southern Denmark	8.1	18.0	.83
Central Jutland	7.9	17.8	.80
Zealand	6.7	10.5	.68
Northern Jutland	5.5	5.8	.56
Denmark	9.8	*100*	*1.0*

Source: Danish Ministry of Refugee, Immigration and Integration Affairs 2010: 30.

Against the backdrop of Europeanization and increasing ethnic and religious diversity, popular anxieties about both the scope and pace of European integration and the societal consequences of mass immigration seem to be accelerating and intersecting for at least two reasons. First, the free circulation of EU citizens has objectively resulted in the greater penetration of national and regional communities by "outsiders." Second, greater European economic and political integration – and particularly the Europeanization of immigration policy making – has fostered a widely held popular view that the state has lost control over *who* and *how many persons* can enter its territory. Given these shifting and often unsettling circumstances, we should perhaps not be surprised to discover two phenomena that portend difficulties for the cause of "ever-closer European union" and, by extension, the emergence of a meaningful European identity. The first is stasis in the propensity of Europeans to embrace a European identity. As numerous opinion surveys have indicated, the number of EU citizens privileging a European identity over a national one – approximately 11-12 percent of the EU's population – has remained relatively unchanged since the early 1990s (Citrin and Sides 2004b: 168). Relatively constant too has been the 85 percent or so of EU citizens who privilege a national identity over a European one.

A second and perhaps an even more important phenomenon is the tendency of a critical number of Europeans to perceive few, if any, meaningful distinctions among the many ethnic, linguistic, racial, and religious groups that are defined as "the other." Ivarsflaten (2005: 42), for example, has discovered that "driving force behind Western Europeans' support for restrictive immigration and asylum policies is their concern about the unity of their national community." In this regard, the opponents of new immigration and/or immigrant settlement are no more favorably disposed toward economic migrants than asylum seekers. Moreover, as Table 3.4 reveals, distrust of the "other" is not exclusively directed toward immigrants. For example, when asked if Scotland would begin to lose its identity if more Muslims, blacks and Asians, or East Europeans came to settle in the region, ethnic Scots, quite remarkably, did

TABLE 3.4. *Scotland Will Lose Its Identity If More "Outsiders" Settle in the Region, 2006 (in percent)*

	Muslims	Blacks and Asians	East Europeans
Agree strongly	14	11	11
Agree	35	35	34
Neither agree nor disagree	19	18	20
Disagree	27	31	30
Disagree strongly	4	4	4
Don't know	1	1	1

Source: Bromley, Curtice, and Given 2007: 140-1.

not choose to discriminate. Every outsider group irrespective of its citizenship status, religious features, racial characteristics, and/or national origin was viewed as equally threatening to Scottish identity. Indeed, a sizeable plurality (49/46/45 percent) of respondents agreed that an increase in the number of permanent settlers from every group would erode Scotland's regional identity. Moreover, reinforcing research findings from the Italian and Dutch cases revealing that threats to cultural identity are more salient than threats to economic well-being (Sniderman et al. 2000; Sniderman and Hagendoorn 2007), ethnic Scots were more likely to perceive the aforementioned outsiders as more of a threat to Scottish identity than an economic challenge (Table 3.5). With regard to the latter, ethnic Scots again were not disposed to discriminate. British ethnic minorities (27%) were about as equally likely as their fellow EU citizens from Eastern Europe (31%) to be perceived as taking "jobs away from other people in Scotland."

As has been extensively documented, ethnic Scots are not especially ethnically, racially, or religiously intolerant. To the contrary, there is abundant evidence that they are *less* exclusionary than many, if not most, of the majority and regional minority populations of Europe (Hussain and Miller 2006: 73-5). Nevertheless, beneath this otherwise positive environment lies the reality that, like their fellow Britons and Europeans, relatively few Scots primarily see themselves as Europeans; moreover, the approximately 12 percent of Scots who identify as European has not increased since the late 1990s (Mahendran and McIver 2007: 12). The further bad news for the advocates of a European identity is that 80 percent of Scots view themselves as having no more in common than with people who see themselves as European than they do with anyone else (Mahendran and McIver 2007: 12).

Against this backdrop, a key question is whether conditions of "super" diversity in the European Union are conducive to the intra- and intersocietal solidarity and cohesion necessary for the emergence of a meaningful European identity and political community. What is super diversity? In the British context, Vertovec (2007: 1024) describes super diversity as a "condition distinguished

TABLE 3.5. *"Outsiders" Take Jobs Away from Other People in Scotland, 2002–6 (in percent)*

	British Ethnic Minorities		East Europeans EU Citizens
	2002	2006	2006
Agree strongly	5	7	7
Agree	15	20	24
Neither agree nor disagree	32	32	28
Disagree	34	30	28
Disagree strongly	9	7	8
Can't choose	4	2	2
Not answered	1	2	3

Source: Bromley, Curtice, and Given 2007: 151–2.

by a dynamic interplay of variables among an increased number of new, small and scattered, multiple-origin, transnationally connected, socioeconomically differentiated, and legally stratified immigrants" who have migrated to the UK since the 1990s. As more broadly defined here, super diversity is the unprecedented proliferation of ethnic, religious, and/or racial cultures and identities (Vertovec 2007: 1048) within and across traditional territorial boundaries (Sniderman and Hagendoorn 2007: 124). As such, the tipping point of diversity – or the point at which it becomes super – has an objective foundation in the proliferation of subcultures and identities *within* and *across* the traditional "nation" states of Europe.

There is little doubt that ethnic diversity has significantly increased within Europe since WWII. As cited in the introduction to this volume, contemporary London, as the home of more than fifty ethnic groups of at least 10,000 persons communicating in more than 300 different languages, is the most diverse city in the history of the world and, hence, especially well deserving of the label "super diverse." In metropolitan Copenhagen, approximately 13 percent of the population is foreign born, with nine countries (Turkey, Pakistan, Yugoslavia, Iraq, Sweden, Lebanon, Germany, Morocco, and Norway) accounting for half of the immigrant population (Price and Benton-Short 2007: 113). With nearly 30 percent of its population foreign born, Amsterdam too exhibits super diversity. Across Europe as a whole, about one third of the population below the age of thirty-five has an immigrant background, with at least thirty cities having populations of more than 100,000 foreign-born persons (Price and Benton-Short 2007: 109). Moreover, more than 300 different ethnic and national minorities currently reside within the EU.

This said, the starting point of this chapter is that super diversity is not simply an objective phenomenon. Rather, the point at which it arrives will vary from one society to another and from one period to the next depending upon the intersection of historical, political, and social factors that either

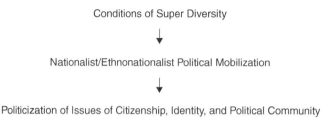

Conditions of Super Diversity

↓

Nationalist/Ethnonationalist Political Mobilization

↓

Politicization of Issues of Citizenship, Identity, and Political Community

↓

Euroscepticism

↓

Lack of Affective European Identity

FIGURE 3.1. Implications of super diversity.

increase or decrease a particular society's carrying capacity for diversity. As such, this chapter argues that it is not the objective conditions of super diversity that potentially and/or directly imperil a European identity and political community, as Putnam (2007) and others (Goodhart 2004) seem to claim, but rather, as Figure 3.1 suggests, the broad field of opportunity that it ploughs for the political ascension of exclusionary nationalist ideologies and nationalist groups and parties (Csergo and Goldgeier 2004). More specifically, conditions of super diversity feed the popular embrace of exclusionary nationalisms, which, in turn, impede the embrace of an affective European identity among Europeans (Green 2007: 25) and the emergence a meaningful European political community (Cinpoes 2008). In so doing, these conditions indirectly frustrate the aspiration of the EU's founding fathers to have a European identity eventually displace national ones among the citizens of Europe (Duchesne and Frognier 1995: 193).

ENTREPRENEURS OF DIFFERENCE AND DIVISION: ETHNONATIONAL AND ANTI-IMMIGRANT PARTIES

Which political vehicles are the principal carriers of these exclusionary nationalisms within the contemporary European Union? Two vehicles are politically prominent and especially salient for the project of ever-greater European union and the emergence of a meaningful European identity: ethnonationalist and anti-immigrant political parties.

Ethnonationalist Parties

Ethnonationalism, according to Leslie (1989: 45), is a broad-based sentiment inspired by "a form of group solidarity or community feeling *based on ethnicity rather than territory*; it refers to subjective attachments that demarcate one particular group from other groups within a total population" (emphasis in the original). Prominent examples of ethnonationalist groups in Europe include the Scottish (SNP) and Welsh (PC) nationalist parties in the United Kingdom, the Basque Nationalist Party (PNV) in Spain, the Breton Democratic Union (UDB) in France, and the Northern League (LN) in Italy.

The primary aspiration of most ethnonationalist groups is to redistribute political authority and power away from central governments in favor of the traditional region or "periphery" (De Winter, Gómez-Reino, and Lynch 2006b: 14). As political antagonists of the integrity and authority of the traditional nation-state, ethnonationalist parties therefore need to erect psychological walls between regional communities and majority and/or other minority populations. As De Winter and colleagues (2006b: 16) astutely observe:

> As ethnic entrepreneurs ... ethnoregionalist parties play a central role in the (re-) construction of the regionalist "imagined community" and its subsequent claims for changing the existing centre/periphery power arrangements.... The widespread stereotypes of Catalans vis-à-vis Andalusians and of Flemish vis-à-vis Walloons, Lombards vis-à-vis Sicilians, do not seem to differ much from those of the extreme-right nationalist-populist parties vis-à-vis Turks and North-African "guest workers."

Contemporary ethnonationalist political parties, however, are not exclusively preoccupied with demands for regional autonomy and/or broader claims for reconfiguring existing center-periphery relations (De Winter et al. 2006b: 15). As examples of ethnonationalist political parties in Belgium, Britain, and France illustrate (Tables 3.6–3.8), many are also very much concerned with Europe and, specifically, with the recent trends and currents connected to the project for greater economic and political European integration (Tarchi 2007: 188). Along these lines and consistent with patterns elsewhere (De Winter and Gómez-Reino 2002: 491; Marks, Wilson, and Ray 2002: 587), the ethnonationalist parties of Belgium, Britain, and France are generally pro–Europe and tend to support greater European economic, if not political, integration.

This said, the preferences of these and other ethnonationalist parties on Europe are far from fixed or unambiguously supportive of the European project (Chari, Iltanen, and Kritzinger 2004; Hoppe 2007). To the contrary, the historical record suggests that ethnonationalist parties tend to hold changing, often contradictory, and predominantly instrumental positions on European integration (Chari et al. 2004); moreover, an analysis of regionalist political party manifestoes reveal these parties to be "only the fourth-most pro-European party family" (see Gómez-Reino, Chapter 6 in this volume). For most ethnonationalist parties, European integration primarily offers but an opportunity to weaken the political authority of the traditional nation-state and make their region more economically viable in the event that it eventually gains greater political and legal/or autonomy (De Winter et al. 2006b: 16; Haesly 2001: 97;

TABLE 3.6. *Belgian Ethnonational Political Parties' Views toward Europe and Immigration, 2007*

Party	Region	General Views on Europe	Specific Views on Europe	Immigration
Lijst Dedecker	Flanders	Pro-Europe, but critical	Believes structural reforms of the European Union should be implemented before it is expanded further east. Against Turkish membership in the EU. Promotes strong respect for the principle of subsidiarity.	Proposes integrating immigrants by teaching them the Flemish language and cultural traditions. Believes that being Flemish is based not on ethnicity but on participation in the Flemish community and acceptance of the Flemish culture. Will only grant political asylum to those who are truly needy, according to the pertinent international agreements. Illegal immigration is condemned; however, legal immigration is permitted without regard to intellect or economic or social status. Favors general European immigration quotas and criteria to facilitate entry into Europe.
Nieuw-Vlaamse Alliantie	Flanders	Pro-Europe	Envisions an independent Flanders that participates fully in all European institutions as a member-state of a democratic and confederate Europe. Supports European integration so long as the European Union respects the individuality and cultural identity of each of its member-states. Wants Flanders to have a more visible presence in Europe.	

Vlaams Belang	Flanders	Critical	Believes the European Union is too bureaucratic and involved in areas in which the sovereignty of the people should prevail. Opposes the extension of the European Union beyond the geographical boundaries of Europe. Wants EU to respect the right of self-determination of each of its member-states. Supports a clear division of responsibilities and a separation of power between the Union and its members. Considers Europe a poorly functioning and cumbersome bureaucracy and out of touch with its citizens. Does not believe that the growing transfer of power to Brussels leads to more efficiency. Besides the euro currency, does not know what the value of Europe really is. Rejects a European superstate and favors instead a confederal grouping of sovereign states that can leave the EU at any time. Believes only European countries should be allowed to join the Union and rejects Turkish EU membership because Turkey is not a European country. Proposes limiting the power of the European Commission and wants the Council of Ministers to be more open in their decision-making process. Supports the veto right of member-states.	Supports preserving Flemish cultural identity and is opposed to multiculturalism. Foreigners expected to adapt to the Flemish culture, values, and lifestyle and to respect certain European principles such as the separation of church and state, democracy, free speech, and equality between the sexes. Proposes a citizenship test, to include the Dutch language and European values, for all non-EU members who want to settle permanently in Flanders. Believes illegal immigrants should be repatriated and reserves the right to vote for citizens. Opposes a Flemish immigration policy that attracts immigrants. However, supports immigration. The slow institutionalization of Islam must be undone, and in certain situations Islamic headscarves must be prohibited. The system of family reunification has gotten completely out of hand, and it was a mistake for the government to regularize tens of thousands of illegal immigrants.

(continued)

TABLE 3.6. (*continued*)

Party	Region	General Views on Europe	Specific Views on Europe	Immigration
			Opposes a European citizenship and a European constitution.	
			Considers the establishment of European institutions in Brussels a disaster for the livability of the city and a threat to Flemish identity and wants a wider distribution of European institutions in more cities.	
			Advocates creating a European defense force and close cooperation between the EU member-states in matters relating to security.	
			Believes a strong Europe is the best defense against international terrorism.	
Vlaams Progressieven	Flanders	Pro-Europe, but critical	Considers Europe to be the first political defense against the alienation created by globalization.	Supports economic migration to Europe through quotas, in partnership with the countries of origin, so as not to create a brain drain.
			Believes in a Europe that respects the rights of its regions and the identity of each nation.	
			Favors a Europe with a senate of the regions and a government based on a political majority and constitutional pluralism.	

			Promotes respect for the principle of subsidiarity.
			Proposes a European defense force to replace national armies. The force should be modern, efficient, and quickly deployable and focus on conflict prevention and management.
			Supports creation of a European group to promote renewable energy.
			Advocates the enlargement of the EU to include the states created from the former Yugoslavia.
			Opposes Turkish membership in EU because it does not satisfy the conditions of the Copenhagen treaty.
VLOTT	Flanders	Pro-Europe, but wary of it	Favors the European Union so long as it is not overbearing and permits the free market to run its course.
			Against the accession of Turkey into the Union, because it believes the country does not hold European standards and values.
			Believes in open-mindedness and condemns intolerance.
			Expects immigrants to respect the region's cultural ideals and add value to the society in exchange for seeking a new life in the area.

Sources: Lijst Dedecker: http://www2.lijstdedecker.com; Nieuw-Vlaamse Alliantie: http://www.n-va.be; Vlaams Belang: http://www.vlaamsbelang.be; Vlaams Progressieven: http://www.vlaamsprogressieven.be; VLOTT: http://www.vlott.be; Google Translate: http://translate.google.com; Yahoo! Babel Fish: http:// babelfish.yahoo.com.

TABLE 3.7. *British Ethnonational Parties' Views toward Europe and Immigration, 2007*

Party	Region	General Views on Europe	Specific Views on Europe	Immigration
Scottish National Party	Scotland	Pro-Europe, but critical	Believes having a stronger voice in European affairs would be one of the greatest benefits of Scottish independence. Promotes European Union as a "confederation of sovereign states" and recognizes the right of nations to protect their sovereignty. Opposed to "unnecessary centralization." Critical of Europe's handling of Scottish fisheries and wants their control to be handed back to Scotland. Promotes a common European security policy to support peacekeeping and humanitarian missions. Believes the euro would be more beneficial to Scotland than the pound. Recognizes EU membership has greatly benefited the economies of small nations such as Finland and believes Scotland could reap these same benefits as an independent EU member. Believes that all EU member-states should meet their commitments to international development aid, which few are currently doing.	
Plaid Cymru	Wales	Pro-Europe, but critical	Wants full European Union membership for Wales. Supports creating a more democratic EU through a written constitution and a Charter of Fundamental Rights incorporated into the Treaty. Wants the decision-making process of the Council of Ministers to become more "accountable and transparent." Advocates strengthening the powers of the European Parliament.	Considers every person living in Wales a Welsh citizen and invites everyone to commit to building a better Wales. Believes that every asylum seeker and refugee should be treated according to the United Nations Refugee Charter.

Sources: Scottish National Party: http://snp.org; Plaid Cymru: http://plaidcymru.org.

TABLE 3.8. *French Ethnonational Political Parties' Views toward Europe and Immigration, 2007*

Party	Region	General Views on Europe	Specific Views on Europe	Immigration
Union du Peuple Alsacien	Alsace	Pro-Europe	Recognizes that Alsace is in the heart of Europe and has been enriched by its past relations with the continent.	
Alsace d'Abord	Alsace	Pro-Europe	Opposed to a "technocratic Europe" that embodies what it sees as the errors of centralized states and favors the construction of a political Europe. Opposes extending the right to vote to non-European citizens. Opposes Turkey, an "Islamic power," joining the EU.	Opposed to the migration of non-Europeans into Europe.
Union Démocratique Bretonne	Brittany, Pays de la Loire	Pro-Europe	Wants a "federal and interconnected" Europe.	
Emgann	Brittany, Pays de la Loire	Pro-Europe, but not in its current form	Wants a Europe that serves its people, not one composed of nation-states that serves the privileged. Promotes a social Europe based on the federalism of the peoples that compose it. Believes that Europe cannot benefit the people of Brittany until the region is free to act as it wants on the international scene.	
Bloc Català	Eastern Pyrenees	Pro-Europe	Wants to construct a stronger Catalonia within a European context and promotes social democrat European policies.	
Unitat Catalana	Eastern Pyrenees	Pro-Europe	Since 1991, has been in favor of the construction of a Europe of solidarity.	

(continued)

TABLE 3.8. (continued)

Party	Region	General Views on Europe	Specific Views on Europe	Immigration
Corsica Nazione	Corsica	Pro-Europe	Wants Corsican independence in a European context.	Welcomes into Corsica anyone willing to learn the Corsican language and culture.
Accolta Naziunale Corsa	Corsica	Pro-Europe	Promotes a strategy of Corsican autodetermination in partnership with Europe.	Anyone who has lived in country for ten years and is willing to integrate into Corsican life is welcome.
Partit Occitan	Southern France	Pro-Europe	Supports construction of a federal Europe composed of different peoples and regions. Desires the recognition of the Occitan community by the European Union. Wants direct representation of the Occitan community in European institutions.	
Ligue Savoisienne	Savoy	Pro-Europe	Recognizes that Savoy is in the heart of Europe and has always been European. Believes that a stronger Europe does not exclude their right to a sovereign Savoy.	Recognizes the right of the Savoyards to decide, through referendum, questions concerning immigration, such as whether to give citizenship to the Savoy-born children of foreign parents. Believes annexation by France led to uncontrolled immigration into Savoy, with negative social consequences.
La Région Savoie, j'y crois!	Savoy	Skeptical	Remains wary of European tendency towards supranationality. However, prefers a European regional equalization to a French one.	

Sources: Union du Peuple Alsacien: http://fers.elsass.free.fr; Alsace d'Abord: http://www.alsacedabord.org; Union Démocratique Bretonne: http://www.udb-bzh.net; Emgann: http://www.chez.com/emgann; Bloc Català: http://www.bloc-catala.com; Unitat Catalana: http://www.galeon.com/unitatcatalana; Corsica Nazione: http://www.corsica-nazione.com; Accolta Naziunale Corsa: http://www.anc-corsica.com/index2.htm; Partit Occitan: http://partitoccitan.free.fr; Ligue Savoisienne: http://www.ligue.savoie.com; La Région Savoie, j'y crois!: http://www.regionsavoie.com.

Paquin 2002: 71). They perceive Europe as providing a "home within which to assert 'regional/national identities' that had been undervalued or trapped inside existing national states" (Laffan 1996: 90). As a consequence, whenever and wherever ethnonationalist parties conclude that either the cause or direction of European integration is incompatible with these objectives or, alternatively, whenever they decide that the progress of European integration seriously threatens their region's cultural autonomy, they do not fail to distance themselves from the European project (Hepburn 2007: 243; Swyngedouw, Abts, and Van Craen 2007: 84). As they do so, a critical number of their supporters follow suit (e.g., Vlaams Belang supporters in the region of Flanders).

Most ethnonational parties also focus, albeit to a lesser degree, on issues of immigration and immigrant settlement. Why they have become increasingly attentive to these issues in recent years is no mystery; as the data in Tables 3.1 through 3.3 reveal, ethnonationalist groups are often embedded within traditional regions, which are also home to an increasing number of Europe's new ethnic, racial, and religious minorities. Many ethnonationalist parties are understandably ambivalent about immigration. On the one hand, foreign workers are oftentimes recruited by regional authorities to alleviate labor shortages, ameliorate declining birthrates, and spur greater economic growth and productivity (Fernández-Huertas Moraga and Ferrer-i-Carbonell 2007). On the other hand, as the formal policy positions of Belgium's ethnonationalist parties demonstrate (Table 3.7), ethnonationalists can sometimes view immigrants as a potential threat to their region's cultural homogeneity and social solidarity (Núñez 2002: 229; Tarchi 2007: 189). Recognizing this ambivalence, Kymlicka (2001a: 75) has been inspired to prescribe that regional minorities should exercise some control over both the volume of immigration and the terms of immigrant settlement, the former "to ensure that the numbers of immigrants are not so great as to overwhelm the ability of society to integrate them."

An important exception to the rule of the ethnonationalist party ambivalence toward immigration is represented in the example of the ethnonationalist right, however. Included among these groups are Italy's Northern League (*Lega Nord*), Belgium's Flemish Interest (*Vlaams Belang*), France's Savoisian League (*Ligue Savoisienne*), and several others. In contrast to other ethnonationalist parties, the ethnonationalist right marries traditional appeals for greater regional autonomy or self-governance with a highly visible animus toward immigration and settled immigrants. Specifically, they explicitly link the cultural, economic, and political "penetration" of the periphery (i.e., the traditional regions) by the metropole (i.e., central government) with its simultaneous human "invasion" by unwanted and undesirable immigrants. Although its racial illiberalism and xenophobia are sufficient reasons for mainstream political parties to shun them, it is, in fact, the ethnonationalist agenda that makes the ethnonationalist right an unattractive, although – as the case of Italy's Northern League well demonstrates – not an entirely unfit partner in national governing coalitions.

Anti-Immigrant Parties.

In contrast to ethnonationalist parties, immigration-related issues are at the top of the agenda of anti-immigrant parties. Indeed, these parties are in the vanguard of the domestic political actors within the EU attempting to politicize state immigration policies and other issues related to the permanent settlement of the new ethnic, racial, and religious minorities. Although the circumstances of their founding, organizational structure, ideological proclivities, programmatic orientation, and core political strategies differ, all contemporary anti-immigrant groups within the contemporary EU share at least three characteristics. First, they are overtly hostile toward settled immigrants and opposed to all new immigration. Second, they owe much, if not the greater part, of their modest political success during the past three decades to their exploitation of the social tensions that have accompanied the settlement of post–World War II immigrants (Betz 1994: 67; Bjørklund and Andersen 2002: 128-9). Finally, to varying degrees, the major anti-immigrant groups of Europe have successfully cultivated and fostered a climate of public hostility toward immigrants that, in turn, has created a more favorable political context for themselves (Williams 2006).

In accounting for the relatively recent surge of popular support for anti-immigrant groups within the European Union, it is fair to conclude on the basis of the evidence (Messina 2007: 54-96) that this phenomenon is less the product of "objective" conditions (e.g., the state of the economy or the objective economic burden of immigration) than a result of "subjective" perceptions and anxieties within the majority population (e.g., the fear that national identity and/or racial or cultural homogeneity are eroding). Along these lines, most anti-immigrant groups propagate "the idea of nation and national belonging by radicalizing ethnic, religious, lingual, and other cultural and political criteria of exclusion in order to bring about a congruence between state and nation, and to condense the idea of nation into an image of extreme collective homogeneity" (Minkenberg 2007: 263).

Like ethnonationalist groups, anti-immigrant actors in Europe are not single issue oriented; to the contrary, they also propagate controversial, if not extreme, views on many other major public policy questions, including issues pertaining to European cooperation and integration. Indeed, Marks and colleagues (2006: 165) appropriately categorize the political far right as the most Eurosceptical party family in Europe.

Fears about the perceived loss of national sovereignty, dilution of national cultures, and prospect of increased immigration from within and outside the European Union motivates most anti-immigrant groups to be the most vociferous opponents of the project for greater European integration. Much as they do with immigration-related questions, anti-immigrant groups articulate and amplify the public's doubts about the current course and pace of the ongoing project of ever-closer European union. To date, the efforts to exploit anti-European public sentiment politically by anti-immigrant groups and far right parties in general have yielded uneven political returns, however. Few anti-immigrant groups have directly profited politically by opposing the quickening pace of European integration, including the adoption and introduction of the single currency (Messina 2006). However, this is not to say that they do not influence the domestic politics of European integration.

Influence of Ethnonationalist and Anti-Immigrant Parties.

How do ethnonationalist and anti-immigrant parties influence popular support for Europe and European integration? Although the empirical evidence is not entirely straightforward, political parties organized around issues of identity and political community, as ethnonationalist and anti-immigrant parties are, do seem to influence negatively the public's perceptions of Europe. Netjes and Edwards (2009), for example, have empirically demonstrated that partisan cueing is essential to "understanding the conditions under which ... national identity considerations are mobilized against European integration." As a result of their cueing of the national electorate, Eurosceptical right-wing parties – that is, predominantly anti-immigrant parties including the ethnonational right – sway "popular opinion against Europe by mobilizing the growing uncertainties about the future of European integration amongst the mass public" (De Vries and Edwards 2009: 22). In this vein, Carey and Lebo (2001) offer evidence demonstrating that declining public support for European integration is explained by attachments to national identity. On the basis of their research, they conclude (2001: 3) that nationalism is "negatively related to support for the European project because of conflicts over sovereignty that developed in this era, such as the creation of a single European currency, the European central bank, and the increasing primacy of European law." Hooghe and Marks (2005: 437) offer the additional insight that "the extent to which national identity bites on support for European integration depends on how divided national elites are. Where elites are united on Europe, national identity and European integration tend to coexist; where they are divided, national identity produces Euroscepticism."

Anti-immigrant and some ethnonationalist parties also seem to circumscribe policy making on Europe. On this score, the influence of ethnonationalist and anti-immigrant parties on public policy outcomes pertaining to Europe and European integration appears to follow from their politicization of the aforementioned themes and, in turn, the effect that politicization has on policy choice. Specifically, flanked by vocal critics of the European project on their political right, national governments are constrained in pursuing policies to foster ever-closer European union. Along these lines, Hooghe and Marks (2009: 22) argue that "the mobilization of exclusive national identity among mass publics is likely to raise the heat of debate, narrow the substantive ground of possible agreement, and make key actors, including particularly national governments, less willing to compromise.... As European multi-level governance has become more closely coupled, so leaders have less room to maneuver." More generally, Hooghe and Marks observe (2006: 248) that "as a result of politicization and populism territorial identities have come to play a decisive role in European integration …. Parties appealing to exclusive national identity have taken the initiative in public debate."

Territorial Identities: Fractures Across and Within European States

How fertile is the political soil for the exclusionary nationalisms fostered by all anti-immigrant parties and the ethnonationalist right? With regard to the former, it is now well known that persons identifying exclusively with the nation-state are more likely than not to be hostile toward Europe and European integration (Hooghe and Marks 2004a). As research by McLaren (2007: 248) has discovered, for these EU citizens, European integration poses "a threat to their key terminal identities." The primary reason is clear. As Carey (2002: 391) argues, "the stronger the bond that an individual feels toward the nation, the less likely that individual will approve of measures that decrease national influence over economics and politics. The growth of the scope of the European Union in the realm of economics, politics and culture, which have previously been under the sole control of the nation-state, impinges on this view of the nation."

The ubiquity of and often robust electoral support for ethnonationalist political parties (De Winter et al. 2006a, 2006b) also suggest that differences of territorial identification within and across national populations have political consequences, although whether ethnonationalist political parties surpass a critical threshold of electoral support ultimately depends upon many variables, including the political and electoral competition strategies adopted by mainstream parties (Meguid 2008). While the pervasiveness and strength of regional identities within a given country is *not* perfectly correlated with the electoral fortunes of ethnonationalist political parties, it is nevertheless self-evident that the most virulent political manifestations of ethnonationalism could never take root in the absence of a critical mass of citizens who strongly identify with their region.

In this vein, the survey data represented in Tables 3.9 through 3.11 indicate that significant differences of public opinion exist across countries – and, within countries, across regions – on issues pertaining to national cohesion and solidarity, or issues that underpin citizenship, identity, and political community. For example, with respect to the question of whether a citizenship and language test should be required of noncitizens (Table 3.9), a supermajority of Germans (86%) and Britons (83%) agree that it should, while many fewer Italians (61%), Frenchmen (61%), and Spaniards (50%) concur. Spaniards and Frenchmen are the most regionally divided and Britons least regionally conflicted on this question, with Germans and Italians falling between these two poles.

Intercountry differences also are evident with respect to whether civics courses should be part of the standard school curriculum. As the data in Table 3.10 indicate, Italians are virtually unanimous (99%) in endorsing mandatory civics courses. At the other end of the spectrum, fewer than three of

TABLE 3.9. *Citizenship and Language Test Should Be Required for Continued Residence in Country, 2007 (in percent)*

Great Britain				Italy			
Region	Yes	No	Not Sure	Region	Yes	No	Not Sure
North	81	8	11	North	66	24	11
Midlands	83	9	8	Central	57	32	11
South	84	8	10	South	54	36	9
Total	83	8	10	Total	61	29	10

Germany				France				Spain			
Region	Y	N	NS	Region	Y	N	NS	Region	Y	N	NS
North	87	8	5	Paris	57	28	15	N. West	38	49	13
Central	89	8	3	N. East	70	13	17	N. Central	47	36	17
South	82	9	9	N. West	53	22	25	N. East	58	26	17
East	90	5	5	Central	67	22	11	Central	52	34	14
West	73	21	6	S. East	66	15	18	Central Coast	41	39	21
				S. West	41	44	15	South	52	33	15
				Mediterranean	8	–	92	Islands	55	40	6
Total	86	9	5	Total	61	21	18	Total	50	35	15

Source: Harris 2007.

TABLE 3.10. *Civics Courses Should Be Part of Standard School Curriculum, 2007 (in percent)*

Great Britain				Italy			
Region	Yes	No	Not Sure	Region	Yes	No	Not Sure
North	77	8	15	North	98	1	2
Midlands	68	16	16	Central	100	–	–
South	74	9	17	South	99	–	–
Total	73	11	16	Total	99	1	1

Germany				France				Spain			
Region	Y	N	NS	Region	Y	N	NS	Region	Y	N	NS
North	93	2	6	Paris	83	9	8	N. West	83	12	4
Central	90	6	5	N. East	85	7	8	N. Central	89	6	4
South	85	10	5	N. West	84	5	10	N. East	89	7	4
East	94	5	2	Central	92	7	1	Central	82	14	4
West	90	6	4	S. East	86	7	7	C. Coast	82	12	5
				S. West	89	11	–	South	80	11	9
				Mediterranean	100	–	–	Islands	79	15	7
Total	92	4	5	Total	86	7	7	Total	84	10	5

Source: Harris 2007.

TABLE 3.11. *Different Communities Should Be Allowed to Abide by Different Laws, 2007 (in percent)*

Great Britain			Italy		
Region	Agree	Disagree	Region	Agree	Disagree
North	38	50	North	49	38
Midlands	40	44	Central	48	38
South	32	54	South	23	52
Total	37	49	*Total*	41	42

Germany			France			Spain		
Region	Agree	Dis.	Region	Agree	Dis.	Region	Agree	Dis.
North	37	31	Paris	34	48	N. West	39	38
Central	33	39	N. East	30	50	N. Central	23	58
South	31	29	N. West	22	52	N. East	44	40
East	33	40	Central	45	47	Central	34	49
West	36	36	S. East	44	48	C. Coast	29	43
			S. West	48	40	South	36	45
			Mediterranean	–	–	Islands	61	20
Total	36	33	*Total*	35	49	*Total*	37	44

Source: Harris 2007.

four Britons (73%) embrace this position, with Spaniards (84%), Frenchmen (86%), and Germans (92%) supporting it more widely. In every country, the general population is less internally divided on the question of mandatory civics courses than the issue of administering citizenship and language tests.

Yet a third pattern of public attitudes prevails on the question of whether "different communities should be allowed to abide by different laws according to their own cultural and religious identity." As Table 3.11 reveals, West Europeans are least unified on this question. Almost half of Britons (49%) and Frenchmen (49%) and approximately two fifths of Italians (42%) and Spaniards (44%) *disagree* that different communities should be allowed to abide by different laws, while only a third of Germans (33%) dissent. In Italy and Germany, the percentage of those who agree and disagree are approximately equal; in France, Britain, and Spain, the balance between the two is decidedly less so. Even more interesting are the interregional differences of opinion on the question. It is universally true – and conspicuously so in Spain and Italy – that fairly wide interregional differences of opinion exist about whether different communities should be allowed to abide by different laws according to their own cultural and religious identity. Along these lines, near majorities *favoring* the proposition are present only in northern and central Italy (including Lombardy and Umbria, respectively), southwestern France

TABLE 3.12. *Rational Distribution of Policy Issue Preferences among Groups*

Policy Issues	Tend to Support	Tend to Oppose
Mandatory citizenship and language test	Nationalists Ethnonationalists	Immigrants
Mandatory civics courses	Nationalists Ethnonationalists	Immigrants Ethnonationalists
Different communities/different laws	Immigrants Ethnonationalists	Nationalists Ethnonationalists

(including Aquitaine), and Spain's Canary Islands. Conversely, majorities *dissenting* from the proposition that different laws should apply to different communities are found within only one region in four of the five countries: southern Britain (including London), southern Italy (including Sicily), northwest France (including Basse-Normandie), and north central Spain (including Cantabria).

Why are West Europeans much more conflicted on the third question than the first two? One possibility is that on the first two questions, nationalists (or at least a large fraction of the majority population) and ethnonationalists may share a similar perspective (i.e., against immigrants?), while the third question possibly pits nationalists against ethnonationalists *and* immigrants and, depending upon the circumstances, ethnonationalists against immigrants *and* the majority population. The potential mix of group interests regarding the three questions is represented in Table 3.12. As these tables suggest, nationalists and ethnonationalists are potentially of a similar mind concerning the proposal for a mandatory citizenship and language test for new immigrants for the fairly obvious reason that both groups generally expect immigrants to integrate into and therefore embrace to some degree the larger social and political community to which they've migrated (i.e., Belgium or Flanders; Britain or Wales; Spain or Catalonia, etc.). Mandating citizenship and language tests for new immigrants is one means of achieving this goal.

With respect to the proposal to require civics courses, nationalists are likely to support it, but so too are ethnonationalists *if and only so long as* the "civic" values promoted within these courses reflect those of the regional rather than the national community; otherwise, they will likely oppose it. Put differently, ethnonationalists are likely to support making civics courses mandatory if these courses have a regional orientation (e.g., they focus on and celebrate Basque, Corsican, or Welsh culture and history) and oppose them if they primarily reinforce national founding myths and values. Thus, depending upon on their content and who is designing and administering them, mandatory civics courses can possibly enhance *either* a nationalist *or* an ethnonationalist social/political agenda by reinforcing an individual's attachments either to the national or regional political community.

Conversely, allowing different communities to abide by different laws according to their own cultural and religious identity potentially threatens the identity and interests of both nationalists and ethnonationalists by permitting, on one tier, ethnonationalists *and/or* immigrants the freedom to undermine national political and social cohesion and, on a second tier, immigrants *and/or* members of the national majority population (a critical number of whom may permanently reside within the historical region) the leverage to undermine regional political unity and cultural homogeneity. As Table 3.12 suggests, in every scenario, nationalists "lose" and immigrants, and particularly devout religious ethnics (e.g., Muslims), "win" if different communities are allowed to abide by different laws. On the other hand, for perfectly rational and self-interested reasons, ethnonationalists are predisposed to deny immigrants and/or members of the national majority population residing within the traditional region the same cultural, legal, and/or political autonomy to which they aspire for themselves and their region within the legal and constitutional framework of the national political community. As Kymlicka suggests (2001a: 63), to do otherwise is to allow nonindigenous populations to challenge "the self-conceptions and political aspirations of those [regional] groups which see themselves as distinct and self-governing nations within a larger state."

CONCLUSION

So what can be concluded about the future of these forces of European disunion? Before addressing this question, it must be underscored that it is not super diversity per se that threatens European identity and political community but rather the political framing, manipulation, and exploitation of conditions of super diversity by anti–European political actors. Whatever the objective or subjective tensions among majority populations, ethnonationalists, and immigrants, these tensions are unlikely to achieve a high degree of political salience within a particular country absent the intervention and influence of ethnic or other entrepreneurs (Messina and Fraga 1992: 11). As McCrone and Bechhofer (2008: 1262) observe, "cultural and social differences per se are not enough to create a conflagration." Hooghe and Marks (2009: 13) make the similar point that:

> [I]dentity does not speak for itself in relation to most political objects, but must be politically constructed.... Public opinion on Europe is particularly susceptible to construction: i.e. priming (making a consideration salient), framing (connecting a particular consideration to a political object) and cueing (instilling a bias).

On this score, few political actors are more invested in issues of identity and political community across contemporary Europe than ethnonationalist and anti-immigrant groups and political parties. Although on opposite sides of most public policy questions, ethnonationalist and anti-immigrant parties are simultaneously the products, political instigators, and beneficiaries of the ethnic, cultural, and social differences that obtain within a particular society. Indeed, ethnonationalist and anti-immigrant groups, whatever their differences, share at least two characteristics. First, both groups tend to politicize issues of identity and political community that were previously outside of the parameters of mainstream political party competition (Meguid 2005: 347). Second, ethnonationalist and anti-immigrant groups are often arbiters of whether cultural and social differences are politically mobilized, how so, and for which purposes (McCrone and Bechhofer 2008: 1262). Put simply, these differences must first be politically framed, filtered, and mediated in ways that suggest that a national or a regional identity and a European one are in tension. Unfortunately for the causes of ever-closer European union and the emergence of a meaningful European identity, it is very much the mission of the ethnonationalist right and almost all anti-immigrant political parties to foster, exacerbate, and politically exploit such tension to varying degrees.

The good news, of course, is that most of Europe's traditional regional communities, including ethnic Scots, do not now support a significant anti-immigrant or ethnonational right political party. The further good news is that most regional minority parties across Europe are positively inclined toward Europe and European integration. This said, one might reasonably ask: Under which circumstances and for how long will the aforementioned conditions persist? Specifically, can a regional identity and an increasingly politically assertive ethnonationalism indefinitely coexist with greater intraregional cultural and social diversity – an inevitable outcome given current conditions – and without eroding the relatively supportive posture toward Europe that most Scots and other ethnonationalists currently hold?

If, as Hooghe and Marks (2007: 126) argue, a strong territorial identity is compatible with support for greater regional integration only in circumstances in which national or subnational identity is nonexclusive and it is *not* cued by a Eurosceptical party or parties, then the answers to the above questions are highly conditional. Specifically, so long as ethnonationalist identities do not become more exclusive as a result of the continuing struggle in political center–periphery relations within the traditional nation-state and the ethnonationalist parties do not find cause to play the anti-immigration card as a reaction to continuing migration to the regions and/or the anti–Europe card as a result of its concerns about a loss of regional cultural or political autonomy – as has occurred in the not-too-distant past (Lynch 2006: 241) – then most ethnonationalists are likely to remain supportive of European integration. If, on the other hand, ethnonational parties choose the opposite, negative course – that is, one similar to that of several ethnonational parties in Europe – then the prospects for greater European union will most likely be different. In either event, one outcome will likely be the same: Ethnonationalists, like most other Europeans, will continue to privilege a nationalist identity over a supranational one and, in so doing, deny Europe the "affection" they willingly and so much more easily extend to their nation.

So what does the future hold for these actors? First, it is highly unlikely that they will be exiting the European political stage any time soon. For reasons exogenous and only indirectly related to European integration, the number of and popular support for ethnonationalist and anti-immigrant groups are currently expanding. Ethnonationalist sentiment continues to spread across Europe, and the countries experiencing a popular backlash to mass immigration continues to multiply. Second, whether political and electoral support for these anti-European forces continues to grow is linked, at least in part, to the responses to these forces and their messages by mainstream political elites and political parties. Specifically, to the extent that mainstream political actors are united and forward thinking on issues of diversity and Europe, it is less likely the potential forces of disunion will be able to indefinitely exacerbate and exploit intra- and intersocietal conflict over these issues. In sum, the extent to which super diversity in Europe is or will be ultimately detrimental to the cause of ever-closer European Union and a meaningful European identity will, in part, be politically determined.

PART II

ETHNOREGIONAL CHALLENGES

4

Strange Bedfellows

Public Support for the EU among Regionalists

Seth Kincaid Jolly

Between 1979 and 1997, Scottish public support for European integration increased by 25 percent (Jowell, Heath, and Curtice 1998; Miller and Brand 1981), while support for European integration among all Europeans dropped nearly 14 percent (Schmitt and Scholz 2005). At the same time, Scottish public support for independence also increased dramatically, from 6.9 percent in 1979 to 34.3 percent in 1997. In addition, as early as 1997, a majority of Scottish citizens thought Scotland would be completely independent within twenty years (Brown, McCrone, and Patterson 1999: 147). While the European Union (EU) deepens, the United Kingdom itself seems ever more likely to fragment, or, at the very least, devolve further.

Are these two trends linked? Regionalists, resentful of centralization and threats of homogenization, could perceive a deeper European Union either as yet another threat to their culture or as an ally in their broader bargaining game with the state.[1] If regionalists view the EU as a threat, then they should be skeptical of European integration, especially regarding political integration. I argue that substate nationalists more often view the EU as an ally, in large part by diminishing the advantages of incorporation in a large, multinational state. By this logic, substate nationalists should not only be supportive of the EU project, but they should also find autonomy itself, whether devolution or independence, a more viable and plausible prospect within a deeper European Union. In this chapter, I first test these competing logics and find that regionalists in Western Europe are Europhiles. Then I analyze the Scottish case in more detail

---

[1] In this chapter, I focus on movements within a state that seek greater autonomy, either in cultural terms, like language rights, or in constitutional terms, such as formal devolution or even independence. As a group, these movements go by many names, including substate nationalist, regionalist, and autonomist. For this chapter, I use the regionalist term to follow the literature (see, for example, De Winter and Türsan 1998).

and find that perceptions of Europe and Scotland's role in it play an important role in the evolving attitudes toward devolution and independence.

Extending from Gabel's initial work on public support for European integration (Gabel 1998a, 1998b) to ever more intricate models (Brinegar and Jolly 2005; Gabel and Scheve 2007a, 2007b; Ray 2004; Steenbergen and Jones 2002), scholars find that economic interest drives public opinion on European integration. Recently, though, scholars have focused more attention on identity to explain support for the EU (Carey 2002; Hooghe and Marks 2004a, 2005, 2009; McLaren 2002). This literature tends to focus on conceptions of national or state identity, with little or no emphasis on substate, or regional, identity; thus, this chapter's focus on substate identities supplements this literature.

Due to data limitations on regional identity questions in surveys, I both directly and indirectly evaluate whether regionalists are pro-European. In addition to using respondents' intention to vote for a regionalist party as an explanatory variable for EU support, I take advantage of a sophisticated literature that evaluates whether elite cues drive public opinion on European integration (Gabel and Scheve 2007a, 2007b; Hooghe and Marks 2005; Steenbergen, Edwards, and De Vries 2007; De Vries and Edwards 2009). After dealing with the obvious endogeneity issues between public and elite attitudes, these studies demonstrate that parties and elites do cue their supporters with either elite Euroscepticism or support. In earlier work (Jolly 2007), I demonstrated that, on average, the regionalist party family is pro-European and, further, regionalist parties use the EU rhetorically to strengthen their case for independence or greater autonomy. Hence, I leverage these earlier findings to evaluate the effectiveness of these cues on attitudes toward the European Union.

In many ways, this research fits neatly in Hooghe and Marks's (2009) postfunctional theory of integration. They argue that European integration is increasingly politicized and that political party and public attitudes toward the European Union are crucial for Europeanization. Among other arguments, they argue that this contestation over Europe is shaped by identity, in particular whether individuals hold inclusive or exclusive conceptions of national identity (Hooghe and Marks 2008). By showing that regionalist partisans (and parties) are, on average, pro-EU, this chapter bolsters their finding, suggesting that the EU may find allies precisely among those groups that are commonly seen as opponents of centralization.

Next, I use the Scottish case to test the second observable implication of the theory: Regionalists should find regional autonomy, even independence, more viable in a deeper European Union than in autarky. The devolution referenda in Scotland in two distinct periods provide a unique opportunity to compare attitudes and actions regarding devolution and independence. In the first referendum, a slight majority voted for devolution, but the margin was not enough to overcome the electoral threshold set by Westminster. In 1997, though, the result was overwhelmingly pro-devolution. In the ethnic politics literature, cultural heterogeneity is the leading explanation of regionalist or autonomy movement support. But in the Scottish case, that factor is held constant over time. Supranational integration, however, is not. With public opinion surveys from each referendum available, I show that the devolution referendum succeeded in 1997 precisely because Scots find an independent Scotland to be a more viable prospect. Following the logic of the size-of-states argument and the elite cueing literature, I argue that deeper European integration is responsible for revised Scottish attitudes toward independence and, therefore, a positive outcome in the devolution referendum.

The chapter proceeds as follows. First, I introduce the size-of-states theory that explains why European integration encourages support for independence among regionalist citizens and therefore increase support for European integration among regionalists. Second, I analyze public support for European integration using the Mannheim Eurobarometer Trend File (Schmitt and Scholz 2005). In the final section, using data from the 1979 Scottish Election Study and the 1997 Scottish Referendum Study (Jowell, Heath and Curtice 1998; Miller and Brand 1981), I demonstrate that voters support devolution at higher rates, in terms of voting behavior, and they also have much more favorable attitudes toward independence from the United Kingdom, albeit within the European Union, in the survey data. This finding suggests that the increased viability of an independent Scotland within a deeper European Union encourages support for autonomy in Scotland.

MULTILEVEL GOVERNANCE AND REGIONALIST MOVEMENTS

European Integration and the Optimal Size of States

Theoretically, the European Union makes smaller states more viable by diminishing the advantages of larger state size (Alesina and Spolaore 1997, 2003; Bolton and Roland 1997). In the past, "[t]he types of arguments used against minority nationalist and regionalist demands have often centered around the impracticalities of upsetting administrative and political traditions constructed around central institutions" (Lynch 1996: 12). Thus, for regionalist political entrepreneurs, European integration increases the credibility of demands for greater autonomy and therefore individual support for self-government.

Following Alesina and Spolaore's (1997, 2003) size-of-states argument, I argue that the European Union decreases subnational dependency on the nation-state in both economic (e.g., international trade and monetary policy) and political terms (e.g., defense, foreign policy, and minority rights). In other words, the European Union system of multilevel governance increases the viability of smaller states, thereby creating additional incentive for citizens to support devolution or even independence. For economists, the theoretical result is a smaller optimal size of states in Europe under the umbrella of the European Union and a system of free(er) trade (Alesina and Spolaore 1997, 2003; Alesina, Spolaore, and Wacziarg 2000; Alesina and Wacziarg 1998; Casella and Feinstein 2002; Wittman 2000). Thus far, though, many of the empirical implications of these theoretical models have remained largely untested.

According to Alesina and Spolaore (2003), the optimal size of a state "emerges from a trade-off between the benefits of scale and the costs of heterogeneity in the population" (175). Via membership in the European Union, the advantages of large states vis-à-vis small states are diminished.[2] However, the key cost of a larger state, namely heterogeneity of preferences, remains. Political economists find that economic growth and public policies suffer with greater ethnic heterogeneity (Easterly and Levine 1997). A government of a homogeneous population tends to be more successful at public policies because the day-to-day lives of the people are more similar (Tilly 1975: 79), while larger, more heterogeneous states are less efficient at public good provision (Bolton, Roland, and Spolaore 1996: 701). As a result of this comparative advantage, European regions may see themselves as more capable of providing sustained economic growth than the traditional nation-states (Newhouse 1997: 69), yielding political separatism as an unintended consequence of economic integration (Alesina and Spolaore 1997).

Though not explicitly modeled, the size-of-states theory hinges on rational behavior by two sets of actors, regionalist political elites and citizens. Regionalist political elites must perceive the changing political opportunity structure and support European integration, in part as an ally against the central state. Using the Chapel Hill Expert Survey (CHES) data for 1984 to 2002, Jolly (2007) showed that the regionalist party family is surprisingly and consistently pro-Europe at least through the early 2000s. Drawing on the CHES data, Figure 4.1 replicates one of the summary findings of that study. As shown in Figure 4.1, regionalist parties send a positive signal to voters regarding European integration, particularly when compared with other niche party families.

Their attitudes are similar to those of mainstream families, such as the Socialist or Liberal party families, as opposed to the Eurosceptic attitudes common to other fringe party families, such as the Radical Right or Left. Certainly, some notable exceptions exist. For instance, Liang (2007) discusses the hard Euroscepticism of the Vlaams Blok and the relatively soft Euroscepticism of the Lega Nord (i.e., not anti–Europe per se but not supportive of the direction the EU is going). Further, the regionalist party support for the EU is not naive or inflexible but rather tactical or even cyclical (Hepburn 2007, 2008). The Scottish National Party, for instance, held negative attitudes towards the EU in the 1970s, only shifting in the 1980s (Hepburn 2008; Jolly 2007).[3]

---

[2] In historical terms, several factors encouraged economically larger states (Alesina and Spolaore 2003), including economic market size, economies of scale for public goods, insurance against asymmetric regional economic shocks, and security. For each of these factors, the EU has reduced – though certainly not eliminated – the advantage of large states vis-à-vis small states. See Alesina and Spolaore (2003) or Jolly (2006) for more on this model.

[3] As discussed in Hepburn (2007, 2008), regionalist attitudes toward the EU may be cyclical and may in fact currently be in a less pro-Europe part of the cycle. However, given that the Mannheim Eurobarometer data end in 2002, this shift does not affect the analysis in this article.

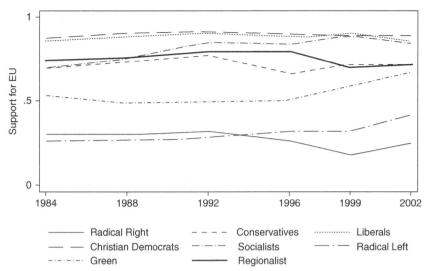

FIGURE 4.1. Support for the European Union by party family.
Source: Jolly 2007.

Nevertheless, the CHES data show the standard deviation of the family's attitude toward Europe is smaller than that of nearly all other party families, implying a relatively coherent party family, at least on this issue. In comparison, the excellent volume edited by De Winter, Gómez-Reino, and Lynch (2006a) makes the diversity of the regionalist party family on many other issues and goals abundantly clear.

More than just pro-European attitudes, though, the regionalist parties tend to use rhetoric that supports the causal mechanism proposed in this article. In tracing the official party positions of the Scottish National Party, in particular, Jolly (2007) finds that European integration becomes an integral component in their strategy and rhetoric for independence. Similarly, the Plaid Cymru in Wales remained hostile to the EU until party elites realized the EU could "serve as a wedge between Wales and the controlling authorities in London," which in turn increased the viability of Plaid Cymru's autonomist goals (Van Morgan 2006: 277).

In addition to elites, citizens must perceive that European integration changes the political opportunity structure in favor of substate regions. If so, public opinion among regionalist supporters should also be in favor of European integration. In addition to the size-of-states argument, Hooghe and Marks's (2004a, 2005, 2008) postfunctional theory also predicts that individuals with nonexclusive national identities (i.e., regional identities) will be more supportive of European integration. Generally, then, I expect that respondents with regionalist identity will be pro-EU.

Unfortunately, while the Eurobarometer is a valuable resource, it does present some problems for this analysis. The Eurobarometer includes a very small number of regionalist supporters in 2000 ($N = 388/32,145$ or 1.21 percent). In addition, there are few questions regarding substate identification available, which restricts a more direct test of the theory in the cross-sectional time-series. As an alternative observable implication, therefore, I focus on party cues. By testing for an effect of party cues on support for European integration, I can indirectly test a critical link in the theory, namely that citizens catch the pro-EU signals of regionalist elites.

Analysis

With evidence from the Mannheim Eurobarometer Trend File (Schmitt and Scholz 2005), which tracks public opinion in the EU from 1970 through 2002, and the 1996 and 2002 Chapel Hill Expert Surveys (CHES) (Ray 1999; Steenbergen and Marks 2007), I begin to address this question. In this section, I focus on two questions: whether regionalists, or substate nationalists, are pro-EU and whether respondents' public attitudes match their party elites' cues.

As Matt Gabel (1998a: 333) points out, public attitudes are an ever-increasing constraint on the European integration project; thus, it is not surprising to find a large and growing literature on the subject (Brinegar and Jolly 2005; Gabel 1998b; Marks and Steenbergen 2004; McLaren 2002). This prior literature provides a starting point for the current analysis of public attitudes toward European integration. Replicating Gabel (1998a), I extend the baseline model by adding whether respondents are regionalist party supporters.[4] Based on the viability theory and the Scottish evidence, I expect to find that regionalist party supporters, ceteris paribus, are more likely to support the European Union.

In the first test of this hypothesis, I utilize Eurobarometer data from 2000, the most recent data in the Mannheim Eurobarometer Trend File for which respondents answer party affiliation and the classic EU support question: Is the EU a good thing or a bad thing?[5] Similar to McLaren (2002), the other variables and controls simply replicate the Gabel model (1998a) and provide a starting point to analyze regionalist sentiment toward the EU.[6] Table 4.1 provides the results of this model.

---

[4] Intention to vote for a regionalist party is simply a proxy for regionalist or substate nationalist sentiment. Though imperfect, it provides a cross-temporal and cross-sectional measure of identification with a regionalist organization.

[5] See Brinegar and Jolly (2004) or Brinegar, Jolly, and Kitschelt (2004) for further discussion of this dependent variable. Perfect, it is not. However, it is largely correlated with other systematic measures of support for European integration (Gabel 1998a). Further, it is the only measure collected consistently through the time series.

[6] In addition to the regionalist party variable, three other exceptions to a perfect replication stand out. The materialism/postmaterialism questions used in the Gabel model are not collected consistently after 1992, the end date of his study. Therefore, I exclude these out of necessity, but even in the original model, they are weak in terms of statistical significance and magnitude. Second, the border variable used in Gabel's original study is not available. Finally, rather than the simple, support proletariat/bourgeois/governing party dummy variables, I use a party cue variable

TABLE 4.1. *OLS Regression of EU Support in 2000*

Variable	Coefficient	(S.E.)
Discuss politics never	-4.722***	(0.441)
Discuss politics frequently	1.979**	(0.587)
Professional	5.974***	(1.210)
Executive	6.568***	(0.798)
Manual laborer	-1.810**	(0.733)
Unemployed	-2.016*	(0.891)
Low education	-4.155***	(0.587)
High-mid education	2.817***	(0.650)
High education	5.664***	(0.557)
Low income	-2.631***	(0.560)
Hi-mid income	3.125***	(0.537)
Hi income	5.088***	(0.520)
Party cue	17.908***	(1.242)
Regionalist Party	4.401**	(1.746)
Female	-2.336***	(0.406)
Retired	1.635*	(0.742)
Small business owner	0.717	(0.897)
Farmer	-1.785	(1.621)
Student	7.281***	(0.755)
Housewife	1.185	(0.723)
Age	-0.078***	(0.017)
Country dummies	Included	
Constant	44.506***	(1.407)
N	32,145	
Adjusted R^2	0.1371	

Note: Table entries are unstandardized regression coefficients with standard errors in parentheses. $*p \leq 0.05$, $**p \leq 0.01$, $***p \leq 0.001$.
Source: Eurobarometer 2001.

Briefly, what is apparent from the replication is the robustness of the original model. Nearly every variable matches the original results in sign and significance. Of particular importance are the occupational, skill, and income variables. In short, higher-skilled, better-positioned citizens are more likely to support European integration in 2000, just as they were from 1973 to 1992 in the original model (Gabel 1998b). With new data, this replication provides further evidence in favor of the robustness of the economic interest explanation.

The two party variables warrant closer attention. First, the positive and significant party cue variable suggests that when parties are supportive of the EU,

developed in Brinegar and Jolly (2005), which matches a respondent's vote intentions with their party's EU position, drawn from the Chapel Hill Expert Survey data (Ray 1999; Steenbergen, Edwards, and De Vries 2007). For this paper, this revised variable better captures the theoretical justification for party cues.

their supporters follow that cue. This variable matches a voter's party intention with the chosen party's position on the EU. In general, then, if the respondent's party supports the EU, the variable will have a positive value. Since regionalist parties tend to be pro-Europe and, in fact, utilize the viability logic to bolster their own credibility while encouraging support of the European project, this variable indicates that regionalist party supporters are more likely to support the EU than any of the other fringe party supporters, such as Radical Right, Green, or Radical Left. Alternatively, if the regionalist parties become more Eurosceptical, then pro-EU forces will lose an important ally.

Also included is a simple dummy variable, measuring 1 if the respondent intends to vote for a regionalist party in the next election. This variable is also statistically significant and positive, again suggesting that regionalist party supporters hold more positive attitudes about the EU than their fellow citizens do. In the next section, I evaluate this conclusion more fully within the Scottish case.

Nevertheless, the number of self-identified regionalist supporters is small. Therefore, I turn to the larger time series available in the Mannheim Eurobarometer Trend file, starting in 1984 to match the CHES data. As the 2000 regression suggests, I expect party cue to be significant across time in the larger dataset. I reran the model from Table 4.1 separately for each year of the Mannheim Eurobarometer Trend File. This alternative to standard time series regression was inspired by Andrew Gelman's (2005) discussion of a secret weapon to consider the changing effect of variables over time.[7] In doing so, I find that the party cue coefficient is statistically significant throughout the time series and has a powerful effect on the dependent variable. Figure 4.2 represents the size of the coefficient for each year's model, with a 95 percent confidence interval.

Figure 4.2 is striking for two reasons tangential to this chapter. First, despite the common perception that parties have lost much of their influence in Western Europe during this period, their attitudes toward the EU continue to have a powerful effect on their supporters' attitudes.[8] Second, there is interesting variation in the magnitude of this variable, with parties having more influence over voters during the 1980s than in the 1990s. Both observations warrant more research.

However, for the purposes of this article, Figure 4.2 demonstrates that party cues have a significant and powerful effect throughout the period. Given the

---

[7] Each individual regression is available upon request of the author, as are the Stata do-files.
[8] As a discussant at the 2008 Midwest Political Science Association annual meeting pointed out, there are at least two plausible alternative explanations. First, rather than parties cueing voters, parties could simply be pandering to the public by choosing policies they support (or oppose). Second, voter preferences on European integration could drive their partisan preferences. However, recent work, using statistical tools designed to test for this type of endogeneity, suggests that there is an effect of elite cues on partisan attitudes (Gabel and Scheve 2007a, 2007b; Steenbergen, Edwards and De Vries 2007; De Vries and Edwards 2009).

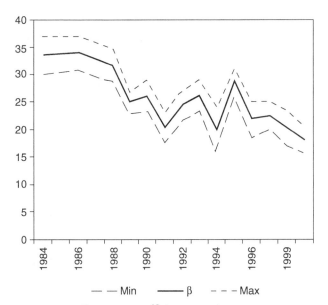

FIGURE 4.2. Party cue coefficient over time.
Source: Mannheim Eurobarometer Trend File, 1970–2002.

knowledge that regionalist parties are pro-EU, on average, this finding suggests that regionalists throughout Western Europe are likely to be pro-EU as well. As noted above, though, where exceptions exist or if regionalist parties change tactics to Euroscepticism, this positive effect will vanish. In the next section, I turn to the Scottish case to test these results for validity.

SCOTLAND

Theoretically, the revised political opportunity structure should affect attitudes toward independence within Scotland. An observable implication of the optimal size-of-states logic is that citizens perceive greater viability of an independent small country within the European Union than outside. In 1979, not only was European integration itself at a less developed stage, but the Scottish National Party did not yet see the EU as a potential partner in making its case for independence. By 1997, the Scottish National Party framed the EU as an integral component of its "Independence in Europe" policy (Jolly 2007). In part, Scottish National Party elites intended this strategy to demonstrate that Scotland would be a viable independent country apart from the United Kingdom. If this viability mechanism is at work, I should find evidence in multiple observable implications.

First, Scottish respondents should be more likely to support European integration. Scottish National Party elites frame the European Union as a

TABLE 4.2. *Scottish Perceptions of European Union as a Good Thing*

Year	Conservative	Labour	SNP	Liberal Democrats	All
1979	29.29	15.97	12.66	25.33	21.12
1997	49.59	43.75	47.54	50.98	45.86
Change	+20.30	+27.78	+34.88	+25.65	24.74

Sources: Jowell, Heath, and Curtice 1998; Miller and Brand 1981.

mechanism to achieve independence without economic upheaval (Jolly 2006). In other words, European integration increases the viability of Scotland as an independent country. Thus, nationalists should perceive the European Union more positively in 1997 than in 1979. Using data from the 1979 and 1997 Scottish Referendum Surveys, Table 4.2 provides some simple statistics regarding attitudes toward the EU.[9]

Across party types, Scottish citizens have far more favorable attitudes toward the EU in 1997 than 1979. In contrast, support for European integration among all Europeans dropped nearly 12 percent during the same timeframe (Schmitt and Scholz 2005).[10] In particular, regionalists are much more favorably disposed to European integration. Only 13 percent of Scottish National Party supporters thought the European Union was a "good thing" in 1979, but 48 percent did so in 1997.[11] This trend follows the rhetoric of the Scottish National Party, which shifted from being anti-integration to supporting the European Union specifically as a lever against the United Kingdom and suggests the citizens caught the cue sent by party elites.

Second, support for independence should be related to European integration. Dardanelli (2005b: 328) argues that attitudes toward the European Union actually determine perceived costs of secession. Certainly, Scottish National Party officials used the European Union to diminish fears of economic displacement

---

[9] For 1979, 729 respondents are included. The breakdown by party is 239 Conservatives, 288 Labour, 79 SNP, and 75 Liberal. For 1997, the total *N* is 676, with 123 Conservatives, 336 Labour, 122 SNP, and 51 Liberal Democrats.

[10] According to the Mannheim Eurobarometer Trend File, which compiles and standardizes the many individual Eurobarometer surveys, approximately 58 percent of Europeans surveyed thought the EU was a "good thing" in 1979 (58.9 percent in Eurobarometer 11 and 57.9 percent in Eurobarometer 12), while 50 percent or fewer respondents thought it was a "good thing" in 1997 (48.2 percent in Eurobarometer 47, 48.6 percent in EB 47.1, 47.2 percent in EB 47.2, and 50.8 percent in EB 48) (Schmitt and Scholz 2005).

[11] In 1997, the survey asked the standard Eurobarometer question about European integration that is commonly used in analysis of support for European integration (Brinegar, Jolly, and Kitschelt 2004; Brinegar and Jolly 2005; Gabel 1998b): whether the respondent thinks the EU is a "good thing," a "bad thing," or neither. In 1979, the survey asked respondents to score the Common Market on a ten-point scale (v467). Following Dardanelli (2005b), I standardized this variable to compare to the 1997 version by grouping 0–3 as bad for Scotland, 4–6 as neither good nor bad, and 7–10 as good for Scotland.

associated with independence (Harvie and Jones 2000: 152; Pittock 2001: 127). In other words, deeper European integration implies lower costs of secession (i.e., increased viability of independence), thereby making both independence and devolution more attractive options.

In the following pages, I will demonstrate that it is the "Independence in Europe" option that drives the increased support for independence. Many fewer respondents prefer independence outside of Europe to independence in Europe as their first or second option. The existence of the EU as an alternative political opportunity structure allows citizens to favor independence much more strongly, either as a first or second option. By convincing its supporters that the European Union was a "good thing," the Scottish National Party shifted the debate over self-government itself, making independence a more reasonable option and increasing support for devolution in the referendum in the process (Dardanelli 2001: 14).

Two related empirical implications present themselves. First, I expect to see more Scottish citizens view independence as a viable option in 1997 than in 1979. Second, the distribution of supporters should change, as well, with the middle class, or those most concerned about potential economic upheaval due to independence, more likely to support devolution in the context of a more viable Scotland.

THE SCOTTISH REFERENDA ON DEVOLUTION

Scotland presents a unique opportunity to test the main alternative causal mechanisms. First, Scotland is a region in Western Europe with a long and rich tradition of a regional autonomy movement. Second, the referenda on devolution at two different points in time provide an opportunity to analyze both attitudes toward autonomy and how those attitudes are translated into votes on devolution, as well as their change over time. Comparing the failed referendum in 1979 to the successful 1997 vote yields variation in both the dependent variable and the explanatory variable of interest (Dardanelli 2001: 2). Finally, the questions available in the 1979 and 1997 surveys allow exploration of the European Union's role in determining attitudes toward self-government.

In both 1979 and 1997, the Labour party introduced a referendum for Scottish citizens to decide whether to establish a Scottish Parliament. While a majority of voters supported devolution in both referenda, it failed in 1979 because of the "Cunningham amendment," which stipulated that devolution must not only achieve a majority of support among voters but also meet at least a 40 percent threshold of the entire potential electorate (Harvie and Jones 2000: 115). In other words, abstention served as a de facto "No" vote.[12] As a result

---

[12] This poison pill, "a brilliant act of anti-democratic political manipulation" (Mitchell 1996: 47), influenced the outcome of the referendum as well as perceptions about the outcome. When newspapers referenced the vote, they gave the result as percentages of the electorate rather than

of the threshold, the referendum failed in 1979 and, after the Conservatives won that year's general election, the government promptly removed devolution from the agenda.

During the 1997 general election campaign, Labour, under Tony Blair, promised another referendum on devolution.[13] The 1997 version of the devolution referendum passed by large majorities in every district in Scotland (Taylor, Curtice, and Thomson 1999: xxvii). Considering that during both years Scottish citizens claimed to support devolution, the positive outcome of the devolution referendum in 1997 compared to the negative outcome in 1979 yields a puzzle. In the next section, I consider the alternative explanations for the different outcomes and then explain why the European Union is a significant factor.

SIMILAR PREFERENCES, DIFFERENT OUTCOMES?

Since at least 1947, a majority of Scots have consistently supported devolution in opinion polls.[14] In 1979, 61 percent of respondents, a clear majority, in the Scottish Election Survey supported self-government, with 54.1 percent in favor of devolution and 6.9 percent supporting independence (Miller and Brand 1981). Yet, despite this consistent support of devolution in theory, a plurality of respondents in that same poll either voted "No" or favored the "No" position, with 44.7 percent against the referendum and only 38.1 percent in favor.

By 1997, this disconnect between attitudes and action virtually disappeared, yielding a near consensus on the devolution referendum questions (Surridge and McCrone 1999: 44). What explanations might account for this disconnect in 1979? Paolo Dardanelli (2005b: 321–3) introduces several explanations prevalent in the literature. First, the actual content of the devolution package was more contentious in 1979, with the first-past-the-post electoral system perceived as heavily Labour biased (Harvie and Jones 2000: 186). The observable implications of the Labour bias logic are that non–Labour party supporters

---

percentages of voters. Therefore, instead of a 52 percent–48 percent outcome in favor of devolution, it appeared that only one third of Scots supported devolution (Pittock 2001: 123). Indeed, even Scottish voters saw the result as indicative of a negative result (Mitchell 1996: 46–47).

[13] Labour supported a referendum rather than simply legislating devolution for multiple reasons. Uncertain of their eventual Parliamentary majority from the 1997 general election, they feared a difficult parliamentary battle over devolution as they faced in the 1970s. In addition, a referendum could secure decentralization in the face of future Tory governments. Presumably, if devolution were granted after a referendum, then only a referendum could reverse the decision (Taylor, Curtice, and Thomson 1999: xxv–xxvi). Labour also used the referendum to avoid association with the potential higher taxes of a Scottish Parliament, the so-called Tartan tax. The two-part referendum asked voters first to choose whether to support a Scottish Parliament and then decide whether the Parliament should have tax-varying authority.

[14] In a 1947 survey, three-quarters of Scots supported a Scottish parliament. In 1949, a Scottish Plebiscite Society poll in Kirriemuir in Angus found that 23 percent were in favor of an independent Parliament, 69 percent supported a Parliament to deal with Scottish affairs, and only 5 percent favored the status quo (Mitchell 1996: 149).

would be expected to be anti-devolution while Labour party supporters would be supportive (Dardanelli 2005b: 322). But in fact, apart from Tory support-ers, who were strongly anti-devolution in each referendum, Liberal Democrats were just slightly less supportive of devolution than Labour supporters while SNP supporters were much more favorable. In addition, Labour supporters themselves were split, with a plurality – not a majority – in favor of devolution. The evidence casts doubt on this explanation.

Second, many scholars point to Scotland's increasingly strong sense of being a perpetual political minority in the United Kingdom as the reason devo-lution gained support from 1979 to 1997 (McCrone and Lewis 1999: 18). Scotland voted for Labour in every general election from 1979 to 1992, but the Conservatives won in the rest of the United Kingdom and therefore governed, leaving Scottish voters feeling disenfranchised and the Conservatives increas-ingly unpopular in Scotland (Mitchell et al. 1998: 178; Taylor, Curtice, and Thomson 1999: xxiv). These anti-Tory sentiments could potentially fuel pro-devolution sentiment. If true, then Scots, especially non-Conservatives, should be less satisfied with the United Kingdom and devolution should be a higher priority for citizens. However, Scottish nationalists are actually more satisfied in 1997 than 1979, and the issue of self-government is no more or less salient, suggesting this hypothesis is not sufficient either (Dardanelli 2005b: 323).

The third main explanation is the incoherence and ineffectiveness of the pro-devolution campaign. In 1979, the political parties, especially Labour, sent mixed signals to the electorate, with a faction of the Labour Party oppos-ing the referendum with a "Labour Vote No" campaign (Denver 2002: 830). In addition, little cross-party coordination existed among the Yes campaign, with as many divisions among the pro-devolution parties as between them and the anti-devolution campaign. A Labour party official disdainfully stated that Labour would not be "'soiling our hands by joining any umbrella Yes group'" (Mitchell et al. 1998: 167). In all, the No campaign in 1979 was more effective in terms of funding, coordination, and campaigning than the Yes campaign (Mitchell 1996: 163).

In 1997, on the other hand, the pro-devolution parties, Labour, Liberal Democrats, and the Scottish National Party, supported a double Yes – for a Scottish Parliament and for tax-varying authority – and coordinated their cam-paign as "Scotland FORward" (McCrone and Lewis 1999: 24). In doing so, they sent clearer messages to their party supporters as to their constitutional preferences. In the 1997 campaign, 90 percent of Labour Party and 86 per-cent of Scottish National Party supporters knew their party favored devolution (Denver 2002: 830). The pro-devolution campaign also successfully convinced businesses that devolution was not a threat to their livelihood, undercutting a major supporter of the No campaign in 1979 (Mitchell et al. 1998: 175). This change, detailed in Dardanelli (2005a), is yet more evidence that business inter-ests no longer feared an independent Scotland as they did in the late 1970s, in part due to the "Independence in Europe" option.

Finally, the Think Twice campaign against devolution, led by the Conservative Party, lacked sufficient resources or supporters to oppose the devolution referendum (Mitchell et al. 1998: 174). Thus, the strength and coordination of the campaigns clearly shifted in favor of a Yes vote. Nonetheless, this explanation still has some difficulty explaining why so many Scots voted against devolution even though they favored the concept in surveys (Dardanelli 2005b: 323).

This gap between supporters of devolution in theory and practice in 1979 is stark and demands explanation. In 1979, 61 percent claimed to support self-government but only 39 percent either voted for or favored the devolution referendum. Dardanelli (2001, 2005a) argues that preference orderings are the key to understanding this gap between expected and actual behavior in the failed referendum vote of 1979.

Whereas attitudes about devolution, independence, and the status quo can be kept conceptually distinct in surveys, the preference ordering actually affected voting behavior (Dardanelli 2005b: 326). For instance, if a citizen preferred devolution to the status quo, then observers would expect that citizen to vote for the referendum. However, if that citizen preferred the status quo to independence and expected independence to be a likely outcome of devolution, then the citizen would be more likely to oppose the referendum. In other words, if citizens perceive a high probability of devolution leading to independence, then the referendum vote appears to be a choice between the status quo and independence rather than status quo and devolution (Dardanelli 2001: 10). Moreover, voters in both referenda thought that independence was a likely outcome of devolution (Dardanelli 2005b: 326). This perception provided reason for citizens with this preference ordering to strategically oppose rather than sincerely support the referendum.

To determine the distribution of voter preferences, I reconstructed the preference orderings in Table 4.3 using a series of questions in the 1979 survey that asks respondents to rank each constitutional option from highly unfavorable to very much in favor.[15] Not surprisingly, Scottish voters who favored the status quo preferred devolution as their second-best alternative. Similarly, nationalist Scots, or those who chose independence as their first preference, much preferred devolution to the status quo. These preference orderings yield little

---

[15] See Appendix A for question wording. To extract a preference ordering for 1979, I used the attitude-toward-devolution question above to determine first preference, then turned to the follow-up questions (v323–v327) (Miller and Brand 1981), which asked the respondent to say whether they were very much in favor of (or against), somewhat in favor of, or somewhat against each constitutional option. Knowing each respondent's first preference, I evaluated which constitutional option they favored second best and created an index variable for the various preference orderings. For example, if a respondent favored the status quo, I determined whether they ranked independence or devolution higher. If the respondent ranked devolution higher, then I coded them as Status Quo > Devolution > Independence. In the case of ties, I coded the respondent as "don't know." Coding is available upon request.

TABLE 4.3. *Preference Ordering on Devolution, 1979*

1st Preference	2nd Preference				
	Status Quo	Devolution	Independence	Don't Know	N
Status quo	—	78.3%	0.0%	21.7%	(189)
Devolution	59.4%	—	25.1%	15.5%	(394)
Independence	4.0%	80.0%	—	16.0%	(50)
(N)	(236)	(188)	(99)	(206)	

Source: Miller and Brand 1981.

explanatory power, though, for respondents in both categories are strongly in their respective camps regardless of their second preference.

However, as Dardanelli (2001: 9) contends, for devolution supporters, the second preference may be critical in determining behavior on the referendum. Devolution supporters who consider independence their second-best preference should be supportive of the referendum, because even if independence is a likely outcome of devolution, it is preferable to the status quo. However, Table 4.3 shows that only 25 percent of the devolution supporters share this preference ordering. By contrast, devolution supporters who fear independence and favor the status quo over independence should be more skeptical of the referendum (Dardanelli 2005a: ch. 4). Nearly 60 percent of Scottish devolution supporters consider the status quo to be their second-best option.

More significantly, those devolution supporters who favored the status quo over independence were actually slightly opposed to the referendum, with 50 percent voting against the referendum compared to 45 percent voting in favor. Combined with the consistent opposition of status quo supporters, the divided cohort of devolution supporters contributed to the gap between expected and actual support for the referendum.[16]

By 1997, preference orderings shifted to a degree that the majority of citizens either favored independence as their first or second most preferred constitutional option.[17] Whereas devolution supporters in 1979 preferred the status

[16] Because the Parliament instituted the threshold on the referendum vote in 1979, abstentions acted as de facto votes against devolution. Forty-six percent of abstentions did not know their attitude toward devolution. However, 40 percent favored the status quo as their first (16 percent) or second best constitutional option (24 percent). Only 14 percent favored independence as their first- (4 percent) or second-favorite option (10 percent). The abstentions, therefore, provide further support that those who feared independence or at least considered it their least preferred constitutional option did not support the referendum, yielding a cumulative negative vote on devolution in 1979.

[17] For 1997, the preference ordering was much more straightforward than in 1979 because the survey asked a follow-up question (21b) to the attitudes-toward-devolution question that asked respondents to list their second-most-preferred constitutional option (Jowell, Heath, and Curtice 1998).

TABLE 4.4. *Constitutional Attitudes, 1979 and 1997*

	1979	1997	Change
Status quo	25.9	18.6	−7.3
Self-government	60.9	77.1	16.2
Devolution	*54.1*	42.8	−11.3
Independence	6.9	34.3	27.5
in EU		25.6	
from EU		8.7	
Don't know	13.2	4.3	−8.9
(N)	(729)	(676)	

Note: The Self-government category includes the Devolution and Independence questions.
Sources: Jowell, Heath, and Curtice 1998; Miller and Brand 1981.

quo to independence, the majority of devolution supporters preferred indepen-dence to the status quo in 1997. Excluding the alternative devolution option, for those who favor a Scottish Parliament with tax-varying authority – which comprises 78 percent of the devolution cohort – independence is the preferred second option. For those who favor the weaker devolution option – 22 percent of the devolution cohort – more prefer the status quo to independence, but there are significantly fewer respondents in this category. In the end, 86 per-cent of those who favor either type of devolution either voted for or favored the referendum.

To summarize, the success of the 1997 referendum can be linked to a dimin-ished fear of independence. This significant shift is relevant to the size-of-states argument. In 1979, a majority of respondents claimed to support devolution as their most preferred constitutional option, with a sizable group favoring the status quo and a very a small minority favoring independence. By 1997, this distribution of first preferences changed dramatically. Support for the status quo and devolution decreased 7 percent and 11 percent, respectively, while sup-port for independence increased 28 percent. I present these data in Table 4.4.

Significantly, the increase in support for independence occurs across all party groups. Only 4 percent of Labour party supporters favored independence in 1979 while 36 percent did so in 1997. For Scottish National Party supporters, independence became the most preferred option, increasing from 35 percent to 72 percent. Even 6 percent more Conservatives supported independence in 1997 than in 1979. Because many respondents believe independence is a likely consequence of devolution, the increased support for independence as a first option significantly affected the outcome of the 1997 referendum. But this find-ing only raises another question: Why is independence so much more popular in 1997 than 1979? I contend that European integration and its strategic use by the Scottish National Party play important roles.

TABLE 4.5. *Referendum Positions by Group Identity, 1979 and 1997*

	1979			1997			Change in Yes
	Yes	No	(N)	Yes	No	(N)	
Class identity							
Middle class	29.6%	62.5%	(152)	55.8%	41.0%	(156)	26.2%
Working class	46.5%	44.1%	(458)	77.5%	17.3%	(457)	31.0%
Other	20.2%	24.4%	(119)	65.1%	19.0%	(63)	44.9%
All	38.7%	44.7%	(729)	71.3%	22.9%	(676)	32.6

Sources: Jowell, Heath, and Curtice 1998; Miller and Brand 1981.

First, notice the disaggregated independence options in Table 4.4. Very little of the increased independence support arises from an autarkic, non-EU, version of independence. In fact, independence in EU, the policy espoused by the SNP, is actually more preferred than the status quo by itself. This finding suggests that citizens recognize the significant change in the political opportunity structure that the EU created.

Further, the viability theory predicts that the distribution of supporters should change as well. If independence is a more viable option economically, then capitalists in particular will be more favorably disposed to independence. For example, traditionally in the Basque country, industrialists, fearing the economic disruption that may result from independence, have been less supportive of Basque nationalism (da Silva 1975: 24; Linz 1973). However, capitalists or industrialists should be more supportive of autonomy if the European Union provides more economic security than independence without such a union. Thus, I expect a new "bourgeois regionalism" should emerge in response to the changing economic context (van Houten 2003: 10). Table 4.5 demonstrates that such a shift occurred in Scotland.[18]

A mere 30 percent of the middle class supported the referendum in 1979, while more than 56 percent favored devolution in 1997. Hence, this finding provides additional evidence for the theoretical argument regarding the optimal size of states.

DISCUSSION

Using the Mannheim Eurobarometer Trend file, I established that regionalists are pro-EU, ceteris paribus, and that respondents' attitudes are linked to their preferred party's position on the EU. Then, using the 1979 Scottish Election Survey and the 1997 Scottish Referendum Study, I evaluated why the

[18] Class identity is derived from questions 62a and 62b in 1979 and 29a and 29b in 1997. For each identity question, the respondent had an option to self-identify and then, if no choice was made, a follow-up question asked the respondent which option they would choose if forced (Jowell, Heath, and Curtice 1998; Miller and Brand 1981).

referendum failed in 1979 but passed in 1997 despite having a majority in favor of devolution in both years. Similar to Dardanelli (2005a), I contend that the fear of independence, coupled with a preference ordering in which the second choice for devolution supporters was the status quo, explained the strategic voting behavior in 1979. Between 1979 and 1997, the European Union project fundamentally altered the political opportunity structure for autonomy movements, making devolution and independence a more viable prospect for regionalists. In turn, increased support for independence, as both a first and second option for Scots, fuelled the dramatic increase in sincere voting for devolution in 1997.

I also presented evidence to support the contention that European integration, especially the Scottish National Party's successful framing of the EU as a mechanism to reduce the costs of secession, contributed to this increase in support for independence. Both in the Scottish case and in Western Europe, generally, regionalist supporters perceive the EU positively. Though substate nationalists, who want greater autonomy in one form or another, and supranational integration supporters seem natural opponents, this research suggests they are, in fact, yet another example of the old adage: An enemy of my enemy is my friend. Strange bedfellows? Perhaps. However, they are an unusual alliance that modern multinational states, wary of secession movements, must take into greater account.

Appendix A: Survey Questions

For 1979, I use the following questions to determine actual voting positions:

"30a. Did you vote in the recent Referendum on Devolution for Scotland?
   IF YES Did you vote 'Yes' or 'No'?
   IF NO Did you favour the 'Yes' side or the 'No' side?" (v315)
   For 1997, I use the following questions:

"6a) The questions asked in the Referendum are set out on this card. How did you vote on the first question?" (refvote)

If the respondent did not vote, the survey followed up with this question:

"7a) The questions asked in the Referendum are set out on this card. If you had voted, how would you have voted on the first question?" (nvrefvote)

For both questions, I group spoiled ballots, "would not vote," "refused to answer," and "don't knows" into the "don't know" category. In Table 4.1 and other tables in this chapter, actual voting numbers include those who either voted for or favored (or voted against or opposed) the referendum in the Yes (or No) category.

To determine attitudes toward devolution, I used the following question on the 1979 survey:

"3la) Here are a number of suggestions which have been made about different ways of governing Scotland. Can you tell me which one comes closest to your own view?

1. No devolution or Scottish Assembly of any sort.
2. Have Scottish Committees of the House of Commons come up to Scotland for their meetings.
3. An elected Scottish Assembly which would handle some Scottish affairs and would be responsible to Parliament at Westminster.
4. A Scottish Parliament which would handle most Scottish affairs, including many economic affairs, leaving the Westminster Parliament responsible for defence, foreign policy and international economic policy.
5. A completely independent Scotland with a Scottish Parliament.
8. DK" (v322)

Following Dardanelli (2005b), I group "No devolution" and Scottish Committees as status quo and the Scottish Assembly and Scottish parliament options as devolution.

For 1997, I use the following survey question:

"21a) Which of these statements comes closest to your view?

1. Scotland should become independent, separate from the UK and the European Union.
2. Scotland should become independent, separate from the UK but part of the EU.
3. Scotland should remain part of the UK, with its own elected parliament which has some taxation powers.
4. Scotland should remain part of the UK, with its own elected parliament which has no taxation powers.
5. Scotland should remain part of the UK without an elected parliament.
8. (Don't know)" (srrefvw1)

For Table 4.1, the two independence and two devolution options are combined. All questions and survey responses are drawn from the 1979 Scottish Election Study and the 1997 Scottish Devolution Study (Jowell, Heath and Curtice 1998; Miller and Brand 1981).

5

Institutional Change and Ethnoterritorial Party Representation at the European Level

Bonnie M. Meguid

Over the past forty years, the countries of Western Europe have faced multiple challenges to the power of their national governments. With the deepening of European integration, control over fiscal, social, immigration, and certain dimensions of foreign policy has been relocated from the national to the supranational level. At the same time, demands for greater regional autonomy have led, in many of these countries, to the adoption of decentralization schemes, with policy competencies over areas such as health, education, and other social programs devolved to subnational levels. The power of national governments is being hollowed out both from above and from below.

Despite the joint occurrence of these two processes, the scholarly literature has typically explored the impact of Europeanization and decentralization separately.[1] In terms of political party fortunes, research (Kousser 2004; Marsh 1998) has shown that governing parties are punished in European Parliamentary elections, whereas smaller parties tend to benefit, especially relative to their national support levels. The effects of decentralization have been less well established, but there is evidence that greater regional autonomy is expected to (and often does) hurt governmental parties and strengthen the support of ethnoterritorial actors at the subnational level (Meguid 2009). However, there is no research to date on whether, across countries and over time, these processes reinforce each other or whether, by changing the structure of the institutional environment and the geographic focus of the actors and voters, they undermine each other.

The goal of this chapter is to shed light on the interaction between decentralization and further European integration and, specifically, their effects on party fortunes. While these processes could influence the support of any set of parties that competes at multiple levels (i.e., subnational and European elections), the

---

[1] Notable exceptions are Lynch (1996) and De Winter and Gómez-Reino (2002).

ramifications are particularly interesting for the set of ethnoterritorial parties, which has championed the strengthening of the region and, conversely, the weakening of the national-level of government. In the absence of decentralization, these parties often appealed over the heads of their national governments to the European level for both financial support and reinforcement of the legitimacy of their regional identities and concerns. The implementation of decentralization or stronger degrees of regional autonomy in many countries signaled the achievement of some or all of these parties' policy goals, with, for instance, the transfer of political and often fiscal powers to the region and the reinforcement of the primacy of the regional identity and regional level. In light of the spread of decentralization and the deepening of existing regional autonomy structures across parts of Western Europe, the question becomes how central is the European level in the minds of the ethnoterritorial parties and their voters. What effect does decentralization have on the electoral support for these parties in the European Parliamentary (EP) elections?

The chapter begins by examining the incentives introduced by EU integration and decentralization for ethnoterritorial party mobilization and electoral support. I then derive hypotheses about the expected effect of decentralization on the electoral performance of ethnoterritorial parties in EP elections. Cross-sectional time-series analyses of the effects of decentralization support the claim that ethnoterritorial parties still see the European Union as an arena for expressing regionalist identities and pursuing additional political and financial legitimacy; controlling for the diverse national, European, and party-specific incentives for ethnoterritorial party performance in EP elections, this chapter finds that the vote share of ethnoterritorial parties increases with decentralization. Thus, rather than creating competing arenas of power and interest, these results suggest that the multiplication of levels of government can be a complementary process, at least for some political parties.

EUROPEANIZATION AND DECENTRALIZATION: INCENTIVES FOR ETHNOTERRITORIAL PARTY SUPPORT

In 1979, the nine member-states of the European Community first conducted direct elections for the European Parliament. Eight ethnoterritorial parties from four countries were among the approximately ninety-three parties that contested the elections.[2] Over the next twenty-five years, as the European Community and then European Union enlarged, the number of ethnoterritorial parties presenting candidates in the EP elections likewise increased. Some of these ethnoterritorial parties came from the new EU members Spain and Finland, while others were new parties, or at least new EP contestants, from the older member-states. By the EP elections of 2004, there were twelve lists

---

[2] These four countries are Belgium, Denmark, Great Britain, and Italy.

of ethnoterritorial parties (comprising at least thirty-one parties) from across Western Europe competing.

The Advantages of European Integration

For ethnoterritorial parties, the European Union provides political and even financial opportunities. The European Parliament opens up the possibility of ethnoterritorial party political representation and influence over a growing number of policy areas. While many of these regionalist actors already partic-ipate in elections in their own countries, the institutional structure of the EP provides advantages for these parties over national political arenas.

First, in some countries, the rules used to elect MEPs are more permissive, and thus more favorable to smaller parties, than the rules employed in national elections.[3] In his analysis of the post-1999 EP, Kousser (2004: 12) identifies three cases – Belgium, France, and Great Britain[4] – in which the electoral rules and structure of the electoral constituencies employed in the EP elections advantage minor parties.[5] Applying this same logic to the pre-1999 period, we find that the number of such countries is two – Belgium and France. Minor parties are favored when PR rules are employed in the EP elections but not at the national level, as is the case in France and Great Britain (the latter from 1999 onward). The fact that EP districts are typically larger than constituencies for national elections further enhances the proportionality of the EP elections, again benefit-ing minor parties; this determines the more propitious European electoral envi-ronment facing the Belgian parties, according to Kousser (2004).[6]

Second, smaller parties are advantaged by the "second-order" nature of the EP elections. This term, coined by Reif and Schmitt (1980), refers to the fact that the European Parliament has fewer competencies, and thus is a less impor-tant body, than national legislatures.[7] It follows, Reif and Schmitt argue, that

---

[3] These conclusions are based on the fact that (1) while there is no uniform electoral system in place for EP elections across countries, most of the countries have adopted some form of propor-tional representation, and (2) the electoral systems employed by countries for EP elections do not always match those used in national elections.

[4] Kousser refers to the United Kingdom, but his comments are germane only to Great Britain. Whereas both Great Britain and Northern Ireland use plurality laws for national elections, Northern Ireland has employed a more permissive single-transferable-vote system, or STV, for its EP elections since direct elections began in 1979.

[5] In the 1999 EP elections, Great Britain employed proportional representation rules, bringing it into line with all the other member-states. Prior to this time, EP elections in Great Britain were conducted under plurality rules in single-member districts.

[6] This conclusion depends on there being a large enough number of seats to allow the larger dis-trict size to provide more proportional outcomes. Kousser (2004: 12) argues that an inadequate number of seats is behind the higher threshold of office attainment in EP than national elections in the countries of Denmark, Luxembourg, the Netherlands, and Portugal.

[7] This term has also come to be associated with the idea that voters cast ballots on the basis of national issues rather than European issues.

voters will be less likely to turn out to EP elections than national ones and, more germane for our analysis, that those voters who do turn out will be more likely to vote sincerely than strategically; without having to worry about which parties could form a government, voters in EP elections can cast their ballots for the party closest to their preferences. This effect disproportionately advantages smaller parties, including ethnoterritorial parties, which often fall victim to voters' concerns about "wasting votes" in national elections. Alternatively, it has been argued that the low importance level of these elections encourages protest voting and that the minor party boost in EP elections comes from the fact that protest votes are likely to be given to smaller, non-mainstream parties.

The European Union also provides advantages to ethnoterritorial parties outside of elections to the European Parliament. The creation of the Committee of Regions (COR) by the 1992 Maastricht Treaty formally recognized the role of regions in the governance of the European Union. The body, which consists of members of regional and local governments of the member-states, serves in an advisory capacity on EU legislation on a range of issues relevant to European regions. Moreover, outside of representation channels, the EU provides direct financial opportunities for regions and their ethnoterritorial parties. Established in 1975, the European Regional Development Fund (ERDF) allocates funds to aid economically disadvantaged regions and localities. This funding is not trivial. For the period of 2000 to 2006, the amount of funding available to regions through the ERDF made up 49 percent of the EU Structural Fund operations, or approximately 17 percent of the total EU budget (Nugent 2003: 312).

Together, the institutional features of the European Union create political and financial opportunity structures in which ethnoterritorial parties in particular can voice their policy demands, gain legitimacy, and acquire financial support for their regions. Because the EU provides an institutional environment over the head of national government, these advantages should accrue to ethnoterritorial parties in centralized as well as decentralized national political arenas. The expectation, therefore, is that ethnoterritorial parties across EU member-states will be likely to contest EP elections and should gain nontrivial degrees of support.[8]

The Advantages of Decentralization

The European level is not, however, the only nonnational arena in which ethnoterritorial parties have political and financial opportunities. Across Western Europe over the past four decades, countries have been creating subnational, or regional governmental structures through the process of decentralization. While the exact configuration differs across and even within countries, five countries – Italy, Spain, France, Belgium, and Great Britain – during this period

---

[8] I model the determinants of the precise level of ethnoterritorial EP support later in this chapter.

established a subnational level of government with directly elected officials who have control over executive, legislative, and, in some cases, even financial decisions on a circumscribed set of policy areas. An additional seven countries increased the autonomy of their existing regions.[9] In other words, regions have gained powers that were previously held by the national governments.

The creation of these regional governments is expected to have a positive effect on ethnoterritorial parties. Decentralization multiplies the number of governmental offices and the number of elected governmental officials with control over significant policy-making and implementing capabilities. While all parties that compete at the regional level have access to these offices, eth-noterritorial parties are particularly well placed to benefit from these reforms. The process of decentralization reinforces the importance of the region politi-cally and in the minds of the voters. It provides incentives for regionally based demands and identities. This coincides with and, therefore, serves to legitimize and strengthen the ethnoterritorial parties' longtime message that the region is the natural unit of politics and society.[10] Combine this with the fact that most Western European governments adopted decentralization to appease elector-ally threatening ethnoterritorial parties (Heller 2002; Meguid 2009), and we would expect these parties to prosper electorally from the decentralization pro-cess at the subnational level.

Although this topic has not been the subject of much research to date, there is evidence of the office advantages of decentralization (both anticipated and realized) for ethnoterritorial parties relative to other parties. Research into the decision by the British Labour Party to decentralize to Scotland highlights how the Labour elites anticipated their party losing support and the ethnoterri-torial Scottish National Party (SNP) gaining support at the new subnational level (Meguid 2009). Labour's expectations were borne out, with Labour votes and seat shares in elections to the Scottish Parliament declining relative to their national performance in this region as well as over time (Outlaw 2005; Paterson et al. 2001; http://www.scottish.parliament.uk/msp/elections/2003/analysis/index.htm). Concurrently, voter support at the subnational level for the ethnoterritorial champion of decentralization, the SNP, has increased. In 2007, the SNP took over control of the regional Scottish government, replac-ing a Labour-Liberal Democrat coalition government. This case is not unique in Western Europe. Decentralization in Spain has also led to mainstream party losses at the regional level and the regular control of Spanish regional govern-ments by ethnoterritorial parties.

---

[9] This calculation is based on the number of Western European countries whose degree of region-al autonomy, as measured by Hooghe, Marks, and Schakel's (2008) Regional Authority Index variable, increased between 1970 and 2006. As discussed more extensively in the data section of this chapter, this measure captures the degree of self- and shared rule of subnational units in a country.

[10] This effect would also extend to other parties that are regionally concentrated.

Based on the institutional features of decentralization as reinforced by this preliminary evidence, decentralization is expected to boost the legitimacy, electoral support, and political power of ethnoterritorial parties. These parties are now in a position to benefit from the political and financial opportunities that come from influencing policy or, in cases of more limited decentralization in which the region has only executive powers, from participating in a system focusing on the specific needs of the region.

INTERACTION OF MULTIPLE LEVELS OF GOVERNANCE: THE EFFECTS OF DECENTRALIZATION ON ETHNOTERRITORIAL PARTY SUPPORT IN THE EUROPEAN PARLIAMENTARY ELECTIONS

Both European integration and decentralization provide significant opportunities for the set of parties that campaign for the strengthening of the region and the weakening of the national government. But it has yet to be studied whether these processes are complementary or conflicting. Since the participation of European member-states in their first directly elected European Parliamentary elections, three countries have undergone significant decentralization reforms, establishing directly elected regional governments in thirty regions. The other two Western European countries to decentralize since 1970 have also increased the autonomy of their regions since contesting EP elections.[11] With decentralization reinforcing the regional focus of politics in these countries and satisfying, to some degree, the political demands of the ethnoterritorial parties, what role does the European Union continue to play for the ethnoterritorial parties? To what extent are ethnoterritorial parties and their voters still mobilizing at the European level? There are two possible and contradictory answers to these questions. In this section, I spell out the two sets of hypotheses and the mechanisms behind each.

Decentralization changes the need of ethnoterritorial parties for the European level and for representation in the European Parliament. This observation is at the heart of both sets of hypotheses. But the implications of this observation for ethnoterritorial participation and success at the European level and in the EP differ depending on whether the two institutions are seen as substitutes or complements. For those of the first opinion, ethnoterritorial party commitment to the EU and vote shares in EP elections should decline with higher levels of regional decentralization. This prediction rests on the idea that the European Union was always seen as a second-best environment for ethnoterritorial parties unable to achieve their primary goal of regional autonomy or even regional independence. Participation at the European level was a means for ethnoterritorial parties to pressure national governments for increased regional recognition

[11] Italy and Spain initiated their decentralization processes in 1972 and 1979, respectively, before they contested their first EP elections (in 1979 and 1987, respectively).

and autonomy. Funds from the European Regional Development Fund were a substitute for the lack of national-level support for regional improvement.[12]

This perspective is supported by evidence that the ethnoterritorial party commitment to the European Union is not necessarily strong and has varied within the party family and over time. Based on an assessment of Eurobarometer data for 1996, De Winter and Gómez-Reino (2002: 492) find that ethnoterritorial party voters are not necessarily champions of the EU. While supporters of some regionalist parties in Flanders, Wales, Catalonia, and the Basque Country are the most pro-EU voters in the region, voters of ethnoterritorial parties in Finland, Italy, Scotland, the Canary Islands, and Valencia are the least pro-EU. Expert survey data also reveal variation in the degree of EU support in the ethnoterritorial party family over time. According to De Winter and Gómez-Reino (2002: 491), ethnoterritorial parties were only considered to have "the most-outspoken pro-EU attitudes" of any party family for the year 1984.

With decentralization increasing the focus on regional politics and boosting regional powers and the availability of regional resources, ethnoterritorial parties have less need for the European level. As a result, we can expect the retreat of these parties and their voters to the regional level. Less effort and attention will be paid to nonregional levels, including the European level, and we can expect the turnout of ethnoterritorial party voters, and consequently the support for these parties, in EP elections to decline. It is important to note that these expectations do not depend on the ethnoterritorial party having secured all of its regional autonomy policy goals. For ethnoterritorial parties ultimately seeking regional independence, decentralization may only be the first step. However, the ethnoterritorial party may gamble that this objective can be best achieved from within the country and the region; these parties will look to the region, and not to the EU, to champion independence or to pass a referendum on secession.

While this is one perspective on the effects of decentralization on ethnoterritorial party mobilization at the European level, it is not the only possibility. The second set of hypotheses is based on the view that these institutions are complementary. Having achieved decentralization, ethnoterritorial parties and their voters will remain engaged with and mobilized at the European level. The anticipated result is a positive relationship between decentralization and EP vote share; the electoral support of ethnoterritorial parties will increase along with the degree of regional autonomy.

This outcome can emerge for both expressive and instrumental reasons. With regard to the former, voters whose regional identity and identification with the ethnoterritorial parties has been boosted as a result of decentralization may demonstrate that allegiance in other electoral arenas. This rests on the

---

[12] De Winter (2002: 131) provides an additional reason. He notes that European integration is another form of power centralization and that this runs counter to the decentralizing policy goals of ethnoterritorial parties.

idea that the electoral advantages that ethnoterritorial parties have at the new subnational level translate into advantages at other levels; more voters support ethnoterritorial parties in the subnational elections, thereby increasing voter loyalty for these parties, and this results in more voters supporting these parties in the European Parliament elections.[13]

Continued and increased engagement at the European level by ethnoterritorial parties and their voters may also be driven by more instrumental objectives. While the implementation of a decentralization scheme in a country may be consistent with the goals of an ethnoterritorial party, it may not fully satisfy them. In regions such as Wales in which, until recently, few political powers were devolved, the ethnoterritorial party may seek a more extensive transfer of policy-making competencies. Even at the other extreme in which countries have effectively become federal, ethnoterritorial parties may desire more financial responsibilities or even demand independence, as in the Basque Country. Given the legitimacy, representation, and financial support that are available from the European Union, ethnoterritorial parties may continue to prioritize participation at the European level. Ethnoterritorial voters are also likely to recognize the importance of continued support at the supranational level for champions of decentralization. The adoption of decentralization will have helped validate the voters' past support for the ethnoterritorial parties. Consequently, further support for ethnoterritorial parties is unlikely to be seen as a waste.

Survey evidence highlights another important use of the ethnoterritorial party's continued engagement with the European level: Voters are likely to be less fearful of the regionalist party's desire for regional independence if independence occurs within the context of the European Union. For example, according to the Scottish Social Attitudes Survey of 2001, which was conducted since the creation of the subnational Scottish Parliament, 18 percent of respondents supported Scottish independence within the European Union, as opposed to only 9 percent who favored being independent from the UK and the EU.[14] This two-to-one split was also present among SNP partisans: 41 percent of SNP identifiers preferred independence within the EU versus 21 percent preferring it outside of the EU.[15] And this conclusion is not limited to Scotland. According to De Winter and Gómez-Reino (2002: 488), "[Europeanization]

---

[13] Based on this logic, we might expect decentralization to lead to an increase in ethnoterritorial party support at all levels. However, given that ethnoterritorial parties call into question the primacy of the national level, it seems more likely that their support would increase only at nonnational levels, such as regional, local, and supranational levels.

[14] Calculations from National Centre for Social Research (2004).

[15] The same relationships emerge if we examine respondent and SNP partisan preferences from before the creation of the Scottish Parliament. According to the 1997 Scottish Election Survey, 18 percent of respondents and 47 percent of SNP partisans preferred independence within the EU versus 8 percent of respondents and 20 percent of SNP partisans who preferred independence outside of the EU context. Calculations from McCrone et al. (1999).

has also reduced the economic and military costs of the option of 'independence within Europe.'"

DATA AND CASE SELECTION

The above discussions have spelled out two contradictory sets of expectations about the effect of decentralization on ethnoterritorial party performance in EP elections. The focus of the rest of the chapter is on testing these propositions. The dependent variable for my analyses is the percentage of votes received by an ethnoterritorial party in a European Parliament election.[16] Following the definitions advanced by Müller-Rommel (1998) and De Winter (2002), an ethnoterritorial party is defined as a regional party that prioritizes and champions regional identity and autonomy in its varying degrees. For this analysis, I consider all ethnoterritorial parties or party lists that contested at least two consecutive EP elections between 1979 and 2004.[17] Note that in EP elections, while some parties present their own lists, others often combine to present common lists of candidates. I include as ethnoterritorial those lists that are identified as representing an ethnoterritorial party or have a majority of their candidates drawn from ethnoterritorial parties.

For substantive and statistical reasons, I am interested in the support received by ethnoterritorial parties as a party family.[18] Thus, in countries in which multiple ethnoterritorial parties compete against each other in the same EP electoral district, the value of the dependent variable is the sum of those parties' vote shares.[19] While this situation emerges for ethnoterritorial parties in elections at all levels, it is particularly germane for EP elections in which many countries aggregate votes and assign seats on the basis of a nationwide district. This is the situation in Spain. Thus, I analyze the support for its myriad ethnoterritorial parties together.[20] The resulting set of ethnoterritorial parties included in the analysis is listed in Table 5.1.

---

[16] Data are taken from Braun (2008).

[17] Data from two consecutive elections are necessary for modeling an ethnoterritorial party's vote in cross-sectional time-series analyses using lagged dependent variable models.

[18] With the data organized as party panels, the separate inclusion of multiple ethnoterritorial parties contesting the same district might violate the assumed independence of the observations. It could introduce the possibility that the electoral success of one ethnoterritorial party simply reflects the failure of a different ethnoterritorial party in the same district.

[19] The Lega Nord poses an exception to this rule. Unlike most regionalist parties, it contests electoral districts outside of its regional "homeland." In the 2004 EP elections, for example, the LN ran lists in all five Italian districts. However, it was not competing with the other ethnoterritorial parties included in this dataset in three of those regions. In light of this fact and the recognition that combining all Italian parties would lead to the loss of ten observations from the data analysis, LN has been included as a distinct party in the regressions.

[20] Even if we were willing to ignore the statistical problems of modeling the vote share of competing regionalist Spanish parties, it would be impossible to include these parties separately. Spanish ethnoterritorial parties often form national party lists with other ethnoterritorial parties

TABLE 5.1. *Western European Ethnoterritorial Parties Included in the Analysis of EP Vote*

Country	Ethnoterritorial Party
Belgium	Front Démocratique des Francophones/Mouvement Réformateur, Rassemblement Wallon
	Volksunie/Spirit
Denmark	Siumut
Finland	Svenska Folkpartiet
Great Britain	Plaid Cymru, Forward Wales
	Scottish National Party
Italy	Lega d'Azione Meridionale
	Lega Nord
	Südtiroler Volkspartei
	Union Valdôtaine
Spain	All Spanish Ethnoterritorial Parties contesting EP elections (e.g., Herri Batasuna, Partido Nacionalista Vasco, Eusko Alkartasuna, Convergència I Unió, Esquerra Republicana de Catalunya, Bloc Nacionalista Valencià, Coalicion Andalucista Poder Andaluz, Chunta Aragonesista, Esquerra Republicana del País Valencià, Coalición Canaria, Unio Mallorquina, Union Renovadora Asturiana, Union Valencia, Bloque Nacionalista Galego, Partido Andalucista, Andecha Astur)

Source: Braun 2008.

Explanatory Variables

An assessment of how ethnoterritorial party support changes in response to domestic institutional change requires a measure of that change. The main explanatory variable of interest is, therefore, a measure of the degree of decentralization in a country and region. As seen across the countries and regions of Western Europe, decentralization is not a black-or-white phenomenon. National governments transfer different configurations and degrees of competencies to the subnational level. Moreover, these differences exist not only between countries but also within countries and over time. Based on these observations, crude indicators of federal versus nonfederal systems used in other contexts (e.g., Castles 1999) are not appropriate. Rather, the variable must provide a more nuanced measure of the degree of powers decentralized to the subnational level (e.g., administrative, executive, legislative and/or financial powers) and the structure of those subnational offices (whether the office is directly

---

from the same and different regions. For instance, in the 2004 EP elections, the ethnoterritorial party lists were GALEUSCA, Europa de los Pueblos, and Coalición Europea. As a result, parties do not individually accrue votes, and thus the percentage of voters casting ballots to support a particular party in a given list cannot be determined.

elected). Moreover, the variable must account for regional differences within a country by providing data at the regional level.[21] To avoid losing observations in the already limited six-point time series of EP elections (1979–2004), data should be available yearly or approximately every five years for the entire time period under analysis.

While many nuanced measures of decentralization and regional autonomy have been created over the past decade (e.g., Arzaghi and Henderson 2005; Brancati 2006; Hooghe and Marks 2001; Lane and Ersson 1999; Lijphart 1999), only one provides data for the regions, countries, and time period under examination in this chapter.[22] Based on its fulfillment of these criteria, I use the Regional Authority Index (RAI) constructed by Hooghe, Marks, and Schakel (2008). This variable captures a region's degree of self- and shared rule. The former is defined as "the authority exercised by a regional government over those who live in the region," and the latter is "the authority exercised by a regional government or its representatives in the country as a whole" (Hooghe et al. 2008: 260–1). The eight measures that comprise the index are indicators of a regional government's administrative autonomy, executive and legislative representation, fiscal autonomy, range of policy competencies, role in national legislation, participation in intergovernmental meetings, determination of national tax revenue distribution, and ability to influence constitution change.[23] This measure is available for regions in all Western European EU member-states from 1979 to 2004.

For the analysis, I use the RAI measure for the region with which the ethnoterritorial party in question identifies and in which the ethnoterritorial party presents candidates in national and regional elections. For those parties that represent geographically diverse peoples or that contest elections nationwide, such as the SFP in Finland, the LN in Italy, and ethnoterritorial parties of Spain, I use the RAI values for the basic regional level.[24] The possible values of the

---

[21] This is particularly important for countries with asymmetrical decentralization, where the powers devolved to one region may be very different from the powers devolved to another.

[22] Gerring and Thacker (2008) differentiate themselves from the other decentralization datasets because they fully cover Western Europe and have yearly data. However, their decentralization index (called "unitarism") includes a measure of bicameralism, which is irrelevant to this discussion and muddies its ability to capture decentralization differences. Equally important, their data do not account for and, thus, do not measure regional variation in the degree of decentralization within countries.

[23] For a more detailed discussion of the components of the Index and its coding, see Hooghe et al. (2008: 123–42).

[24] In the Finnish case, I use the values for the regions (i.e., maakuntien). For the parties in Spain, I use the RAI value for the general autonomous community. For the Lega Nord, I use the values provided for the nonhistorical regions of Italy (the regions of "ordinary status" as opposed to the regions of "special status"). The RAI figures for the LN case may underestimate the degree of decentralization in the regions comprising Lega Nord's "homeland" of Padania. However, because the party contests EP elections in districts composed of "ordinary regions," I made the decision to err on the side of underestimating the degree of regional autonomy and thus the true effect of decentralization on the party's EP vote.

RAI measure for a given region range from 0 to 24, where 0 is no regional authority and 24 is extreme regional authority.[25]

The expected relationships between the RAI variable and ethnoterritorial party vote vary by hypothesis. If, on the one hand, decentralization and European integration are substitutes, then the EP vote of ethnoterritorial parties should decline as the RAI increases. If, on the other hand, these two processes are complementary, ethnoterritorial party vote shares should remain the same or increase with higher levels of RAI.

Institutional Control Variables

The advantages that ethnoterritorial parties are expected to have in EP elections, and thus the effects of decentralization on their vote shares, turn on the institutional features of those European elections. To account for the differences in ethnoterritorial party vote over time and across countries, it is important to control for these institutional features. These factors can be divided into country-specific, party-specific, and period effects.

As discussed previously, the electoral system facing parties contesting EP elections is not uniform across the EU member-states (or over time). Prior to 1999, Great Britain used plurality rules, while the rest of the countries used a variety of proportional representation rules; all countries employed some form of PR after this time. Likewise, countries differ in the number of constituencies that they have. Many have a single national district whereby parties compete in national lists. In other countries, there are regional or even smaller districts.

Both the electoral rules and the organization of the EP constituencies are expected to influence the vote shares of ethnoterritorial parties. The vast literature on the effect of electoral systems in general (e.g., Cox 1997; Duverger 1954; Lijphart 1994; Ordeshook and Shvetsova 1994) suggests that parties do better under more permissive electoral rules, such as proportional representation, and large electoral districts, which enhance the proportional effect. Moreover, Kousser's (2004) analysis of EP elections reveals that minor parties in particular gain higher levels of support in EP than in national elections when the EP system is more proportional and has larger constituencies.

There is reason to believe, however, that the relationships between these variables and the vote of ethnoterritorial parties in particular may be different. As noted by Rae (1971) and Sartori (1976), countries with regionally concentrated parties, such as ethnoterritorial parties, are the exception to Duverger's law; their support levels are expected to be higher under plurality rules than PR rules. This claim is substantiated by Meguid (2008: 74) for ethnoterritorial

---

[25] While there are cases in the Hooghe et al. (2008: Appendix B) dataset that have RAI scores of zero (e.g., Iceland and Luxembourg), there are no subnational units that have the highest possible score of 24. The German Länder and the "entities" of Bosnia and Herzegovina come closest with scores of 21 and 22, respectively.

party support in national elections in Western Europe.[26] Similarly, nationwide districts may hinder regional parties that have difficulties appealing to voters across the country or even coming up with enough potential MEPs to populate or resources to mount a national list; these issues have repeatedly frustrated the efforts of French ethnoterritorial parties to contest EP elections (see Lynch 1996: 170). Regional districts present fewer monetary or list-populating problems and serve to reinforce the regional identity of many ethnoterritorial parties.

To test these conflicting hypotheses and control for the varied institutional setting in which the ethnoterritorial parties compete, I include two dummy variables.[27] The first is coded 1 if the electoral system is PR and 0 if it is plurality. The second variable is coded 1 if a country employs subnational constituencies for the EP elections and 0 if it has one nationwide district. These codings are based on data from Bowler and Farrell (1993) and Nugent (2003; 2006). Building on the minor party-specific logic, we expect a positive relationship between EP vote and the first variable and a negative relationship between EP vote and the second variable. The predictions are the opposite if ethnoterritorial parties benefit from plurality rules and smaller, geographically concentrated constituencies.

Just as the EP elections have institutional characteristics that should affect the electoral support of any ethnoterritorial party, research demonstrates that their institutional features also have party-specific effects. Parties in national government consistently receive lower electoral support in EP elections than nongoverning parties (Kousser 2004; Marsh 1998).[28] While the literature has focused its discussions almost exclusively on the mainstream parties leading the government, its rationale suggests that the same effect should emerge for any party represented in the government or government coalition. Thus, I include a variable indicating whether the ethnoterritorial party was a formal member of the governing coalition during the time of the EP election.[29] This information

---

[26] In a similar vein, Gómez-Reino, De Winter, and Lynch (2006: 256) conclude: "In comparison with other newcomers, ethnoregionalist parties seem to suffer less in a majoritarian system."

[27] An alternative approach suggested by the parties' literature for capturing both country-specific electoral institutions is to employ a measure of district magnitude (DM). However, while the district magnitude measure allows the researcher to model differences in the permissiveness of electoral rules, it does not adequately capture differences between the national and subnational structure of EP electoral districts. In particular, the DM measure fails to allow us to distinguish countries with a small number of MEPs elected in one national district from countries with a large number of MEPs elected from across several subnational districts. As argued in the text, the incentives for regionalist party support are expected to be very different in these two circumstances. Because the fortunes of regionalist parties are expected to be sensitive to these differences, I employ the two separate electoral institution variables rather than the combined DM measure.

[28] Voters are thought to turn against governing parties because of midterm malaise or retrospective assessments.

[29] I do not code an ethnoterritorial party informally supporting a minority government, such as was regularly seen in Spain, as being a governing party.

is taken from Woldendorp, Keman, and Budge (1998), supplemented for the 1995 through 2004 period with data from the annual country summaries in the *European Journal of Political Research* and *Electoral Studies*. If the hypothesis applies to ethnoterritorial parties as well, I would expect a negative relationship to emerge.

The EU is an evolving institution. Changes to the power of the EP and its emphasis on regions should have an effect on the electoral support of political parties and ethnoterritorial parties in particular. The passage of the Maastricht Treaty in 1992 ushered in such changes. The Treaty introduced the co-decision procedure of legislation, increasing the role of the European Parliament in EU decision making. The Treaty also created the Committee of Regions. Both of these reforms provide ethnoterritorial parties with greater opportunities to advance their policy objectives at the European level, and thus we might expect an increase in ethnoterritorial party vote share in EP elections held after 1992.

This is not the only possible implication for the support of these parties, though. The increase in the power of the European Parliament after Maastricht challenges the second-order nature of its elections. With MEPs having more power, voters might have become more strategic in their voting decisions, leading to a decline in support for minor parties, ethnoterritorial parties included. This conclusion relies, however, on the assumption that the average European voter is aware of the changes in the EP. It is more likely that the ethnoterritorial parties are motivated by the increase in EP power and EU attention to the region and that they, in turn, mobilize their specialized electorate. Thus, I expect a positive relationship between ethnoterritorial party vote and a dummy variable coded 1 for EP elections held after 1992 and 0 before.

STATISTICAL ANALYSES OF ETHNOTERRITORIAL PARTY VOTE IN EUROPEAN ELECTIONS

Clues about the effects of these variables emerge from an initial analysis of the data. As shown in the bivariate correlations in Table 5.2, the degree of decentralization is positively and significantly correlated with the vote percentage received by an ethnoterritorial party in the European elections. This outcome suggests that ethnoterritorial parties and their voters may be motivated by (1) the strengthening of their regional identification triggered by decentralization and/or (2) the advantages of the EU for decentralized regions, which serve to increase voters' support of the regionalist parties in EP elections.

The bivariate correlations also reveal some expected and unexpected findings about the control variables. Consistent with our hypotheses, ethnoterritorial party vote is significantly higher after the passage of the Maastricht Treaty and its enhancement of the powers of the EP and creation of the Committee of Regions. Supporting the claims by Kousser (2004) for the vote share of minor parties but running counter to the claim based on the regional advantages of

TABLE 5.2. *Bivariate Correlations of Ethnoterritorial Party EP Vote and the Independent Variables*

	Ethnoterritorial Party EP Vote
Decentralization	0.2706*
PR electoral rules	0.2483
Subnational electoral districts	−0.5643***
Member of the government	0.3698**
Maastricht/COR creation	0.2827*

*** $p \leq 0.001$ ** $p \leq 0.01$ * $p \leq 0.1$.

ethnoterritorial parties, the presence of subnational electoral districts is correlated with a reduction in ethnoterritorial party vote share. No statistically significant relationship emerges between vote and the electoral rules variable.

Surprisingly, the governmental status of an ethnoterritorial party turns out to have a positive and significant effect on its EP vote share, contrary to the findings of the literature (e.g., Kousser 2004; Marsh 1998). While we will need to see if this positive relationship is robust to multivariate analysis, it suggests that ethnoterritorial parties are not being punished for their involvement in government, like the mainstream governmental actors examined by Kousser. Given that these ethnoterritorial parties are only ruling as part of a coalition government and that the voters' ability to assign policy responsibility and blame is lower in coalition governments than in single-party governments (Powell 2000), it is logical that voters may only hold the larger, more visible governmental parties responsible, downplaying the power or even forgetting about the presence of the smaller, ethnoterritorial coalition partners. Of course, further investigation is necessary into why governmental status would actually boost – rather than just not harm – the ethnoterritorial parties' support.

The bivariate correlations provide some hints about the explanatory power of decentralization. However, to fully understand the effects of this institutional reform on the electoral support of ethnoterritorial parties, we need to consider its influence when the other factors shaping the general EP electoral environment are controlled for. To test my hypotheses, I employ pooled cross-sectional time-series analyses. I ran ordinary least squares (OLS) regressions with lagged dependent variables and panel-corrected standard errors. I followed the advice of Beck and Katz (1995, 1996) and included a lagged dependent variable to eliminate autocorrelation in the underlying data.[30]

---

[30] Because the decentralization variable is often time invariant within party panels and has similar values across ethnoterritorial party panels within the same country, we cannot include country fixed effects (Beck and Katz 2001: 492). But any concerns about having unmodeled country-specific effects are allayed. The institutional control variables added to the model provide a more theoretically rigorous and substantive way of capturing any country-specific factors in an ethnoterritorial party's vote than would the set of substantively empty placeholder country

TABLE 5.3. *Models of Ethnoterritorial Party Vote Percentage in the European Parliament Elections, 1979–2004*

	Expected Sign	Model I	Model II
Decentralization (Regional RAI)	+	0.07*	0.17*
		(0.05)	(0.09)
PR electoral rules	+ (Marsh, Kousser)		−2.09*
	− (ethnoterritorial lit.)		(1.23)
Subnational electoral districts	+ (ethnoterritorial lit.)		−1.28
	− (Kousser)		(1.65)
Member of the government	−		1.44
			(1.18)
Maastricht/COR creation	+		0.67*
			(0.39)
Vote % $_{t-1}$		0.85***	0.74***
		(0.09)	(0.16)
Constant		−0.08	1.47
		(0.59)	(1.99)
R^2		0.7552	0.7895
N		41	41

*** $p \leq 0.001$ ** $p \leq 0.01$ * $p \leq 0.1$.

Table 5.3 presents the results of my multivariate analyses of ethnoterritorial party vote share, with the predicted signs of the explanatory variables listed in column two. As revealed by both Models I and II, decentralization has a positive and statistically significant effect on the EP vote share of an ethnoterritorial party: As the degree of decentralization in a region increases, voter support for the ethnoterritorial party in that region also increases. These results offer support for the claim that the European Union remains important for ethnoterritorial parties even as they achieve (some of) their regional goals.

This positive effect of decentralization translates into a significant boost in an ethnoterritorial party's vote share. Based on the results from the more complete Model II, a change in the RAI measure from one standard deviation below the mean (RAI = 5) to one standard deviation above it (RAI = 18) results in an increase in ethnoterritorial party vote of 2.18 percentage points.[31] With the mean vote share of the ethnoterritorial party panels in my dataset at 4.05 percent, this jump caused by decentralization is equivalent to a more than 50 percent increase in party vote. Clearly, this domestic institutional reform has significant supranational effects.

dummies. Indeed, as a rule, Beck and Katz (2001: 493) recommend including substantive predictors of country-level effects over country dummies.

[31] This change in RAI is equivalent to going from a level of regional autonomy less than that enjoyed by provinces in centralized Finland to the level found in Brussels post-decentralization.

The results from Model II also highlight the importance of the institutional environment in which EP electoral competition takes place. As foreshadowed by the bivariate correlations, the Maastricht Treaty variable has the expected positive effect on ethnoterritorial party vote. Consistent with the idea that these regionalist parties view the European Union as a source of political and financial resources – both before and especially after decentralization – their support is estimated to increase by 0.67 percentage points when the EP has more powers and when the importance of regions is explicitly recognized within the European decision-making process. There is no evidence therefore that voters shy away from supporting ethnoterritorial parties as the importance of the EP, and the possibility of wasting a vote, increases.

A country's electoral rules also have a significant effect on regionalist party EP vote shares. Table 5.3 shows that ethnoterritorial party vote is weaker in EP elections held under proportional representation than under plurality rules. While this finding runs counter to general theories on minor party performance, it reinforces the recent work on ethnoterritorial parties. As shown by De Winter (1998: 219) and Meguid (2008) for national-level elections, these regionalist parties benefit from electoral systems that reward geographic concentration.

There is no support for the hypotheses that ethnoterritorial EP vote share is significantly different in countries with subnational than nationwide districts. Similarly, although the sign is positive as was seen in the bivariate correlations, being a member of a national government has no statistically significant effect on the EP vote share of an ethnoterritorial party.

DISCUSSION

The twin processes of European integration and decentralization have come to shape the political and electoral opportunities for political parties across Western Europe over the past forty years. Yet no research to date has systematically explored the interaction of these two institutional reforms across countries and over time. This chapter fills this lacuna by examining the degree to which decentralization alters the vote shares of ethnoterritorial parties in European Parliament elections from 1979 to 2004. These parties are the most susceptible to the effects of decentralization at the EP level, as they are typically the champions of decentralization and their engagement at the European Union has been influenced by their pursuit of regionalist policies.

This chapter finds evidence that domestic processes have an effect on ethnoterritorial party performance at the European level. Specifically, higher levels of decentralization are associated with higher levels of party support in the EP elections. This evidence is consistent with the argument that, even for parties moving closer to achieving their main policy goals, the European level still proves useful and attractive. Voters are building upon heightened regionalist identification and expressing their identity and ethnoterritorial partisanship at new levels of governance, and/or the parties and their voters view the EU as providing further resources and political support for their next goals of greater regional autonomy or independence. While confirmation of the individual mechanisms behind this result requires further analyses using individual-level survey data or interview data, the findings of this chapter suggest that multiple levels of governance can reinforce each other rather than providing competing arenas that undermine each other.

My analyses also highlight the importance of European institutions for the electoral support of ethnoterritorial parties. Voter support increases after 1992 when MEPs gain more power and the EU prioritizes regional interests in the legislating process. Although we might expect that the increase in MEPs' power boosts support among all political parties, the zero-sum nature of elections suggests that the vote percentage increases experienced by ethnoterritorial parties should serve to distinguish them from other political actors. Ethnoterritorial party fortunes are also affected by the electoral rules in EP elections, specifically in a way that runs counter to their effect on other minor parties as reported in the literature. While the coefficient is not statistically significant, there is tentative evidence that even governmental membership influences ethnoterritorial parties differently from other parties. Additional analyses are, however, necessary to confirm this observation.

This chapter represents a first step in the exploration of the effect of decentralization on political party performance. For the ethnoterritorial parties that contest EP elections, decentralization has had a positive effect, at least electorally. The regional logic behind this vote boost is not conceptually limited to ethnoterritorial parties, however. Indeed, although ethnoterritorial parties are the most obvious and often were the earliest versions of regional parties, they are not the only ones. Regional parties of various political stripes have emerged in many EU member-states. Moreover, this chapter's claims about the effects of decentralization on EP vote should, for the most part, apply to these cases. Although nonethnic regional parties may be less motivated by the EU's legitimization of independence movements, regional party voters should be equally likely to take advantage of the increased EU attention to the regions and the opportunity to express an already enhanced regional party allegiance at the European level. Whether decentralization's reach extends beyond ethnoterritorial to other regional parties is, thus, a promising subject that awaits future research.

6

European Integration and an Alternative Party Family

Regionalist Parties and the European Question

Margarita Gómez-Reino

In the past decade, the pro-Europeanness of the regionalist party family was taken for granted in academic writing.[1] The earliest study on party families and European integration (EI) discovered a Europeanist vanguard, since the regionalist party family was 'unambiguously and unanimously' pro-European (Hix and Lord 1997: 27). The position of the regionalist party family as pro-European has been empirically demonstrated by several quantitative and qualitative studies (De Winter and Gómez-Reino Cachafeiro 2002; Lynch 1996; Marks, Wilson and Ray 2002). More recent studies confirmed the pro-European position of the regionalist party family and the continuity of its support over time (Jolly 2007: 121). However, the consideration of regionalist parties as natural supporters of European integration has been recently and increasingly questioned (Hepburn 2008). The support for European integration is more conditional and ambiguous than unqualified (Elias 2008; Hepburn 2008). Not only are some regionalist parties Eurosceptical and critical of European integration, but also they lack consistent positions on Europe (Hepburn 2008). Finally, rather than a continuous support over time, pro-Europeanist positions are cyclical or evolving towards critical views (Elias 2008; Hepburn 2008).

The contrasting arguments and evidence about the position of regionalist parties towards European integration are rather puzzling. They offer completely opposing views on the position of the regionalist party family towards European integration. In the past, some ambiguities and negative views of European integration were already highlighted, either because of the alleged effects of European integration on the party family (De Winter and

---

[1] In this chapter I use the label 'regionalist' to refer to ethnoregionalist, minority nationalist or autonomous parties. The multiplication of labels in the literature is not problematic as long as the exact meaning of these parties is defined: parties claiming territorial autonomy and demands of self-government. Non–statewide parties are not included in this group because they are only defined by the level at which claims are made (De Winter, Gómez-Reino and Lynch 2006a).

Gómez-Reino Cachafeiro 2002), the presence of different types of reactions at the regional level, from rejectionist regionalism to resource-based support regionalism (Keating and Hooghe 2006: 272), or the existence of clear cases of Euroscepticism within the family (De Winter, Gómez-Reino and Lynch 2006a). However, the consideration of the regionalist party family as pro-European was not so consistently challenged until now. Are regionalist parties still and *really* pro-European? Are regionalist parties changing their position on European integration and if so, in which direction? Which factors drive the position of these parties towards European integration?

This chapter examines the position of regionalist parties on European integration. It analytically distinguishes between the aggregate EU position of the regionalist party family and individual positions within the party family. At the aggregate level and in comparison with other party families, EU positions are pro-European. However, they are neither very positive nor homogeneous. This chapter argues that the regionalist party family is historically and intrinsically characterized by the co-existence of pro– and anti–European positions regarding European integration. The regionalist party family includes both some of the most Euro-enthusiasts and Eurosceptical parties in Europe. This chapter seeks to investigate the sources of this mild EU position and the striking differences in positions towards European integration within the party family. While at the aggregate level the EU position has suffered minor changes over time, significant shifts in individual party positions towards European integration (both pro- and anti-European integration) took place within the family over the past decades.

The results of comparative studies on regionalist parties are sensitive to research design, unit of analysis and instruments used to measure party positions.[2] As minor and small parties, the lack of empirical data has been one of the standard problems in analysing the regionalist party family at the aggregate level (De Winter 1998). One of the intrinsic problems is the under-representation of regionalist parties in comparative studies. The Comparative Manifesto Research Project does not include many regionalist cases, so they are not a standard tool of analysis of the position of regionalist parties (see exceptionally Dandoy and Sandri 2008). The lack of comparative data at the aggregate level is translated in the reliance on expert surveys, a standard tool that has improved over time (Marks, Hooghe, Nelson and Edwards 2006; Marks, Wilson and Ray 2002; Ray 1999). The validity and reliability expert surveys are usually brought to the fore compared to Manifesto analysis (Marks, Hooghe and Bakker 2007; Whitefield et al. 2006). Other types of comparative analysis measuring other aspects of the position of party voters on European integration are lacking. There is limited comparative evidence on party voters,

[2] One of the difficulties emerges from the different unit of analysis (the party family in itself and individual political parties) and the different research designs that range from the larger-N party family to small-N comparisons or case studies.

but De Winter and Gómez-Reino Cachafeiro (2002) suggested that party elites were more supportive of European integration than party voters were. Thus, at the aggregate level, the evidence is skewed towards expert surveys and party elites, while qualitative analysis has provided a wealth of evidence and detailed knowledge of some of the cases, emphasizing the process by which certain party positions are adopted. The chapter seeks to combine available evidence from the waves of the UNC-Chapel Hill expert surveys and evidence from party programs.

Unlike mainstream traditional party families, the regionalist party family is like an alternative type of family whose members are very heterogeneous (Mair and Mudde 1998; Von Beyme 1986). Some scholars even question its nature as a single party family given the differences among regionalist parties in Europe. Mair and Mudde suggest to disaggregate and to distribute the parties among the traditional party families (Mair and Mudde 1998: 222). The specificity of the regionalist party family is built on the center-periphery cleavage: territorial claims and demands of autonomy on the basis of a core ethnic nationalism (De Winter and Türsan 1998). However, these territorial claims are tied to very different ideologies, issues and programs. The ideology of regionalist parties is multidimensional because it combines several dimensions of conflict for regionalist parties: one related to category space (identity), others related to left-/right-wing (socioeconomic issues) and new politics (De Winter 1998).

There are two sources of heterogeneity in the positions towards EI. On the one hand, the ethnoregionalist family has as its defining characteristic demands of self-government and autonomy from European states. In principle, European integration is an opportunity to surpass state boundaries.[3] Yet the center-periphery cleavage has been reshaped, with territorial restructuring in Europe producing mixed effects and different opportunities and costs associated with European integration (Bartolini 2005; Keating 1998). Under the umbrella of Europe of Regions, or Europe of Peoples, a general positive attitude exists hand in hand with ambiguities and critical attitudes towards the institutional design and the policies of the EU (Elias 2008). On the other hand, the positions on the EU are associated with other dimensions of conflict, in particular the left-/right-wing dimension.

Specifying party positions on European integration is not an easy task, because parties can be treated alternatively as Eurorealist, Eurosceptical or moderate pro-European in different analyses. The literature on attitudes towards European integration is divided over the precise meaning of pro-European support and Euroscepticism which – given conceptual stretching – is problematic.

---

[3] This is a wider logic than the one provided by the viability argument that predicts support for the EU as small countries become more viable. It should be taken into account that within the regionalist party family, 'autonomy' is an encompassing term to define independentists, federalists, protectionists and so on. Less than half of regionalist parties can be defined as independentists (De Winter, Gómez-Reino Cachafeiro and Lynch 2006).

Different classifications and typologies account for differences in party support (Kopecki and Mudde 2002; Szczerbiak and Taggart 2008). Taggart and Szczerbiak (2008) distinguished between hard and soft Euroscepticism but left out pro-European positions. Kopecki and Mudde (2002) aimed at reformulating the concepts with a typology that includes pro- and anti-EU positions. In some cases, the distinction is blurred because it is a matter of slight nuance, for example, the difference between critics and soft Eurosceptical parties.[4]

Today research on party based Euroscepticism is divided between what Mudde defines as the Sussex and North Carolina "schools." These schools differ in definition, data, scope and findings of positions on European integration. North Carolina's is a basic definition on "overall orientation of party leadership," a continuum of party stances on European integration ranging from extreme opposition to marvelous support for integration (Ray 1999). In the surveys, country experts were asked to place parties in their own country on a seven-point scale ranging from complete opposition to European integration to complete support. While North Carolina's operationalization of Soft Euroscepticism is between the values of 2 and 4, (no opinion on European integration, a 4 on this scale) (Mudde 2012:197). Mudde argues that it would make at least as much sense to argue that a score of 5 measures Soft Euroscepticism, as it indicates that the party is only "somewhat in favor" of European integration (Mudde 2011:197). In contrast, 5 is the cut-off point for North Carolina to define pro-Europeanness.

The next section reviews two standard analytical frameworks to explain the position of regionalist towards European integration. The chapter examines the contemporary position of the regionalist party family at the aggregate level with data from the UNC-Chapel Hill expert surveys (Marks et al. 2006). Then it presents two cases of the impact of left-/right-wing ideologies on positions towards the EU within the regionalist party family. The combination of ideological (the center-periphery cleavage with the left-/right-wing dimension of competition) shaped these divergent trajectories towards European integration. This emphasis is on reversed trajectories of party positions within the regionalist party family: one trajectory from hard to soft Euroscepticism, the case of the Bloque Nacionalista Galego (BNG), and its inverse, from pro–Europeanness to increasing Euroscepticism, the case of Lega Nord.

EXPLAINING THE POSITION OF THE REGIONALIST PARTY FAMILY TOWARDS EI

The two most widespread analytical frameworks to explain the position of the regionalist party family towards European integration are cleavage theory and

---

[4] Party positions are defined on a seven-point scale: (1) strongly opposed; (2) opposed; (3) somewhat opposed; (4) neutral, no stance on the issue; (5) somewhat in favor; (6) in favor; and (7) strongly in favor (Ray 1999: 295).

strategic competition. The analytical framework provided by cleavage theory posits that the pre-existing ideology of the regionalist party family explains the position towards European integration. Alternatively, models of strategic competition introduce the location (mainstream or fringe) of regionalist parties in party systems to explain their positions on European integration. The hypotheses derived from these frameworks predict opposing positions on European integration one positive (cleavage theory) and one negative (strategic competition).

Cleavage theory is based on the historical emergence of the cleavages that structured Western European party systems as developed by Lipset and Rokkan (1967). These cleavages gave rise to different party families in Europe. Party ideology filters European integration within its existing ideologies and programs (Marks and Wilson 2000; Marks, Wilson and Ray 2002). Membership in each party family is associated with positions on European integration, so party families are coherent on European integration (Marks and Wilson 2000: 439). The regionalist party family represents the center-periphery cleavage, the defence of the ethnoterritorial minority against the center and demand for regional political autonomy. From the cleavage, Marks, Wilson and Ray (2000) derive the position of the regionalist party family on economic integration as 'strongly in favor' (integration provides an economic framework favorable for regional political autonomy), and on political integration the position is defined as 'moderately in favor' (supranational authority weakens national control and a plural Europe can emerge) (Marks et al. 2002: 587).[5] Thus, the overall position of the family on European integration is defined as 'moderately to strongly in favor' (Marks et al. 2002: 587).

Several studies confirm the pro-European attitudes of the party family (De Winter and Gómez-Reino Cachafeiro 2002; Marks and Wilson 2000; Marks et al. 2002). However, the regionalist party family is not very pro-European, since traditional party families such as Christian democrats or Liberals are more positive towards integration. Different analyses confirm that the regionalist party family is only the fourth most pro-European family (Jolly 2007; Marks et al. 2002). Some scholars argue that the pro-Europeanness of the regionalist party family has decreased over time (Keating and Hooghe 2006: 272). Cleavage theory provides a static view of the center-periphery cleavage and defines positive views on political and, in particular, economic integration. The regionalist party family is less pro-European than expected, given the centrality of undermining central state authority for party programmatic positions. These positive views on political and economic integration are built on the opportunities offered to regions to undermine state authority within the European Union (De Winter and Gómez-Reino Cachafeiro 2002; Hix and Lord 1997; Marks et al. 2002). However, there are also costs involved in the

---

[5] Cleavage theory has been also combined with the viability hypothesis on the optimal size of states. According to Jolly, regionalist parties will be Europhiles because market integration makes autonomous regions more viable economic entities (see Jolly 2007: 112).

process of integration for regions (De Winter and Gómez-Reino Cachafeiro 2002; Keating and Hooghe 2006). Moreover, membership in the family does not translate into homogeneous views on European integration because regionalist parties differ in their views on political and economic integration.

A clearly alternative theoretical framework is provided by models of strategic competition (Meguid 2005; Taggart 1998). Mainstream parties are largely considered as pro-European while fringe families oppose European integration (Taggart 1998). This hypothesis considers regionalist parties as fringe and minor parties and as the source of their anti-European position.[6] As small parties with agendas focusing on the claims of territorial minorities, high specialization of party agendas and party voters was assumed (Lipset and Rokkan 1967; Urwin 1983). Recently regionalist parties were conceptualized as niche parties – minority nationalist, green and radical right parties – exhibiting three main characteristics: absence of traditional politics, novelty of issues and politicisation of a restricted set of issues in electoral competition (Jensen and Spoon 2008; Meguid 2005: 347–8). Unlike traditional parties, ethnoregionalists restricted their claims and demands to encapsulated ethnic and national minorities that are territorially bounded. Here political competition is confined to a very limited political space and marginal and extreme politics.

In fact, the regionalist party family is treated as an exception to the Eurosceptical character of fringe party families (Jolly 2007: 110). The strategic position of regionalist parties in European politics is an elusive one. There is evidence that the peripheral position of some regionalist parties also shapes party Euroscepticism (Gómez-Reino Cachafeiro, Llamazares and Ramiro 2008). The strategic position of regionalist parties in European politics is an elusive one. Beyond their niche, some of these parties behave as mainstream parties, or as 'intrinsically catch-all parties' in the politicisation of issues and competitive dynamics (De Winter 1998: 223). Three waves of political mobilization of ethnoregionalist parties show that they also behave as mainstream or catch-all parties, incorporating all kind of demands into their programs covering other issues, entering regional and even national governments and exhibiting moderate positions (De Winter, Gómez-Reino and Lynch 2006b).[7] The emergence of regional arenas within a multilevel political system offers the opportunity to achieve government (at the regional level). Whether these parties can be treated as fringe or mainstream parties depends on context and political opportunity structures at the regional level, the proper level of analysis to determine their mainstream or fringe positions (exceptions: Svenska folkpartiet [SFP] and Lega Nord [LN] entering coalitions at the national level).[8]

[6] Despite this crucial methodological remark, we can still find empirical studies using the national level as the relevant one (Brancati 2008).

[7] 'Mainstream' can be defined in term of votes, left-right position or government participation (Marks, Wilson and Ray 2002: 588).

[8] Regionalist parties should be analyzed at the regional level, success measured as a proportion of their target electorate and size measured in terms of the regional level as well (De Winter 1998: 211).

The position of regionalist parties towards European integration reflects the combination of the ambivalent and mixed effects of European integration on the center-periphery cleavage (opportunities of empowerment and costs of reduced power within the EU) and other dimensions of conflict relevant in their established ideologies, in particular the left-/right-wing dimension (Gómez-Reino, Llamazares and Ramiro 2008: 139).

The impact of European integration on the center-periphery cleavage is arguably the deepest of all the *familles spirituelles* (De Winter and Gómez-Reino Cachafeiro 2002) because it strikes at the core of this political conflict on the distribution of political authority at the territorial level. The centrality of claims and demands for territorial autonomy offer powerful arguments to support the European Union to undermine state authority. However, the mixed effects of the center-periphery cleavage prevent us from expecting the regionalist party family would be a pro-European vanguard, matching the Eurosceptic vanguard of the extreme right. According to Keating and Hooghe (2006), European integration is ambivalent for regions since it is two sided. The effects of European integration have changed over time: There are more constraints and fewer opportunities associated with European integration (Keating and Hooghe 2006: 272). The costs of European integration involve different aspects of regional autonomy. European integration constrains the empowerment of the regions vis-à-vis the European Union (De Winter and Gómez-Reino Cachafeiro 2002: 490). EU policies that accommodated a regional level of politics through the creation of a Committee of the Regions and the development of structural policies and regional funds had slowly diminished over the past decade (Elias 2008). Moreover, EU enlargement has amplified the different status of 'nations without a state' (De Winter and Lynch 2008).

The demands for some kind of self-government constitute 'the defining characteristic' of ethnoregionalist parties, but regionalist parties insert their claims with wider platforms and policy issues (De Winter 1998: 208). The regionalist party family is the most mimetic party family with regard to both traditional and new politics. The salience of the traditional left-/right-wing dimension to explain ethnoregionalist politics appears in several studies on the party family (De Winter 1998; De Winter, Gómez-Reino Cachafeiro and Lynch 2006; Erk 2010; Newman 1997). Unlike any other party family in Europe, ethnoregionalist parties are located along the entire dimension, spreading along the ideological continuum from the extreme left to the extreme right (De Winter 1998; Guibernau 1996; Tronconi 2006). Centre-left is the most frequent position within the regionalist party family (De Winter, Gómez-Reino and Lynch 2006).[9]

The most important dimension of conflict structuring party positions towards European integration is the socioeconomic cleavage defined as the

---

[9] Some oregionalist parties have developed a clear profile on new politics and the so-called silent counterrevolution (De Winter 1998: 208; Van Atta 2003).

left-right continuum (Marks and Steenbergen 2004). The visibility of the different positions on the left-right dimension in contrast with the rest of the party families was captured by Hix and Lord's analysis (Hix and Lord 1997; Marks and Steenbergen 2004). Hooghe and Marks define a two-dimensional model in which the left-right dimension (pitting regulated capitalism vs. neoliberalism) and national sovereignty dimension both structure actors' positions. Certain aspects of European integration are likely to be absorbed into the left-right dimension (Hooghe, Marks and Wilson 2002; Marks and Steenbergen 2004: 9–10). On the one hand, this explains that centrist families are more pro-European because European integration is a centrist project (Hooghe and Marks 2004b). On the other hand, the evolution of the European Union on this dimension, from a liberal project into a regulatory and social framework in the late 1990s, affected the position of party families towards European integration. This would explain why, as regulatory and social Europe became more important in the late 1990s, social democrats became more pro-European while the right became less so (Hooghe and Marks 2004b).

The left-right dimension also structures the position of regionalist parties towards European integration. The linkage between territorial identity and social policy is a central aspect of the contemporary politics of regionalist parties, both left- and right-wing. The territorialization of political issues affects a wide range of public policies but in particular the so-called regional welfare state. Nationalism and the welfare state are framed in reference to the idea of solidarity (Béland and Lecours 2005: 679). In short, nationalist movements will promote their identity politics – the congruence between cultural and national boundaries – with their views on social citizenship (Béland and Lecours 2005: 680).

The relationship among the left-/right-wing position of party families with positions towards European integration is represented by an inverted-U curve (Figure 6.1) (Marks 2004; Marks, Wilson and Ray 2002: 592). Hooghe, Marks and Wilson (2002) show support among centrist parties and opposition among parties towards both extremes. The explanation for the inverted-U curve is that established ideologies are powerful predictors of the position of party families towards European integration. The regionalist party family reproduces within it the inverted-U curve that shows the relationship between the left-/right-wing dimension and positions on European integration (Marks 2004: 238).

All parties of the regionalist family show differences regarding the model of integration (De Winter 1998: 210). This suggests a specific pattern of adaptation of regionalist parties towards Europe that does not eliminate significant differences in their views regarding the EU (De Winter 1998; Elias 2008; Frampton 2005). In a comparative study of autonomist parties in Europe, De Winter, Gómez-Reino and Lynch (2006) pointed out that in light of the seventeen cases analysed, a convergence on positive attitudes towards the EU among regionalist parties could be advanced (252). However, the pro-European position of the regionalist party family is a thin layer. The heterogeneity of the regionalist

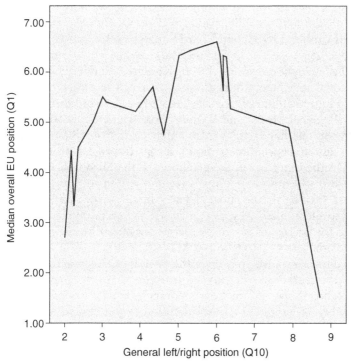

FIGURE 6.1. The inverted U-curve within the regionalist party family: party left-right placements and positions toward European integration.
Source: Questions 1 and 10 in the 2006 UNC-Chapel Hill Expert Survey on national parties and European integration.

party family resurfaces in the differences in models of integration, specific positions regarding the evolution of the EU. Heterogeneity was an intrinsic characteristic of the party family from its origins (De Winter, Gómez-Reino and Lynch 2006; De Winter and Türsan 1998). As Seiler (1980) put it, 'singularity and the expression of difference are the constant features of peripheral parties' (374). Lipset and Rokkan (1967) posited that large-scale processes in state and nation formation left behind encapsulated cultural peripheries in European states. Historically, the European peripheries had very different positions with regard to political and economic centers (Gourevitch 1979; Rokkan and Urwin 1982). Both territorial cultural and economic development were constrained by the relationship of the region with the central state (Gourevitch 1979; Rokkan and Urwin 1982). Thus, the regionalist party family has as its 'core business' claims of self-government based on territorial identities and interests. Yet even the claims of self-government of ethnoregionalist parties include a range of options from independence to decentralization (De Winter, Gómez-Reino and Lynch 2006; De Winter and Türsan 1998; Van Houten 2007). The most frequent claims of ethnoregionalist parties in contemporary European politics are independence, autonomy and federalism (De Winter, Gómez-Reino and Lynch 2006).

The diversity of positions of the regionalist party family towards European integration appears in the different position taken regarding the specific evolution of European integration over time and regarding the socio-economic model of integration. These differences are not well tapped by general positions pro– or anti–European Union. The most recent example is provided by positions on the referendum on the Constitutional Treaty demonstrated in the schisms within the regionalist party family. In the United Kingdom, the SNP was against it but Plaid Cymru was in favor. In Spain, the country that contributes the largest number of cases to the regionalist party family, clear differences also emerged within the party family. In the case of the consultative referendum that took place on 20 February 2005, regionalist parties were neatly divided over it. On the one hand, Partido Nacionalist Vacso (PNV), Convergència i Unió (CiU) and Coalición Canaria (CC) voted for the treaty. On the other hand, BNG, Eusko Alkartasuna (EA), Chunta Aragonesista and Esquerra Republicana de Catalunya (ERC) voted against it. Although all these parties are pro-European to different degrees according to expert surveys, they represent a clear-cut divide on the direction of European integration beyond general positions, forming in the Spanish case two distinctive groups, a right-wing nationalist group and a left-wing nationalist group. Thus, it seems that there are also clear differences within the regionalist party family on European integration.

Thus within the regionalist party family there are a pro-European moderate centrist position (center-right, center-left) and Eurosceptical extremes. The extremes are well represented by contemporary populist right-wing parties, but in the past they were exemplified by extreme-left nationalist ideologies. Unlike most party families, the diversity of positions of regionalist parties towards European integration is also translated by their different institutional location at the European level. The regionalist party family also exhibits a heterogeneous position in parliamentary groups and Euro-parties. The members of the regionalist party family are divided among the European Free Alliance and the different traditional party families in the European parliament.

CONTEMPORARY POSITION OF THE REGIONALIST PARTY
FAMILY TOWARDS EI

The regionalist party family is composed of small and minor parties.[10] Over time, the geography and the number of regionalist parties in comparative

---

[10] There are different problems associated with membership in the party family: some related to double membership in party families (most clearly LN), the confusion between non–statewide parties and regionalist parties and the like, but most importantly, the criteria of relevance for these parties, including the fringe-fringe ethnoregionalist parties in Europe.

studies and in expert surveys studies have expanded.[11] Despite these efforts, many regionalist parties are not included in these studies. The geography of the regionalist party family has also expanded due to EU enlargement (De Winter and Lynch 2008). The presence of the regionalist party family is limited to specific member states. In Western Europe, the regionalist party family has been traditionally represented in five countries. The UNC-Chapel Hill expert surveys conducted in 2002 and 2006 included parties in five other countries in Central and Eastern Europe (Marks et al. 2006). In the past, both comparative studies and expert survey studies show a pro-European party family on average, but the findings are based on different parties.[12]

The regionalist party family included in the University of North Carolina study (Hooghe et al. 2010) is composed of twenty parties from Western and Eastern Europe (Table 6.1). The average position of the regionalist party family towards European integration is pro-European integration (5.11 on a 7-point scale; 5 corresponds to 'somewhat in favor'). The average for the regionalist party family is only slightly above the mean for all party families (5.04). In longitudinal perspective, data from previous waves of the expert surveys show that the average EU position of the regionalist party family is slightly above the mean average for all party families.[13] In 2006, the mean EU position for the regionalist party family ranks 5 on the list of most pro-European families (after Liberals, Socialists, Christian Democrats and Conservatives). If a Europhile is someone who admires the EU, these data certainly do not support the image of strong supporters of European integration. Using data from a previous wave of the UNC–Chapel Hill expert surveys, Jolly's (2007) analysis point to a party family highly supportive of European integration, coherent on Europhile positions and with a very insignificant number of anti-European outliers (Jolly

---

[11] The regionalist party family defined by Hix and Lord in 1997 included thirty-seven parties from seven EU countries, eleven of them represented in the European parliament in 1994. In the first attempt to locate the position of the regionalist party family at the aggregate level, conducted by Hix and Lord, data were very limited and the empirical findings were not robust. Only fifteen out of thirty-seven parties could be placed in the left-right dimension and four out of thirty-seven on the integration-sovereignty dimension (Hix and Lord 1997: 46–7). The retrospective expert survey conducted by Ray (1999) to cover the period 1984 through 1999 included fifteen cases. The 2002 and 2006 University of North Carolina, Chapel Hill expert surveys (2012) included sixteen and twenty cases, respectively, of which nine are regionalist parties covered by the first expert survey by Ray. Jolly includes twenty-one parties from 1984 to 2002.

[12] Again the cases covered by comparative studies and expert surveys only partially coincide: Only nine of the seventeen party cases covered by De Winter, Gómez-Reino and Lynch are included in the last wave of expert surveys (De Winter, Gómez-Reino and Lynch 2006a; Marks et al. 2006). Some parties have disappeared – such as the Volksunie – and others are dropped from the survey – such as the Partido Andalucista.

[13] Until 1999, support for European integration among the regionalist party family was higher than the average party family, but from 1999, support has been lower (Keating and Hooghe 2006: 272).

TABLE 6.1. *Regionalist Party Family*

	EU Position*	EU Salience**
BNG Galician Nationalist Bloc	4.50	2.11
CC Canary Coalition	5.27	2.44
CHA Aragonese Council	5.00	1.88
CiU Convergence and Unity	6.31	2.73
EA Basque Solidarity	4.78	2.00
ERC Republican Left of Catalonia	4.46	2.10
FDGR Democratic Forum of Germans of Romania	6.43	3.29
KP Constitution Party	3.33	2.00
LLRA Election Action of Lithuania's Poles	5.71	2.86
LN Northern League	1.50	3.00
NVA New Flemish Alliance	4.90	2.00
PC Party of Wales	5.40	2.40
PNV Basque Nationalist Party	5.62	2.30
SFP Swedish People's Party	6.33	2.91
SC Harmony Centre	5.50	2.25
SF We Ourselves	2.70	2.10
SMK Party of the Hungarian Coalition	6.36	3.21
SNP Scottish National Party	5.22	2.78
SVP South Tyrolean People's Party	6.33	2.33
UDMR Hungarian Democratic Union of Romania	6.60	3.40
Average	5.125	2.4545
Std deviation	1.33385	.49243

Source: Marks et al. (2006).

* How would you describe the general position on European integration that the party leadership took over the course of 2006?

** We would like you to think about the salience of European integration for a party. Over the course of 2006, how important was the EU to the parties in their public stance?

2007: 120). Rather, in 2006, at the aggregate level, regionalist parties show a mild pro-Europeanness.

Moreover, the results of the 2006 UNC-Chapel Hill expert survey data also show that the salience of the EU for the regionalist party family is remarkably low. The salience of the EU for regional parties is 2.45 (on a 4-point scale) lower than the average for all party families (2.79). Comparing party family scores on EU salience, the regionalist party family on average is the one that attaches less importance to European integration. In longitudinal perspective, EU salience according to previous expert surveys for the regionalist party family was lower than the mean for party families for the period 1984 through 1999 (2.9) However, data for 2006 also reveal that EU salience for the regionalist party family is lower than the average in the previous 2002 and 1999 studies and the lowest since the early 1980s.

Coherence of the Party Family

The heterogeneity of the regionalist party family underlies different positions of regionalist parties towards European integration. The range of positions within party families on European issues reflects party family cohesion.[14] De Winter and Gómez-Reino (2002: 491) used Ray's (1999) expert survey data to establish that the regionalist party family was the most homogeneous party family in terms of standard deviations of their EU attitudes. Jolly (2007) states that the standard deviation around the mean shows a more coherent party family than most party families, only preceded by the Liberal family. However, data from the 2006 wave show that the standard deviation from the mean average of the EU positions of the regionalist party family is rather high (1.33). By 2006, most party families are more coherent on their EU position; only the Confessional, Agrarian and Conservative party families are less coherent than the regionalist party family.

Today the most pro-European parties within the regionalist party family are parties from Central and Eastern Europe. The Hungarian Democratic Alliance is the most pro-European party (6.6 on a 7-point scale), followed by the Democratic Forum of Germans in Romania and then by three parties from the West, the Südtiroler Volkspartei (SVP), the SFP and CiU.[15] Before enlargement, the most pro-European regionalist parties since 1984 in Europe had been the Catalan CiU, a coalition formed by Convergència Democràtica de Catalunya (CDC) and Unió Democràtica de Catalunya (UL), followed by the other Catalan regionalist, ERC (until 1999).[16] The most Eurosceptical parties within the regionalist party family are still in Western Europe. In the 2006 wave of the expert survey, on the side of those less in favor of European integration appear the Lega Nord (1.5) followed by Sinn Fein (2.70).[17] In contrast, according to previous expert waves, the most Eurosceptical parties of the party family since 1984 were only extreme-left parties, both the Basque Herri Batasuna (Euskal Herritarok in 1999) and the Irish Sinn Fein (Ray 1999).

---

[14] The indicators of the coherence of the party family are: standard deviation (average deviation from the mean position of each party family) and range (difference between the lowest and highest party position in each party family).

[15] In the 2002 survey, which included four parties from Central and Eastern Europe, the most pro-European party was the Hungarian Democratic Alliance of Romania, followed by the SFP.

[16] The parties in Central and Eastern Europe included in the party family are not like the standard regionalist parties of the West. The traditional definition of the center-periphery cleavage uncomfortably fits since they lack territorial claims and defend linguistic and cultural minorities such as the Russian-speaking minority in the Baltic state or the Hungarian minorities in Central Europe. In this regard, they are similar to the rather exceptional SFP in Finland, which defends the language rights of the Swedish minority. Thus, arguments about territorial autonomy or a Europe of Regions within the EU are not relevant (Raunio 2006).

[17] After the 2002 survey, Euskal Herritarok (Batasuna since 2000) does not appear. So Sinn Fein clearly defines the interval from the extreme left.

TABLE 6.2. *Regionalist Party Family: EU and Left-Right Position*

Party	EU Position*	Left-Right
BNG Galician Nationalist Bloc	4.50	2.36
CC Canary Coalition	5.27	6.36
CHA Aragonese Council	5.00	2.75
CiU Convergence and Unity	6.31	6.25
EA Basque Solidarity	4.78	4.60
ERC Republican Left of Catalonia	4.46	2.18
FDGR Democratic Forum of Germans of Romania	6.43	5.29
KP Constitution Party	3.33	2.25
LLRA Election Action of Lithuania's Poles	5.71	4.33
LN Northern League	1.50	8.71
NVA New Flemish Alliance	4.90	7.89
PC Party of Wales	5.40	3.10
PNV Basque Nationalist Party	5.62	6.17
SFP Swedish People's Party	6.33	6.18
SC Harmony Centre	5.50	3.00
SF We Ourselves	2.70	2.00
SMK Party of the Hungarian Coalition	6.36	6.08
SNP Scottish National Party	5.22	3.89
SVP South Tyrolean People's Party	6.33	5.00
UDMR Hungarian Democratic Union of Romania	6.60	6.00
Average	5.1125	4.7195
Std deviation	1.33385	1.9863

Source: Marks et al. (2006).

* How would you describe the general position on European integration that the party leadership took over the course of 2006?

Differences in EU position are closely associated with the ideological heterogeneity of the regionalist party family. The regionalist party family average on the general left-right scale is 4.7 (slightly below the average for all party families, 5.04), but the standard deviation from the mean is the highest of all party families, showing the importance of ideological differences along the left-right continuum (Table 6.2).

The location of a regionalist party on the left-right dimension is closely associated with its position in favour or against European integration (see Figure 6.1). At the aggregate level, a pro-European centrist position emerges, while Eurosceptical parties are located at the extreme left and extreme right. In the 1980s, the most hard and soft Eurosceptic parties belong to the extreme left (Ray 1999). Currently, the most Eurosceptical party within the family is the radical right Lega Nord.

Within the regionalist party family, pro- and anti-European positions have always co-existed. In historical perspective, the Europhile views of the regionalist party family also pertain to parties from the right and center-right, such as the CiU or the PNV. In contrast, still in the late 1970s, there was nothing natural or automatic about support for the construction of Europe from the peripheries for left-wing regionalist parties. Some of them started out with clear opposition to European integration. In addition to the Flemish Volksunie, parties such as the Scottish National Party (SNP), Plaid Cymru (P.C.) or BNG are well-known examples of initial rejection of European integration.[18]

These ideological differences along the left-right dimension are reinforced at the European level by the different location of regionalist parties within the EU institutional and political framework. Unlike most party families, the regionalist party family is divided in the European parliament. Some regionalist parties are members of the pro-European integration European Free Alliance-Democratic Party of the Peoples of Europe (EFA-DPPE) created in 1981, a transnational federation (from six original to currently forty members) that seeks to act as the voice of these parties in the EU (De Winter and Gómez-Reino 2002; Lynch and De Winter 2008). The example of the proselytizing work of Maurits Coppieters shows the importance of building support for European integration among regionalist parties. Maurits Coppieters, elected as member of the European parliament for the Volksunie in 1979, played a key role in shaping the pro-European attitudes of oregionalist parties in Europe through the creation of the European Free Alliance (EFA). He is recognized by regionalist parties as a pioneer of a view of Europe able to accommodate the presence of national minorities, a Europe of Regions and a Europe of minorities. His own party, the Volksunie, was an example of critical views and rejection of European integration evolving later towards support (De Winter 1998). His mission was precisely to convince other minor regionalist parties of the advantages that the European Parliament would represent to advance a common European policy for national minorities.

Table 6.3 shows regionalist parties' affiliation to the different groups in the European Parliament. Center-left and left-wing regionalist parties are typically associated with EFA. An exception is the Nieuwe-Vlaamse Alliantie, one of the heirs of the Flemish Volksunie, which belonged to the European Popular party in the period 2004 through 2009 and later became affiliated with EFA. EFA has a common policy platform and a European integration vaguely defined as the promotion of the diversity of peoples, cultures, languages and regions (Lynch and De Winter 2008). EFA endorses a so-called progressive nationalism. It has also adopted policies common with the Greens in light of their past collaboration in the European parliament (Lynch and De Winter 2008: 586). In its 2009 European Elections Manifesto, EFA defines itself as a family of pro-European parties yet a family of critics of certain policies and evolution of European integration. EFA has provided a common platform on European integration and

---

[18] By the same token, within the radical right-wing family, some parties such as the FN, the REP or the FPO initially supported European integration only to turn later into some of the most Eurosceptic parties in Europe (see Mudde 2007).

TABLE 6.3. *Regionalist Party Family in the EU, 2009*

	EFA	Other EU Group
Galician Nationalist Bloc	X	
Canary Coalition		—
Aragonese Council	X	
Convergence and Unity		ELDR
Basque Solidarity	X	
Republican Left of Catalonia	X	
Democratic Forum of Germans of Romania		—
Constitution Party		—
Election Action of Lithuania's Poles		EPP
Northern League		Europe for Freedom and Democracy
New Flemish Alliance	X	
Party of Wales	X	
Basque Nationalist Party		ELDR
Swedish People's Party		ELDR
Harmony Centre		GUE/NGL
We Ourselves		GUE/NGL
Party of the Hungarian Coalition		EPP
Scottish National Party	X	
South Tyrolean People's Party		EPP
Hungarian Democratic Union of Romania		EPP

policy role in shaping positions is also limited, given the ideological differences, the variety of autonomy goals and therefore the intrinsic difficulties in devising a common constitutional model for the EU (it works with the principle of the common minimum denominator) (De Winter and Gómez-Reino 2002; De Winter and Lynch 2008).

In contrast, center-right and right regionalist parties are integrated within the framework of the traditional party families in the European parliament. As Table 6.3 shows, most of them belong to the group of the European Popular party followed by the Liberal group – both more pro-European than the regionalist party family.[19] As Table 6.3 shows, some prominent members and the most pro–European parties within the family do not belong to EFA, such as CiU, SVO or SFP. The significance of the different location of regionalist parties at the EU level, as Lynch and De Winter have pointed out, is that it is ultimately an incomplete party family (Lynch and De Winter 2008: 584).

[19] Some regionalist parties have been loyal to the European Free Alliance (EFA) – PC, the European Popular Party (EPP) – and to the Alliance of Liberal and Democratic Europe (ELDR) – Union Democrática de Catalunya (UDC), Convergéncia Democrática de Catalunya (CDC) – since they were first elected to the European parliament, while others such as Lega Nord have changed over time, from EFA to non-attached, Independence and Democracy and UEN.

The EU position of regionalist parties has changed as they move away and towards the extremes along the left-right continuum. Within the regionalist party family, there are divergent trajectories towards pro–European integration or increasing Euroscepticism. The next section looks more closely at two reversed trajectories, away from the extreme left (BNG) and toward the extreme right (LN) to show how the left-right position of regionalist party can push the position of regionalist parties towards or against European integration. In fact, despite the image of continuity and minor changes on the regionalist party family at the aggregate level, EU positions can be adapted and actually reversed.

EVOLVING ORIENTATIONS TOWARDS THE EU, REVERSED TRAJECTORIES: THE BNG AND LN

The combination of the center-periphery cleavage with the left-/right-wing dimension has led to different varieties of pro– and anti–European positions within the regionalist party family. This section examines two cases, the left nationalist Bloque Nacionalista Galego and the right populist Lega Nord and their divergent positions towards European integration. Both were extremist parties along the left-right dimension, the BNG as a starting point in its evolution, the Lega Nord as the result of its politics over the past decade. The comparison of the two cases shows both how the center-periphery is ambivalent towards European integration (very different views on opportunities and costs associated with European integration) and filtered through broader left-/right-wing ideologies. The influence of left-/right-wing ideology played a role in facilitating and preventing regionalist parties from supporting the European Union across time (from the 1980s up to the present) in these divergent trajectories that share a rejection of the democratic deficit of the European Union, although the meaning attached to it by both parties is very different. The first trajectory, the BNG, explains the shift from hard to soft Euroscepticism, from outward rejection in the 1980s to critical support for European integration from the late 1990s onwards. It focuses on ideological and strategic changes that turned outward opposition towards EI into an adaptation of party goals to European integration, although this adaptation does not erase criticisms regarding the evolution and model of European integration. The second trajectory, LN, illustrates the opposite move from initial support to European integration in the 1980s and early 1990s to increasing Eurosceptical orientations on European integration. Moreover, the 'content' of their rejection of the European Union also reflects their position on the left-/right-wing continuum because the extreme left is mostly based on socioeconomic policies and the extreme right on cultural issues (De Vries and Edwards 2009).

The Bloque Nacionalista Galego is a left-nationalist regionalist party born in 1982. The Bloque Nacionalista Galego represents an anti-European party whose position on integration dramatically shifted in the course of two decades.[20] During its first decade of existence, the BNG was a minor fringe party in the Galician party system, with symbolic representation in the Galician parliament since 1985. Until the mid 1980s, it was an anti-system party that rejected the Spanish constitution and the Galician Statute of Autonomy. The BNG became one of the electoral successes of the third wave of regionalist party mobilization. The BNG was in opposition at the regional level until it entered the Galician government (2005–2009) in coalition with the Socialist party (Gómez-Reino Cachafeiro 2011).

The ideological profile of the BNG is distinctive along two dimensions: national identity and left nationalism. The party front was born out of a coalition of nationalist left-wing parties (Socialist and Communist) that was expanded to include most Galician nationalist parties (Gómez-Reino Cachafiero 2006; Lago 2004). Although the ideological sources of these parties were different, the identity of the party was clearly marked by its left position.

The first BNG period was characterized by extreme-left nationalism and thirldworldism, and views on European integration were based on the consideration of Galicia as a colonized European periphery. In the first 1982 party political principles, the European community appeared as one of the main enemies of Galician nationalism. The BNG denounced then 'the Europeanist ideology of the Europe of Peoples' (Gómez-Reino Cachafiero 2006: 184). Based on the discourse of the peripheries and internal colonies in Europe, the BNG rejected all of what European integration implied: the common market, transnational capital interests and European imperialism.

The party devised a broad platform, *o proxecto comun* or common project, to integrate different views and perspectives within Galician nationalism. Since 1989, early demands of self-government were replaced by demands of further political autonomy within the Spanish framework of the *Estado de las Autonomías* as the BNG searched for moderating its initial anti-system stand. This led to an electoral expansion of the BNG and its consolidation in the Galician party system.

Views on European integration slowly changed in the 1990s. First, the BNG accepted membership in the EU while the party criticized the institutional and economic framework of the European Union. Second, the BNG maintained critical views regarding the European project, integration and institutions. Third, European issues were marginal for both party ideology and strategy. Still in the late 1990s, its first and only MEP, Camilo Nogueira, elected in 1999, represented a minority view within the BNG, a more pro-European (yet

---

[20] There are disagreements on the position of the BNG towards European integration. The most positive derives from expert surveys in which it appears already as pro–European in the 1980s (Ray 1999; the initial score for the BNG in 1984 was 5 on a 7-point scale). In contrast, other qualitative and quantitative studies reflect a more critical and Eurosceptical party (Elias 2008; Gómez-Reino, Llamazares and Ramiro 2008).

critical) view of European integration, in comparison with most members of the party leadership.

For the BNG, European integration always had a negative impact on Galicia because it damages the position of economically dependent and peripheral regions in particular on some of the most crucial economic sectors, such as fishery or agriculture. In this regard, the adaptation of the BNG has turned the European Union into an arena to defend specific territorial and sectoral interests. It has become a pro-European regionalist party that belongs to the European Free Alliance. Yet the BNG defends a democratic and social model of Europe that recognizes 'nations without a state'. The BNG has opposed systematically the EU treaties for these ideological reasons. The Maastricht Treaty showed for the BNG the democratic deficit of the EU and a dominant model of economic integration against the welfare state (Gómez-Reino, Llamazares and Ramiro 2008: 143). Likewise, the BNG opposed the referendum for the Constitutional Treaty along the same lines, denouncing the democratic deficit and the social model embedded in it. The BNG clearly has 'contingent and qualified' critical positions on the EU, qualifying as a soft Eurosceptic for some scholars or as a pro-European but critical party for others.[21]

The BNG illustrates a common trajectory to left-wing regionalist parties that adapted and support the wide EU framework while criticizing specific policies and their impact at the territorial level. Moreover, while Sinn Fein remains the most Eurosceptical party of the regionalist party family, it has certainly followed this path of adaptation to the EU (Frampton 2005).

Lega Nord is also distinctive along the two dimensions analyzed here: its claims of self-government for the north of Italy and its populist radical right position. Lega Nord is a populist regionalist party with double membership in the regionalist party family and radical right-wing family. While at first Lega Nord's claims were mainly cultural, during the 1990s, the position of the party along the left-/right-wing dimension was increasingly defined (Ruzza 2006: 223). Lega Nord has entered national government in right-wing coalitions on three occasions. The first right-wing coalition took place in 1994 with Berlusconi's Forza Italia and Alleanza Nazionale, in coalition during the 2001–2005 and 2008–2011 periods.

Lega Nord was created out of a variety of minor regionalist parties that were born in the Northern Italian regions during the 1980s. These parties were clearly identified by their pro-European views, and they supported by the idea of a Europe of regions and Peoples. Moreover, these regionalist parties were also aware from the start of the opportunities afforded by European integration in terms of institutional and electoral space. Lega Lombarda also benefited quite early from the European arena because it obtained its first MEP in the 1989 European elections (Gómez-Reino Cachafiero 2002). Moreover,

---

[21] According to Gómez-Reino and colleagues (2008: 135), 'even if some of their statements resemble Hard Eurosceptic arguments, they are not guided by principled opposition to the EU.

Lega Nord (since 1991) followed its regional 'identity', searching for a place within the regionalist party family in Europe. Lega Nord was expelled from the European Free Alliance in 1994 with the formation of the Berlusconi government. In the European Parliament, its position shifted among different groups until it entered the Union for Europe of the Nations (UEN) group for the period 2004 through 2009. At present, Lega Nord has formed a new group in the EU Parliament that gathers populist Eurosceptics: Europe for Freedom and Democracy.

The pro-European position of Lega Nord marks its first decade of existence. Lega Nord voted for the Maastricht Treaty in the Italian parliament. The height of support corresponds to the period the party was seeking independence and seeking entering the European Monetary Union (EMU) for Padania. However, it has experienced more abrupt changes in party position on European integration. The trajectory was first clearly pro-European in the 1980s,[22] pro-Europeanness in the early 1990s, dropping since 1998 into soft and even 'hard' Eurosceptical views. Lega Nord has completely changed its position on European integration. The party shift on the EU and the euro is traced back to Italy's acceptance into the EMU (Albertazzi and McDonnell 2005: 965). Lega Nord was not fundamentally or ideologically Eurosceptic; hard Euroscepticism is not entrenched in the party (Quaglia 2003: 15–8). Opposition against Europe has been growing since 1998 to the rejection of the EU as the 'Soviet Union of Europe'. Strategically, Euroscepticism provides LN a way to differentiate the party from its government partners and also a strategy to reconstruct its party identity: from soft to hard Euroscepticism (Quaglia 2003: 18). The Lega Nord opposed the Constitutional Treaty and the Lisbon Treaty, denouncing the democratic deficit of the European Union. Lega Nord demanded the insertion in the document of references to the cultural basis of the EU, 'the Christian roots of the continent'. Moreover, Lega Nord demands the rejection of the entry of Turkey in the European Union. Finally Lega Nord denounces the risks of the erosion of the principle of sovereignty within the European Union.

A comparison of both trajectories shows that EU positions can shift substantially over time and that adaptation to and away from pro-European views is closely associated with party general left- and right-wing positions. The evolution of both the Bloque Nacionalista Galego and the Lega Nord parties shows very different starting points, crossing trajectories and divergent outcomes and patterns of adaptation. They criticize the democratic deficit of European integration, but their divergent positions for and against European integration and on the left and right general continuum mark the different content of this deficit. The BNG still defends a specific leftist model of political and socio-economic integration for Europe and criticizes social and economic policies in the current evolution of the European Union, while the Eurosceptical and

---

[22] Lega Nord properly did not exist in the 1980s; I assume they used the position of the pre-existing regionalist parties in the regions of the north before 1991.

radical-right Lega Nord rejects on cultural grounds the evolving architecture and boundaries of the EU.

CONCLUSIONS

The support of the regionalist party family for European integration seems more modest than expected. The contemporary map of the regionalist party family at the aggregate level is a family with pro-EU centers (left less and right more so) and Eurosceptical extremes. The different positions within the regionalist party family towards European integration are built on established ideologies and strategic moves. These established ideologies are not only the products of the ambivalent center-periphery cleavage but also of other dimensions of conflict, in particular the left-right dimension. The regionalist party family is contributing to the construction of a common European project in a specific piecemeal, fragmented fashion. It defends, and represents too, a Europe of diversities. As this chapter has attempted to highlight, its views on European integration are divided, as they reflect different ideologies and divisions within the party family at the European level. The examination of the position of regionalist party family towards European integration is still incomplete. We lack detailed evidence on manifestos in comparative and longitudinal perspective. More importantly, we need comparative evidence on the attitudes of party voters towards European integration. In this way, we could generate hypotheses about the way party elites factor public opinion on their strategic moves and how fragile the support for the European Union really is.

Moreover, European identity is malleable and in the making. The classic definition of the center-periphery cleavage relies on the existence of two opposing and exclusive territorial identifications: the dominant culture and the peripheral culture of ethnic and national minorities (Lipset and Rokkan 1967; Urwin 1983). According to Hooghe and Marks (2009), a strong territorial identity is consistent with both support for and opposition to integration; what matters is the extent to which identity is exclusive (Hooghe and Marks 2009: 21). However, an exclusive identity is still a requirement in the definition of regionalist parties (Türsan 1998). Future research ought to address the question of the exclusive or multiple identities of regionalist parties in comparative perspective and how a European identity fits within multiple territorial identities. Research has advanced our knowledge about the extent to which regionalist parties endorse multiple identities (Llamazares and Marks 1999; Martínez Herrera 2002). The extent to which a European identity is included in these multiple layers (for both party elites and voters) is still an open question for empirical research. The low salience of the EU for regionalist parties requires further investigation, because one of the starting points in the analysis of the regionalist party family and European integration was the utmost importance of European integration for the center-periphery cleavage and for the evolution of the regionalist party family (De Winter and Gómez-Reino 2002).

PART III

RELIGIOUS CHALLENGES

7

Muslims and Multicultural Nationalism in Scotland

William L. Miller and Asifa M. Hussain

After a Scottish Parliament election (2007) that, for the first time, put the Scottish Nationalist Party (SNP) into office if not into power (the party forms the Scottish Government but holds only 47 of the 129 seats), it is tempting to suppose that the 2007 election result indicates a 'rise of nationalism' in Scotland. Alas, the evidence does not support that interpretation.

Much of the evidence suggests that Scots have indeed become somewhat more nationalist and less unionist since the 1960s – but more so in terms of voting than in anything else. It has got easier to vote Nationalist and more difficult to vote Unionist – in part because the meanings of both Nationalism and Unionism, as defined by the parties, have changed. So even if there had been no change at all in public opinion, there would probably have been a significant change in public behaviour at the polls.

The option of a Nationalist vote became more available as the SNP contested more seats and became more credible in the context of a Scottish Parliament and a new proportional election system. However, most importantly, a Nationalist vote became less frightening as the SNP adopted a much more moderate and inclusive definition of Nationalism. In policy and rhetoric, Nationalists have become very much less nationalist than they were in the 1960s.

The evidence suggests that the apparent rise of Nationalism in Scottish elections owes more to institutional changes and to the SNP's increasingly moderate, internationalist and inclusive redefinition of Nationalism than to rising nationalist sentiment amongst the public (Miller 2008). We can summarize the change in sentiment amongst the public since the 1960s as follows:

1. Their broad political culture and values remain almost indistinguishable from those in England.
2. Their support for a Scottish Parliament – always strong – was more for devolution than independence; it increased only modestly; and it is now past its peak.

3. Their identification with Scotland – always strong – also increased only modestly; and it is past its peak.
4. The greatest change has been in voting rather than in constitutional preferences, broad political values or national identities. None of these potential causes of voting change has changed as dramatically as voting itself: In short, behaviour has changed more than opinion.

At the same time, nationalism has been redefined since the 1960s. We can summarize the changing nature of Nationalism as follows:

1. The concept of independence has been redefined by the SNP. In the 1960s, the SNP favoured complete independence: a Scotland outside the UK and outside the EU. But after a fierce battle between rival factions within the party – which briefly included the expulsion of current leader Alex Salmond – the party now supports his oxymoronic principle of 'independence within' – albeit 'independence within the EU' rather than the Labour Party policy defined by the late Donald Dewar as 'independence within the UK' (otherwise known as devolution).
2. Second, and equally important, the concept of the nation has been redefined by the SNP. The SNP has travelled all the way from an old nationalism that stressed history, people and heritage to a new nationalism that now stresses the future rather than the past, the land rather than the people and, especially important for our present discussion, multiculturalism rather than heritage.

It is a very long way to travel. Murray Leith's comprehensive statistical study of the changing content of SNP manifestos over the last thirty-five years has reached the conclusion that recent SNP manifestos are now only 'half as nationalist' (Leith 2006: chapter 3, section 7) as they were three decades ago. The anti-English tone of earlier manifestoes has been replaced by a less ethnic and more political attack on the Conservative Party (not the English people) for being anti-Scottish. The English themselves are no longer attacked as they were in the 1970s (e.g. for taking student places at Scottish universities) and negative statements about England or Anglicization have, according to Leith, 'almost disappeared'. At the same time, coded phrases like 'new Scots', 'new Scotland' and even the more explicit 'multicultural society' have crept in. (Leith 2006: chapter 6). Moreover, words have been followed by deeds: The first Asian ever to sit in the Scottish Parliament was elected from the SNP list in 2007. He was pictured in the press, wearing the kilt, as he celebrated his victory.

And yet, the genuinely inclusive, multicultural nationalism of SNP leader Alex Salmond may not reach down to grass-roots party members – still less to the street. Devolution was undeniably a move in a nationalist direction, even if it was intended to inoculate Scots against more extreme nationalism. Indeed, opponents had long argued that it was a step onto a slippery slope that would encourage rather than discourage nationalism. In an increasingly self-conscious post-devolution Scotland, English immigrants might feel ill at ease – like the Protestants in the Irish Republic after partition (Fedorowich 1999) or the ethnic Russians in post-Soviet Central Asia or in the Baltic States (Brubaker 1996, 148–78; Sendich and Payin 1994) – an unwelcome 'post-imperial' minority. During the 1990s, SNG (Siol Nan Gaidheal – 'Seed of the Gael') pledged to 'unstintingly campaign against English imperialism' and spawned both 'Scottish watch' and the more clearly titled 'settler watch' to 'expose and oppose' English 'incomers' (Hearn 2000: 65–70). Moreover, an increasingly self-conscious Scotland, increasingly focused on its own history, culture and traditions might regard other minorities as even more culturally alien than the 'auld enemy' (i.e. the English) – especially Muslims after 9/11.

At the top, both advocates of devolution and the more independence-minded nationalists have consistently proclaimed their commitment to a non-ethnic, inclusive, 'civic' concept of nationalism (Henderson 1999: 138). Labour First Minister Jack McConnell declared that Scotland needed more immigrants, asylum seekers and ethnic minorities (McConnell 2003). In addition, leading nationalists have not so far attempted to increase their support by attacking minorities. Indeed, quite the opposite: When John Swinney was SNP leader, he accused Labour of racism in its ill treatment of Muslim asylum seekers (Herald 8 Sept. 2003a), repeatedly describing it as a 'national shame' (Herald 12 Sept. 2003b) or a 'national disgrace' (Herald 10 Oct. 2003c). That was despite the fact that the 2003 Scottish Social Attitudes Survey (SSAS) showed that a large majority of Scots were in favour of detaining asylum seekers: 62 per cent in the SSAS agreed that 'asylum seekers should be kept in detention centers while their cases were being considered' and only 26 per cent disagreed. So there was no short-term political advantage in Swinney's accusation – though such statements helped to define the SNP as a civic rather than an ethnic nationalist party, and in the longer term that may help the SNP retain its position in the mainstream of Scottish politics rather than slipping to the extremist fringe. Following the invasion of Iraq, Muslim voters in Scotland switched overwhelmingly from Labour to the SNP (Hussain and Miller 2006: 165). That Muslim voters abandoned Labour is not remarkable in the circumstances, but that they should opt for the SNP rather than the Liberals (who also opposed that invasion) provides clear evidence that the SNP was not by then regarded as an ethnic nationalist party.

The SNP's inclusive approach extended – even more remarkably – to the English as well. Current SNP leader Alex Salmond, for example, has regularly claimed to be an anglophile. (Try entering 'Alex Salmond' and 'anglophile' into Google and just count the hits.) To take just one from his many public statements: 'I have often pronounced myself one of the most anglophile of all Scottish Members ... We present our case for Scotland in a positive way. We do not spend our time being antagonistic about other nations' (Salmond 1997).

Kellas (1998: 65) distinguishes between ethnic nationalism that he describes as 'in essence exclusive', stressing the ethnic group and common descent, and the civic nationalism of those such as Swinney and Salmond, which, he says, claims to be 'inclusive in the sense that anyone can adopt the culture and join the nation'. The distinction between civic and ethnic nationalism has been drawn so often that it has become 'almost a cliché in the literature' (Kymlicka 2001b: 243), often equated with Gellner's (1983: 99) simple but evocative distinction between 'benign' and 'nasty' nationalism.

Yet there are problems with the apparently simple civic-versus-ethnic distinction. First, minorities may be either unwilling or even unable to 'adopt the culture' or 'join the nation'. Our own research suggests that the Muslim minority in Scotland is unwilling to adopt the culture (though willing to join the nation), while English immigrants in Scotland are psychologically unable to join the nation (though willing to adopt the culture). Neither the Muslim nor the English minority in Scotland can pass the test set by Kellas.

Second, civic nationalism can easily degenerate into ethnic nationalism. For Gellner (1983: 1–2), nationalist sentiment is at root a feeling of anger; for Breuilly (1993: 5–7), although nationalism can be asserted in a 'universalist [i.e. civic] spirit', it has 'not often been so sweetly reasonable'. For Vincent (1997: 294), 'nationalism will always resist being assimilated into liberalism ... and easily collapses into ... shallow expressions of blood, soil and xenophobia'. For Pulzer (1988: 287; see also Porter 2000), 'nationalism degenerates ... often inspired in its first stage by the urge to emancipate, it finds its logical conclusion in a paroxysm of destructiveness'.

Third and perhaps the greatest problem – so very easy to overlook but so very difficult to resolve – is that liberal notions of tolerance and equality, while welcome, may be grossly insufficient: '[O]ne might enjoy all the rights of citizenship and be a formally equal member of the community, and yet feel an outsider who does not belong' (Parekh 2000: 237). Minorities seek acceptance, reassurance, respect, admiration and warmth – not simply cold, liberal, equal justice. Part of the problem is the significance of 'political symbols, images, ceremonies, collective self-understanding and views of national identity' (Parekh 2000: 203; see also Modood and Werbner 1997: 263) for that feeling of warmth, acceptance and belonging. An increasing emphasis on Scottish history and enthusiasm for films like Braveheart (Edensor 1997: 147) claims that the Scottish Parliament is not a new parliament for a new age but only the restoration of an old parliament that merely 'adjourned on 25 March 1707' and now is 'reconvened' (Scottish Parliament 1999: vol. 1, col. 5), or even John Swinney's (Scotsman 2002) own call to use Scotland's patron saint to promote the new Scotland – all of these are necessarily exclusionist for those whose ethnic culture and/or identity makes it impossible for them to identify with historic Scotland – as distinct from contemporary Scotland.

Furthermore, even if political elites take greater care to ensure that political symbols are inclusive and successfully avoid unfortunate lapses such as over-enthusiasm for Christian saints or for military victories over the English, minorities can be made 'to feel outsiders who do not belong' by the way they are treated by ordinary people in everyday life. If minorities feel they are regarded by the public as a burden on the country's resources, as social untouchables or as a disloyal element, they are likely to feel excluded. Street-level prejudice can be just as alienating as elite-level discrimination. So we must investigate street-level prejudice to show how far the inclusive civic nationalism of Scottish political elites reaches down to the street and, in particular, how the street reacts to minorities that cannot or will not adopt the culture and/or join the 'nation'.

Muslim and English minorities constitute, respectively, the largest 'visible' and 'invisible' minorities in post-devolution Scotland. According to the 2001 Scottish census, English immigrants (i.e. born in England, living in Scotland) constitute 8 per cent of Scotland's population, rising to 12 per cent across the whole of the capital city, Edinburgh, and to 18 per cent across all of rural/small-town southern Scotland. By contrast (self-defined), ethnic Pakistanis (overwhelmingly, by self-description, Muslim) constitute just more than 1 per cent of Scotland's population, but they are more 'visible' than the English – by dress code as well as skin colour (though English immigrants are more 'audible' because they, unlike the Scottish Pakistanis, do not speak with a Scottish accent!). Pakistani visibility is enhanced by their concentration in the cities, especially Glasgow, and by generally increasing awareness of Muslim minorities after 9/11 and the invasion of Iraq.

English immigrants in Scotland tend to identify themselves as more British than Scottish, while ethnic Pakistanis in Scotland tend to describe themselves as more Scottish than British (Hussain and Miller 2006: 147). But while the primary identity of native Scots is 'Scottish' and the primary identity of English immigrants is 'British' (significantly, it is not 'English'), the primary identity of ethnic Pakistanis in Scotland is simply 'Muslim' (Hussain and Miller 2006: 157). Thus, the self-identification of ethnic Pakistanis in Scotland is primarily religious rather than any kind of territorial identity – Scottish, British or even Pakistani.

ANALYSIS OF SSAS SURVEY

For direct measurements of street-level Islamophobia and Anglophobia amongst ordinary or majority Scots, we need to focus on something less than the entire population resident in Scotland. In particular, it would be absurd to include English immigrants themselves in any calculation of Anglophobia. They are so numerous as well as so distinctive that including English immigrants and their partners – who together constitute about 12 per cent of the resident population in Scotland – would significantly underestimate Anglophobia. Therefore, to measure Islamophobia and Anglophobia in Scotland, we focus on the attitudes of majority Scots – defined to exclude Muslims (only 1 per cent of the population), English immigrants (8 per cent) and also those whose partners are English immigrants (another 4 per cent). Just 1,158 of the respondents in the 2003 Scottish Social Attitudes Survey sample fit this tight definition of majority Scots.

TABLE 7.1. *Identities of "Majority Scots" and Others in Scotland (in percent)*

	Majority Scots	Others in Scotland	All those in Scotland
Scottish, not British	36	15	31
More Scottish than British	38	17	34
Equally Scottish and British	21	24	22
More British than Scottish	2	11	4
British, not Scottish	1	13	4
Other identity	1	14	4
None of these	*	5	1
Sample size (unweighted)	1,158	350	1,508

The difference between majority Scots and the population of Scotland (including English immigrants and their partners) is evident from a tabulation of 'Moreno identities' – that is, whether they feel more Scottish or more British (Table 7.1).

It should be unnecessary to point out that our analytic procedure is a methodological requirement only, driven by the need for analytical clarity. We do not ourselves equate 'majority Scots' with 'real Scots' or 'true Scots', for example – though many majority Scots do make that equation, recognizing only people 'like themselves' as being 'truly' Scottish.

EQUALITY

Majority Scots, as we have defined them, are overwhelmingly committed to the liberal concept of ethnic equality – for English immigrants as well as Muslims. About 80 per cent support the extension of anti-discrimination laws from race and gender to apply to both religion and sub-UK origin – specifically to cover discrimination against Muslims or against English immigrants (Table 7.2).

Majority Scots are not opposed to having both Muslim and English immigrant MSPs in the Scottish Parliament but are not enthusiastic, either. More than half do not think it matters – a view that is similar to that held by English immigrants themselves but is certainly not similar to the views of Muslims. By a margin of more than two to one, those majority Scots who do have a view divide in favour of having some Muslim MSPs but are evenly divided about English immigrant MSPs. At the time of the survey, there was in fact a disproportionately large number of English immigrant MSPs in the Scottish Parliament but, at that time, no Muslim MSPs.

We should be concerned, however, with something that goes beyond liberal equalities – with recognition and respect rather than rejection and suspicion and with warmth and acceptance rather than cold justice. Liberal justice is not enough.

TABLE 7.2. *Majority Scots' Views on Anti-Discrimination Laws (in percent)*

	About Muslims	About English Immigrants
Should there be a law against Anti–Muslim/Anti–English discrimination?		
definitely should	65	64
probably should	16	15
probably should not	8	9
definitely should not	6	8
Should there be Muslim-/English-born MSPs		
should be	31	22
does not matter either way	52	57
should not	14	19
Sample size (unwted)	1,158	1,158

RECOGNITION

There are some reasons to expect that Anglophobia amongst majority Scots might be less extensive or less virulent than Islamophobia. Muslims are not cut off from the Scottish majority, but they are somewhat less closely connected by ties of friendship and far less by ties of family. Since English immigrants are far more numerous than Muslims or Pakistanis in Scotland – roughly ten times as numerous according to the 2001 census – that alone might explain why most majority Scots know someone who is English but only half know a Muslim (Table 7.3). But while only twice as many know an English person as know a Muslim, fully four times as many have an English friend as a Pakistani friend – and twenty times as many majority Scots have family connections with English people as with Muslims. A remarkable 40 per cent of majority Scots (who by our strict definition exclude those with English immigrant partners) have an English relative, while only 2 per cent have a Pakistani relative.

Yet while friendship and family might tie majority Scots more closely to the English than to Muslims, their perceptions of what it takes to be a 'true' Scot tie them more closely to Scottish Muslims than to English immigrants (Table 7.4). The criteria used to determine whether someone else is a true Brit or a true Scot vary from person to person, but amongst those most frequently cited are birthplace, parentage and race (McCrone et al. 1998; Paterson et al. 2001: 117–9). Majority Scots stress the importance of birthplace: 57 per cent feel that to be 'truly Scottish', it is essential to be born in Scotland, and only 33 per cent disagree. But they put little weight on race: Only 16 per cent feel it is essential to be white and 69 per cent disagree. Although neither ethnic Pakistanis nor English immigrants are mentioned explicitly in these questions, Pakistanis are not 'white' and English immigrants are by definition not Scottish

TABLE 7.3. *Majority Scots' Knowledge of Minorities (in percent)*

	About Muslims	About English Immigrants
know someone who is Muslim/English	49	93
Muslim/English partner	*	2
Muslim/English in family	2	40
Muslim/English friend	15	60
know someone else who is Muslim/English	32	38
know 'not very much/nothing at all' about Muslims in Scotland	86	na
Sample size (unwted)	1,158	1,158

Note: Those with English immigrant partners are excluded by definition from majority Scots, though a few described their partner as English nonetheless. Only 2 out of 1,158 described their partner as Muslim.

TABLE 7.4. *Majority Scots' View of What It Takes to Be "Truly Scottish" (in percent)*

To be truly Scottish it is necessary to be born in Scotland	
Agree strongly	15
Agree	42
Disagree	27
Disagree strongly	5
To be truly Scottish it is necessary to be white	
Agree strongly	4
Agree	12
Disagree	50
Disagree strongly	19
Only 'true Scots' should get a Scottish passport and full Scottish citizenship	29
Sample size (unweighted)	1,158

by birth (although almost half the Pakistanis are). Since Scots put so much more stress on birthplace than on skin colour, it follows that majority Scots could more easily recognize ethnic Pakistanis as Scots than recognize English immigrants as Scots – and we have no reason to think majority Scots would object to that inference from their answers. It was clearly implicit in these by now familiar questions (see also Rosie and Bond 2006 for the importance of spoken accents that would also make it easier for Scots to recognize ethnic Pakistanis than English immigrants as truly Scottish).

Failure to qualify as a true Scot has implications in the eyes of at least some majority Scots. SNP party policy is to give full citizenship and a Scottish

TABLE 7.5. *Majority Scots' View of Cultural Variety (in percent)*

better for the country to share the same customs, religions and traditions	6
	5
	5
(mid-point)	16
	19
	21
better for the country for there to be a variety of customs, religions and traditions	26
Sample size (unwted)	1,158

passport to all who live in Scotland on the day of independence. However, 29 per cent of majority Scots would deny 'a Scottish passport and full Scottish citizenship' to those they felt were not 'truly Scottish'.

Even cultural similarity might not count in favour of the English. We asked on a seven-point scale whether it was 'better for a country if almost everyone shares the same customs, religions and traditions' or 'better for a country if there is a variety of different customs, religions and traditions' (Table 7.5). Majority Scots come down overwhelmingly on the side of cultural diversity. Remarkably indeed, the most popular choice is the most extreme point at the 'variety' end of the scale. In addition, on balance, 66 per cent opted for cultural variety against only 16 per cent for uniformity.

MEASURING AND COMPARING PHOBIAS

We can measure the extent of street-level phobias by using five strictly comparable indicators of Islamophobia and Anglophobia (Tables 7.6–7.9). Since the wording of these questions is critical, we reproduce it in detail. We began:

> People from lots of different backgrounds live in Scotland. I would now like to ask you some questions about two of these groups – English people and Muslims. By Muslims I mean people who follow the Islamic faith, many of whom in Scotland are Pakistani.

To measure Islamophobia, we then asked respondents to place themselves on various five- or seven-point scales:

> M1 (Economic resentment): Muslims who come to live in Scotland (1) take jobs, housing and health care from other people in Scotland or (7) contribute a lot in terms of hard work and much needed skills (7-point numerical scale)
>
> M2 (Nationalist distrust): Muslims in Scotland (1) are really committed to Scotland or (7) could never be really committed to Scotland (7-point numerical scale)

TABLE 7.6. *Economic Resentment (in percent)*

	View of Majority Scots	
	About Muslims	About English Immigrants
Muslims/English immigrants …		
… take jobs, housing, health care	8	3
	4	3
	9	7
(mid-point)	24	23
	25	29
	16	21
… contribute a lot in terms of hard work and skills	9	10
Sample size (unwted)	1,158	1,158

TABLE 7.7. *Commitment and Loyalty (in percent)*

	Views of Majority Scots	
	About Muslims	About English Immigrants
Muslims/English immigrants …		
… are really committed to Scotland	4	6
	11	16
	15	16
(mid-point)	26	28
	15	14
	8	8
… could never be really committed to Scotland	11	8
Muslims living in Britain have done a great deal to condemn Islamic terrorism		
Agree strongly	3	
Agree	23	
Disagree	25	
Disagree strongly	7	
Muslims/English more loyal to other Muslims/ to England than to Scotland		
Agree strongly	10	11
Agree	33	51
Disagree	11	14
Disagree strongly	*	*
Sample size (unwted)	1,158	1,158

TABLE 7.8. *Fears for National Identity (in percent)*

	Views of Majority Scots	
	About Muslims	About English Immigrants
Scotland would begin to lose its identity if more Muslims/English people came to live in Scotland		
Agree strongly	11	7
Agree	31	27
Disagree	33	41
Disagree strongly	4	5
Sample size (unweighted)	1,158	1,158

TABLE 7.9. *Social Exclusion in the Workplace (in percent)*

	Views of 'Majority Scots' About Muslims
Happy or unhappy to work beside a suitably qualified person from a different racial or ethnic background?	
Very happy	29
Happy	45
Unhappy	3
Very unhappy	1
Sample size (unweighted)	1,158

M3 (Nationalist distrust): How much do you agree or disagree: Scottish Muslims are more loyal to other Muslims around the world than they are to other people in this country. (5-point scale from strongly agree to strongly disagree)

M4 (Fears for national identity): How much do you agree or disagree: Scotland would begin to lose its identity if more Muslims came to live in Scotland. (5-point scale from strongly agree to strongly disagree)

M5 (Social exclusion): How would you feel if a close relative of yours married or formed a long-term relationship with a Muslim? (5-point scale from very happy to very unhappy)

Interleaved between these questions were corresponding questions (E1 to E5) about English immigrants, generally substituting 'English people' for 'Muslims', though in the third question substituting 'loyal to England' for 'loyal to other Muslims around the world', and in the fifth '… with an English person now living in Scotland'. While the question wording never uses the brief and accurate but unfamiliar phrase 'English immigrants', it always uses a longer phrase to focus on English immigrants rather than the English in England. That is particularly important in that E5 emphasizes forming a relationship in Scotland albeit with an English person – in order to focus the question on the relationship rather than on the prospect of the relative moving far away.

With these wording adjustments, the five questions provide a comparative index of Islamophobia and Anglophobia. Islamophobia or Anglophobia is indicated by feeling on balance that Muslims/English 'take jobs, housing and health care from other people'; that they 'could never be really committed to Britain/Scotland'; that they 'are more loyal to other Muslims around the world/ to England' than they are to 'this country'; that 'Scotland would begin to lose its identity' if more came to live in Scotland; and that they would 'feel unhappy if a close relative married or formed a long-term relationship with a Muslim/ English person now living in Scotland'.

In addition, we have one indicator that applies specifically to Muslims after 9/11 and is not generalisable to other anti-minority phobias:

M6 (Condemnation of terrorism): How much do you agree or disagree: Muslims living in Britain have done a great deal to condemn Islamic terrorism. (5-point scale from strongly agree to strongly disagree)

The Islamophobic side of the question in M6 is, of course, disagreement.

Economic Resentment

Relatively few majority Scots actually express economic resentment of minorities taking jobs, housing and health care. Only 21 per cent take a negative view of Muslims, and 13 per cent a negative view of English immigrants. By contrast, 50 per cent take a clearly positive view of Muslims and 60 per cent a clearly positive view of English immigrants. So economic resentment is generally low, but it is particularly low with regard to English immigrants.

Commitment and Loyalty

More doubt the minorities' commitment to Scotland: 34 per cent take a negative view of Muslims' commitment to Scotland, and 30 per cent a negative view of English immigrants' commitment. By contrast, only 30 per cent take a clearly positive view of Muslims and 38 per cent a clearly positive view of English immigrants' commitment. So on balance, majority Scots have a marginally positive view of English immigrants' commitment and a marginally negative view of Muslims' commitment. They also take a marginally – but no more than marginally – negative view of British Muslims in regard to condemning Islamic terrorism. Most of all, however, majority Scots suspect that the minorities' primary loyalties lie outside Scotland – with 'other Muslims around the world' or with 'England': Four times as many majority Scots take a negative view of the minorities' loyalty to Scotland as take a positive view. And most significantly, majority Scots doubt the loyalty of English immigrants more than they doubt they loyalty of Muslims.

Fears for National Identity

Majority Scots are apprehensive that 'Scotland would begin to lose its identity if more English/Muslim people came to live in Scotland'. But despite the huge imbalance in the numbers of English immigrants and Muslims already living in Scotland, majority Scots are rather less apprehensive about the impact on Scotland's national identity of a further influx of English immigrants than they are about an increase in the number of Muslims: 42 per cent take a negative view of Muslims coming to Scotland, and 34 per cent a negative view of more English immigrants. By contrast, 37 per cent take a positive view of Muslims coming to Scotland and 46 per cent a positive view of more English immigrants. So on balance, majority Scots have a moderately positive view of further English immigration and a marginally negative view towards more Muslims coming to Scotland.

Social Exclusion

There is scant evidence of support for social exclusion in the workplace: Only a mere 4 per cent say they would be unhappy to work beside 'a suitably qualified person from a different racial or ethnic background' (Table 7.9). Moreover, 29 per cent say they would not just be 'happy' but actually 'very happy' to do so.

But there is much more evidence of social exclusion in regard to relationships with Muslims (Table 7.10). Most Scots doubt the loyalty of English immigrants to Scotland and many regard them as a threat to Scotland's own national identity. But social exclusion is not part of Anglophobia, nor indeed of sectarianism in Scotland. A mere 3 per cent of majority Scots say they would be at all 'unhappy' to have a close relative form a long-term relationship with an English immigrant. That compares closely with the current state of the classic sectarian divide in Scotland: 3 per cent of Catholics would be unhappy about acquiring a Protestant relative; and 5 per cent of those brought up in the (Presbyterian) Church of Scotland would be unhappy about acquiring a Catholic relative.

All of that contrasts sharply with attitudes towards relationships with Muslims: 22 per cent of majority Scots would be unhappy if a close relative married or formed a long-term relationship with a Muslim. The degree of social exclusion should not be overstated, however: 45 per cent said they would be at least happy to acquire a Muslim relative, 17 per cent of them very happy.

TABLE 7.10. *Social Exclusion in Relationships (in percent)*

	Views of Majority Scots about			
	Muslims	English immigrants	Catholics	Protestants
If close relative formed long-term relationship with Catholic/Protestant/ Muslim/English person now living in Scotland, would feel …				
Very happy	17	23	30	31
Happy	28	43	35	38
Unhappy	15	2	3	1
Very unhappy	7	1	1	*
Sample size (unweighted)	1,158	1,158	1,158	1,158

PERCEPTIONS OF CONFLICT

Large numbers of majority Scots regard conflicts between Scots and English, Muslims and non-Muslims or Protestants and Catholics as at least 'fairly serious'. But by any measure, they rate conflict with the English as far less serious than the sectarian conflict between Catholics and Protestants (Table 7.11).

They are less clear in their assessment of the conflict between Muslims and non-Muslims in Scotland, however. Relatively few rate Muslim/non-Muslim conflict as 'very serious', but there are a significant number who simply 'do not know'. Overall, they rate Muslim/non-Muslim conflict in Scotland as only marginally more serious than Catholic/Protestant conflict in Scotland.

On the other hand, majority Scots are very clear that Muslim/non-Muslim conflict in England is much more serious than in Scotland and that Muslim/ non-Muslim conflict 'around the world' is far more serious still than in England. The numbers of majority Scots who rate Muslim/non-Muslim conflict as 'very serious' rise from a mere 3 per cent with regard to conflict within Scotland to 12 per cent with regard to conflict within England and to 28 per cent with regard to conflict within the rest of the world.

Conversely, the numbers who rate Muslim/non-Muslim conflict as 'not very serious' or non-existent decline from 50 per cent with regard to conflict within Scotland to 22 per cent with regard to conflict within England and to a mere 13 per cent with regard to conflict within the rest of the world.

Perceptions of conflict are not quite the same as phobias, although they may be closely related as either cause or effect. But this pattern of perceptions of conflict would at least be consistent with greater Islamophobia than Anglophobia within Scotland. At the same time, these patterns of conflict perceptions would be consistent with Islamophobia being no greater than sectarian (i.e. Catholic/Protestant) phobias in Scotland. And these patterns of conflict

TABLE 7.11. *Majority Scots' Perceptions of Interethnic Conflicts (in percent)*

	Between Protestants and Catholics in Scotland – apart from football and sport	Scots and the English – apart from football and sport	Between Muslims and non-Muslims		
	(excl sport)	(excl sport)	… in Scotland	… in England	… around the world
Very serious	10	5	3	12	28
Fairly serious	31	20	32	43	44
Not very serious	51	66	46	21	12
No conflict	8	8	4	1	1
DK	1	1	15	22	15
Sample size (unweighted)	1,158	1,158	1,158	1,158	1,158

perceptions would be consistent with Islamophobia being greater in England than in Scotland and still greater around the world than in England. Rightly or wrongly, majority Scots think Islamophobia is more intense outside Scotland than inside.

Significantly, our interviews with Muslims in Scotland show that they also feel that Muslim/non-Muslim conflict is greater in England than in Scotland and greater still outside Britain. Indeed, Scottish Pakistanis' and majority Scots' perceptions of Muslim/non-Muslim conflict within Scotland are very similar. But Scottish Pakistanis' perceptions of Muslim/non-Muslim conflict outside Scotland, in England and around the world are very much greater than majority Scots' perceptions of Muslim/non-Muslim conflict outside Scotland. Majority Scots clearly regard Scotland as a relatively safe haven for Muslims, but Muslims in Scotland hold that view even more strongly than majority Scots (Hussain and Miller 2006: 115).

OVERALL INDICES OF ISLAMOPHOBIA AND ANGLOPHOBIA

Overall indices of Islamophobia and Anglophobia are crude but useful measures for comparing the two phobias and for simplifying our discussion of how they vary across different social and political groups amongst majority Scots (Table 7.12). To construct these summary indices, we use the five fully comparable questions M1–5 and E1–5. For each question, we exclude those with no opinion or with neutral opinions and calculate the percentage that take the Islamophobic/Anglophobic side as a percentage of the total who take one side or the other.

TABLE 7.12. *Comparative Indices of Majority Scots' Islamophobia and Anglophobia (in percent)*

	Of Majority Scots with Clear Positive or Negative views		Diff.
	Islamophobic	Anglophobic	I-A
(Economic resentment) take jobs etc. from Scots	30	18	+12
(Nationalist distrust) never really committed to Scotland	53	44	+9
(Nationalist distrust) more loyal to other Muslims/England	79	81	−2
(Fears for national identity) Scotland would lose its identity if more came	52	42	+10
(Social exclusion): Unhappy if a close relative formed long-term relationship with a Muslim/English person	32	5	+27
Average	49	38	+11
Sample size (unweighted)	1,158	1,158	

That provides very simple, easily interpretable and fully comparable measures of the two phobias:

Index of Islamophobia = the average across the five questions of the percentages that hold negative rather than positive views of Muslims

Index of Anglophobia = the average across the five questions of the percentages that hold negative rather than positive views of English immigrants

Excluding those with no opinion or mixed opinions, an average of 49 per cent across the five questions hold negative rather than positive views of Muslims (Islamophobia) and an average of 38 per cent hold negative rather than positive views of English immigrants (Anglophobia). So, on these strictly comparable indicators, Islamophobia in Scotland runs just 11 per cent ahead of Anglophobia. (By inserting the same questions into the British Social Attitudes Survey, we were able to calculate a similar index of Islamophobia in England; it runs 14 per cent ahead of Islamophobia in Scotland.)

HOW ISLAMOPHOBIA AND ANGLOPHOBIA VARY

Generally narrow, limited and parochial backgrounds are likely to foster narrow, limited, inward-looking and parochial attitudes. Too much focus on the familiar may stimulate a fear of the foreign, the different, the 'other'. Nationalism need not entail xenophobia, but it has often done so. And xenophobia tends to be indiscriminate, targeting anyone and everyone who is 'not like us'. Consequently, all anti-minority phobias may vary together and in particular the same factors that make people relatively Islamophobic are likely to make them Anglophobic.

But while the English might be judged less culturally different than Muslims from majority Scots, England has a far larger role than Pakistan or Islam as the 'significant other' that defines Scottish identity itself. So cultural parochialism – as indicated by age and generation, low education and lack of minority knowledge or friendship, along with religion, perhaps – might be expected to have a greater impact on Islamophobia than on Anglophobia. Yet at the same time, historical or political nationalism – indicated by exclusively Scottish identities or SNP voting – might be expected to have a greater impact on Anglophobia than on Islamophobia.

The impacts of age and generation, education, knowledge and contact with minorities are universal. There is nothing specifically Scottish about them. We would expect to find similar patterns in many societies. But the impact of Scottish nationalism on Anglophobia and Islamophobia is uniquely Scottish, and it is important for the insight it gives us into the character of both Scottish national identity and political nationalism in Scotland. It provides the critical test of the claim that twenty-first-century Scottish nationalism – unlike so many other nationalisms – is civic, inclusive and benign.

AGE AND GENERATION

Conceptually, it is important to distinguish between the impact of age and the impact of generation (sometimes termed 'cohort'), though in a single-wave cross-sectional survey, age and generation are both measured by asking respondents how old they are. Despite the measurement problem, we can at least bear the conceptual distinction in mind and look at the shape of the relationship between years of age and phobias. If there is a steady tendency for older people to be more phobic, we might speculate that this was the consequence of aging. But if there were a sharp difference that coincides with significantly different periods in which different people had grown up, we might speculate that this was a consequence of the different early-life experiences of different cohorts or generations. Statistics alone cannot determine if the impact of aging or the impact of significantly different experiences is the correct explanation. But we do not have to rely on statistics alone. We can, should, indeed must bring outside knowledge to bear on the raw survey statistics (Table 7.13).

Age and generation have very little impact on Anglophobia. Only one of the five indicators of Anglophobia – doubts about the English immigrants' commitment to Scotland – varies consistently across the age cohorts. That contrasts with the much greater impact of age and especially of generation on Islamophobia in Scotland.

There are certainly some indisputably generational effects. The old are far less likely than the young to claim some knowledge of Muslims or to have a

TABLE 7.13. *Impact of Age and Generation on Anglophobia and Islamophobia (in percent)*

	Age 25–34	35–44	45–54	55–64	65+	Impact
M1: Muslims take jobs, housing, health care from others in Scotland	37	29	26	32	22	−15
M5: Unhappy at relative forming relationship with Muslim	16	23	19	48	64	+48
Anglophobia: average E1–5	35	39	37	39	41	+6
Islamophobia: average M1–5	42	46	45	55	62	+20
Know nothing about Muslims	26	20	22	32	44	+18
Have a Muslim friend	24	18	19	8	4	+20
At least 'fairly serious' conflict between Muslims and non-Muslims in Scotland	50	44	38	36	37	+13
Sample size (unweighted)	255	237	193	206	264	

Note: Based on the numbers of those who take the Islamophobic or Anglophobic side as percentages of those who take sides.

Muslim friend. It is beyond reason to suppose that is because older people have forgotten what they once knew about Muslims or have lost the friendships they once had with them. Instead, these patterns reflect the fact that they grew up in a society in which there were far fewer Muslims and far less interaction between Muslims and non-Muslims: It is the imprint of history.

Overall, the old are 20 per cent more Islamophobic but only 6 per cent more Anglophobic than the young. But the pattern is more complex than that in two ways. First, the old are actually less likely (15 per cent less) than the young to fear that Muslims might take jobs, health care and housing from other Scots. But the old have greater doubts about Muslims' commitment to Scotland. They are much more apprehensive (21 per cent more) that Scotland would begin to lose its identity if there were an influx of Muslims; they are much more likely (24 per cent more) to feel that true Scots must be white. And by the huge margin of 48 per cent, the old are very much more unhappy at the thought of acquiring a Muslim relative.

Secondly, the variation with age is not smooth and continuous. On the three indicators that display the greatest variation, there is a sharp 'step effect' at around age fifty-five, implying a generational effect rather than an age effect.

The overall pattern points to a cultural difference between the generations that affects cultural or racial cosmopolitanism (especially intermarriage) but is partially offset by the old feeling less fearful than the young about competition for jobs, probably by reason of age (as they leave the job market) rather than generation.

TABLE 7.14. *Impact of Education on Anglophobia and Islamophobia (in percent)*

	Degree Equiv	Higher Educ Below Degree	Higher Grade Equiv	Standard Grades 1–3 Equiv	Standard Grades 4–7 Equiv	None	Impact
Anglophobia: average E1–5	22	35	30	42	45	47	+25
Islamophobia: average M1–5	28	44	38	54	57	62	+34
Have English friend	78	71	66	66	56	41	+37
Have Muslim friend	32	21	20	12	8	6	+26
Unhappy to acquire English relative	3	2	1	6	8	7	+4
Unhappy to acquire Muslim relative	17	24	11	31	38	56	+39
Sample size (unweighted)	131	170	169	145	189	342	

Note: Based on the numbers of those who take the Islamophobic or Anglophobic side as percentages of those who take sides.

This tentative conclusion gains some corroboration from the pattern of age variation in friendship, knowledge and perceived conflict. The old have much less knowledge of or friendship with minorities. That is especially true for friendship with Muslims. And again, there is a sharp generational cleavage at age fifty-five – especially with respect to Muslims. But at the same time, the old are less likely to perceive serious conflict with either minority – and again especially with respect to Muslims.

These patterns fit the model of a culture-based generational cleavage at age fifty-five, offset by less fear of economic competition and less fear of conflict amongst the old by reason of age rather than generation.

EDUCATION

Friendship with and knowledge of minorities varies more sharply with education than anything else (Table 7.14). Compared to those with no qualifications, graduates are 37 per cent more likely to have an English friend and more than five times more likely to have a Muslim friend (32 per cent compared to only 6 per cent). Conversely, those without qualifications are 25 per cent more Anglophobic than university graduates as well as 34 per cent more Islamophobic. Both phobias run at more than twice the level amongst the unqualified as amongst university graduates.

The impact is large and, with one reservation, steadily monotonic across education levels. The sole exception to monotonicity is that those with 'higher education below university degree level' display greater levels of both Islamophobia and Anglophobia than those with Higher Grade (or equivalent) school qualifications.

And the impact is large on every individual indicator of Islamophobia and Anglophobia with one exception only: Attitudes of social exclusion towards English immigrants remain very low at all levels of education. The contrast with attitudes of social exclusion towards Muslims is striking, however. Amongst graduates, only 3 per cent would be unhappy to acquire an English relative and only 17 per cent unhappy to acquire a Muslim relative. Amongst those with the least education, the numbers unhappy to acquire an English relative remain very low (at 7 per cent), but the numbers unhappy to acquire a Muslim relative more than triple and rise to 56 per cent.

CONTACTS WITH AND KNOWLEDGE OF MINORITIES

As we might expect, having a minority friend makes a difference to the attitudes of majority Scots towards minorities (Table 7.15). Having a Muslim friend reduces Islamophobia by 21 per cent, and having an English friend reduces Anglophobia by 11 per cent.

Much less obviously, however, having a friend in either minority reduces phobia towards both. That is partly because those who have a friend in one minority are much more likely to also have a friend in the other: 21 per cent of those with English friends also have Muslim friends; by contrast, only 6 per cent of those without English friends have Muslim friends. Conversely, 85 per cent of those with Muslim friends also have English friends, while only 56 per cent of those without Muslim friends have English friends.

But knowledge is far more important than friendship. There are so few Muslims in Scotland that many majority Scots can be sympathetic towards such a small minority without actually having a personal friend within it. It is those who, by their own account, lack knowledge – as well as friendship – who are prey to the most intense phobias.

Most Scots know something about the English, but many – by their own account – do not know much about Muslims. Compared to those who have a Muslim friend, those who say they 'know nothing at all' about Muslims are 34 per cent more Islamophobic (Table 7.16). But they are also 25 per cent more Islamophobic than those who, irrespective of whether they have Muslim friends, claim to know at least 'quite a lot' about Muslims. Most of the variation in Islamophobia occurs across levels of knowledge, not friendship or lack of friendship as such.

Significantly, the 'know nothings' – defined in terms of their confessed lack of knowledge about Muslims – are also 18 per cent more Anglophobic than those with a Muslim friend. Only 51 per cent of the (Muslim-defined) 'know nothings' claim to have an English friend, and the rate of English friendship rises steadily as knowledge of Muslims increases. The pattern points to general

TABLE 7.15. *Impact of Friendship on Anglophobia and Islamophobia (in percent)*

	Have M Friend	Not	Impact	Have E Friend	Not	Impact
Anglophobia: average E1–5	29	40	+11	34	45	+11
Islamophobia: average M1–5	32	53	+21	44	56	+12
Sample size	155	1,001		687	469	

TABLE 7.16. *Impact of Knowledge on Anglophobia and Islamophobia (in percent)*

		Knowledge about Muslims			
	Have M friend	At Least Quite a Lot	Not Very Much	Nothing at All	Impact
Anglophobia: average E1–5	29	33	35	47	+18
Islamophobia: average M1–5	32	41	44	66	+34
Sample size (unwted)	155	144	641	365	

Notes: Based on the numbers of those who take the Islamophobic or Anglophobic side as percentages of those who take sides.

Column 1 (those who have Muslim friends) is based on a different question from columns 2–4. Those with Muslim friends claim varying levels of knowledge about Muslims, though few claim to know nothing about them.

ignorance of 'others' having general consequences, as well as specifically Islamophobic consequences.

RELIGION

Most majority Scots divide into just three religious categories – protestant Presbyterians (overwhelmingly Church of Scotland), Catholics and the largest category, the irreligious. Overall, they differ very little on Anglophobia, though both Catholics (by 17 per cent) and Presbyterians (by 11 per cent) are more inclined than the irreligious to doubt English immigrants' commitment to Scotland. Catholics are the least likely to have an English friend, while Presbyterians are the least likely to have a Muslim friend (Table 7.17).

But they differ more on Islamophobia – especially on whether Scotland 'would begin to lose its identity' if more Muslims came and on social exclusion. On these two matters, Presbyterians are the most Islamophobic, Catholics less

TABLE 7.17. *Impact of Religion on Majority Scots' Anglophobia and Islamophobia (in percent)*

	Presbyterians	Catholics	Irreligious	Impact
Anglophobia: average E1–5	40	41	37	+4
Islamophobia: average M1–5	56	54	42	+14
Scotland would begin to lose its identity if more Muslims came	65	54	42	+23
Unhappy to acquire English relative	6	3	4	+3
Unhappy to acquire Muslim relative	47	33	18	+29
Have English friend	57	51	64	+13
Have Muslim friend	9	17	18	+9
Sample size (unweighted)	439	131	490	

Note: Based on the numbers of those who take the Islamophobic or Anglophobic side as percentages of those who take sides.

so. From the sixteenth to the nineteenth century, Scotland was defined primarily by its Presbyterianism rather than by geography (see, for example, Finlay 2005). Although the simple equation of Scotland with Presbyterianism was finally destroyed by Irish Catholic immigration, Presbyterians may still retain a stronger concept of there being a unified national culture than Catholics, who necessarily had to pioneer multiculturalism in Scotland. At the same time, however, on other matters – on perceptions of loyalty and commitment to contemporary Scotland and on jobs – Catholics are the most Islamophobic, Presbyterians less so. So overall, both Catholics and Presbyterians are around 13 per cent more Islamophobic than the irreligious – though for somewhat different reasons.

Presbyterians are 23 per cent more concerned than the irreligious about the impact of Muslim immigration on Scotland's identity and 29 per cent more unhappy at the prospect of acquiring a Muslim relative. The impact of religion is thus quite powerful within certain restricted issue-domains, but overall it has far less impact than education.

SOCIAL NATIONALISM: SUB-STATE IDENTITIES

Compared to those who identify equally with Britain and Scotland, those who identify themselves as exclusively Scottish are 13 per cent more Anglophobic but scarcely any more (only 4 per cent more) Islamophobic. The impact of national identity is relatively weak. But in contrast to the impact of education, which had significantly more impact on Islamophobia than on Anglophobia, Scottish nationalism has a greater impact on Anglophobia than on Islamophobia (Table 7.18).

Indeed, the impact of Scottish national identity – in complete contrast to the impact of low education – seems to be specifically Anglophobic, focused

TABLE 7.18. *Impact of Scottish National Identity on Majority Scots'*
Anglophobia and Islamophobia (in percent)

	Equally Scottish and British	More Scottish	Exclusively Scottish	Impact
Anglophobia: average E1–5	33	35	46	+13
Islamophobia: average M1–5	50	46	54	+4
Unhappy to acquire English relative	3	3	8	+5
Unhappy to acquire Muslim relative	38	28	36	−2
Sample size (unweighted)	247	431	437	

Comparison: Impact of English National Identity on Majority English's Islamophobia (in England)

	Equally English and British	More English	Exclusively English	Impact
Islamophobia: average M1–5	58	61	78	+20
Unhappy to acquire Muslim relative	47	51	67	+20
Sample size (unwted)	277	169	166	

Note: Based on the numbers of those who take the Islamophobic or Anglophobic side as percentages of those who take sides.

on the historic enemy, the 'significant other' that helps define Scottish identity, rather than on a minority that differs more in terms of race, religion or culture from the majority Scots. The pattern of attitudes towards social exclusion is particularly striking – especially in contrast to the impact of education on these attitudes. Unsurprisingly, the exclusively Scottish are 5 per cent more unhappy at the prospect of acquiring an English relative – but they are actually 2 per cent less unhappy than those who feel equally Scottish and British at the prospect of acquiring a Muslim relative. The figure of 2 per cent is scarcely significant statistically – but that is the point: It is a case of Sherlock Holmes's 'dog that did not bark'. The impact of national identity on social exclusion is 7 per cent greater against the English than against Muslims – in contrast to the impact of low education on social exclusion, which is 35 per cent greater against Muslims than against English immigrants.

There is a further contrast of some significance for our understanding of the impact of national identity: Amongst the majority English within England (defined as majority 'white' non-Muslim), an exclusively English national identity increases Islamophobia in general and social exclusion towards Muslims in particular by 20 per cent (Hussain and Miller 2004). Those who have discovered similar contrasts between the impact of English nationalism in England and Scottish nationalism in Scotland on attitudes towards asylum seekers,

TABLE 7.19. *Impact of Political Nationalism on Anglophobia and Islamophobia (in percent)*

	Vote at 2001 General Election							
	CON	LAB	Lib Dem	SNP	DNV	Hi	Lo	SNP – CON
Anglophobia: average E1–5	33	38	27	43	40	SNP	LD	10
Islamophobia: average M1–5	55	48	35	48	51	CON	LD	–7
Have English friend	66	53	75	55	66			
Have Muslim friend	11	11	26	14	23			
Unhappy to acquire English relative	1	4	2	12	4			
Unhappy to acquire Muslim relative	47	32	24	36	25			
Sample size (unweighted)	138	432	83	163	255			

Notes: Based on the numbers of those who take the Islamophobic or Anglophobic side as percentages of those who take sides.

This table, like all others, is based entirely on the attitudes of majority Scots defined as Scottish born, with Scottish-born partners (if any).

'ethnic minorities', blacks or Asians have been tempted to characterise English nationalism as more ethnic or 'nasty' and Scottish nationalism as more civic and 'benign'.

If we had focused only on Islamophobia, which proves to be almost uncorrelated with Scottish nationalism, we would have concluded that Scottish nationalism is indeed remarkably uncorrelated with anti-minority phobias. But it does correlate more with Anglophobia (Table 7.19). Moreover, the existence of Anglophobia may help to explain why Scottish nationalism is so uncorrelated with Islamophobia. Muslims in Scotland benefit from being 'not English' and thus, in the eyes of majority Scots, a little bit more 'like us' than they would be in the absence of Anglophobia. Mostly, they do at least speak English with a Scottish accent.

POLITICAL NATIONALISM: PARTISANSHIP

Voting choices provide an indicator of political nationalism. Both Anglophobia and Islamophobia are lowest amongst Liberal Democrat voters in Scotland. But while Islamophobia is highest amongst Conservative voters, Anglophobia is highest amongst SNP voters. Anglophobia amongst SNP voters is 10 per cent higher than amongst Conservatives (and 16 per cent higher than amongst Liberal Democrats). Conversely, Islamophobia is 7 per cent higher amongst Conservatives than amongst SNP voters (and 20 per cent higher than amongst Liberal Democrats). Non-voters come second only to SNP voters on Anglophobia and second only to Conservatives on Islamophobia.

PATTERNS OF PERSONAL FRIENDSHIP TELL THE SAME STORY

Conservatives are 11 per cent more likely than SNP voters to have an English friend but 3 per cent less likely than SNP voters to have a Muslim friend. And Liberal Democrats are the most likely to have both English and Muslim friends. Similarly, SNP voters would be the least happy to acquire an English relative: 12 per cent would be unhappy. And Conservative voters would be the least happy to acquire a Muslim relative: 47 per cent would be unhappy. By contrast, only 2 per cent of Liberal Democrats would be unhappy to acquire an English relative and 24 per cent unhappy to acquire a Muslim relative.

Many English people in Scotland vote Conservative, of course, and few vote SNP. So it is extremely important to stress that our analysis of the link between party support and Anglophobia is based – like all our other analyses of Anglophobia and Islamophobia – entirely on majority Scots defined to exclude both English immigrants and their partners. Thus, our finding shows that Conservatives from amongst the 'majority Scots' (born in Scotland and with Scottish-born partners, if any) are much less Anglophobic than other majority Scots. Our findings are robust. There is no English-born contamination of the Conservative voters whom we find so relaxed about acquiring English relatives!

A MULTIVARIATE ANALYSIS

We can usefully summarise and confirm our findings with a multivariate analysis (Table 7.20). For that, we have constructed five-point scales for each of the elements of our indices of Islamophobia and Anglophobia. Some were already five-point agree/disagree scales (agree strongly, agree, neither, disagree, disagree strongly). Others were seven-point semantic-differential scales running, for example, from 'Muslims are really committed to Scotland' to 'Muslims could never be really committed to Scotland' with the intermediate points unlabelled. In these cases, we merged the most extreme points with the adjacent categories to convert them into five-point scales. Numerical values running from -2 to $+2$ were assigned to each scale, with $+2$ being the most phobic. Those with mixed opinions or no opinion were placed at 0, the centre-point of the scale. By averaging across the five questions, we get composite Islamophobic and Anglophobic scales that also run from -2 to $+2$.

Correlations between the components of each composite scale prove to be uniformly high. The individual items contributing to the Islamophobia scale correlate on average at more than 0.70 with the composite Islamophobia scale, and items contributing to the Anglophobia scale correlate on average at more than 0.64 with the composite Anglophobia scale.

Much more interestingly, the two composite scales correlate at 0.65 with each other. We have already seen that the categories of people that are relatively Islamophobic tend also to be relatively Anglophobic. Now we know that

TABLE 7.20. *Multivariate Analysis of Islamophobia and Anglophobia in Scotland*

	Islamophobia	Anglophobia
RSQ (× 100) =	15	17
	Beta (× 100)	Beta (× 100)
Higher education	−26	−25
Not religious	−13	*
Knows little or nothing about Muslims	11	10
Has a Muslim friend	−10	*
Has an English friend	*	−13
Strong/exclusive Scottish identity	*	17

* Blank entries and all variables missing from the table indicate that the beta coefficient was less than 0.10; so the independent and additional impact of such variables is small (if any at all) and relatively unimportant; all beta coefficients displayed in the table are not only large enough to be politically significant, they are also statistically significant at better than the 1% error level.

is true for individuals as well as categories: Individual people who are relatively Islamophobic are likely to be relatively Anglophobic as well – and the correlation, at 0.65, is remarkably strong.

We use regression to see which of the influences we have considered actually explain phobias best and which are redundant once more powerful explanations are taken into account. To do this, we predict levels of Islamophobia and Anglophobia from the following:

1. age both as a seven-point scale from young to old and as a dichotomous generation marker, contrasting those above and below age 55;
2. education as a three-point scale distinguishing university-level education, lower-school qualifications (or none), and those with higher-school qualifications or higher education below university degree level;
3. minority contacts measured by three variables: a four-point scale of knowledge about Muslims and two indicators of whether the respondent had a Muslim friend and/or an English friend;
4. religion measured by three separate indicators of whether the respondent was or was not Presbyterian, Catholic or irreligious;
5. national identity measured by the five-point Moreno scale that runs from exclusively Scottish to exclusively British;
6. political nationalism measured by four separate indicators of whether the respondent voted Conservative, Labour or SNP at the previous general election or abstained – effectively treating Liberal voters as the base against which all others are judged.

The multiple regressions confirm that the most important influence on both phobias is education. But even taking that into account, other factors have their own independent and additional impact. Islamophobia is greater amongst those who know little or nothing about Islam. It is lower amongst those who have a Muslim friend and amongst those who are irreligious. But most significant is the factor that does not exert any substantial impact on Islamophobia: Scottish nationalism.

But by contrast, Scottish identity comes close to rivalling low education as an influence towards Anglophobia. Beyond that, having an English friend reduces Anglophobia by about as much as having a Muslim friend reduces Islamophobia. And lack of knowledge about Islam probably indicates a broader rejection of the 'other', for it has as much impact on Anglophobia as on Islamophobia.

Regression is better at demolishing hypotheses than generating them. In addition to showing that Scottish identity has no important impact on Islamophobia, it also shows (by their absence from Table 7.20) that age and generation do not have an independent impact once education, personal contacts and Scottish identity have been taken into account, nor does political nationalism once Scottish identity has been taken into account.

CONCLUSIONS

Our comparison of Anglophobia and Islamophobia in Scotland suggests four broad conclusions.

Less Anglophobia than Islamophobia: Amongst majority Scots (tightly defined to exclude both English immigrants and their partners), Anglophobia runs at a lower level than Islamophobia. On five strictly comparable indicators, Anglophobia runs 11 per cent behind Islamophobia – at 38 per cent compared to 49 per cent.

But Not Much Less Anglophobia: In Scotland, the level of Anglophobia, though less, is comparable with that of Islamophobia. The difference between Islamophobia in Scotland and England is greater than the difference between the levels of Anglophobia and Islamophobia within Scotland.

And the difference between Anglophobia and Islamophobia in Scotland varies sharply across our five indicators. There is a large difference in social exclusion: Few (only 5 per cent) 'would feel unhappy if a close relative married or formed a long-term relationship with an English person now living in Scotland', but far more (32 per cent) if the relationship was 'with a Muslim'.

There Is Less Difference on Economic Resentment: Almost a fifth (18 per cent) of majority Scots feel that English immigrants 'take jobs, housing and health care from other people in Scotland' rather than 'contributing a lot' to Scotland, but almost a third (30 per cent) feel Muslims do that. Similarly, on fears for national identity: Two fifths (42 per cent) feel 'Scotland would begin to lose its identity' if more English immigrants came to live in Scotland and half (52 per cent) if more Muslims came.

But on two indicators of nationalist distrust, the differences pointed in opposite directions. On commitment to Scotland, Anglophobia is a little less than

Islamophobia: 44 per cent feel the English immigrants 'could never be really committed to Scotland', but 53 per cent feel Muslims could never be really committed to Scotland. Yet on loyalty, Anglophobia exceeds Islamophobia, if only marginally: 81 per cent feel English immigrants are more loyal to England and only 79 per cent feel Muslims are more loyal to other Muslims around the world than they are to Scotland. The difference is too small to be statistically significant, but it shows beyond statistical doubt that majority Scots do not draw any great distinction between the loyalty of English immigrants and Muslims.

Phobias generally go together: Anything that encourages one phobia tends to encourage the other – though not necessarily to the same degree. Having either an English friend or a Muslim friend reduces both Anglophobia and Islamophobia. Both Anglophobia and Islamophobia increase with age and generation (i.e. with older age and generations). Higher education appears to reduce both Anglophobia and Islamophobia. And Liberal Democrat voters are at once the least Anglophobic and the least Islamophobic.

But narrow parochialism and nationalism have significantly different impacts on different phobias: Narrow backgrounds and attitudes have more impact on Islamophobia, but nationalism has more impact on Anglophobia. An exclusively Scottish identity increases phobias. But in sharp contrast to low education, older generations or lack of minority friendships, which might all be interpreted as indicators of narrow parochialism, a more Scottish nationalist identity has much more impact on Anglophobia (13 per cent) than on Islamophobia (only 4 per cent) – though Scottish nationalist identity has much less impact on Anglophobia (13 per cent) than English nationalist identity (in England) has on Islamophobia (20 per cent) in England.

Similarly, while SNP voters are the most Anglophobic (16 per cent more so than LibDems), Conservative voters are the most Islamophobic in Scotland (12 per cent more so than LibDems) – though Conservative voters in England are even more Islamophobic (14 per cent more so than even those relatively Islamophobic Scottish Conservative voters).

Is Scottish nationalism, unlike English nationalism, benign rather than nasty as so many writers suggest? Towards Muslims, the answer must be an unequivocal 'yes'. But towards English immigrants, perhaps not. Scottish nationalism, unlike English nationalism, does not make people significantly more Islamophobic. But at street level, if not at Alex Salmond's SNP leadership level, it does make them more Anglophobic.

There is one final caveat, however. All our statistical evidence suggests that education has the most powerful impact on reducing phobias, including Islamophobia. That is what the regression analysis of the survey data shows so clearly. And yet our focus group discussions with both Muslims and English immigrants in Scotland cast some doubts on this apparently robust statistical finding. Focus group participants suggested that the well-educated 'talked the talk' but did not 'walk the walk': '[R]acism is very subtle and you get it across the board ... in colleges and universities'(PK4-E: participant E in Pakistani Focus Group 4); 'the less educated are the ones that slag you in the streets, but the professionals will be the ones that do not give you the job' (PK1-B); 'less educated people will openly curse the person ... but educated people can control their tongue easier ... show racism in a subtle way that you might not realize' (PK6-E); 'teachers in the High School have this really strong, deep anti-English feeling ... [which] has to be really well concealed because of their profession, but its there' (E6-E: participant E in English-Immigrant Focus Group 6); 'I got an interview, but the minute I opened my mouth [exposing an English accent] you could see the shutters come down' (E6-G). (For these and other sceptical quotes from minority focus groups in Scotland, see chapters 5 and 6 of Hussain and Miller 2006.)

Our statistical evidence shows beyond doubt that Scottish discourse is significantly less Islamophobic than English. Scots in general, like the well-educated in particular, are good at talking the talk. But perhaps Scots, like the well-educated in particular, are just better at hiding their phobias – always excepting their Anglophobia, of course!

8

Are All Britons Reluctant Europeans?

Exploring European Identity and Attitudes to Europe among British Citizens of South Asian Ethnicity

Marco Cinnirella and Saira Hamilton

There is evidence from UK opinion survey data that the majority of British citizens are, at best, ambivalent about the European Union (EU) and European integration (Cinnirella 2001; Eichenberg and Dalton 1993) and, at worst, often openly negative and sceptical about the enterprise (Hewstone 1986). Thus, Barzini's observation that the British are 'reluctant Europeans' seems compatible with empirical evidence (Barzini 1983). Furthermore, the EU's Eurobarometer surveys usually indicate that the British public are one of the least enthusiastic of all EU populations when it comes to support for further integration. For example, in Eurobarometer report 52 (1999), support for EU membership in the UK was 29 per cent, the lowest of all EU member states, compared, for example, to 82 per cent support in the Republic of Ireland. More recently, the Eurobarometer 56 (2001) reported that, out of all current EU member states, the level of European identity in the United Kingdom was the lowest, with UK participants indicating that, given the choice of a European and a national identity or a sense of national identity alone, 71 per cent would prefer to retain national identity alone; only 28 per cent indicated feeling any sense of European identity. In contrast, national pride in the UK is strong – Eurobarometer 56 (2001) reports that 93 per cent of participants indicated feeling either 'fairly' or 'very' proud of their nationality in the UK.

However, there has been a tendency to tarnish all British citizens with the same brush and to assume that a broadly Eurosceptical stance, coupled with high levels of national pride, is shared equally among the British population. This is not a safe assumption, however. Evans (1996), for example, presented evidence that some demographic factors (e.g. age, education) are associated with differences in attitudes towards Europe, and these observations are confirmed in several Eurobarometer findings. However, while advances in this area have been made and have demonstrated, for example, that the Scots may be more pro–European than the English (Hopkins and Reicher 1996, 1997), on the dimension of ethnicity and its relationship with attitudes towards and identification with Europe, psychologists have been largely silent (unlike theoretical sociologists, such as A.D. Smith, who have explored some issues surrounding ethnicity, nationalism and European integration – see, for example, Smith 1991).

This is a particularly pertinent question when one turns to the topic of European identity. Cinnirella (1997) argued that issues surrounding national and European identities have become almost inseparable in the UK in the sense that their perceived compatibility is a central psychological backdrop for the formation of attitudes towards Europe and identification with other Europeans and has increasingly formed a backdrop for current constructions of British national identity. For his white British participants, national and European identities were negatively correlated. This perception seemed partly based on a construction of British national identity that was grounded in reverence of the national past.

Cinnirella (1997) also argued that his white British participants appeared to perceive national and European identities as if they operated at the same level of abstraction: Rather than seeing them, respectively, as national- and international-level social categories, British participants seemed to perceive them both as national-level categories, essentially necessitating a choice be made between one or the other and negating the possibility of identification with both. In contrast, white Italian participants in Cinnirella's study seemed to perceive Italian and European identities as national- and supra-national-level social categories and were usually happy to profess loyalty to both identities. This illustrates that the level of abstraction of a social category is not an objective property of the respective category but is socially constructed and open to contestation (see Rutland and Cinnirella 2000).

One might well wonder whether this would be reflected in the constructions of national and European identities manifested by British citizens of an ethnic minority background. Schlesinger (1987) suggests that if a European identity is to be forged, it will necessitate the rewriting of social history (in a manner similar to Hobsbawm and Ranger's notion of 'the invention of tradition', outlined in their 1992 edited volume of the same title). This might be difficult for white Britons if they are enamoured of Britain's past and if they wish to cling to the psychological remnants of history (Cinnirella 1997; Hewstone 1986; see also Samuel 1989). However, in contrast, British citizens of an ethnic minority background might not wish to dwell on Britain's imperial past, evaluating aspects of this past negatively and instead wishing to focus on the present and/or future (as the Italian participants in Cinnirella 1996 did). Thus, Asian Britons, for example, may find the adoption of a European identity easier to reconcile with any sense of British identity they possess, if such a national identity is not as past oriented as it often seems to be for white Britons. They may, therefore, perceive that psychological attachment to Europe presents less of a threat to national identity than white Britons think it does. Furthermore,

British Asians may not perceive the level of abstraction of British and European social categories in the same way that white Britons do – perhaps they do not share the tendency of white Britons to construct European identity at the national as opposed to supra-national level of abstraction? These are all important questions in the quest to understand the psychology of British reactions to European integration, yet at present they remain, empirically, unanswered.

One of our aims in this chapter is to further elucidate the manner in which individuals and social groups attempt to 'manage' multiple social identifications in multicultural settings (part of Brown's proposal for a future research agenda for social identity theory; see Brown 2000). Through examining constructions by our participants of their ethnic, national and European social identities and their relationship with other variables in the study, such as attitudes towards European integration, we hope to contribute to the ongoing debate in social psychology about the optimal way of reconciling multiple identities (see, for example, Mummendey and Wenzel 1999 and Berry's model of acculturation as, for example, outlined in Berry et al. 1989). In conceptualising the different ways in which social identities might be associated with each other in the minds of individuals, we feel that Hofman's ideas are useful (Hofman 1988). In particular, Hofman suggested that there are essentially three ways in which multiple social identifications might be related in the minds of individuals: They may be consonant (i.e. compatible), indifferent (i.e. unrelated) or dissonant (in some way incompatible). Although individuals must attempt to reconcile and 'manage' their individual identity repertoires (or what Roccas and Brewer 2002 term 'social identity complexity'), it is also likely that social groups will come to generate and foster shared social representations about the relations between different identities (Chryssochoou 2003), and this validates the level of analysis adopted in the present study, which essentially focuses on the identity dynamics manifested at the group rather than individual level.

In principle, at least, there is no reason members of ethnic minorities cannot hold a sense of both ethnic and national identification (Nesdale and Mak 2000). In fact, according to 'dual identity' models, this would be a desirable outcome (Hornsey and Hogg 2000). However, the possibility that British national identity might not be as important or easy to construct for ethnic minority citizens as it is for the white majority was a focus for Hutnik's (1985) study of identity, in which she was able to demonstrate that 'British' or 'English' identity was not a frequent component of the self-concept for British Asian participants. More recently, social scientists from a variety of disciplines have suggested that the construction of British national identity by members of ethnic minority groups in the United Kingdom is not always straightforward (see, for example, Modood 2000). If British national identity is less important to British Asians than it is for the white indigenous population, then perhaps British Asians may be more willing to embrace a European identity or, at the very least, be more positive attitudinally towards the EU and European integration. This is one of the questions we investigated empirically in the present study using a social survey approach.

Sociological research hints at the possibility of different attitudes towards European institutions held by immigrants in comparison to the attitudes of indigenous populations. Soysal (2000), for example, talks of particularistic identities held by immigrants rather than national identities and argues that multiculturalism has led to increasing legitimacy in 'the right to one's own culture'. These rights of personhood, as Soysal (2000) describes them, have been formalised in some EU institutions, such as the European Court. To the extent that the EU might be seen as representing the preservation of human rights, then it may be that immigrant populations could, as a consequence, be enthusiastic towards the EU and the idea of European integration.

The children of immigrants, who have been born, raised and educated in the United Kingdom, are sometimes seen as being suspended between two cultures. While it will not be possible in the context of the current research to explore all the intricacies of respondents' precise ethnic backgrounds, it is possible to investigate any possible differences between attitudes held by first- and second-generation immigrants. Phinney and associates (2001; see also Ghuman 2003), for example, argue that first-generation immigrants are often found to have a stronger sense of ethnic identity, with second-generation migrants often developing a sense of identity that incorporates aspects of both national and ethnic identity. Baumann (1996) reports that young adults in Southall, West London, were more likely to cross boundaries of specific ethnic backgrounds by placing themselves in broader categories of ethnicity than perhaps their parents were likely to. Second-generation immigrants are more likely to see themselves as 'British Asians' rather than simply 'Asians' and may extend this blurring of boundaries. Social identity research has indicated that larger macro-societal units (e.g. Europe) are more likely to be associated with future rather than preceding generations (Bolfikova and Frankovsky 1997). It is proposed that the ability to expand and develop self-identity in younger generations will therefore be associated with more positive attitudes towards European integration.

HYPOTHESES

Our broad empirical aim is to assess differences in attitudes towards Europe and the EU in immigrant versus indigenous white British groups as well as look at differences in national and European identities. The ethnic minority population studied is the South Asian minority, comprising those whose ethnic origins are within the Indian sub-continent (i.e. India, Pakistan, Bangladesh and Sri Lanka). For our purposes, this group will henceforth be referred to simply as 'Asian' and the indigenous population group as 'white'. The analyses focused on exploring the following six key hypotheses:

On the basis of previous research on white British samples (Cinnirella 1996, 1997, 1998) and trends prevalent in Eurobarometer opinion polls, it is predicted that white participants will manifest a national identity significantly stronger than their European identification. It is expected that this will be manifested in both the social identity scale scores and the placement of symbols on the visual identity task (H1).

On the basis of previous research (Hutnik 1985, 1986), we predict that the Asian sample will manifest a weaker British identity than the white sample (H2) and that their ethnic identity will be stronger than their national identity (H3). These differences are also expected to appear in the visual identity task, where the proximity of symbols to the centre of the diagram is predicted to mirror the predictions about identity above.

Since previous research has suggested that strong British national identity is a barrier to European identity (Cinnirella 1997), we predict that Asians, who are expected to manifest a weaker British identity than whites, will subsequently hold more favourable attitudes towards European integration and a stronger European identity than the white group (H4). We expect this to be manifested in both Likert measures of attitudes and identity and a mean placement of the European identity symbol on the visual task, closer to the centre of the diagram than for the white group.

While we expect national identity for white participants to correlate negatively with European identity (based on Cinnirella 1997), we predict that this correlation will be either non-significant or else positive for Asian participants, since Asian constructions of British identity are likely to be less based on idealizing the British past and should therefore be more compatible with a European identification (H5).

Finally, based on evidence from studies of generational effects on Asian identity (e.g. Baumann 1996; Bolfikova and Frankovsky 1997), we predict that second-generation Asians will manifest stronger national and European levels of identity than first-generation Asians (H6).

METHOD

An attitudinal social survey approach was employed and administered to volunteer participants of white or else South-Asian ethnic background, obtained by means of convenience sampling.

Participants

An opportunity sample of volunteers was obtained by means of snowball sampling using established community and business contacts, mostly in Southern England. A total of 210 questionnaires were sent out with reply paid envelopes. The response rate was 49 per cent (102 participants), which is above average for postal surveys (Czaja and Blair 1996). Two main groups of respondents were targeted: indigenous white British respondents (referred to as 'white'; $n = 58$) and respondents from the South Asian ethnic minority (referred to as 'Asian'; $n = 44$). Of the Asian respondents, 51 per cent were first and 47

per cent were second generation. The age range of all respondents was eighteen to seventy-four years, with a mean age of forty years. The gender distribution was forty-four male, fifty-seven female. The socio-demographic spread
of respondents was fairly wide, with professionals recruited through different
business organizations (66.7 per cent), university students (17.6 per cent) and
retired (6.9 per cent) respondents constituting the main employment categories.
The geographical composition of the respondents was also fairly wide, with
respondents from Devon to Scotland, although the majority of respondents
(59 per cent) were from London and the Home Counties. Statistical analysis
using *t*-tests confirmed that there were no significant age or gender differences
between the Asian and white participant groups.

Procedure

The questionnaire was administered in a cascade fashion in a variety of loca-
tions. Clusters of the relevant ethnic minorities were identified throughout the
UK, and snowball sampling was utilised to boost numbers.

The self-report questionnaire was constructed specifically for this study. It
is now generally accepted by social identity scholars that national and ethnic
identities can be usefully explored, empirically, using concepts and research
tools from the social identity paradigm (see, for example, Bar-Tal and Staub
1997; Hewstone, Islam and Judd 1993; Mummendey, Klink and Brown 2001;
Salazar 1998). The three social identity sections were based on fixed-response
Likert-type scales previously employed by Cinnirella (1997); see also Rutland
and Cinnirella (2000). These scales included seven items relating to perceived
importance, socio-emotional connotation, similarity judgements between self
and other members of the in-group and interdependence between self and other
in-group members. The same fixed-response scales were used to assess all three
social identities and were reworded to measure levels of British, European and
ethnic identity (the latter was only measured for Asian participants, as pilot
work indicated that it was problematic to devise and implement such a scale
for white participants).

The seven fixed-response Likert-type social identity measures (here worded
for British national identity) were: To what extent do you feel British? To what
extent do you feel strong ties with other British people? To what extent do you
feel pleased to be British? How similar do you think you are to the average
British person? How important to you is being British? To what extent do you
feel proud to be British? When you hear someone who is not British criticize
the British people, to what extent do you feel personally criticized? Each measure used a seven-point bipolar response scale.

The next section of the questionnaire comprised seven fixed-response Likert-
type items relating to attitudes toward the EU or 'Europe'. This scale included
items relating to perceived importance (e.g. 'How important is the EU to the
future of Britain?'; response scale = 'not at all important' – 'extremely important'), value judgements about the benefits of Europe, socio-cultural connection

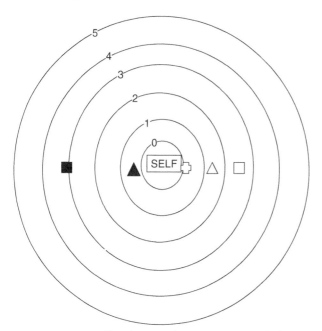

FIGURE 8.1. Wording for visual representation of identities task and mean scores by ethnic group.

'In this section you are invited to think about how your sense of identification with your ethnic group, your nation, and with Europe, relate to your overall sense of who you are – i.e. your overall sense of self. Please show on the chart where you feel the different identities represented by the symbols occur in relation to the self, which is shown at the centre of the chart. Place the symbol for an identity closer to the center of the diagram; the more important you feel it is to your sense of who you are. The further away from the centre you place the symbol for an identity the less central you feel that identity is to your sense of self. Please place the symbols wherever you want within the circles – there are no correct or incorrect answers to this question. Please ignore the ethnic identity if you are not a member of the Indian/Pakistani/Bangladeshi group'.

Note: In the diagram above we have added the mean scores/placement of symbols for the white (filled shapes) and Asian (outline shapes) participant groups, and the scores associated with each ring. Naturally, participants would not have seen either of these pieces of information on their diagrams.

and expectations of possible further political proximity with Europe. All items were answered on seven-point bipolar scales, and the direction in which scale labels were printed varied from item to item in order to protect against response sets.

The final section of the questionnaire was a custom-written visual identity task in which respondents were asked to indicate, on a background of five concentric circles with the word 'SELF' printed at the centre, where they felt the three possible social identities occurred in relation to their self (see Figure 8.1).

Figure 8.1 indicates the position of each of the three identities based on the mean scores for the two participant groups.

In some ways, this task taps into what Hofman (1988) has called the 'centrality' of an identity, by which is meant the degree to which a social identity is at the very core of a person's self-concept. This is congruent with the notion in Sellers and associates' model of racial identity that centrality is an indicator of the comparative importance of an identity for self-definition (Sellers et al. 1998) and connects with Stryker's identity model (Stryker and Serpe 1994), in which psychological centrality refers to the comparative importance of an identity within a person's identity 'repertoire'. Additionally, the act of placing the symbols on the diagram may be conceived as one of self-definition and self-labelling. This is an important psychological construct, especially for national identity (Feather 1993, 1994).

The three possible identities were British, European and ethnic. This task was tested and refined during pilot work. A similar measure has been successfully employed in other studies of social identification, such as Marson's (2001) work on organizational identity and the work of Cassidy and Trew (1998), which successfully used the task to explore a range of identities, including national and religious. On this occasion, we used the placement of symbols for each identity as an interval-level quantitative scale, allowing the generated data to be utilised in inferential statistical tests.

The questionnaire scales were assessed for face validity and ease of administration by means of a small-scale pilot study using the questionnaire in an interview administered format with white and South Asian participants ($n = 11$). In the main study, Cronbach's alpha levels for sub-scales were as follows: national (British) identity = 0.92; European identity = 0.74; ethnic identity = 0.94; European attitudes scale = 0.86. An alpha of 0.7 or above is typically deemed an adequate indicator of satisfactory internal-consistency reliability (see Loewenthal 1995).

RESULTS

We first explored whether there was evidence for any differences in attitudinal and identification items between the first- and second-generation Asian participants (as predicted in H6). None of these analyses proved significant, and consequently this issue is not focused on in the remainder of this section (all analyses had p-values of more than 0.4).

Visual Representation of Identities Task

The distribution of responses for this task is illustrated using bar charts (Figures 8.2 and 8.3), with the mean responses for each ethnic group also indicated on Figure 8.1. Ninety per cent of participants completed this task appropriately (no differences by ethnic group), and thus sample sizes in the reported analyses vary depending on the number of missing/spoiled responses.

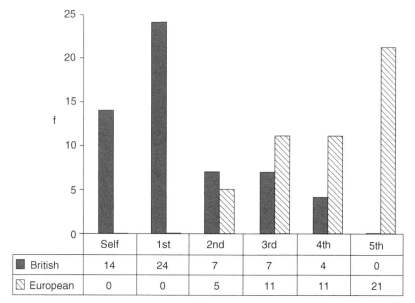

	Self	1st	2nd	3rd	4th	5th
■ British	14	24	7	7	4	0
◤ European	0	0	5	11	11	21

Ring chosen

FIGURE 8.2. Visual representation of identities task: White participants.

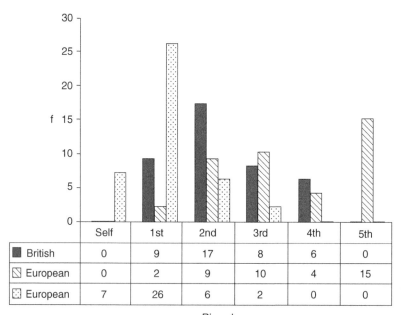

	Self	1st	2nd	3rd	4th	5th
■ British	0	9	17	8	6	0
◤ European	0	2	9	10	4	15
⋮ European	7	26	6	2	0	0

Ring chosen

FIGURE 8.3. Visual representation of identities task: Asian participants.

Figure 8.2 shows the distribution of responses for the white group. Lower scores indicate placement of a symbol closer to the centre of the diagram and the area labelled 'self'. Firstly, the distribution for British identity is positively skewed, indicating that most white participants placed their symbol for British identity close to the self. In contrast, the distribution for European identity is negatively skewed so that most of the responses are further from the self. White participants clearly perceived British identity (M = 1.37, SD = 1.19) as closer to their 'core self' than European identity (M = 4.02, SD = 1.17; $t(50) = -/13.13$, p $B/.001$, two-tailed).

Figure 8.3 summarizes the placement of symbols by Asian participants, and it can be seen that this sample saw British identity as more distant from their core self than the white sample, with a distribution approximating a normal curve (t-test comparing white versus Asian participants confirms this: white M = 1.37, SD = 1.19, Asian M = 2.29, SD = 1.11; $t(96) = -/4.00$, p $B/.001$, two-tailed).

The distribution of scores for the placement of the European identity symbol for the Asian group was slightly negatively skewed, as it was for white participants. However, our Asian respondents on average placed this symbol closer to their core self than our white participants: white M = 4.02, SD = 1.17, Asian M = 3.50, SD = 1.38; $t(90) = 1.68$, p $B/.05$, 1-tailed). Nevertheless, on average, our Asian participants, like our white group, placed the symbol for British identity closer to the core self part of the diagram than the symbol for European identity ($t(39) = -/5.86$, p $B/.001$, two-tailed).

Our Asian participants also placed a symbol on the diagram to represent their ethnic identity. From Figure 8.3, it can be seen that the distribution of responses for this were positively skewed, with many Asian respondents placing their ethnic identity close to the core self part of the diagram. In comparison to their other two identities in the task, on average, the placement of ethnic identity (M = 1.17, SD = 0.93) was closer to the core self than British identity (M = 2.29, SD = 1.11, $t(39) = 4.64$, p $B/.001$, two-tailed) and also closer than European identity (M = 3.59, SD = 1.38, $t(40) = 10.31$, p $B/.001$, two-tailed). Thus, on average, our Asian respondents ordered their identities in the following way: ethnic identity > British > European.

LIKERT SCALE MEASURES OF BRITISH, ETHNIC AND EUROPEAN IDENTITIES

Identity scores were totalled for each participant and then compared across groups. Each scale was scored in the same direction: 7 (very strong identity) through 49 (very weak). The white group showed a stronger sense of British identity (M = 19.24, SD = 7.88) than the Asian group (M = 25.43, SD = 10.02; $t(100) = -/3.49$, p $B/.01$, two-tailed). European identity was weaker in the white group (M = 36.26, SD = 8.67) than the Asian group (M = 31.16, SD = 11.61; $t(100) = 2.44$, p $B/.01$, one-tailed).

Turning to an examination of some of the Pearson correlations between these identities provides us with a window on their psychological compatibility for our participants. In the white group, British and European identities were negatively correlated ($r = -/.25$, $n = 51$, p $B/.05$, one-tailed). However, in the Asian group, they were significantly positively correlated ($r = .735$, $n = 44$, p $B/.001$, two-tailed). Interestingly, for Asian participants, the correlations between ethnic and European identity ($r = .22$, $n = 44$, NS) and between ethnic and British identity ($r = .13$, $n = 44$, NS) were not significant.

THE RELATIONSHIP BETWEEN IDENTITY AND ATTITUDINAL VARIABLES

Unsurprisingly, European identity and attitudes towards Europe were significantly positively correlated for both groups (white: $r = .745$, $n = 51$, p $B/.001$, two-tailed; Asian: $r = .687$, $n = 44$, p $B/.001$, two-tailed).

Ethnic identity for the Asian group was not correlated with attitudes towards Europe ($r = .258$, NS). However, the relationship between British identity and attitudes towards Europe was found to follow a very different pattern for the two groups. In the white group, British identity and attitudes towards Europe were significantly negatively correlated ($r = -/.456$, $n = 51$, p $B/.001$, two-tailed). In the Asian group however, British identity was significantly positively correlated with attitudes towards Europe ($r = .411$, $n = 44$, p $B/.01$, two-tailed). The difference between the groups in the 'attitudes towards Europe' scale was confirmed by comparing the mean scores on the scale. The white group displayed significantly less favourable attitudes towards Europe (M = 32.36, SD = 10.31) than the Asian group (M = 22.52, SD = 10.64; $t(100) = 4.71$, p $B/.001$, two-tailed).

DISCUSSION

In considering our findings, it should be noted that one cannot generalize them to the UK population without caution, given the convenience nature and small scale of our samples. Nevertheless, our findings are grounded in hypotheses emerging out of previous research or well-established theoretical phenomena and, as such, at least point towards trends that are worthy of investigation with larger samples. It was not, however, our intention to provide a definitive picture of what British Asians think about European integration or about being British. Rather, we wished to explore whether it is time to question the continuing tendency to ignore ethnic minorities when making generalizations about British public opinion and the construction of a European identity in the United Kingdom. We believe that our data provide strong support for this view and that they raise some general methodological and theoretical issues for the study of multiple social identifications.

The visual representation of identities task explored both the centrality (Hofman 1988) of each identity and explicit perceptions of the interrelations between them. With our white participants, as expected, average placement of identity symbols suggested that national identity was more important and closer to the core self than European identity (supporting H1). Analysis of Likert identity scales confirmed that, overall, national identity was significantly stronger than European identity for white participants. Although previous research did not allow a prediction concerning these measures in our Asian sample, the same pattern emerged in this group. This finding echoes previous research with white British samples, which has suggested that European identity in the United Kingdom is still in an embryonic state and as such is unlikely to be at the centre of British self-concepts (see Rutland and Cinnirella, 2000), perhaps partly because it fails to offer opportunities for the motivation of distinctiveness to be satisfied, therefore failing to provide what Brewer (1991) has called 'optimal distinctiveness'. However, it extends the former research by providing suggestive evidence that these features of European identity constructions in the United Kingdom may be manifested by British Asians as well as white Britons. This finding is one of the few ways in which our white and Asian samples are alike in terms of their sense of national and European identities. It should be noted, however, that it is possible that British South Asians orient themselves differently to European identity, compared to white Britons, despite the similar levels of identification. For example, British citizens of South Asian descent may feel that the European 'prototype' is white, and this may be a barrier for the internalisation of European identity in such cases. In contrast, British South Asians may perceive the concept of British identity as more multicultural, and this could explain their higher levels of national than European identity, suggesting that future research would benefit from an examination of the perceived content dimensions of these identities.

Our Asian sample clearly manifested a preference for ethnic identity over British national identity, evident in significant differences from the white sample scores on both the British identity scale and the placement of symbols on the visual task. This supports our second and third hypotheses and previous research suggesting that ethnic identity is often stronger and more central to ethnic minorities in the United Kingdom than a sense of British identity (e.g. Hutnik 1985, 1986). One possible reason for this may be that the boundaries of British identity are perceived by some ethnic minority citizens to be defined, at least in part, along racial lines, such that one cannot be 'truly British' unless one is white (see Gilroy 1987; Jacobson 1997; Miles and Dunlop 1986; Tizard and Phoenix 1993).

Alternatively, could our finding of a stronger ethnic than national identity be explained by a methodological artefact, such as the task of rating ethnic, British and European identities, leading respondents to differentiate each identity more than they would normally do (perhaps motivated by a desire for positive distinctiveness)? We would argue not – our scales were piloted using in-depth interviewing on a sub-sample, and it was found that different variants of the rating scales did not affect the relative magnitude of manifested identities. Our participants did not report perceiving our measures as artificial, and we would argue that for many Britons of an ethnic minority background, thinking about the relationship between the three social identities focused on here is not something strange and alien – rather, it is actually something that is done on a fairly regular basis.

Our fourth hypothesis was supported – Asian participants, in comparison to our white group, had a stronger European identity as measured by Likert items, indicated on the visual task that their European identity was closer to the core self, and had more positive attitudes towards European integration and the EU. Our findings failed to provide support for our sixth hypothesis, since we did not find any evidence for generational differences in responding among our Asian sample (although our sample sizes were small for these analyses and this issue requires more detailed exploration in the future with larger, representative samples).

Thus, both attitudinally and in terms of identification, our British Asians were more pro-European than our white British participants, regardless of whether they were first or second generation, a finding that requires a reappraisal of previous research on European identity and public opinion about the EU in the United Kingdom. We have demonstrated that it is not wise to assume, in a multicultural nation, that the construction of European and national identities, as well as associated attitudes, will be broadly similar throughout all ethnic groups. Our findings provide at least exploratory evidence suggesting that by no means are all Britons resistant to a sense of European identity or to cultivating pro-European attitudes.

Our fifth hypothesis was supported, indicating that the relationship between British and European identities was different in our two samples, being manifested in a negative correlation for the white group and a positive correlation for the Asian group. This is strong evidence for a difference in the relations between national and European identities for our two groups: To use Hofman's terminology, national and European identities appeared to be 'consonant' for our Asian group and 'dissonant' for our white group. These correlations between national and European identities were complemented by the analyses exploring the correlations between identities and attitudinal support for European integration and the EU. In both samples, degree of identification with Europe was strongly correlated with attitudinal support, in line with Cinnirella's previous findings (Cinnirella 1997) but also extending them to an ethnic minority sample. Similarly, British identity was strongly correlated with attitudes towards European integration. However, we found that for our Asians, British identity was positively correlated with pro-European attitudes, while for our white participants, this correlation was negative (as it was for the white sample in Cinnirella 1997). This provided yet further evidence that our Asian participants seemed to perceive British national identity as compatible with a pro-European stance, in stark contrast to white participants.

Why might our Asians have manifested a higher European identity than our white participants, and one that appeared to be compatible with national identity, again, in contrast to white constructions of incompatibility between the two? As indicated earlier, one major stumbling block for European identity to flourish in the UK has been a tendency by citizens, probably fuelled by the mass media (Hardt-Mautner 1995), to perceive an incompatibility between the United Kingdom's imperial past (essentially a notion of 'shared history' – see Wallwork and Dixon 2004) and a future that could involve devolving power and control to the EU (Cinnirella 2001; Hewstone 1986; Lyons 1996). There is good reason to expect this to be less of an issue for members of ethnic minorities who, in contrast, may well perceive an imperial past as something to deplore rather than derive pride from. In this sense, like Cinnirella's (1997) Italians, it may be that their more positive stance towards Europe could in part derive from a temporal orientation that is more future oriented, in comparison to the often past-oriented perspective of white citizens in the United Kingdom.

It may also be the case that negative stereotypes of other Western European nationalities (such as the French and Germans), held by many white Britons and often purveyed vividly in the UK mass media (see, for example, Hardt-Mautner 1995; Hewstone 1986), may be less eagerly adopted by ethnic minority citizens in the United Kingdom, who, for example, may not have a desire to continue to revive stereotypical imagery associated with World War II. For white Britons, in contrast, these same social stereotypes seem more readily accessible and embraced, thus presenting psychological barriers to the acceptance of European integration, given the central role played by France and Germany in the European movement (Cinnirella 2001; see also Hedetoft 1993).

Thus, many white Britons seem to construct European identity as a potential threat to British national identity (Cinnirella 1997). This may not be as common among ethnic minority groups in the United Kingdom, such as South Asians. Thus, as Sanchez-Mazas (1996) has argued, if European identity is perceived as compatible with and non-threatening towards national identity, then it may be more readily embraced. It may also be the case that British Asians construct their sense of British identity somewhat differently than their white British compatriots do, perhaps basing their loyalties more on a sense of civic national identity (see Cinnirella 2001; Kelman 1997; Smith 1991) that is less entrenched in emotional ties to national culture and symbols – this is an issue that needs to be explored in the future. In addition, we did not seek to examine the content dimension of these identities in the present study, but it is important not to ignore this aspect of identification (see, for example, Condor 2001; Jacobson 1997; Reicher and Hopkins 2001). Further research, for example, could explore the degree to which the meaning of ethnic, national and European identities varies across different demographic sub-groups in the United Kingdom. We would not wish to argue that the perceived relations between these identities manifested in our data are set in stone and thus immutable; as has been argued in the past (e.g. Cinnirella 1997), the compatibility of European and national identifications is contested daily in the rhetoric of politicians and the mass media.

There are wider implications for our findings, particularly in relation to the measurement of social identification and the issue of how individuals 'manage' multiple identifications. Considering the issue of methodology, it has been demonstrated that a visual identity task can be a useful tool for tapping into perceptions of the relations between multiple social identities/social categories. In this case, the data generated were compatible with those emerging from more traditional Likert-type scale measures, and this 'triangulation' from different measures of identity adds weight to our findings (Hofman 1988). This kind of visual task could be employed to further explore multiple social identifications in multicultural contexts, an issue that is undeniably important (Brown 2000; see also Crisp and Hewstone 2000).

Theoretically, our findings raise questions for future research into multiple identifications. For example, how important is collective memory for the past in determining the perceived compatibility of multiple social identifications? And to what extent might sub-groups within the in-group interpret the group's past in different ways? In addition, it is worth exploring whether ethnic minorities within nations might tend towards a greater willingness to adopt supra-national levels of identification (such as European). One weakness with our study was that the Asian participants rated British, ethnic and European identities, whereas white British participants rated only British and national identities. Further research could usefully profit from also asking white British participants to rate their sense of white ethnic identity and by also including Scottish, Welsh and Northern Irish participants.

In conclusion, our findings suggest that the perceived relations between multiple identifications may be affected by a diversity of socio-demographic variables within a nation. While previous research on European identity and attitudes has highlighted the importance of education, age, gender and the rural–urban distinction (see Evans 1996 and Eurobarometer surveys), our research suggests that ethnic background is another important variable to be considered. Finally, one thing that our white and Asian participants had in common was a tendency for identification with the nation and with Europe to be intertwined, supporting the idea that the ultimate fate of national identity in European nations is now inextricably bound up with questions of European integration (see also Chryssochoou 2000a, 2000b; Ros, Huici and Gómez 2000).

9

Islam and Political Ideologies in Europe

Andrew C. Gould

Muslim elites in Ireland, Portugal, and Spain acknowledge intellectuals, politicians, and religious figures from diverse traditions and backgrounds as inspirational for their own thinking about the proper relationships between religion and politics. The acknowledged influences include proponents of universalist syntheses of liberalism and Islam but also secular anticlericalism and antimodernist political Islamism. Research on who Muslim leaders say has helped them formulate their religious and political ideas helps us to assess the influence of Muslim civic organizations, Muslim activists and their pan-European networks, and European states and political parties. No single intellectual, organization, or even ideology can demonstrate complete success so far. Endorsements for novel syntheses of Islam and liberalism are more prevalent than the vocal critics of Islam in Europe contend. Yet the distribution of views also shows that any overlapping consensus between liberalism and Islam has not yet become the majority position, even among Europe's Muslim leaders. Muslim elites in Europe show distinctive signs of adopting and elaborating European worldviews and identities, yet they are doing so in ways that redefine what it means to be European.

Scholarship on the interaction between European states and Muslim communities suggests two possible paths for the development European ideals among Muslim elites. One body of scholarship emphasizes national differences and varied patterns of accommodation for Islam in European countries (Aluffi-Beck Peccoz and Zincone 2004; Fetzer and Soper 2005). For these scholars, the differences in the relations between Muslims and various European countries are more significant than the similarities. According to scholars working within this tradition, the causes of the different national patterns derive in large measure from varied national traditions for handling relations between religious and political institutions, as well as from other policies that shaped Muslim communities, notably those related to colonialism and decolonization. A second body of scholarship emphasizes pan–European trends and cross-national similarities

(Klausen 2005; Laurence 2005, 2006). Klausen (2005) contends that the attitudes of Muslim civic leaders on political and religious matters exhibit general patterns that cross rather than coincide with national boundaries. For Laurence, European states all desire to exert new control over transnational religious communities and organizations through parallel policies of enhanced monitoring by security services and greater outreach by interior ministries.

The relative weights of national differences and pan-European trends can be assessed with the new information in this chapter. The country-cases of Ireland, Portugal, and Spain have not been included in the previous analyses, and these cases permit one to observe Muslim communities in settings different from those that have spawned the greatest outpouring of research.[1] Ireland and Iberia exhibit comparatively vibrant religious belief and practice, in contrast to Scandinavia, Germany, the Netherlands, and the United Kingdom. These are also overwhelmingly Catholic societies in which relations between political and religious institutions are the subject of much greater national and partisan consensus than in France. If national political and religious settings shape Muslim communities, as the national-difference scholarship contends, then the effects of strong religious institutions in the host societies with favorable treatment of religion by national political institutions should be associated with Muslim political and religious elites that strongly favor integration of Muslim religious institutions into modified forms of the national models for the political regulation of religious institutions. If pan-European trends and common policy initiatives are the primary determinants of the developments within European Muslim communities, then the political and religious attitudes of Muslim elites in Ireland and Iberia should flow from the degree to which these similar policies have been followed and should largely resemble the attitudes of Muslim elites that have been observed in other cases.

The rest of this chapter is organized as follows. The next section considers scholarship on political ideologies and on Muslims in Europe to develop the expectations that can be elaborated and tested with new research on Muslim elites. The section on methods reviews the techniques for selecting countries and interview respondents and for the construction of the interview protocol. The section on the ideologies of Muslim leaders presents some of the key results from the interviews, focusing in particular on the evidence regarding the influences on their thinking acknowledged by Muslim elites. The final section points the way to further research.

MAKING AND SPREADING IDEAS

This chapter speaks to an emerging body of scholarship about the production, dissemination, and reception of ideas regarding Islam in Europe, especially

---

[1] For more on the Irish case and its literature, see Ciciora (2009); for more on the Portuguese and Spanish cases and scholarship on them, see Gould (2009).

among Muslims themselves. European and Muslim self-understandings are changing in a context in which political and religious conflict within Europe but also elsewhere in the world make interactions among Muslims and non-Muslims in Europe highly charged. While the transformations have not reached their endpoints yet, scholars are seeking to understand the origins of ideas and the processes by which particular ideas come to be accepted (or rejected) over time and across different social groups. Indeed, the developments in Europe and among Europe's Muslim communities provide an exceptional opportunity for social scientists to observe whether, how, and to what degree leaders of a religious community are reinforcing and/or reformulating political and religious belief systems in the face of new challenges and opportunities. The research in this chapter provides new evidence regarding key conjectures in the literature.

The research focuses on a critical intersection of ideologies and cultures. Europe's Muslim elites are attempting to recraft conceptions of citizenship and belonging for their religious communities and for the European societies to which they belong on contested terms. They must confront novel and in some instances unsympathetic cultural realities as they attempt to work out formal religious and political belief systems, which can also be termed ideologies (Geertz 1968: 61; Swidler 1986: 279). The anthropologists' and sociologists' distinction between culture and ideology is usefully drawn in political science by Stephen Hanson: Cultures are the "informal, implicit, and relatively inconsistent understandings of political community held by people within a given institutional setting," whereas ideologies are "formal, explicit, and relatively consistent definitions of political community articulated by political elites" (Hanson 2003: 356). Muslim elites in Europe do not command political regimes, political parties, or comprehensive, hierocratic religious institutions, so their ability to enforce broad conformity to any particular political and religious ideology is quite limited; moreover, as we shall see in section 4 below, there is no ideological consensus upon which they may build. They draw from ideologies that have little explicit to say with respect to Islam (such as liberalism and communism) along with relatively newer ideologies that take account of Islam in more explicit and differing ways (such as modernism, political Islamism, and universalism). Yet we are observing a moment of potential creativity in the development of religious and political ideologies in Europe. In an unsettled period of social transformation – to use Swidler's terms (1986: 278–9) – for new Muslim communities and for European societies generally, Muslim elites will be among the first to adopt and put into practice any new understandings of political community.

Scholars who study the making of ideas by Muslim public intellectuals (an even smaller group than Muslim elites more generally) distinguish between different styles of reasoning. On the one hand, according to John Bowen (2004), jurisprudential reasoning begins with one of the traditions of legal scholarship in Islam, such as the Hanafî, Hanbalî, and Mâliki schools, and draws guidance from that tradition for Muslims in Europe. Jurisprudential approaches require creative modifications for the European context but emphasize knowledge of existing rules as they have been implemented in Muslim-majority countries. On the other hand, a different intellectual style seeks to provide guidance by elevating the general ethical values in Islam. Reasoning from general values requires that new intellectual production begin with "the general meaning or intent of an Islamic rule rather than the social form that a rule has taken in what are considered as 'Muslim countries'" (Bowen 2004: 337). While the mode of intellectual production based in jurisprudence or in ethical reasoning does not determine the compatibility of an idea with a particular political ideology, Bowen suggests that ethical reasoning (rather than jurisprudential reasoning) is more amenable to building bridges across cultural and religious divides.

The successful dissemination of political belief systems depends on organization. Some scholars point the way to an optimistic scenario for the dissemination of a universalist synthesis of liberal principles with Islam. According to Peter Mandaville (2005: 303), important pluralist and cosmopolitan trends within Muslim transnationalism are "compatible with civil, pluralist norms" and key figures supporting these ideas are "socially positioned to scale up their influence over the next generation." Robert W. Hefner (2005) contends that pluralist and democratic Muslim politics will depend on "the emergence of public intellectuals backed by mass organizations with the social and discursive resources to convince fellow Muslims of the compatibility of Islam with pluralism and democracy" (6–7).

New bodies are seeking to become recognized authorities that can establish the proper directions for European Muslim communities and that can promulgate a widely accepted set of rules to govern the interaction of religious and political institutions. Alexandre Caeiro (2003) examines the efforts of leading figures in the European Council for Fatwa and Research (ECFR), such as Yusuf al-Qaradawi, to establish that body as a *fiqh* council with pan–European *shari'atic* authority. The Union of Islamic Organizations of France (UIOF) and the Federation of Islamic Organizations of Europe (FIOE) helped to found the ECFR in 1997 in London. Caeiro (2004) studies a 1999 *fatwa* of the ECFR permitting Muslims to take interest-bearing mortgages in the West and examines the production of this fatwa within the council, the debates surrounding the fatwa, and its reception in European Muslim communities. The FIOE sponsored the Muslims of Europe Charter that outlined the rights and responsibilities of European Muslims and their expectations from European states.[2] The FIOE claimed that 400 Muslim organizations from twenty-eight states signed the charter when it was presented at the Parliament of the European Union in January 2008. The document emphasizes tolerance and contains articles compatible with liberalism, but it has been skeptically received. The EU Parliament

[2] The Muslims of Europe Charter has been available at http://www.methaq.eu/index.html

official who welcomed the document in his public remarks disparaged the document and the FIOE as a "wolf in sheep's clothing" in a private conversation with the author (September 2008). It is important to assess the degree to which Muslim leaders cite the FIOE and its initiatives as valuable.

In a view that I share, the development of Islam in Europe cannot be fully understood without exploring the statements of Muslim leaders themselves. This is the approach taken by Klausen (2005) and Tiesler (2009). Tielser (2009: 18–19) finds a complex interplay between Muslim self-understandings and the development of transnational scholarly understandings of these phenomena:

> What makes this dynamic interesting is the fact that representatives of a new generation of European-Muslim intellectuals are analyzing the new social conditions and experiences of culturally and ethno-linguistically heterogeneous religious minorities not through conventional Islamic-theological and –legal categories, but through the language of secular discourse and its conceptual creations of transnationality and diasporicity (my translation).[3]

In reviewing both her own interview data and the writings of leading Muslim public intellectuals (such as Tariq Ramadan and Salman Bobby Sayyid), Tiesler finds crucial roles for such concepts as ethnicity, diaspora, transnationality, self, and other, all of which figure prominently in secular intellectual traditions. Gould (2009) also presents evidence from interviews regarding the distribution of political and religious beliefs among Muslim elites in Portugal and Spain and finds diverse sets of intellectual influences that bear strong imprints of European influences.

Direct evidence regarding political and religious ideas among Muslims provides crucial tests for (dis)confirming competing claims about what Muslims believe. To what extent do European-Muslim elites have European worldviews and identities? Which modes of reasoning in Islamic traditions resonate among prominent Muslim elites? Do organizations that seek to provide guidance to European Muslims have any influence on their thinking? These are questions this research aims to answer. With interview data from 2007 and 2008, the research reported in this chapter provides early indications of which widely known public intellectuals and organizations are successfully reaching out to and finding support within the next stratum of Muslim elites. The research also points to several influences on Muslim leaders that have been largely overlooked in previous scholarship. In contrast to approaches that assume which public intellectuals and organizations have been influential, the research reported here emphasizes what can be learned by exploring the ideas articulated by the

---

[3] "*O que torna esta dinâmica interessante é o facto de estarmos perante representantes de uma nova geração de intelectuais euro-muçulmanos que analisam as novas condições sociais e as práticas de minorias religiosas heterogéneas em termos culturais e etno-linguísticos, não através das tradicionais categorias islâmicas do foro teológico e jurídico, mas antes recorrendo à linguagem do discurso secular e às suas noções de transnacionalidade e diasporicidade.*"

members of the Muslim elite. In this way, the research strategy provides new information about which ideas can actually be observed in the field and which ideas indeed resonate among those who seek to provide leadership in Europe's Muslim communities.

INTERVIEW METHODS

The evidence regarding political belief systems emerges from interviews with Muslim elites in Ireland, Portugal, and Spain.[4] The respondents were selected as persons of Muslim faith or background who hold or held elected or appointed office in national, regional, or local political or civic organizations. The respondents include office-holders in political parties and deputies in national or regional parliaments (indeed, the respondents include the only such persons in Ireland and in Spain – there are no Muslims serving as officials in political parties or as parliamentary deputies in Portugal). The respondents also include leaders of the main national and municipal institutions of representation for Muslims and Islamic religious institutions in all three countries. The interview methods were developed to maximize comparability with Jytte Klausen's (2005) pioneering interviews in Scandinavia, Britain, France, and Germany. I use Klausen's definition of Muslim elite and her networking procedures for selecting interview subjects. For each country, a goal of the research is to identify every elected or appointed leader in a national or regional civic or political organization who is of Muslim faith or background and to interview as many of them as is possible. In-depth interviews permit the close examination of ideas, especially via responses to open-ended items, and the structured interview protocol, including closed-ended items, enhances comparability across interviews and national contexts.

I wrote new survey items that probe the intellectual influences on the views of Muslim elites and that help me to analyze the characteristics of the religious and political belief systems of Muslim elites. The novel method in these items is to ask respondents to place themselves with respect to ideologies by proxy, that is, by asking respondents to name the intellectuals or political figures that have influenced their thinking. Several of the questions in the interview protocol were drawn from Klausen's (2005) surveys. Other questions were adapted

[4] In particular, the data in this chapter are drawn from twenty-three interviews conducted in 2007 and 2008 by two student researchers and myself, using a fixed interview protocol with both closed-ended and open-ended items. Each interview lasted approximately two hours. In Ireland, the interviews took place in English and were conducted by Alice Ciciora (one interview was conducted with an Arabic translator); in Portugal, I conducted the interviews (some in English – with Portuguese versions of the questionnaire also available – and some in Portuguese); in Spain, the interviews were conducted in Spanish by John Grothaus. At the beginning of each interview, the respondent was promised (and we have maintained) confidentiality in the reporting of results.

from Gallup and Pew surveys of public opinion among Muslims in Europe and Muslim-majority countries. Questions that referred to specific national events and characteristics were modified to fit each country.

The exact text of the question regarding intellectual influences was: "Who are the writers, thinkers, or political figures, if any, who have been most helpful in formulating your own views about religion and politics?" The respondents' answers regarding their intellectual influences were not cued by the questionnaire. Several respondents did say that the question was difficult or surprising; interviewers encouraged reluctant respondents to answer the question. No previous items in the interview questionnaire included a proper name (neither did later items). Some of the question's difficulty came from being open ended – there was no interviewer-supplied list of likely influences. Nor did the questionnaire use well-known phrases that would cue respondents to name particular persons. The questionnaire eschewed expressions such as "to be a European Muslim," which evokes Tariq Ramadan's 1999 book, and "clash of civilizations," which echoes Samuel P. Huntington's (1996). The phrase "if any" in the question provided justification for giving responses in which no particular person was identified.

As an open-ended question, the text did not name ideologies or prompt respondents to choose consciously among a specified set of political and religious belief systems. An advantage of this instrument is that it permits coding the responses according to many different criteria. A possible disadvantage is that the coding is performed after the interview by the researcher, without an opportunity for the respondent to make explicit choices about self-placement on a stated scale; other closed-ended items did provide such opportunities. Respondents did not know that their responses to this item would be coded according to the ideological family of the named influences, the origins of those named influences, the era of the named influences, the number of named influences, and so on.

Respondents were certainly aware of the strong associations of particular names, and respondents were likely to know which names are controversial and which names are not. Muslim leaders are self-selected for having (or being willing to develop) views on religion and politics, notably by their willingness to serve in elected or appointed offices of political or civic organizations. There were also likely selection effects of the interview process, as potential respondents were informed prior to the interview of the general subject matter and could choose to be interviewed or to decline to be interviewed. In the context of the survey itself, respondents had already answered twenty-nine questions about religion and politics and so had been primed by considering their own views on controversial topics.

Among the twenty-three persons surveyed, there are eighteen – six from each of the three countries – who named specific influences on their thinking that were identified by proper names. While the number of respondents is small, these respondents included the most highly placed Muslim community leaders in each country. Thus, the results in this research can be interpreted as indicating what the leaders of Muslim communities in three countries say they believe. Whether the results of the present study also obtain among broader populations awaits research among those populations; there are certainly many other influences and trends at work among Muslim communities at large that are not as evident among a selective sample of the leadership. Nevertheless, understanding the intellectual frames and general belief systems of elites is important because of the role of elites in influencing nonelite Muslim thinking. Moreover, many Muslim elites work closely with national political bodies, and if those contacts are having any effects, they should be evident in this sample. Additional sources of variation in the influences cited by a respondent are the respondent's country of birth, the origins of the respondent's family, and the country in which the respondent received formal education.

IDEOLOGIES AND ISLAM AMONG MUSLIM LEADERS IN THREE COUNTRIES

The interviews provide insight into the nature and diffusion of ideologies among European Muslim leaders. The officeholders in Muslim political and civic organizations are consciously intellectual, in the sense that they indeed point to specific individuals as influencing their thinking (Table 9.1). Moreover, they are oriented to recent developments as well as older sources, as a slight majority of influences that they cite were contemporary figures. Similarly, the respondents are influenced by traditions and trends within Islam, as shown by the tendency to cite influences that are themselves Muslim. Muslim leaders are also wide ranging in their influences, predominantly representatives of major political ideologies – such as liberals ranging from Victor Hugo (1802–1885) to Samuel Huntington (1927–2008) and political Islamists like Hassan Al Banna (1906–1949) and Yusuf al-Qaradawi (1926) – and a few notable figures in older intellectual traditions – such as Socrates (469 BCE–399 BCE), René Descartes (1596–1650), the Prophet Muhammad (570–632), and Abū Hāmid Muhammad ibn Muhammad al-Ghazālī (1058–1111). There are also frequent references to people such as Tariq Ramadan (1962), Feisal Abdul Rauf (1948), and others seeking to establish broad areas of overlapping consensus between liberalism and Islam. Several people were mentioned by more than one respondent (see Table 9.1), while most people were mentioned just once (see Table 9.2). The evidence thus points to Islamic, contemporary, and diverse influences on the thinking of Muslim elites.

Despite the difficulty of the question, respondents indeed cited individual names and discussed the influences on their own views. Taken together, the responses produced eighty-two mentions of proper names, of which

TABLE 9.1. *Most Frequently Cited Influences*

Tariq Ramadan (1962) [6x]
Nelson Mandela (1918) [4x]
Mohandas K. Gandhi (1869–1948) [3x]
Yusuf al-Qaradawi (1926) [3x]
Feisal Abdul Rauf (1948) [3x]
Muhammad Iqbal (1877–1938) [2x]
Martin Luther King, Jr. (1929–1968) [2x]
Abdool Karim Vakil (1965) [2x]

TABLE 9.2. *Influences Cited Once, by Date of Birth*

Socrates (469 BCE–399 BCE)	John F. Kennedy (1917–1963)
Plato (428/427 BCE–348/347 BCE)	Pope John Paul II (1920–2005)
Muhammad (570–632)	Mário Soares (1924)
Umar ibn al-Khattāb (581/83–644)	Olof Palme (1927–1986)
Malik ibn Anas ibn Malik ibn 'Amr al-Asbahi (715–796)	Samuel Huntington (1927–2008)
	M. Sa'id Ramadan al-Bouti (1929)
Abū Hāmid Muhammad ibn Muhammad al-Ghazālī (1058–1111)	Hassan 'Abd Allah al-Turabi (1932)
	José Saramago (1922–2010)
Dante Alighieri (1265–1321)	Ali Shariati (1933–1977)
Thomas More (1478–1535)	Kofi Annan (1938)
René Descartes (1596–1650)	Aníbal António Cavaco Silva (1939)
Victor Hugo (1802–1885)	José Gil (1939)
Karl Marx (1818–1883)	John Esposito (1940)
Friedrich Engels (1820–1895)	John Lennon (1940–1980)
Eça de Queirós (1845–1900)	António Lobo Antunes (1942)
Max Weber (1864–1920)	Amin Maalouf (1949)
John Maynard Keynes (1883–1946)	Archbishop Rowan Williams (1950)
Dale Carnegie (1888–1955)	Bertie Ahern (1951)
Fernando Pessoa (1888–1935)	Francis Fukuyama (1952)
Abbas Mahmoud al-Aqqad (1889–1964)	Gema Martín-Muñoz (1955)
Taha Hussein (1889–1973)	João Carlos Espada (1955)
Karl Popper (1902–1994)	José Manuel Durão Barroso (1956)
Sayyid Abul A'la Maududi (1903–1979)	Brian Joseph Lenihan (1959)
Jean-Paul Sartre (1905–1980)	Vali Nasr (1960)
Hassan al-Banna (1906–1949)	Philip Watt (1962)
Naguib Mahfouz (1911–2006)	Conor Lenihan (1963)
Willy Brandt (1913–1992)	David Munir (1966)
	Amr Khaled (1967)

seventy-eight were recognized and coded on all relevant variables.[5] Almost all of the respondents explained who had influenced their own thinking about religion and politics. Nineteen respondents identified one or more individuals as intellectual influences, and respondents typically offered two or three such names (the modal number of names was two or three; the median was three; the mean was four). The upper-end outlier was a respondent who identified twenty influences. Two respondents answered the question but did not name specific individuals as being particularly influential: "My ideas aren't based in any expert. Experience and a vision of the European reality – France, Holland, Belgium – a little of everything," said one respondent. Another said: "In politics, none. In religion, imams, mullahs, the wise in the religion. These are the people who will make you understand religion. In politics, what occurs in wars will make you understand politics." Of the nineteen respondents who answered the question with one or more specific persons, one mentioned a family member only, "my father," leaving eighteen respondents who provided identifiable proper names of persons whom they acknowledged as intellectual influences. Just two respondents declined to answer the question at all.

Respondents typically named a mix of influences in terms of religious background and in terms of historical era, with slightly greater representation for Muslim and contemporary references. A heuristic two-by-two typology of influences is formed by religious background (Muslim and non-Muslim) and era (alive and deceased) of the named person. The mean proportions of named influences of each type were as follows: living Muslims 0.29, living non-Muslims 0.27, deceased Muslims 0.23, and deceased non-Muslims 0.22. For instance, one respondent named seven influences, four of whom were Muslim and four of whom were alive: the Prophet Muhammad (570–632), Feisal Abdul Rauf (1948), Tariq Ramadan (1962), the imam of Lisbon's Central Mosque, David Munir (1966), Dale Carnegie (1888–1955), Mohandas K. Gandhi (1869–1948), and Nelson Mandela (1918). In the case of this respondent, the proportions of Muslim persons and living persons named as influences were each 0.57. These are similar to the 0.56 mean proportion of Muslim persons named per respondent and to the 0.52 mean proportion of living persons named per respondent.

Most of the respondents naming public figures (twelve of eighteen) provided influences from two or more of the four categories of religion and era. The

---

[5] Proportions and means are based on the seventy-eight recognized names. Four other names remain unrecognized: "Fader ben-Assur" (possibly Abdul-Wahid ibn 'Ashir – Moroccan Maliki scholar), "Najib Kilani" (possibly Najeeb al-Keelani – Islamic revivalist poet, 1931–1995), "Couls," and "Dolores Ramon." A respondent who cited four liberals and two universalists has a proportion of liberal influences that is 0.67 and a proportion of universalists that is 0.33. The mean of liberal influences is the numerical average of the proportions of liberal influences in several response sets. This method of calculating means gives more weight to a name if the respondent cites few other names and less weight to a name if the respondent cites many other names. If one were instead to calculate proportions based on the raw list of named influences, the summary statistics would be biased toward the names cited by the more prolix respondents.

influences of two respondents covered all four categories, answers from two more respondents spanned three, and eight respondents' responses appeared in two categories. Seven respondents provided influences from just one of the four categories: Two respondents indicated just one influence each and five choose two or more influences that were each from the same category. Six respondents named living influences only, while just three respondents named deceased influences only. Six respondents named Muslim influences only, while five respondents named non-Muslim influences only.

The influences were of several political types. The first two types are historical categories that predate the emergence of modern ideologies. Classical Greek and Roman and Renaissance European thought are broad and pre-ideological categories that include all non-Muslims from ancient Greece and Rome and premodern Europe who lived before 1700. Classical Islam is a similarly broad and pre-ideological group that includes all Muslims from the Prophet Muhammad up to 1700. These two nonideological groupings are necessary for coding such persons as Plato (428/427 BCE–348/347 BCE), the Prophet Muhammad (570–632), and Thomas More (1478–1535), who lived prior to the development of modern ideologies and whose ideas have been invoked in support of varied ideologies.

Three ideologies emerged in the predominantly Christian and secular societies of Western Europe after 1700 and had little to say specifically about Islam: Liberalism involves constitutional and representative government, separation of religious and political institutions, and free markets. Nationalism favors political dictatorship and capitalist markets in which the state plays a leading role. Communism opposes capitalism and seeks a revolution, led by a vanguard party, culminating in rule by the working class and ultimately a classless society. None of the three primary ideologies that originally developed in Western Europe devoted sustained attention to the question of whether and how Islam should be incorporated into the polity and society.

Three modern ideologies do seriously engage with Islam. First, modernism takes an evolutionary view of social development and views religion as an element of traditional society that is to be superseded in the course of a transition to modern social order.[6] Modernism seeks to elaborate modern institutions within predominantly Muslim societies, often by diminishing the role and influence of religion in favor of strongly secular liberalism. Second, political Islamism developed in reaction to colonialism and exposure to Western societies; its proponents seek an explicitly Islamic political regime governed in accordance with the Shari'a (Kuru and Kuru 2008: 100). Political Islamism combines the modern, authoritarian elements of nationalism and/or communism with a significant and positive role for Islam. Third, universalism articulates a broad

---

[6] For the purposes of this chapter, the two modernist influences, Taha Hussein (1889–1973) and Naguib Mahfouz (1911–2006), are grouped along with other liberals. For more on aggressively secular versions of liberalism and modernism, see Kuru (2009: 173–4, 221).

and overlapping consensus between liberalism and Islam that involves representative and constitutional government and mutually recognized autonomy
for religious and political institutions. Universalism builds on traditions within
Islamic thought that run "parallel to" elements of Western liberalism, notably
support for democracy, human rights (including for women and non-Muslims
in predominantly Muslim societies), freedom of thought, and belief in human
progress (Kurzman 1998: 4).

Each ideology has implications for the elaboration of European worldviews
and identities among Muslim elites. Modernism and universalism are consonant with European and Western world views, although in both cases Muslim
Europeans must grapple with important complications. Modernism is difficult
to join with advocacy of a strong role for public religion, while universalism's positive evaluation of religious inspiration for shared values is rejected
by many secular liberals. In strong contrast to liberalism, modernism, and universalism, political Islamism abjures contemporary European worldviews and
identities, even though in historical perspective political Islamism owes a great
deal to European models of nationalism and communism that are partly or
more completely outdated according to currently reigning European ideals.

Among the respondents in this study, the most frequently cited influences
were liberals, followed by universalists and political Islamists. Each of these
categories was mentioned by about half of the respondents, and together, the
influences in these main categories comprised three fourths of the names in the
response sets. The rest of the named influences included leading figures from
classical Greece, classical Islam, Renaissance Europe, and Marxism-Leninism.
These others were much less frequently cited, with persons in each category
receiving mentions from just two or three respondents. No nationalist influences were mentioned.

The mean proportion of liberal influences in the response sets was 0.33.
Nine of the respondents included one or more liberals in their list of influences – seven of them naming a majority of liberal influences. One respondent, for instance, named two people coded as liberals – Francis Fukuyama
(1952) and Samuel Huntington (1927–2008) – along with one person coded
as a universalist – Vali Nasr (1960). Another respondent named four people
in the broadly liberal category – Mohandas K. Gandhi (1869–1948), Nelson
Mandela (1918), Pope John Paul II (1920–2005), and Martin Luther King, Jr.
(1929–1968), along with two in the universalist category: Feisal Abdul Rauf
(1948) and Tariq Ramadan (1962). Nine respondents named no influence
coded as a liberal.

The mean proportion of universalist influences was 0.24. Nine respondents
included one or more universalists in their answer sets. For example, one
respondent named three people in the universalist category – Amin Maalouf
(1949), Tariq Ramadan (1962), and Gema Martín-Muñoz (1955) – along with
one political Islamist, Yusuf al-Qaradawi (1926). The respondent who cited
twenty names overall included two universalists, Tariq Ramadan and Abdool

Karim Vakil (1965). The response sets of nine respondents did not include any universalists.

The mean proportion of political Islamist influences named by respondents was 0.19. Eight respondents named one or more of the seven political Islamist influences mentioned in the interviews, and two of those respondents named only political Islamist influences in their short lists of one or two influences. Three respondents named Yusuf al-Qaradawi (1926) and two named Muhammad Iqbal (1877–1938). One respondent each named the other five political Islamists: Ali Shariati (1933–1977), Hassan al-Banna (1906–1949), M. Sa'id Ramadan al-Bouti (1929), Sayyid Abul A'la Maududi (1903–1979), and Hassan 'Abd Allah al-Turabi (1932). Ten respondents named no political Islamists; one would expect no mention of political Islamists among the intellectual influences of non–Muslim European elites.

References to persons from the period of classical Islam were few, yielding a mean proportion of 0.10. Just three respondents mentioned such persons, each of whom was named just once: the Prophet Muhammad (570–632), Umar ibn al-Khattāb (581/83–644), Malik ibn Anas ibn Malik ibn 'Amr al-Asbahi (715–796), and Abū Hāmid Muhammad ibn Muhammad al-Ghazālī (1058–1111). Classical Greek and Renaissance European references comprised a mean proportion of just 0.06. They appeared in the response sets of two respondents and included Socrates (469 BCE–399 BCE), Plato (428/427 BCE–348/347 BCE), Dante Alighieri (1265–1321), Thomas More (1478–1535), and René Descartes (1596–1650). Communist influences were rare, with a mean proportion of just 0.05. Just two of the respondents included such influences. A former MP in a labor party cited Karl Marx (1818–1883), Friedrich Engels (1820–1895), and Jean-Paul Sartre (1905–1980). The largest response set of twenty names included left-wing political leaders and intellectuals such as Willy Brandt (1913–1992), Olof Palme (1927–1986), and José Saramago (1922–2010).

The pan-European trends perspective fits with some commonalities across the three countries. In all three countries, Muslim elites cite contemporary intellectual influences from a mix of Muslim and non-Muslim sources. About half of the weighted response sets contain living persons in all three countries, and the response sets in all three countries include Muslims and non-Muslims. Moreover, Muslim elites across these countries accept as influences representative figures from the same main intellectual traditions. Each major class of influences – liberal, universalist, and political Islamist – received mentions in all three countries. The contemporary influences least likely to be observed among non-Muslim Europeans, namely political Islamists, were present among the influences of some Muslim elites.

Yet there are also country-level specificities and limits to cross-national trends so far. The Muslim elites in Portugal named the lowest proportion of Muslim influences in their response sets (0.34 on average), compared to Irish Muslim elites (0.56) and Spanish Muslim elites (0.69). No single person was mentioned as an intellectual influence in all three countries. And just three people were mentioned in any two countries: Tariq Ramadan (1962) received four mentions in Portugal and two in Spain. Nelson Mandela (1918) was mentioned three times in Portugal and once in Ireland. Muhammad Iqbal (1877–1938) was mentioned once in Portugal and Spain. The other figures receiving multiple mentions were confined to one country each: Feisal Abdul Rauf (1948) and Mohandas K. Gandhi (1869–1948) were mentioned three times each in Portugal, Yusuf al-Qaradawi (1926) was cited by three respondents in Spain, and Abdool Karim Vakil (1965) and Martin Luther King, Jr. (1929–1968) were each mentioned twice in Portugal. It is noteworthy that Yusuf al-Qaradawi, president of the ECFR located in Dublin, was not mentioned by any Portuguese-Muslim elite or by any member of the Muslim elite in Ireland.

Country-level differences are observed as well in the varied strengths of the main intellectual traditions in each country. Portugal's Muslim elite is the most liberal and cosmopolitan of the three communities. Portugal's Muslim elite cite influences that are predominantly liberal (0.61 of their response sets on average) and universalist (0.31), with most of the remaining figures from classical Islam. The liberal influences named by Portugal's elites include political and intellectual figures from many world regions. As a group, Spain's Muslim elite is the least exclusively liberal. Instead, Spanish Muslim elites are more strongly oriented to competing contemporary intellectual developments that seek to deal explicitly with the role of Islam in a modern society: universalists (0.35 of their response sets on average) and Islamists (also 0.35), with most of the remainder from historical European sources. Ireland's Muslim elite are not as concentrated on the leading intellectual traditions of liberalism, universalism, and political Islamism; instead, they are influenced by Irish-national political figures and a diverse array of other influences. Ireland's Muslim elites acknowledge liberal influences (0.32) that are mainly Irish political figures or US-based scholars, with the remainder distributed widely among Communist, classical Islamic, liberal, and universalist sources.

The acknowledged intellectual influences of the Muslim elite respondents distinctively span regional boundaries. One measure is the country or region in which the named influence was born. For example, a Spanish respondent cited intellectual influences originating mainly from the Arab world: He named Abbas Mahmoud al-Aqqad (1889–1964), Taha Hussein (1889–1973), Hassan al-Banna (1906–1949), and Naguib Mahfouz (1911–2006), all of whom were born in Egypt, along with French-born Victor Hugo (1802–1885). In contrast to this predominantly Muslim-majority-origin response set, on average the respondents cited people who were born in Muslim-majority countries and people who were born in Europe with roughly equal frequency. Muslim-majority-born influences appeared in thirteen of eighteen response sets with a mean proportion of 0.43, and European-born influences appeared in twelve response sets with a mean proportion of 0.41. The remaining influences were born in the US (five response sets with a mean proportion of 0.09) or in non–Muslim-majority developing countries (four response sets; mean proportion of 0.07).

CONCLUSION

States, other political organizations, and intellectuals are all seeking to influence prominent European Muslims, and the research reported here provides some new evidence regarding the characteristics of some successful efforts to do so. Direct and face-to-face interactions between those who wish to be influential and European-Muslim leaders are strongly associated with who indeed becomes an acknowledged influence. Where national-level politicians have met with Muslim leaders, as notably in Ireland and Portugal, Muslim leaders cite them as being influential in the context of research interviews focused on religion and politics. A similar relationship obtains for public intellectuals such as Tariq Ramadan – their influence is acknowledged where they have themselves interacted with leaders in Muslim communities, as especially in Portugal. Direct diplomacy across borders, national- and subnational outreach by domestic government officials, and personal visits by intellectuals are among the attempts to influence the thinking of European Muslims that indeed leave memorable impressions on the thinking of European-Muslim leaders.

The research also provides evidence regarding the choices that European-Muslim elites have been making in selecting their intellectual guidance, and the results are that liberalism, universalism, and political Islamism are the most widely acknowledged sources of ideas about religion and politics. Muslim elites are frequently asked for their views on Islam and politics, and this takes place in a context in which the main terms of reference provide only limited and/or controversial guidance: Liberalism, nationalism, and communism were initially propounded for predominantly non-Muslim societies, while universalism, modernism, and political Islamism remain highly contested. The level of influence that has been achieved by universalism, the newest of these ideological families, is impressive, yet it is noteworthy that this perspective is not a majority position even among the European-Muslim elite (nor is it the dominant ideology in any western European state). Other potential sources of ideas about the proper relationships between religion and politics – including aggressively secular liberalism, versions of liberalism that are largely silent on Islam, and political Islamism – have longer histories, better-known leading figures, and stronger institutions to support them. By contrast, universalists (and also liberals and who assert the compatibility of Islam and vibrant constitutional and representative democracy) cannot rely on the influence of existing institutions to carry the day.

In an unsettled time, such as the one that European societies are currently experiencing, research on the views of religious and political elites provides a window into ongoing processes of ideological conflict and creativity. Further research is necessary to develop a more complete analysis of the alternative modes of reasoning – jurisprudential or ethical to use Bowen's terms (2004) – that resonate among Muslim leaders. We have seen that prominent juris-prudentialists, such as Yusuf al-Qaradawi, are cited, but so are those whose reasoning is primarily ethical, such as Tariq Ramadan. Further research is also necessary to understand how sources that predate the emergence of modern ideologies are being incorporated and elaborated within modern frameworks. Abū Hāmid Muhammad ibn Muhammad al-Ghazālī (1058–1111) and Malik ibn Anas ibn Malik ibn 'Amr al-Asbahi (715–796) are two cases in point. For instance, the Mâliki legal school can be said to be a both source of jurispruden-tial reasoning and one of the more flexible Islamic legal traditions. The compet-ing uses and references to Islamic authorities within the political belief systems of European-Muslim elites (and among Muslims more broadly) deserve further study through in-depth analysis of how people assert and defend their concep-tions of the proper relationships among religious and political institutions.

The findings present a mixed picture with respect to the development of European identities and worldviews among Muslim elites that some will see as a glass half full and others as a glass half empty. The officeholders of Muslim faith or background in political and civic organizations in Europe are just as likely to cite influences from Europe as from Muslim-majority regions. They are just as likely to refer to figures associated with universal syntheses of Islam and liberalism as to political Islamists. Muslim elites in these three differ-ent European countries all draw on the same main intellectual traditions in European and Islamic thought, but they do so in varied proportions, with sub-stantially greater liberalism in Portugal, divisions between universalists and Islamists in Spain, and local political references in Ireland. The task of explain-ing just what it means to be European and Muslim remains unfinished, for there is no consensus on how exactly to join these religious and political iden-tities, even among the officeholders in the organizations that take such projects as central to their mission. Critics on each side of the religious and political divide contend that a vibrant and mutually reinforcing combination is impossi-ble; according to them, a person can be authentically Islamic or European only to the extent that he or she diminishes the other commitment. For those who believe otherwise, elaborating an alternative vision of reinforcing contributions and providing institutional support for such a conception in religious, political, and educational institutions are tasks that remain to be accomplished.

PART IV

NEW NATIONALIST CHALLENGES

10

Nationalism versus Multiculturalism

European Identity and the Impact of the Radical Right on Antidiscrimination Policy in Europe

Terri E. Givens

European identity has been challenged by the influx of immigrants since World War II and the growth of ethnic minority communities. Two important trends constitute the political response to Europe's increasing racial and cultural diversity. First, many countries have been part of a worrying trend, the rise of right-wing, anti-immigrant political parties (Givens 2005). France's Jean-Marie Le Pen and Austria's late Jörg Haider have attained the greatest international notoriety, but reactionary political figures across Europe have enjoyed increasing degrees of success over the past several years. Second, several countries have enacted laws that prohibit racial discrimination comparable to what is commonly known in America as "civil rights" legislation. These two trends appear to be interrelated. For example, Erik Bleich (2003: 49) suggests that in the mid-1960s, British political elites sought to "defuse" the race issue, stoked by MP Enoch Powell among others, "by pursuing Parliamentary consensus over an antidiscrimination law." Likewise, scholars suggest that the entry of Jörg Haider's Freedom Party into a governing coalition in Austria fueled the European Union (EU) consensus on the Racial Equality Directive (RED) (Bell 2002: 74; Guild 2000: 416).

The 1980s saw the dramatic rise of racist, nationalist radical right parties, particularly in France, Germany, Austria, and Denmark. As this chapter will show, paradoxically, these parties pushed European governments to take on the issue of racial discrimination at the European Union level. In general, the literature on radical right parties has tended to focus on their electoral successes, but these parties have also had an impact on policy. With the rise of anti-immigrant parties and increases in popular anti-immigrant sentiment, government leaders increased their emphasis on immigration control. Whether that actually led to decreases in immigration is debatable, but certainly the

With research support from Rhonda Evans-Case, Adam Luedtke, and Marko Papic.

salience of the issues increased (Givens and Luedtke 2004), which led to more restrictive policies. However, the rise of the radical right is not only linked to restrictive immigration control policies, it can also be linked to measures that were designed to improve the situation for immigrants and ethnic minorities who had already settled in European countries. A clear example of this is the EU's Racial Equality Directive.

Right-wing politics casts immigrants as foreign objects within the body politic and blames them for a litany of social ills, including high rates of crime and unemployment. In his quest for the French presidency in 2002, Jean-Marie Le Pen of the National Front won enough votes to propel him into a runoff election against Jacques Chirac. Although he ultimately lost by a wide margin, he was for a two-week period the second most popular politician in France. In October 1996, Austria held its first direct election for Members of the European Parliament, and Haider's Freedom Party (*Freiheitliche Partei Österreichs* or FPÖ) gained 27.6 percent of the vote. In 1999, Haider's Freedom Party entered into a national coalition in Austria after garnering 26 percent of the vote. More recently, Haider's new party and the Freedom Party won a combined score of 29 percent of the vote in the 2008 federal elections. These relatively recent successes serve to underscore the persistence of these parties.

One can argue that the popularity of the radical right, along with an increase in terror attacks, also led many countries to abandon more multicultural approaches to immigrant and ethnic minority communities. However, multiculturalism and immigrant integration can be approached in many ways. Perhaps one of the more important factors in integration is an acknowledgement of discrimination and measures to address access to the workforce, fair housing, and equal opportunities more generally. Certainly, the activists who pursued the passage of the Racial Equality Directive felt that this was an important step in the development of equal rights.

The success of radical right parties, increases in immigration control, and changes in approach to immigrant integration can all be considered moves indicating a more "integralist" approach to European political identity. Holmes (2009: 56) identifies the leader of the French National Front, Jean Marie Le Pen, as the figure who "'re-functioned' the nature of European identity, imparting an experimental ethos and an illiberal dynamic." However, the actions taken by European governments to pass an antidiscrimination directive provide a counterpoint to this type of narrative. Castiglione (2009: 37) has noted that "Issues such as migration and how to deal with a multicultural society provide the integralist position with ammunition for their defense of traditional conceptions of national sovereignty, territorial integrity, and cultural nativism, thus making discourses of a dominant European identity rather vulnerable for the foreseeable future." These two trends are indicative of the ongoing tensions within the development of a European political identity.

This chapter will examine how the rise of the radical right led to the development of antidiscrimination policy at the EU level. The development of

Britain's race relations policies in the 1960s and 1970s (which drew on civil rights policy in the United States) became the basis for EU-level antidiscrimination policy, but it was the success of the radical right, particularly in Austria, that became the catalyst for a Left-party dominated European Council to push forward antidiscrimination policy. After transnational activists had pursued the development of antidiscrimination policy, the European Council adopted the Racial Equality Directive in June 2000.

The RED represents a significant development as it involves issues of race and European integration, both of which can serve as lightening rods within national politics. Whereas the push for laws prohibiting sex discrimination was driven by labor market considerations (see Bell 2002: 8–9, 30), the RED was largely driven by calls for greater "social cohesion and solidarity" (The Council of the European Union 2000: Preamble). Moreover, it addresses racial discrimination in the areas of social protection, housing, education, and associations, as well as in employment.[3] In terms of scope, it thus represents a significant advance in European integration and helps to define a more inclusive European political identity. Premised as it is upon rights-creation and enforcement, the RED is emblematic of a broader effort to use state guarantees of fundamental rights as a means of fostering a sense of citizenship. Based upon survey data and the number of "hits" experienced by EU antidiscrimination websites, "antidiscrimination has become one of the most widely known areas of EU employment and social policy" (The Council of the European Union 2000: Article 3).

The European Council unanimously adopted the RED in record time as a response to the electoral success of the Austrian Freedom Party in parliamentary elections (Geddes and Giraudon 2004). The directive required member-states to adopt national legal protections against racial discrimination within two years. As with many EU directives, most countries did not meet this deadline, but it was adopted in the EU-15 as of 2007. As originally conceived by a group of nongovernmental organizations (NGOs), known as the Starting Line Group (SLG), the RED not only prohibited discrimination against racial minorities, but it also prohibited discrimination on grounds of religion and provided protection to "third-country nationals" (TCNs) (see Chopin 1999b: 111). In addition, the SLG also proposed two additional legal instruments, one on free movement and another on the participation of TCNs in elections. Ultimately, however, in its final form, key provisions desired by the SLG were omitted from the RED. Although the RED's protection against discrimination extends to TCNs, the Directive does not cover differences of treatment based on nationality and is without prejudice to provisions governing the entry and residence of third-country nationals and their access to employment and to occupation. The RED constitutes a significant victory for transnational NGOs in the EU policy-making process, but it also illustrates the fraught relationship between immigration and antidiscrimination policies.

The European populace continues to send very mixed signals with regard to both race and EU integration. On the one hand, radical right parties have done well in elections to both national and European parliaments, but on the other hand, the May 2003 results from a Eurobarometer survey indicate that a majority of Europeans oppose discrimination in all forms (European Commission 2004: 8). I will argue that the rise of the radical right did have some impact on the agenda related to immigration policy at the national level but that it also had the impact of focusing Left parties on immigrant integration and antidiscrimination and encouraged activists to focus their efforts for immigrant rights at the EU level. This focus moves forward the idea of a *European* approach to citizenship and political identity.

IMMIGRATION, RACE, AND IMMIGRANT INTEGRATION IN EUROPE

Since the end of World War II, millions of immigrants from developing countries have settled in Western Europe. Immigration and issues related to the integration of those settlers have become some of the most salient political issues in Europe over the last two decades. During the postwar recovery, many European countries began to import labor, initially from Southern Europe and later from former colonies and other developing countries. With the economic slowdown of the 1970s, most European countries stopped the importation of labor and had policies of zero immigration. However, due to family reunification and asylum policies, large flows of immigrants and asylum seekers continued to enter Europe as settlers. These populations, many from Muslim backgrounds, have led to the development of various policies of integration in combination with citizenship laws, creating different European approaches to immigrant integration.

Ethnic and racial conflict has accompanied the development of new minority communities in Europe. Riots have occurred on a regular basis in Britain since the 1950s. Despite the media frenzy surrounding the Paris "riots" (a.k.a. "uprising") in 2005 and again in 2007, these events were only the most recent incidents in which police violence had touched off a response in the suburbs. These realities point to shortcomings in the development and implementation of policies designed to integrate and deal with issues of discrimination against minorities.

Of course, countries like Britain and France have had very different approaches to the concept of race. Britain has generally followed the U.S. model in its approach to "race relations," while France has resisted any references to race in policy making. It is no secret that race is a highly charged concept, and even in the negotiations over the RED, it was made clear that race was not accepted as a biological concept. In this chapter, the use of the term "race" comes partially from an American perspective. It is clear that race is a social and cultural construction, but it is useful in understanding key aspects of this analysis, mainly racism and discrimination. Although not a biological fact, race is a "social fact" (Durkheim 1982). As Frederickson argues, "race

... is commonly used as a criterion to justify a dominant and privileged position – accompanied by the notion that 'we' are superior to 'them' and need to be protected from real or imagined threats to our privileged group position that might arise if 'they' were to gain in resources and rights. Here we have 'racism' in the full and unambiguous sense of the term" (as cited by Foner 2005: 12).

The study of race has been a difficult topic in Europe (outside of Britain) for social scientists. The French case is illustrative of some of the issues arising from the experience of genocide in World War II. Social scientists Valerie Amiraux and Patrick Simon note that studies of racism in France "remained marginalized in the academic 'field' until the early 1990s" (Amiraux and Simon 2006: 191). Studying race, immigration and immigrants is considered illegitimate unless the researchers remain in the realm of ideas. The collection of statistics on race, never practiced by postwar French governments, has been seen as harkening back to the Vichy era, and new attempts to begin collecting these data have led to open battles in the French media between those like Simon who argue for this collection, particularly in the context of antidiscrimination policy, and those who feel that mentioning race in order to fight racism only reaffirms it. As Amiraux and Simon (2006: 204) note, "[W]hile choosing not to use ethnic and racial categories in statistics, the French scientific community prevents the accumulation of discrimination data and contributes to euphemizing the social impacts of racism."

The British case is nearly the opposite of France, in that "there is now a massive catalogue of publications on [immigration and race relations]" (Small and Solomos 2006: 249). There has been an ongoing focus on issues related to immigration and "race relations" as these issues have risen on the political agenda. However, Small and Solomos (2006: 250) also point out that "researchers working in this field have found it hard to i) establish a rounded research agenda that included all facets of race and racism in British society and ii) have been pulled in different directions by contrasting political and academic pressures."

Germany's history of the Holocaust and the country's ethnicity-based citizenship have made the issue of race a difficult topic. As Wright (2004: 184–5) notes, "The Americans, French, and British, to one degree or another, most often pretend to (and to some degree do) overlook race in determining national belonging, instead bringing in a different set of signifiers such as political beliefs, cultural mores, and economic status.... Germany, on the other hand, while not prohibiting all non-Germans from becoming citizens, nonetheless has trouble viewing those who do not share a specific racial heritage as 'true' Germans."

Although racism is often based on color in Europe, it is also important to look at issues of cultural racism (Modood 2005: 7). As Muslims have become more defined as a group rather than as part of their respective nationalities and ethnicities, they have become the focus of restrictive immigration policies, punitive integration measures, and citizenship tests designed to test for "antiliberal" values. Although much attention goes to the issue of Muslims in Europe, many groups face issues of racism and political exclusion. Anti-Semitism continues to be an issue in Europe, despite the history of the Holocaust and efforts to recover from that period of genocide. The basis for discrimination is often perceived race, as well as religion and culture.

As authors like Foner (2005: 216) note, "immigrants are more likely to be stigmatized on the basis of culture than of color-coded race." Foner (2005: 16) also notes: "In Fredrickson's conceptualization of racism, culture and even religion can become essentialized to the point that they can serve as a functional equivalent of biological racism – culture, put another way, can do the work of race, when peoples or ways of life are seen as unchangeable as pigmentation." The concept of race is complex, but as a term it is useful for defining the rationale behind antidiscrimination policies in Europe, and I use it in this context.

Immigrant Integration

Most European countries are looking at how they have integrated immigrants in the past and how they might change their policies to avoid some of the problems exhibited in immigrant and minority communities today. High levels of unemployment and other manifestations of discrimination including negative attitudes in the broader communities are challenges for policy makers. Immigrants, particularly noncitizens, tend to face higher levels of unemployment than the general population, as well as exclusion from many aspects of society. Cultural and religious issues have come to the fore as Muslims and other religious groups look for ways to practice their faith in societies with strong Christian underpinnings.

What is meant by immigrant integration? This can generally be considered to be the processes that take place after an immigrant has moved to a new country. Integration is also considered a two-way process, requiring accommodation on the part of both the native and the immigrant populations. Ireland (2004: 15) has described it as a goal that leads to overall social cohesiveness. Authors have used terms such as "assimilation," "incorporation," and "multiculturalism" to describe the processes that lead to an immigrant becoming an integrated part of his or her adopted community. However, these are tenuous concepts, mainly used by policy makers to describe a particular policy outcome, such as immigrants who can speak the language, are sending their children to school, and in general are not causing problems in a society.

Although policy has moved away from a more multicultural approach to an assimilationist approach, encouraging immigrants (and ethnic and religious minorities) to adopt the language, culture, and morals (however they may be defined) of the host society, there has also been recognition of the discrimination faced by these populations. Clearly, issues of immigrant integration range from citizenship policy to employment issues to housing issues. Antidiscrimination policy is one means of addressing immigrant integration issues and has often been seen by the left as a way to soften the impact of restrictive immigration control measures.

IMMIGRATION CONTROL AND ANTIDISCRIMINATION POLICY: IMPACT OF THE RADICAL RIGHT

In his article on the impact of the extreme right on immigration policy, Martin Schain examines the *Front National* (FN) in France as an agent of electoral realignment. He argues, "the FN succeeded in realigning voting and issue patterns, as well as the relationship among parties in France" (Schain 2008: 278). He finds that the electoral success of the FN forced parties of the right and left to take on the issue of immigration, thus impacting the policy agenda, noting that "the dynamics of party competition resulted in redefinition of the issue of immigration in national politics, from a labor market problem, to a problem of integration and national identity, to problems of education, housing, law and order, and citizenship" (Schain 2006: 283).

Although he focuses on the extreme right in France, Schain argues that the French case has implications for comparative study. He notes: "In virtually every case where there has been an electoral breakthrough of the extreme-right, established parties have reacted by co-opting some aspects of their programme in an attempt to undermine their support" (Schain 2006: 286). Other examples come from countries in which radical right parties have actually become part of government, such as Austria and Denmark.

Jeannette Money (1999) has pointed out that increasing restrictions on immigration predated the emergence of the extreme right (referenced in Schain 2008: 286). Certainly, in countries in which there has been no electoral breakthrough for radical right parties, there has been a push for more restrictive immigration policies, for example in Germany and Britain. Money also points out that Left parties have an incentive to push for integration policies in order to develop these new constituencies of immigrants who are becoming voters (Money 1999).

In general, political parties have rarely argued over whether there should be more immigration control. This makes it rather difficult to tie immigration control directly to the rise of the radical right. There certainly can be no clear claim of causality. However, it is clear that the period during which the radical right has been more active has seen more restrictive immigration policies developed not only at the national level but also at the EU level. In the next section, the focus is on immigration control policy at the EU level. The following section focuses on antidiscrimination policy, in which the causal link is much clearer.

Immigration Control versus Integration

Perhaps one of the more clear-cut areas of increasingly restrictive policies has been harmonization at the EU level. However, this comparison also provides an example of the tensions between control and integration. Table 10.1 lays out policies on immigration, asylum, and other areas of immigration policy. In a 2004 article, Givens and Luedtke examined the development of EU immigration policy and the impact of issue salience, finding that the high salience of immigration control led to more restrictive policies, while the low level of salience of integration policies led to less restrictive policies like the Racial Equality Directive.

The halting and contested harmonization of European Union immigration policy is not a monolithic process. There is unexplained variation in four areas of this harmonization: throughout time, across countries, across policy areas, and between "subjects" (EU nationals versus TCNs, who are legally resident in an EU country but do not hold citizenship). This variation takes two forms. First, the success of harmonization proposals is variable, since much of the proposed EU legislation has not been enacted. Some harmonization restricts immigrant rights by enacting a standardized policy with low "standards" for the protection of immigrant rights, by not providing judicial remedy, and by obligating some member-states to "lower" their standards. For instance, Germany used EU harmonization in 1993 to tighten its expansive political asylum rules, which had previously been protected by domestic judges (Joppke 1999). Other harmonization is expansive toward immigrant rights by obligating member-states to "raise" their standards. For instance, the 2000 Racial Equality Directive (RED), while not protecting all immigrants (since it is based on race and not nationality), provides judicial remedy for ethnic minority immigrants and obligates all member-states (including those who previously had no racial discrimination legislation) to implement the RED into national law (Niessen 2003). Not all harmonization proposals have been successful, and not all successful harmonization proposals have been expansive toward immigrant rights.

How do harmonization proposals vary on these two dimensions, success and restrictiveness? Throughout time, harmonization has gathered pace and has advanced in some policy areas after years of blockage. Across countries, there is variation in the support of EU member-states for harmonization proposals, with some member-states supporting expansive harmonization proposals, some supporting only restrictive harmonization proposals, and some blocking harmonization proposals altogether. There has been more success in policy areas, like the societal integration of immigrants versus controlling the inflow of new immigrants. And finally, between "subjects": EU nationals, in the last few decades, are increasingly able to exercise full freedom of movement rights, as long as they are participating in the labor market, meaning that member-states are now unable to prevent each other's citizens from living

TABLE 10.1. *Proposed EU Immigration Policies and Their Outcomes*

Policy Area	EU Proposal	Adopted by Council?	If Adopted, Restrictive or Expansive?
Asylum	Common asylum procedure (COM(2000)755)	Yes	Restrictive
	Minimum standards for conditions for the reception of asylum-seekers (COM(2001)181)	Yes	Restrictive
	Determining the member-state responsible for examining an asylum application (COM(2001)447)	Yes	Restrictive
	Granting refugee status (COM(2002)326)	No	
	Status of third country nationals and stateless persons as refugees (COM(2001)510)	No	
	Granting temporary protection in case of mass influx (COM(2000)303)	Yes	Restrictive
	Council Regulation No 2725/2000, the establishment of "Eurodac" for the comparison of fingerprints	Yes	Restrictive
Legal migration	European Refugee Fund (COM(1999)686)	Yes	Neither
	Family Reunification (COM(2002)225)	No	
	Status of third-country nationals who are long-term residents (COM(2001)127)	No	
	Coordination of Social Security Benefits (COM(2002)59)	No	
	Conditions of entry and residence of TCNs for paid employment (COM(2001)386)	No	
	Residence permit for victims of illegal immigration who cooperate with authorities (COM(2002)71)	No	
	Council Regulation (EC) No 2424/2001, development of Schengen Information System II (fingerprint database)	Yes	Restrictive
	Admission for scientific research (COM(2004)178)	Yes	Expansive
	Admission for study/training (COM(2002)548)	Yes	Expansive

(continued)

TABLE 10.1. *(continued)*

Policy Area	EU Proposal	Adopted by Council?	If Adopted, Restrictive or Expansive?
Visas and border control	Council Regulation amending Regulation 1683/95 uniform format for visas (2002/C 51 E/03) (COM(2001)577)	Yes	Neither
	Listing third countries whose nationals must possess visas (COM(2002)679)	Yes	Restrictive
	Common Consular Instruction for examining visa applications (2000/C 164)	Yes	Neither
	Common Border Guard Manual (2001/C 73)	Yes	Restrictive
	Travel by nationals exempt from the visa requirement (2000/C 164)	No	
Illegal Immigration	Transit Assistance for Removal by Air (2003/C 4)	No	
	Mutual recognition of expulsion orders (2000/C 243)	Yes	Restrictive
	Compensating financial imbalances resulting from mutual recognition (COM(2003)49)	No	
	Residence permit for victims of illegal immigration who cooperate with authorities (COM(2002)71)	No	
	Penalties for Carriers of Illegal Immigrants (2000/C 269)	Yes	Restrictive
	Obligation of Carriers to Communicate Passenger Data (2003/C 82)	No	
	Combating Human Trafficking (COM(2000)854)	Yes	Restrictive
	Strengthening of Penal Framework (2000/C 253)	Yes	Restrictive
Antidiscrimination	Treaty of Amsterdam – EU can fight any discrimination, including on the basis of nationality (Article 12, TEC)	Yes	Expansive
	EU can fight discrimination based on sex, race, religion, disability, age, or sexual orientation (Art. 13, TEC).	Yes	Expansive
	Charter of Fundamental Rights of the European Union (2000 / C 364 / 01)	Yes	Expansive
	Racial Equality Directive (COM(1999)566)	Yes	Expansive
	Community Action Program to combat discrimination (COM(1999)649)	Yes	Expansive
	Common Agenda for Integration (COM(2005)389)	No	

in their territory, holding jobs, and even voting in local elections. However, TCNs, despite having legal residence, cannot exercise this freedom of movement, despite calls by the European Commission, European Parliament, and many of the member-states to grant this freedom (Geddes 2003).

The harmonization of immigration policy that has occurred has tended to be restrictive in nature, designed only to enhance national sovereignty and control over immigration by allowing state actors to circumvent national-level institutional constraints. Germany's use of EU harmonization in 1993 to tighten its expansive political asylum rules (which had previously been protected by domestic judges and the constitution) is a perfect example of this paradoxical development, whereby EU harmonization enhances de facto national sovereignty as opposed to eroding it (Joppke 1999). A country like the United Kingdom, on the other hand, with no strong, independent judiciary to protect immigrant rights, has no need of the EU's "venue" to legitimize its immigration crackdown and thus has tended to block even the most restrictive harmonization proposals that have been on the table, preferring to maximize pure sovereignty instead of strategic policy cooperation (Hix and Niessen 1997).

Antidiscrimination Policy

Prior to 1999, the EU did not explicitly possess authority to act with regard to an increasingly important issue in the region, racial discrimination. In that year, Article 13 entered into effect. It empowers the European Council to take action to combat discrimination based on a number of ascriptive grounds, including race. Thirteen months later, a record speed for the EU, the Council unanimously adopted the Racial Equality Directive, which sets a supranational standard for national laws that protect against racial and ethnic discrimination. Member-states were required to transpose the Directive's terms into national law within a period of three years. The willingness of EU lawmakers to act and the speed with which they moved may be explained, in part, by contemporaneous events.

Across Europe in the late 1990s, issues involving racism garnered significant public attention. In 1999, for example, the Stephen Lawrence Inquiry released its damning report on racism within the British police force, and Jörg Haider's extreme right-wing Freedom Party won a position in Austria's governing coalition. Moreover, during this period, twelve of the fifteen member-state governments were dominated by left or center-left political parties. These factors combined to create a unique political opportunity for action against racism at the European level.

In order to understand the politics that shaped negotiations over the Directive, it first helps to know the developments that preceded its adoption and made it feasible, as well as the precise terms of the Directive in its final form. The RED was the product of a nearly twenty-year effort begun by the European Parliament to legislate against racial discrimination at the EU level.

The effort would be taken up by a group of transnational activists that would push the policy through to the passage of the RED.

The European Parliament played a key role in putting and keeping the issue of racism on the European agenda (European Commission 1997). The issue was first raised by a 1985 Committee of Inquiry, which produced the so-called Evrigenis Report that documented the growing problem of xenophobia among member-states. The following year, after a series of dramatic electoral gains by extreme right-wing parties, most notably in France, the European Commission, the Council of Ministers, and the European Parliament signed the *Joint Declaration against racism and xenophobia*.[1] Over the ensuing years, however, the Council of Ministers refused to enact new antidiscrimination legislation covering racial discrimination despite repeated requests by the European Parliament. Although there was consensus that racism and xenophobia presented serious problems requiring redress, within the Council of Ministers there was disagreement as to the appropriate form of that redress and the legal competence of European institutions to deliver it.

As a new decade dawned, the European Parliament redoubled its efforts and was joined by a coalition of NGOs. Undeterred by the Council's recalcitrance, in 1990, the European Parliament convened a second Committee of Inquiry, which produced the Ford Report that revisited issues of rising racism, the electoral successes of extreme right-wing parties, and the need for European legislation against racial discrimination (European Parliament 1991). Thereafter, as had been recommended in the report, an annual Parliamentary debate on racism was instituted, and the Parliament continued to press for legislative action. In 1991, a new ally emerged. The Starting Line Group (SLG) was formed by the British Commission for Racial Equality (CRE), the Dutch National Bureau against Racism, and the Churches Commission for Migrants in Europe (CCME) (Chopin 1999a).[2]

The SLG promptly organized a group of legal experts from across member-states to draft a directive targeting racial discrimination, and by 1993, its draft was endorsed by more than 200 NGOs and submitted to the European Parliament, which explicitly approved it in two separate resolutions.[3] The

---

[1] Joint Declaration by the European Parliament, the Council and the Commission against racism and xenophobia, June 11, 1986 (OJ C 158, 25.6.1986).

[2] Founded in 1964, the CCME is an organization of churches and ecumenical councils from Austria, Belgium, Czech Republic, Finland, France, Germany, Greece, Italy, the Netherlands, Norway, Romania Switzerland, Spain, Sweden, the United Kingdom, and Ireland. There are contacts with the Ecumenical Patriarchate (Brussels/Istanbul) and with church partners in Denmark and Russia. The General Assembly of CCME, October 1999 in Järvenpää, Finland, decided in conjunction with the Conference of European Churches and the World Council of Churches to expand its mandate to cover the whole area of migration and integration, refugees and asylum, and racism and xenophobia.

[3] 1993 resolution, OJ 1993 C 342/19, 20.12.93; 1994 resolution, para. o, OJ 1994 C 323/154, 20.11.94.

original SLG proposal relied upon Article 308 (formerly Article 235) as its legal basis. That Article empowers the European Community (EC) to take actions not explicitly authorized in the EC Treaty if such action is proven "necessary to attain, in the course of the operation of the common market, one of the objectives of the Community." When it became clear in 1993 that there was insufficient political will to use Article 308, the SLG shifted its strategy and sought an amendment to the EC Treaty that would provide clear authority for a directive on racial discrimination. From the beginning, the SLG's "founding organizations were convinced of the need to combat racism by means of binding legal measures including enforceable sanctions, that is by legislative means," as well as "of the necessity of action at the European level" (Chopin 1999b: 2). They further believed that racism and xenophobia threatened to undermine "the process of social integration taking place in the member-states of the European Union" (Chopin 1999b: 2). The SLG sought a directive as the best means of achieving the harmonization of national laws. Other directives already protect against sex discrimination.[4] In discussion with actors involved in the SLG, it appears that they were putting all of their eggs in the EU basket rather than pushing for new laws at the national level.

To those developments, the Council of Ministers responded with a series of symbolic gestures rather than substantive legislative proposals. In 1994, however, more consequential action was taken by the Council with the establishment of the Consultative Commission on Racism and Xenophobia, or Kahn Commission as it came to be known after its chair, Jean Kahn, President of the European Jewish Congress. In its final report, the Kahn Commission issued a number of recommendations, three of which are of particular importance here. First, it recommended that the EC treaty be amended to authorize the EC to fight racial discrimination. This would resolve uncertainties concerning the EC's legal competence. Second, borrowing largely from the EC's sex equality legislation, the Commission recommended a particular model. Specifically, it proposed the use of directives, similar to the Equal Pay and Equal Treatment Directives, in order to institutionalize in EC law the principle that "all individuals regardless of their colour, race, nationality, ethnic or national origins or religion should have the right of equal access to employment, equal pay and fair treatment from an employer." Third, the Kahn Commission concluded that "effective record keeping and monitoring are central to the effective implementation of equal opportunities policies and action plans." This, however, proved quite controversial. France and other countries objected, arguing that such record keeping would reinforce difference. Moreover, in the absence of national data, such records would be difficult to interpret.

---

[4] Council Directive 76/207/EEC on the implementation of the principle of equal treatment for men and women as regards access to employment, vocational training and promotion, and working conditions. Council Directive 97/80/EC on the burden of proof in cases of discrimination based on sex.

Both the Parliament and Commission subsequently endorsed the first of the two recommendations, and at the 1996 intergovernmental conference, member-states took the important step of amending the EC Treaty. As a result, the Treaty of Amsterdam provides for a new Article 6a (subsequently known as Article 13). Article 13 provides:

> Without prejudice to the other provisions of this Treaty and within the limits of the powers conferred by it upon the Community, the Council, acting unanimously on a proposal from the Commission and after consulting the European Parliament, may take appropriate action to combat discrimination based on sex, racial or ethnic origin, religion or belief, disability, age or sexual orientation.

Although it did not fulfill all of the activists' wishes, it does represent "a turning point" in EU antidiscrimination policy (Bell 1998). The SLG had hoped that the new Article would possess direct effect as does Article 119, which requires equal pay between women and men, for that would have enabled individuals to invoke the Article in national legal proceedings and ultimately to appeal to the European Court of Justice. Instead, Article 13 "simply provides a discretionary power to the Council to adopt measures as they see fit." Additionally, the SLG, as well as many commentators, had also wanted the Directive to include nationality as a prohibited ground of discrimination. The SLG revised its original draft to include religion as a prohibited category of discrimination (Bell 1998: 24–5).

In 1996, the council of the European Union adopted a joint action enjoining member-states to ensure judicial cooperation in pursuing expressive racist crimes, as well as in pursuing parties that participate in racist organizations (96/443/JHA). With the input of more than 600 NGOs, the European Network against Racism (ENAR) was founded in October 1998, and its official secretariat was installed in September 1999. Permanent national networks have been formed in each EU member-state. The ENAR is financially supported by the European Community under the Community Action Programme to Combat Discrimination.

In October 1999, the month before the Commission released its proposals for implementing Article 13, radical right parties stunned Europe by making dramatic gains at the polls in Austria and Switzerland. At Austria's October 1999 parliamentary election, the FPÖ, led by anti-immigrant politician Jörg Haider, won the second-largest number of votes. After protracted negotiations, it formed a coalition government with the Austrian People's Party in February 2000. Three weeks after Austrians went to the polls, Swiss voters reinforced perceptions of a rising radical right in Europe. Campaigning against the country's asylum policy and efforts to join the EU, the Swiss People's Party (SVP) won 23 percent of the vote, up from 15 percent at the previous election, making it the second-largest bloc in the lower house of Parliament and undermining a long-standing power-sharing arrangement. Although Switzerland was not a member of the EU, these developments stoked fears among European political elites.

The EU responded to the FPÖ's electoral performance with unprecedented action, including a bilateral diplomatic boycott. At the time, the Council was composed of largely left-leaning governments, and all three of Europe's major powers were controlled by social democratic governments. In 1997, Tony Blair's New Labour had defeated Britain's Conservatives, and the *Parti socialiste* won control of the French National Assembly; the following year, the government of German Chancellor Helmut Kohl was replaced by a coalition of the Social Democrats (SPD) and Greens. Fourteen of the EU's foreign ministers threatened to isolate Austria if it let the FPÖ into government. Some national governments took especially prominent public positions against Austria. For example, Belgian foreign minister Louis Michel called for a boycott of Austrian skiing holidays (Black 2000: 16). The French and Belgian ministers made a point of leaving the room when Austria's Social Affairs Minister, Elisabeth Sickl, a member of the FPÖ, started to address an EU meeting (Staunton 2000: 15). In March 2000, a month after the coalition government was formed, Haider stepped down as the FPÖ's party leader, although he retained his position as governor of the province of Carinthia.

Discussions on the RED began on February 13, 2000, the very month that the FPÖ entered into a coalition government. The timing of these events created a perfect opportunity for the members of the European Commission and the SLG to shame member-states into action on the proposed directive. On February 4, the *Deutsche Presse-Agentur* quoted a spokesperson for EU Social Affairs Commissioner Anna Diamantopoulou: "'[I]t is very important that given the current situation in Austria that the EU does not delay adoption of the directives on non-discrimination on grounds of race.'" On February 24, 2000, Diamantopoulou called upon member-states to adopt the directives in response to the events in Austria. In the words of one unnamed EU official, according to the *Deutsche Presse-Agentur*, "adoption of the proposals 'are a test for how far we are prepared to go to turn our principles into reality.'" On March 13, 2000, in the midst of the negotiations, Diamantopoulou again invoked the message that adoption of the directives would send in the midst of Haider. "'To weaken these proposals,'" she warned, "'would send entirely the wrong message at this sensitive time'" (*Deutsche Presse-Agentur*, 2000).

According to Niessen (2000: 212), the SLG believed that the Austrian situation created a favorable environment for the RED's adoption in two ways. First, it expected that Austria's new government "would not dare oppose the Race Directive out of fear that this would legitimize the reproach by the governments of the other fourteen member-states that the Austrian government cannot be trusted because it includes a racist party." Second, if the other governments sought to oppose the Directive, "they would be blamed and shamed for not putting their political powers where their mouth is." The SLG considered this opportunity to be short-lived. Again, according to Niessen (2000: 212), the blaming and shaming strategy could be employed only so long as the fourteen member-states maintained their pressure on Austria, a situation that the SLG estimated would "probably not last longer than one year."

In February 2000, the European Commission was pushing the European Council to negotiate on both the Racial Equality Directive and the Equal Employment Directive. The Portuguese presidency felt that it was important to split the directives in order to make the negotiations easier. With the Haider situation in the background, it was felt that Council members could not say no, particularly Austria. France was initially opposed to the RED because it took an Anglo-Saxon approach to race, singling out minority groups and emphasizing the use of civil law. However, the French were supportive of the Equal Employment directive since it was more general and fit with France's ideas of *égalité* or equality.

France had the most philosophical difficulties with the directive and the biggest shift to make in terms of the shift from criminal to civil law. Credit is due to the negotiators in Brussels who played a pivotal role in getting Paris to make the shift. In particular, French and Belgian negotiators were committed to getting the directive through in response to the formation of the People's Party-Freedom Party (OeVP-FPOe) government in Austria. The Race Equality Directive (Directive 2000/43/EC) was adopted on June 29, 2000, by the Council of the European Union, "implementing the principle of equal treatment between persons irrespective of racial or ethnic origin."

CONCLUSIONS

This chapter has focused on the impact of the rise of radical right parties on immigration control and the passage of the EU's racial equality directive. However, it should be made clear that this is a partial picture of a complex set of issues that have impacted the issue of European identity at both the national and transnational levels. What I have tried to show in this chapter is that the rise of anti-immigrant sentiment not only led to an increase in restrictive immigration policies but also created an opportunity for policies that were supportive of immigrants and ethnic minorities.

What does the development of antidiscrimination policy say about European political identity? First, it was a clear repudiation of the racist, nationalist position of the radical right. Second, it is clearly a step in defining Europe and European political identity more broadly by opening up pathways to full citizenship for minority groups. However, the passage of the RED does not take away from the fact that there are still tensions around the issue of immigration and immigrant integration. The nationalist perspective of radical right parties, and in particular politicians like Jean Marie Le Pen, has had influence across Europe. The RED, however, was more of a top-down exercise in policy making. It is clear that many elites favor a broader definition of European political identity; it is not clear that this view will be supported at the grass roots. In fact, implementation of the RED at the national level has run into many hurdles. However, it is still in the relatively early stages of being implemented, and only time will tell if it will be successful.

11

New Europe, Enduring Conflicts

The Politics of European Integration in the Enlarged EU

Nicole Lindstrom

The expansion of the European Union in 2004 to eight post-communist states of Central and Eastern Europe was heralded as the end to Europe's post-war divide. The European federalist campaigns of the 1940s had appealed to *all* European peoples to build a "free and peaceful community." Yet the Iron Curtain would exclude those falling east of it from participating in post-war European integration efforts over the next four decades. This finally changed in 1989. On the eve of the fall of the Berlin Wall, President George H. W. Bush (1989) declared in Mainz, Germany, "the Cold War began with the division of Europe. It can only end when Europe is whole." European leaders reiterated their commitment to "overcome the divisions of Europe."[1] Concretely, this first entailed offering free trade agreements and aid packages to East European states. By 1993, the European Union offered full membership to any peoples willing and able to join. Leaders of the newly independent states, in turn, heralded the end of the Cold War as "returning to Europe." Over the next decade, they set out to fulfil all the requirements of EU membership, from the protection of minority rights to adopting environmental requirements. With the accession of Croatia into the EU in 2013, the EU-28 now extends from the Atlantic to the Adriatic to the Black Sea.[2]

The process of EU enlargement has not proceeded without conflicts. One of the most intense crises emerged in the lead-up to the Iraq War. Most EU member governments (with the notable exceptions of the United Kingdom, Italy and Spain) strongly opposed the American plans for military intervention in Iraq. It also spurred large public protests across European capitals. In the face

---

[1] Margaret Thatcher declared in an August 1990 speech to the Aspen Institute, for instance, that "The European Community has reconciled antagonisms within Western Europe; it should now help to overcome divisions between East and West in Europe," accessed at www.margaretthatcher.org/speeches/.

[2] This distinction draws on Scharpf (1999).

of overwhelming West European opposition to the US intervention in Iraq, attention turned east. Central and East European states had strong foreign and security ties to the United States. However, they were also at the doorstep of joining the European Union. Many commentators at the time predicted that these states would prioritize their relations with the EU over the US. They were wrong. On 6 February 2003, the ten post-communist applicants signed a collective declaration in Vilnius pledging full support for the US intervention. The so-called Vilnius Declaration sparked prompt and critical reactions among West European leaders. French President Chirac exclaimed that East European states had "missed their opportunity to remain silent." Donald Rumsfeld's provocative demarcation a month earlier between "new" versus "old" Europe appeared prescient.

Conflicts over Iraq raised fears that not only had post-war divisions of Europe failed to be overcome, but enlargement now seemed to compromise the project of an "ever closer Union" by dividing Europe between old and new states (Habermas and Derrida 2005) This chapter argues that such a concern is unwarranted. Indeed, in the case of Iraq, new members aligned together. However, this was exceptional (Roter and Žabič 2004). We can expect that just as "old" member-states diverge daily on a host of EU-related issues, "new" Europe finds itself divided just as often. As in Western Europe, states and societies that comprise the region exhibit as many differences as similarities in their domestic policies. This chapter focuses on one source of differences that shape different views on European integration: type of capitalism. Since at least the 1970s, one of the most salient cleavages within the EU has been between more neo-liberal-oriented member-states, such as the UK, that envision the EU primarily in terms of furthering the single market, and more socially oriented states, like the Nordic states, that seek to preserve strong social welfare models against liberalizing pressures of European (and global) integration. Scholars of European integration have shown how varieties of West European capitalisms shape different positions on European integration. Given that a similar variety of capitalisms has emerged in Eastern Europe, this chapter considers whether we can observe similar patterns of political positions towards European integration among its newest members.

This chapter considers this question through a comparison of two new EU member-states: Estonia and Slovenia. These two small, newly independent states were heralded as economic success stories upon joining the EU. Yet each state can attribute its economic "success" to a very different transition strategy: Estonia pursued the most neo-liberal reform agenda of all Central and East European (CEE) states, pursuing a "shock therapy" strategy of stabilization, liberalization and privatization, while Slovenia fashioned a more gradualist strategy that used state power to simultaneously build market economies and preserve social cohesion (Bohle and Greskovits 2012). With the start of formal EU accession negotiations in 1998, each state was forced to adapt its emerging market economy differently. In general, the EU accession process led Estonia to make its economy less open, while in Slovenia it prompted further liberal reforms. The chapter considers how EU pressures inspired domestic resistance in each state around the perceived negative consequences of Europeanization to the national political economic status quo. It examines these political conflicts over single-market laws and regulations related to the free movement of capital, goods, services and labor, which comprise the core competencies, and many would argue the raison d'état, of the EU.

ENLARGEMENT VERSUS THE EUROPEAN SOCIAL MODEL?

An inherent tension underlies the European project: between promoting the free movement of goods, capital, services and labor (the single market) and maintaining social cohesion within and across its member-states (the European Social Model or ESM). To achieve the first task, European institutions seek to remove existing barriers to trade and investment across borders (or *negative* integration). To achieve the second, they seek to introduce new regulatory policies to correct market failures, creating supranational rules on consumer protection, environment or health and safety at work (or *positive* integration). Since the former President of the European Commission Jacques Delors stressed that a social dimension must be at the heart of the Single European Act, the European Union has expanded its scope in economic terms through the expansion of the common market and the introduction of a single currency in 1999 and in social terms through the introduction of strategies on employment, social inclusion and pensions. What has come to be termed the European Social Model signifies a unique, or *European*, compromise between promoting market liberalization while preserving labor and social protections embedded in European social welfare states.

While EU scholars have cited internal demographic changes, the introduction of a single currency and globalization pressures as the main threats to the European Social Model, enlargement has now been added to the list. Enlargement is argued to pose a threat in three main ways. For one, due to their lower wages and higher rates of unemployment, new member-states may threaten to put downward pressure on wages in the EU as a whole by Western firms moving east and Eastern workers moving west. With almost all barriers to trade and investment eliminated, West European-based firms will continue to take advantage of far lower wage costs and move production east. This places pressure, in turn, on Western labor to reduce its costs in order to compete. Provision for free movement of workers is also predicted to spur mass migration of East European workers to seek higher wages in the West. Migration, according to this view, will lead to reduced wages and increased unemployment in West European states as employers lay off domestic workers and replace them with migrants willing to work at a lower rate of pay. Studies seeking to measure the impact of enlargement on Western labor markets are inconclusive, documenting varying degrees of impact. Accurate assessments are difficult given that enlargement is so recent, transitional periods are still in effect and migration data are incomplete. Yet elite and popular *perceptions* of this relationship between enlargement and labor markets may be as important as reality in setting the policy agenda. With the exception of the United Kingdom, Ireland and Sweden, most EU member-state governments negotiated transitional arrangements limiting freedom of movement for new EU members for up to seven years.[3] Restrictions are tighter for Romanian and Bulgarian citizens. Despite these transition periods, the emblematic "Polish plumber" – along with the "Slovak mason," "Czech nurse" or "Estonian programmer" – appear in different guises in popular debates over the free movement of labor across the EU.

A second and related issue is the impact of enlargement on economic and social cohesion. Commonly referred to as "social dumping" or "regime competition," this argument posits that new member-states' lower tax rates, laxer environmental and labor standards and weaker social provisions will lead to a European-wide "race to the bottom." That is, in order to prevent capital from exiting, West European leaders will be motivated to slash taxes, weaken state regulations and attempt to constrain wages. Tensions over social dumping erupted in a diplomatic imbroglio in 2005 when then Finance Minister Nicolas Sarkozy stated that if new member-states could "afford" a flat tax – suggesting that such a tax would lead to subsequent decline in tax revenues – then they would not require financial help from the EU in the form of structural and cohesion funds. (Adding fuel to the fire, just weeks after Sarkozy's outburst, George H. W. Bush arrived in Bratislava to praise Slovakia's flat tax as a model for Europe.) Chancellor Gerhard Schröder also criticized the new member-states for taking aid from Brussels while reducing their tax rates to attract business from Western Europe, stating: "It is certainly unreasonable that we finance an unbridled tax competition among each other via the budget of the European Union" (Stojaspal 2004).

A third perceived impact of enlargement on the ESM is that because new member-states are far more neo-liberal in orientation, they will join forces with member-states like the United Kingdom and Ireland to push for further liberalization in the EU. This view of new member-states being more closely aligned to Anglo-Saxon than Continental values was reinforced by their positions on the Iraq war. This view also extends to economic ideals. Soon after the start of the Iraq war, Habermas and Derrida (2005) published a manifesto differentiating "core Europe" from the UK and new member-states in many of its core

---

[3] Under the so-called "2+3+2" arrangement, member-states had two years (2004–06) to open up domestic labor markets or use national legislation to restrict migration from the eight new East European states. In the next three years, states could either end the initial arrangements or keep them in place. The final two-year escape clause allowed states to defer lifting restrictions if migration is deemed to pose a threat to domestic labor markets.

values, including its social-democratic traditions. The perceived proclivity of new member-states towards neo-liberal rather than social democratic ideals is often attributed to the legacy of state socialism, where decades under communist rule leave liberal reformers sceptical of state interventions of any sort. This tendency is also attributed to the neo-liberal "shock therapy" reform agenda introduced and overseen by U.S.-based advisors in the early 1990s. EU accession was promoted as a means to reunite Europe not only in symbolic terms but also to harmonize socio-economic rules and norms across the continent. Yet in practice, the harmonization of the single market proceeded faster than the harmonization of labor and social policies. Scholars have attributed this outcome to external factors, namely the Commission's prioritization of single-market harmonization over and above softer social policies and to internal dynamics, namely the strength of transnational capital vis-à-vis labor in new member-states. According to Meardi (2000), this outcome is also a matter of will on the part of post-socialist elites: Rather than lagging behind old EU states in creating free markets, new member governments are in the vanguard of economic liberalizers.

In sum, enlargement is viewed to pose a threat to the existing and future ESM by placing downward pressure on wages, spurring regime competition and bolstering neo-liberal ideals. The divide between "new" Europe versus "old" Europe is now commonly portrayed in political-economic terms. Yet many of these accounts overlook the significant degree of variation across different new member-states in terms of their economic characteristics, political-economic institutions and prevailing norms. Bohle and Greskovits (2012) argue that we can observe at least three types of capitalism in Central and Eastern Europe: a "neoliberal" type in the Baltic, an "embedded neoliberal" type in the Visegrad states and a "neocorporatist" model in Slovenia. Similarly, applying the varieties of capitalism framework to Estonia and Slovenia, Feldmann (2006) demonstrates that Estonia exhibits characteristics of "liberal market economies" like the United Kingdom and Slovenia rather than those of a "coordinated market economy" like Germany and the Scandinavian states. The question then arises: How have these varieties of capitalism among new member-states shaped their responses to the common pressures of European integration? The following sections compare responses to the EU between two most different cases: Estonia and Slovenia.

NEO-LIBERAL OPPOSITION TO THE EU: THE CASE OF ESTONIA

Estonia's "return to Europe" was inextricably linked to its exit from the Soviet Union. Europe was framed as a "saviour" in the early stages of transition, a means for Estonia to escape its geopolitical position in the post-Soviet sphere. Estonia was the most economically developed Soviet republic. However, decades under Soviet rule left it unprepared to face new market pressures. When Estonia seceded in 1991, exports outside the Soviet Union accounted for only 2 per cent of the Estonian GDP. With its access to Russian markets blocked, Estonia experienced a radical decline in industrial production, a drastic increase in gas prices and inflation rates up to 1,000 per cent per year. Estonia's economic strategy at this critical juncture was based on a rapid opening of its markets and withdrawal of the state from the economy. By 1993, Estonia had abolished *all* tariff and non-tariff barriers to trade, including on agricultural products. Moreover, Estonians pursued rapid privatization and ensured equal treatment of foreign investors. As a result, foreign owners played a prominent role in the Estonian privatization process, purchasing around 40 per cent of the sale value of all privatized enterprises by the end of 1994. In line with this approach, poorly performing domestic firms were not extended government subsidies.

Estonia's radical unilateral trade-and-investment liberalization is unique among all CEE countries. Only the Czech Republic came close to Estonia's level of liberalization among the CEE states. By 1999, with a 0 per cent of average weighted tariffs, the only competitors to Estonia's non-discrimination between foreigners and its own citizens were Hong Kong and Singapore. How then did a country whose leaders aspired to become the "Nordic Singapore" negotiate their accession into an economic and political union whose economic policies were far less liberal? From the late 1990s, Estonia was forced to gradually *de*liberalize its economy. Because of an extraordinarily high degree of internal consensus around Estonia's neo-liberal reform agenda, the impetus for change was almost exclusively externally imposed. Estonian ruling governments fully abided by EU conditions, completely harmonizing their trade policies in conformity with the EU by 2004. However, these changes did not go uncontested. Prominent architects of Estonia's radical shock therapy strategy argued that EU membership would undermine Estonia's successful neo-liberal model.

Estonia's transition was marked by a remarkable degree of political continuity, with right-leaning parties remaining in power from independence until EU accession. All governments were pro-EU in their party platforms. Yet all had numerous EU critics among their leaders. Ivar Raig is illustrative. As long-time chair of the parliamentary economic committee, Raig was one of the founders and active supporters of Estonia's trade policy. From 1993 to 1996, he was also the chair of the government working group preparing Estonia's EU membership application. In Raig's (2003) account: "We created a very liberal trade policy. My vision was Estonia as the Nordic Singapore. Membership of the EU will threaten us economically because we enter a market with many trade restrictions. Duty free sale, free import of metal from Russia, and free trade with Ukraine will be threatened." Raig advocated that the government should push for transition periods on eliminating Estonia's bilateral trade agreements with Russia and Ukraine upon entering the EU. He pointed to a number of precedents such as Finland successfully negotiating a permanent derogation in 1995, preserving the duty-free and tax-free status of the Åland Islands. Raig also argued forcefully that in order to maintain Estonia's "attractiveness for foreign investors," both from within and outside the EU, it should opt out of "positive" integration measures when it could, and Raig evoked the United Kingdom opting out of the Social Charter as an example. Short of obtaining permanent derogations or opt-outs, Raig advocated that Estonia pursue a strategy of "minimal compliance" with EU laws and regulations.

Movements also emerged outside of government to promote anti-EU agendas. For instance, the Estonian "No to the EU Movement" (or LEIEL in Estonian), a small, independently financed non-governmental organization, sought to capitalize on anti-Soviet sentiment in its campaigns. One LEIEL leaflet donned an image of the Soviet hammer and sickle in the middle of the European Union flag. The leaflet lists fifteen ways in which the Soviet Union and the EU are alike. One likens Europol to the KGB; another compares the European Commission to the Politburo. Uno Silberg, a professor of economics and leader of LEIEL, made such comparisons at the 30th Anniversary of the People's Movement against the EU in Denmark in 2002:

> The European Union is very like a disguised Soviet Union – a form of federal bureaucratic socialism. The advocates of Estonia's independence and sovereignty are against such a super-project. They regard it as downright harmful to the harmonious development of Estonia, Denmark and other European countries that aspire to maintain their national democracy and national independence.[4]

Silberg warns that "the break-up of the old Soviet Union started from Estonia, and you can be certain that the European Union and its architects will not have an easy time either of trying to manipulate our country."[5]

Another prominent EU critic, Igor Gräzin, joined forces with Raig to create the Eurosceptic think tank Research Center Free Europe in 2003. Gräzin, a law professor at Tallin State University, suggests that the allegedly socialist – and expansionist – nature of the European project will have adverse affects on the Estonian economy. An advocate of unfettered free markets, Gräzin complains: "To qualify for EU entry, we'll have to ditch the liberal market system that has made us so successful" (Skov 2005). Estimating that "over 10 to 15 current EU governments are socialist-oriented," Gräzin says one of the reasons the EU has pressed Estonia to abandon its ultra-low-regulation, low-tax policies is that "socialism is expansionist by nature. The European Union needs Estonia more than Estonia needs the EU" (Skov 2005). He continues:

> It remains to be seen how much further the servitude Eastern Europe and the feudal superiority of the EU will expand given all the international legal tools to control the newly acquired colonies from the former Communist and Soviet bloc.

---

[4] Silberg was previously head of the department of economics in the Estonian Ministry of Agriculture for four years, a job he claims he lost because he "became active against Estonia's accession in the EU" (Skov 2005). The speech can be accessed at http://www.teameurope.info/node/214.

[5] Speech at The People's Movement against the EU's 30th Anniversary, 21 April 2002, in Copenhagen. Accessed at www.teameurope.com.

> How much new humiliation is Eastern Europeans ready to bear and how deeply
> rooted is their passive resistance? This is the silence of the lambs! (Skov 2005).

Estonian EU critics thus integrate two main critiques against the EU: that the
sovereignty-constricting nature of the EU threatens Estonia's newly won sovereignty in general and Estonia's particular and successful neo-liberal variety
of capitalism in particular. Given the high degree of consensus around neo-
liberal reforms – and the lack of resistance to these reforms by domestic interest groups or opposition parties – EU critics could portray EU pressures to
deliberalize the Estonian economy as a threat to a cohesive as well as successful
national economic policy. The elite scepticism towards the EU seemed to mirror public opinion. In 1999, 13 per cent of Estonian respondents reported that
Estonia's membership in the EU would be a "bad thing," a percentage that rose
to 21 per cent by the time Estonia entered in 2004. The popular support surrounding the "return to Europe" in the early 1990s seemed to dissipate by the
time EU membership was a reality. By 2004, less than a third of all Estonian
respondents believed the EU membership would be a "good thing" for Estonia
(Eurobarometer 2004: 1).

SOCIAL OPPOSITION TO THE EU: THE CASE OF SLOVENIA

Slovenia's initial transition strategy differed significantly from Estonia's. Instead
of following a strict doctrine of macroeconomic stabilization or market liberalization, the Slovenian government implemented a floating exchange rate,
protected domestic industries through formal and informal trade barriers, sub-
sidized "national champions" and launched a privatization scheme that kept
most ownership shares in domestic hands. Unlike Estonia that sought a sharp
break from previous political regimes, a higher degree of political continuity
existed in Slovenia, with former Yugoslav elites remaining in power throughout the 1990s and the corporatist legacy of Yugoslav worker self-management
kept largely intact. Once Slovenia entered formal EU accession negotiations
in 1997, it faced the same pressures as other CEE applicant states to eliminate barriers to the free movement of capital, goods and services. Given that
Slovenia's transition was guided by granting the state an active role in protecting domestic capital against foreign competition, liberalizing pressure from the
EU was portrayed as a threat to Slovenia's particular model of capitalism.

Like Estonia, Slovenia experienced a transition recession and high inflation
after gaining independence in 1991. However, this recession period was far
shorter and far less severe than in other post-socialist states. While Slovenia
lost important Yugoslav markets with the violent dissolution of the Socialist
Federation of Yugoslavia, these losses were partially offset with Slovenian
firms' already-established trade links with the West brought about by liberalizing reforms in the 1970s. Initial starting conditions are undoubtedly a significant factor in shaping Slovenia's gradual transition path. Yet political choices

mattered. The government's economic strategy was supported by an early consensus among employers, trade unions, political parties and economic experts. Like in Estonia, the Slovenian transition was characterized by remarkable political continuity, but with left- rather than right-leaning coalitions retaining power almost uninterrupted between 1991 and 2004. Slovenian leaders also actively rejected the "shock therapy" formula for reforms. Given that Slovenia's voucher privatization policy that favoured domestic owners went against the prevailing IMF wisdom, in 1992, Jeffrey Sachs, an economist, travelled to Ljubljana to propose an alternative IMF-endorsed plan for privatization. Then deputy prime minister, Jože Mencinger, along with other influential Slovenian economists, strongly opposed Sach's blueprint. Mencinger recalls, "We listened to them, but didn't follow their advice. Their agenda was based on ideology, not economics. And the US advisors didn't see a difference between Slovenia and Mongolia."[6] Mencinger went on to join the Board of Governors of the Slovenian Central Bank, where he pushed a macroeconomic policy agenda that continued to diverge from IMF advice.

As Slovenia entered formal accession negotiations with the EU in 1998, the EU exerted more active leverage on Slovenian economic policy. One of the earliest and most contentious episodes in Slovenia's path to Europe occurred when the European Commission, at the behest of Italy, forced Slovenia to amend its Constitution, eliminating a clause that prohibited foreigners from buying land, in order to enter EU negotiations. The Slovenian government complied, but not without prompting a heated parliamentary and public debate that raised concerns about the threat of EU membership to national interests. Opening the state-owned Slovenian banking sector to foreign competition became one of the most contentious issues in EU accession negotiations. After entering formal EU negotiations in 1998 and facing EU pressures to conform to conditions set out in the competition chapters of the *acquis*, the government began to substantially liberalize the banking sector and dismantle many of the barriers to entry that were kept in force throughout the 1990s. Yet by 2001, the government still owned nearly 90 per cent of the banking sector. Although liberalization of the banking sector in other CEE countries generated little public concern, in Slovenia a joint media campaign, public protest and political opposition obstructed the privatization of Slovenia's nationally owned banks. Public opinion polls showed that Slovenians were, along with Estonians, among the least enthusiastic East Europeans towards the EU. By the time Slovenia entered the EU in 2004, only 40 per cent of respondents reported that Slovenia's membership in the EU would be a "good thing", with 13 per cent reporting it would be a "bad thing" (European Commission 2004: 1).

Architects of Slovenia's initial transition strategy figured prominently in public debates over liberalizing measures. Mencinger continued to advocate,

---

[6] Author's interview with Jože Mencinger, Ljubljana, 13 September 2006.

now as rector of the University of Ljubljana and head of a leading economic think tank, for a greater state role in Central Bank, monetary policy and bank ownership and argued against yielding to EU pressure to privatize the banks and open the sector to foreign competition. Mencinger frequently cited a comparison of bank ownership in Western and Eastern European states to suggest that Slovenia looked quite similar to West European states. The 10 per cent of foreign bank assets in Slovenia compared favourably with the EU-15 average of 12.7 per cent and was actually higher than neighbouring Austria (3.3 per cent) and Germany (4.3 per cent). These percentages were in marked contrast to East European states in which the percentage of foreign bank ownership exceeded 75 per cent by 1997, in Estonia reaching 100 per cent. In its 2003 evaluation of Slovenia's progress in meeting EU membership criteria, the Commission stated that the "competitiveness of the economy would be supported by speeding up structural reforms," in particular the "further privatization in the financial sector." Soon after Slovenia entered the EU in 2004, a new right-leaning coalition came to power, ending the twelve-year reign of the Liberal Democratic Party. The new government immediately launched an ambitious national restructuring program, with bank liberalization at the center of reforms. In January 2005, the Slovenian Prime Minister travelled to Estonia, where he acknowledged that although Slovenia and Estonia took very different development paths, they now share the same views. Slovenia is "facing the second wave of reforms, which Estonia has already implemented," he remarked. The government appointed key neo-liberal economists to guide the measures. Yet just three months after being appointed head of the Office for Development and Growth, a leading neo-liberal economist, Jože Damijan, resigned in protest, allegedly over a disagreement with the finance minister over the slow pace of privatization. Damijan remarked to the business daily *Finance* on his resignation: "My personal views regarding the withdrawal of the state from the economy are somewhat different from the views of some ministers" (Slovenian Public Relations and Media Office 2006). In a personal interview, Damijan reflected on the government failing to push through economic reforms. Given that the government and the public are "socialist in mindset," according to Damijan, "to really change this mentality and liberalize the economy will take decades."[7] Meanwhile, Mencinger reflected on the failed reforms by saying that the government's strategy, like the EU's competitiveness strategy on which it was based, with its "abundance of empty words, newly invented phraseology and concepts, action plans and priorities, and similar claptraps" will go in to the dustbin of history as a "worthless and harmless document."[8]

---

[7] Author's interview, 11 February 2006.
[8] Author's interview, 12 February 2006. See also Mencinger (2006).

CONCLUSIONS

Through an in-depth comparison of political debates within Estonia and Slovenia over European integration, the chapter suggests that patterns of opposition to the EU based on varieties of capitalism among EU-15 states can also be found in the newest members. While Estonian critics portray European integration as an interventionist threat to Estonia's successful neo-liberal reform agenda, their Slovenian counterparts portray the European project as a neo-liberalizing threat to Slovenia's more protectionist social welfare model. Critics in both states, therefore, contest the EU as a threat to their particular national development paths but frame their critiques around different conceptions of the purpose of the EU. This suggests that conflicts over the current and future political-economic trajectory of the EU will not be waged between new and old member-states. Instead, enlargement has expanded long-standing divisions among advocates of further economic liberalization and proponents of social cohesion to include the diverse new member-states of the EU.

To what extent might we generalize beyond the cases of Estonia and Slovenia to other new EU member-states? Indeed, size matters. Generally, the smaller the state in terms of population and territory, the easier it is to achieve consensus among elites and their populations. Estonia and Slovenia are also exceptional cases for being relatively economically successful in terms of growth and cohesion despite their very different methods of achieving this success. Certainly, the better states perform economically, the less their populations will be inclined to accept externally imposed changes that may alter the status quo. In states such as Romania and Bulgaria, where economic development has lagged far behind other East European states, *any change* might appear preferable to what exists now. Estonia and Slovenia are also unique among East European states for each having exceptional political continuity from the early 1990s to 2004. Other states experienced a more typical regular alternation between right- and left-leaning governments, a factor that contributed to the creation of more "mixed" forms of capitalism, combining liberalizing measures with varying degrees of commitment towards social cohesion. Yet like in Estonia and Slovenia, the architects of a state's initial transition path tend to emerge as the most outspoken critics of EU pressures. For instance, Czech President Vaclav Klaus or Polish "shock therapist" Leszek Balcerowicz have become prominent supporters of economic neo-liberal policies and, likewise, outspoken critics of stronger EU regulatory agendas or social cohesion policies.

A final question concerns how different new member-states might be advocating for a particular balance between the single market and the European Social Model in EU decision making. Returning to our two cases, while formally Estonia and Slovenia have equal representation rights within EU bodies, in practice they are too small and weak to shape EU agendas on their own. Yet they can ally with like-minded states. One of the most salient alliances to emerge after enlargement is among proponents of further liberalization within the EU. Estonian and British leaders have spoken out openly against any move towards harmonization of tax and social policy at the EU level.[9] They have also joined forces to push for further liberalization of the service sector, first through EU legislative channels and more recently in their submitted opinions of a number of important European Court of Justice cases that ultimately ruled in favor of East European firms seeking to freely provide services in West European states (see Lindstrom 2011). Slovenian leaders have generally been far more passive. The Slovenian government coined a new slogan: "Slovenia: The New Star of Europe," but this stardom is rarely imbued with substantive claims about the "Slovenian way" to Europe. Yet Slovenian actors, including prominent economists, politicians and labor leaders, have joined forces with their counterparts across Europe to advance a model of the EU based on the principles of social cohesion. As Mencinger, one of the leading architects of the Slovenian economic model, put it, the rallying cry for Europe should be: "Plumbers of all countries, unite!"

[9] Estonian EU critics have also formed close links with their British counterparts, such as the Bruges Group, named after Margaret Thatcher's famous 1988 speech, in which she remarked: "We have not successfully rolled back the frontiers of the state in Britain, only to see them re-imposed at a European level" http://www.brugesgroup.com/about/index.live.

12

Conclusions

Regional, National, and Religious Challenges to European Identity

Andrew C. Gould

You love Italy?" Rinaldi asked Miss Ferguson in English.
"Quite well."
"No understand," Rinaldi shook his head.
"Abbastanza bene," I translated. He shook his head.
"That is not good. You love England?"
"Not too well. I'm Scotch, you see."
Rinaldi looked at me blankly.
"She's Scotch, so she loves Scotland better than England," I said in Italian.
"But Scotland is England."
I translated this for Miss Ferguson.
"Pas encore," said Miss Ferguson.
"Not really?"
"Never. We do not like the English."
"Not like the English? Not like Miss Barkley?"
"Oh, that's different. You mustn't take everything so literally."

(Hemingway 1988 [1929]: 20–1)

Each of the preceding chapters explores one part of the path that has brought Europe to where it stands today. Together, the analyses draw a map of European identities with three types of features highlighted: regions, nations, and immigrations. The scholars contributing to this volume, like other careful observers of the European scene, past and present, strive to get beneath the easy labels and explore complex interactions and developments. The example of cross-national, multilingual friendships in Hemmingway's *A Farewell to Arms* highlights the question of whether conventional understandings of identity indeed divide people. Is Europe "united in diversity," as the EU's lowest-common-denominator motto suggests, or are the easy particularisms of region, nation, or culture stronger? Which set of terms should not be taken "so literally," as Miss Ferguson enjoins, and which constructed identities should be seen as natural and real? Are actual interactions among individuals eroding boundaries and assembling new solidarities? European integration has many possible futures, and this volume, which documents the interplay of identity and integration, has many possible conclusions. This is just one.

REGIONAL LIMITS

Regionalism and European integration reinforce each other, and key actors in both processes have shared interests in redirecting the control developed by national states to subnational and supranational institutions. However, this antistate alliance does not show signs of fostering a new conception of European identity that would undermine states' robust abilities to mobilize and orient political loyalties. Instead, the alliance of regionalists and integrationists is tactical and ultimately self-limiting.

The political parties advocating for the interests of subnational regions have been almost as or equally prointegrationist as the mainstream socialist, liberal, Christian democratic, and conservative parties; regionalist parties have been much more supportive of integration than have green parties and radical parties of the right or left (see Jolly, Chapter 4, this volume, Figure 4.1). Scholars disagree whether there is more or less diversity within the regionalist party family compared to other party groupings on support versus opposition to integration, with Jolly stressing coherence (and exceptions) and Gómez-Reino (in Chapter 6) emphasizing contradictions (alongside broad trends). It is worth stating the counterfactual conditions that remain implicit in these arguments: In the absence of regionalist parties, support for integration in Europe's regions would be weaker. This counterfactual conditional is less plausible if regionalist party supporters would otherwise identify with mainstream parties and more plausible if they would otherwise support niche parties. Undeveloped by the arguments in this volume is the even stronger counterfactual: In the absence of regionalist parties, there would be less European integration policy – not just sentiment – than there already is. Regionalism supports supranationalism, if only because both processes benefit from reducing the reach of the national state.

Integration should decrease the importance of the national state in providing certain public goods, such as economic policy (establishing a market and monetary policy), foreign policy, and credible commitment to democratic rule (including the rights of minorities within regions). If the European Union's system of multilevel governance makes smaller states and near-state regional units more viable, then we should observe, as Jolly documents: (1) party elites making this argument in relevant campaigns; (2) key groups changing their support for regional governance; and (3) broader mass-level support for regional governance. Policy making in other areas, such as cultural policy, should be facilitated by creating smaller, more demographically and economically homogeneous political units. Jolly finds the support that should be expected in all three implications. Regionalist party leaders are prointegration, and voters see the EU as lowering the costs of greater autonomy for their regions. In his study of one region – Scotland – at two points in time, Jolly finds that the deepening of European integration changed attitudes toward regional independence: The 1979 devolution referendum failed (even though opinion polling showed that voters already supported devolution in principle), and the 1997 devolution referendum succeeded (despite no increase in polling support for devolution). What changed between the two periods was the voters' confidence that devolution would not lead to an isolated form of independence. Scots supported devolution in both years but actually voted for it the second time because deeper European integration increased the viability of regional autonomy and reduced the likelihood of uncontrolled splintering.

Changes in the structure of authority toward higher levels (supranationalism) and toward lower levels (decentralization) both benefit regionalist parties. These findings fit expectations but run counter to plausible alternative hypotheses. The plausible alternative to Jolly's finding would have been that supranationalism substituted for greater regional autonomy, but the evidence in the Scottish case demonstrates that supranationalism increased the attractiveness of devolution in the Scottish case and led to greater support within Scotland for enhanced regionalism. As Meguid suggests in Chapter 5, it could be that regional administrative autonomy substitutes for enhanced regionalism in European Parliamentary elections, but her evidence is firmly on the side of showing that cross-national positive differences and diachronic positive changes in decentralization increased the vote shares of regionalist parties in the six European Parliamentary elections from 1979 to 2004. Meguid's pooled, cross-sectional time-series analysis (using forty-one election-year groupings of regionalist parties in six countries) demonstrates that decentralization within national states increased the vote shares of regionalist parties in European Parliamentary elections.

Yet the nexus of regionalism, decentralization, and European integration did not foster a new European identity. Rather than encouraging sentiments of a shared future, these interlinked processes sharpened the political salience of divergent economic interests across Europe's regions. Parties representing Europe's regional oppositions to national centers have varied economic situations – ranging from disadvantaged sectors to the most advanced – and have different economic interests and policy preferences over greater market integration. Thus, the family group of regionalist parties is diverse on economic issues and its members take different positions on integration with respect to integration's implications for social and economic policy, notably whether European integration should or will involve transfer payments or protections for backward regions versus greater freedoms for the more economically advanced areas. Regionalist parties disagree because the regions they seek to represent have differing economic interests.

Regionalist parties are still generally pro-European, according to Gómez-Reino analysis in Chapter 6, but they have become less supportive of further integration. The factors that drive the positions of regionalist parties regarding European integration are economic and cultural interests, changes in the policy content of integration, and strategic positioning vis-à-vis other parties. The most important confounding factor is the regionalist party's position on the left-right spectrum. Regionalist parties in the center of the left-right spectrum generally favored integration. Regionalist parties on the extremes of left and right generally opposed integration, albeit for different reasons: Parties on the left emphasized economic issues in their opposition to integration, while parties on the right emphasized cultural issues. Each party's distance from the center on left-right issues and each party's strategic competition with mainstream parties shaped the party's stance on integration, and together these factors created diversity on the integration question across regionalist parties.

The interaction of the left-right split with the changing policy content of integration can be seen in the diachronic evolution of party positions in two illustrative cases. The Bloque Nacionalista Galego (BNG) in Spain is a left regionalist party that began in the 1980s as a critic of integration; the reasoning articulated by the party emphasized opposition to economic exploitation of Galicia and European colonialism of the region. Nevertheless, the BNG shifted its position to one of support for integration, qualified by criticism of specific policies; by the early 1990s, the BNG accepted Spain's membership in the EU. Yet it opposed both the Maastricht Treaty in 1992 and the referendum on the proposed constitutional treaty in 2005. In Italy, the Lega Nord (LN) began as a collection of regionalist parties in support of greater independence for northern Italy and strong support for European integration. The LN supported Maastricht in 1992 but then opposed the proposed constitution and the watered-down treaty that finally emerged, the Lisbon Treaty (2009). Thus, the two parties started at opposite poles: The BNG opposed integration and the LN favored integration. Both parties tempered their views on integration while still disagreeing on Maastricht: The BNG was anti- and the LN pro-Maastricht. Subsequently, they have narrowed and virtually reversed positions: The BNG accepted EU membership but opposed both the primacy of states in decision making and the neoliberal social model of the EU. The LN supported economic integration with the rest of Europe's advanced economy but opposed the erosion of sovereignty in further integration. Its Euroscepticism aided the party in differentiating itself from its coalition partners in government and in tapping into populist concerns over immigration via opposition to the possible EU membership of Turkey as a Muslim-majority country.

Although integration aids regionalism, it simultaneously exposes the limits of cross-regional commonalities. Regionalist political parties have indeed benefitted from the prospect of weakening national powers and the specific gains in European integration; regional elites used integration to provide a new frame for regional autonomy and voters conditioned their support for regionalism on reduced costs for breaking down national markets. Yet the debates over the economic implications of integration – including the key questions of who gains, who loses, and who will be compensated – pulled regionalist parties in different directions. Of the regionalist parties represented in the EU in 2009, seven were members of the European Free Alliance and shared a left-progressive stance, while the other ten parties were members of other groups of more traditional parties with centrist and center-right economic positions (see Gómez-Reino, Chapter 6, this volume, Table 6.1). The absence of agreement on economic issues damaged the consensus-forging ability of any larger institution, such as a more robust European-level organization of regionalist parties. The absence of such an institution, and with none on the horizon for the near future, means that, at the mass level, there is no partisan organization seeking to build a new European identity based on regions to counter identities oriented to national states.

DURABLE NATIONALISM

Nationalism poses a formidable obstacle to the formation of a European identity, and nationalism is not fading away as the founders of community institutions had anticipated. While interstate war among Europeans no longer fuels nationalist sentiments, the increasing internal diversity of European societies, at least in the short and medium run, as Messina shows in Chapter 3, provides new opportunities for nationalist movements to stoke fears of outsiders, force mainstream parties to adjust their appeals, and shape state policies. Europeans who are concerned about too much diversity in religion, ethnicity, and national background do not look to the EU for solutions. Rather, they look to their own national states. Nationalist parties propose that the EU should not be enlarged to incorporate a Muslim-majority country, Turkey, and national governments should tighten rules for immigration, citizenship, and national belonging.

At the level of mass sentiment, exclusive identification with Europe remains rare, while the most common attitudes are to feel both European and national or to feel national alone. According to Citrin and Wright's analysis in Chapter 2, the prevailing sentiment among European publics is "nation first and Europe too." As for the extremes on either side, national resistance to further integration is far more common than is Europeanist support for more integration. There are correlates of pro-European sentiment: leftists, women, city dwellers, and those with an immigrant history are more likely to be pro-European – and such groups are growing – but there is very little Europe-first identity.

The modest trend toward a dual identity of national and European has not increased the small share of those with a Europe-only identification. In responses to Eurobarometer surveys in 1999 and 2007, the share of respondents who say they see themselves as nationals only declined by 6 percent, while the share that see themselves as nationals and European increased 5 percent. Still, the share of respondents who see themselves as European only has not changed (Citrin and Wright, Chapter 2, this volume, Table 2.1). These trends are modest compared to the size of the underlying shares that privilege the nation rather than

Europe in self-reported identity: 43 percent of respondents identify exclusively as nationals and 45 percent identify as nationals first, Europeans second. Some of these data are highly sensitive to category choices. When the measure allows for the possibility that a person could feel equally attached to the nation and to Europe, almost twice as many people feel attached to both (64 percent) as feel attached to the nation alone (28 percent). As with the first measure, however, few people are attached to Europe exclusively (3 percent) or to neither (6 percent; Chapter 2, this volume, Table 2.2).

Related to these trends in attachment to Europe are strong attitudinal limits to European integration as a policy. Respondents to European surveys are concerned about crime, job loss, and the erosion of welfare states, which are amalgams of economic and cultural concerns. However, European publics, including those identifying with both nation and Europe, are also concerned about more exclusively cultural issues, such as the loss of national linguistic and cultural distinctiveness. There is very little antinationalist, pro-European sentiment; if European integration threatens a nation's linguistic and cultural distinctiveness, then the public will choose distinctiveness over integration. Supermajorities – even among those who identify themselves as both nationals and Europeans – want their national state to have authority over education, welfare, and cultural policy.

At the mass level, then, antinationalism is not fueling supranationalism, as positive national feeling remains strong. The popularity of national identification makes it important to understand what people mean by belonging to the nation. Nationalists and Europeanists alike consider language ability and respect for national political institutions to be important for belonging to the nation. Yet beyond this agreement, those who identify with Europe have a reduced conception of what national identity entails. Few Europeanists agree with most nationalists that being born in the country, having the country's citizenship, and feeling like a national are important for being a national. Those who are equally attached to both the nation and Europe resemble those who are attached only to the nation, except that they are less likely to view birth in the country and citizenship to be important for national belonging. Just small minorities of all groups consider being Christian important to being a member of the nation. Those who identify as Europeans first are more likely to hold positive attitudes about immigration and the maintenance of multiple cultures within a single society than are those who place priority on national identification. Self-identified Europeans-first espouse cosmopolitan values. Yet they have a lowest-common-denominator conception of national belonging and have yet to formulate a compelling alternative identity with broad appeal.

The rich, broad-appeal conceptions of identity currently available, however, involve layers of meaning that make European and national identities difficult to blend. The key is that each national identity developed historically in processes linked to interstate rivalry and conflict. Cinnirella and Hamilton in Chapter 8 find evidence for the residues of these processes by comparing the identity assessments that Asian and white residents of Britain make for themselves. Asians report greater compatibility between British and European identities, while white respondents report greater incompatibility between these identities (white respondents put greater distance between their British and European identities, while Asian respondents put both identities close to each other and to their own selves). British and European identities are positively correlated among Asians – that is, those who locate British identity close to the self also locate European identity close to the self. Yet the same identities are negatively correlated among Britons: Those who locate British identity close to the self put greater distance between themselves and European identity.

Among Asians, British identity was uncorrelated with attitudes toward Europe, whereas among Britons, British identity was negatively associated with attitudes toward Europe. Cinnirella and Hamilton argue that the native population has – as encouraged by politicians, media, and cultural institutions – stronger identification with European historical events than does the immigrant population. Thus, the European World Wars and Britain's fraught relationships with Germany and with France weigh on the mind of a native Briton when it comes to locating British and European identities with respect to the self, whereas for an Asian Briton these European conflicts do not create distance between the self and Europe.

Even when national and European identities are both strong, they are nested in an ordering that gives priority to the nation. Asian and white residents of Britain consider their British identity closer to themselves than their European identity. National identity is still the more central identity; it is a gateway to European identity, not the other way around. Even newcomers to the nation and to Europe consider themselves nationals first, Europeans second. Cinnirella and Hamilton's study offers a clear model for testing the centrality and priority ordering of political identities.

The interactions of substate nationalism in Scotland and antipathy to English immigrants and Muslim immigrants (mostly from Pakistan), as laid out by Miller and Hussain in Chapter 7, show the layering of new and old conflicts. In the case of Scotland, nationalism has been redefined by political party elites as being compatible with membership in the EU and with a multicultural Scottish nation. Public opinion on underlying issues has remained relatively constant, but the Scottish National Party has become more viable and more moderate in the eyes of voters. Such findings are supported by evidence about party elites and voting trends. In order to get at "street-level" phenomena, Miller and Hussain investigate the anti-Muslim and anti-English sentiments of majority Scots, that is, Scots who are not themselves or not married to a Muslim or English person.

Anti-outsider sentiments against each group at the mass level are remarkably similar in terms of overall levels of anti-outsider sentiment and the correlates of those sentiments. There is somewhat more resentment against Muslim immigrants than there is resentment against English immigrants, but not much more.

In most matters – such as in fear of economic competition, attitudes toward working with someone from the other group, and assessments of the newcomers' loyalty to Scotland – majority Scots are just as concerned about the English as they are about Muslims. The strongest differences in attitudes toward the two outsider groups are on issues of family relations: Endogamy and opposition to acquiring a relative by marriage into one's family are much stronger with respect to Muslims than to the English. Respondents who espouse Scottish nationalism are more likely to score higher on Anglophobia but not on Islamophobia, which confirms the historic roots of Scottish nationalism and suggests that Scottish nationalism has the possibility of openness to religious and ethnic pluralism. In at least the Scottish case, immigrant diversity and regional nationalism are not locked in a negative spiral of conflict and exclusion.

RELIGION AND OTHERNESS

Who is a real European? The question has as many answers as respondents – citizens and participants, scholars and observers – and even more if one counts what each person answers in different contexts. Yet despite the myriad voices, only a few institutions, notably European member states and the European Union, have the authority to legislate what it means to be a citizen and who shall enjoy the full rights of belonging. As Givens's analysis sustains, the EU has tightened the criteria for joining the European polity in several legal spheres related to immigration – notably in asylum, legal and illegal migration, and visas and border control (see Chapter 10, this volume, Table 10.1). These steps toward narrowing who can become European fall short of the reforms advocated by radical, right-wing parties that achieved some measure of electoral successes in France, Austria, Germany, and Denmark since the 1980s. Mainstream parties in national governments and the EU Council enacted immigration-restricting policies as strategic concessions to deprive right-wing competitors of an electoral appeal.

Yet with respect to antidiscrimination policies, the EU adopted expansive reforms that entrenched a wide reach for the full legal protection of the European Union and its member states. These policies, too, Givens maintains, countered the prospect of even more right-wing electoral successes. The focus on race shamed right-wing parties to assert an inclusive legal-cultural definition of belonging to Europe and raised institutional barriers to restrictive policies. The Racial Equality Directive of 2000 is a clear example, and it fits within a broader set of policies, ranging from the 1999 Charter of Fundamental Rights and Treaty of Amsterdam (especially Articles 12 and 13) to the 2009 Treaty of Lisbon (which gave binding legal effect to the Charter). These and related initiatives sought to invalidate discrimination based in gender, race, color, ethnic origin, social origin, genetic features, language, religion and belief, political and other opinions, membership of a national minority, property, birth, disability, age, sexual orientation, and nationality.

The protections offered to citizens in each category are varied, with minority religions and beliefs enjoying weak authoritative inclusiveness. Religion and belief were relegated to a narrow directive that prohibited discrimination just in occupation and employment; the directive authorized individual legal recourse only at the national level and set a high standard for new EU action, namely unanimity among the member states (Directive 2000/78/EC, 27 November 2000). In contrast, the racial equality directive demanded inclusiveness in many different spheres: employment, union membership, education, social protection, health care, social security, and the supply of goods and services such as housing – all of which are both public and private. Moreover, individuals were given legal assistance via the creation of specialized equality-monitoring bodies in each member state; and the EU can legislate quickly, on the basis of qualified majority voting (Directive 2000/43/EC, 29 June 2000). Gender equality is even more strongly and consistently asserted; sex discrimination is barred in virtually all realms of social and political life, and the model of gender equality protections is the standard against which advocacy groups measure and assess protections for other categories. In practice, results have matched the different levels of institutional commitment: The agency that monitors compliance with full-citizenship directives found that member states, employers, and unions are familiar with and have taken the necessary steps regarding gender equality but have made limited progress in enforcing racial and ethnic inclusiveness and have faltered on ensuring rights for religious and cultural minorities (European Union Agency for Fundamental Rights 2010: 214–17).

In the formerly communist member states, one knew what it meant to be European in the 1980s and 1990s: It meant to be non-Soviet. That is no longer so. The "other" against which identities form had a clear reference for elites and masses in Central and Eastern Europe. Yet with the disappearance of Leninist regimes and then enlargements in 2004 and 2007, Europe's old other fell into history, and political life focused on differences, including over the issue of continued economic liberalization versus social cohesion, both within the new member states and with respect to EU policies. As shown in Lindstrom's (Chapter 11) analysis of Estonia and Slovenia, each new member state had advocates of the neoliberal single market as well as proponents of a European social model. For shock therapists, the EU still contained too much social and economic regulation, while those seeking social cohesion opposed the market-based core elements of the EU *acquis* (the free movement of goods, labor, services, and capital). Taken together, these opposing visions of the EU and the integration of new member states generated a common concern about the challenges to national interests entailed by EU membership that is no longer checked by a coherent ideological and political opponent.

With the fall of Communism, it is Europe's Muslims who now straddle the deepest rift in European identity formation. Until asserted otherwise, they are taken to represent a religious, cultural, and political worldview opposed to Europe's own imagined traditions. Non-Muslim Europeans see Islam – or at least Islamists – as the enemy of their Europe, whichever Europe that is: modern or traditional, secular or Christian (or Jewish), multicultural or monocultural, globalized or solidaristic. The traces of a fraught position can be seen in the intellectual references of Muslims that Gould documents in Chapter 9, including among those elites promoted and self-selected to promulgate the inclusive project of Muslim incorporation into the European polity. Muslim elites cite secular and Christian European founders of free thinking and a religious citizenship alongside Muslim advocates of universal principles in the "overlapping consensus" of contemporary liberalism and Islam, in the borrowed words of John Rawls and that apply, for some analysts, to the thought of Tariq Ramadan (March 2007). Yet Ramadan himself is a polarizing figure, and it remains a matter for vigorous debate where to draw the similarities and differences between his thought and that of self-described conservative Muslims, contemporary state-sponsored clerics in Muslim-majority countries, key figures in the Islamist movements, and historic thinkers in the Muslim tradition from North Africa, Persia, the Arab world, Asia, and Europe's own Muslim past. The contrast between sympathetic treatments (Buruma 2007) and unfavorable interpretations (Berman 2007, 2010; Fourest 2007) could hardly be greater. Absent an emerging consensus on how to combine Muslim faith and European citizenship, Islam is for many a sign of what is excluded from European self-understandings.

FINAL REFLECTIONS

Given the aforementioned challenges, upon which principles is a European political identity – if it ever emerges – more likely than not to be founded? First, a robust European identity must impart some sense of exclusivity. It must develop the idea that Europeans – including Europe's new ethnic, racial, and religious minorities – are distinct from other people (Castiglione 2009: 36). In order for a European identity to take firm root and expand, it is necessary, in Smith's (1992: 75) phrase, that it be in "opposition to the identities of significant others." Indeed, the success or strength of any political identity project – including a European political identity – ultimately "depends upon first, the other identities with which it must compete and, second, the strength of the competing institutions that buttress those identities" (Berezin 2003: 13).

Second, despite the amorphousness of Europe's current borders (Jacobs and Maier 1998: 1), a European identity must likely suggest some sense of shared, geographical neighborhood. According to Shils (1995: 100), every polity is, of necessity, territorially bounded. As Berezin and Schain (2003: vii) argue, "territory unites issues of identity and membership in physical space. Territory excludes and includes, and it is intimately connected to issues of membership." Although the EU currently has no permanent territorial borders, it nevertheless seems reasonable to assume that in the absence of a bounded geographical neighborhood, Europe cannot become a space within which competing interests and actors can pursue acceptance and recognition; hence, it cannot become a true polity. This said, to the degree that a robust European political identity eventually emerges, it is unlikely, even in the most propitious circumstances, to be uniformly embraced across the member state countries (Bruter 2005: 135). Rather, existing intercountry differences will undoubtedly persist (Díez Medrano 2003).

Whether a robust European identity *will* eventually emerge is, of course, unknown and, indeed, unknowable at this point in European history. As the chapters in this volume collectively underscore, the ideational obstacles to this goal remain formidable and are not likely to wane any time soon. Although the notion of a European identity is gradually emerging, it remains to be seen if its progress can keep pace with that of the contemporary forces or potential forces of political and social fragmentation explored in this volume. The economic crisis in Europe since 2008 has been met with policy responses – austerity, bailouts, and uncoordinated strategies for growth – that have not laid institutional foundations for identities beyond nation-states. The crisis and responses to it have been debated in terms of blame and distribution (who caused the problems and who benefits from the solutions) rather than the imperatives of solidarity (our mutual obligations and our duty to respond to a common foe). Even if more strongly prointegrationist policies, such as Eurobonds with collective responsibility, are eventually adopted, the perspectives in this volume suggest that social bonds across political borders will likely remain underdeveloped. The identities of region, religion, and nation are just as constructed as any European identity – and just as immune to weakening through exceptions, as Hemingway's characters observed – yet these forms of belonging and exclusion all have older and denser institutions behind them than does a European identity. The goal of the emergence of a European identity and, with it, the goal of ever-closer European union very much remains unfulfilled.

References

Albertazzi, Danielle and Duncan McDonnell. 2005. "The Lega Nord in the Second Berlusconi Government: In a League of its Own," *West European Politics*, 28, 5: 952–72.

Aleinikoff, Thomas A. 1998. "A Multicultural Nationalism?" *American Prospect*, 36: 80–7.

Alesina, Alberto and Enrico Spolaore. 1997. "On the Number and Size of Nations," *Quarterly Journal of Economics*, 112, 4: 1027–56.

2003. *The Size of Nations*. Cambridge, MA: MIT Press.

Alesina, Alberto, Enrico Spolaore, and Romain Wacziarg. 2000. "Economic Integration and Political Disintegration," *American Economic Review*, 90, 5: 1276–96.

Alesina, Alberto and Romain Wacziarg. 1998. "Openness, Country Size and Government," *Journal of Public Economics*, 69, 3: 305–21.

Alsayyad, Nezar and Manuel Castells, eds. 2002. *Muslim Europe or Euro-Islam: Politics, Culture, and Citizenship in the Age of Globalization*. Lanham, MD: Lexington Books.

Aluffi Beck-Peccoz, Roberta and Giovanna Zincone, eds. 2004. *The Legal Treatment of Islamic Minorities in Europe*. Leuven, Belgium: Peeters.

Amiraux, Valerie and Patrick Simon. 2006. "There Are No Minorities Here," *International Journal of Comparative Sociology*, 47, 3–4: 191–215.

Anderson, Benedict. 2006. *Imagined Communities: Reflections on the Origin and Spread of Nationalism*, revised edition. London and New York: Verso Books.

Archibugi, Daniele. 2009. "Which Language for Europe?" *Open Democracy*. June. http://www.opendemocracy.net/article/which-language-for-europe.

Arzaghi, Mohammed and J. Vernon Henderson. 2005. "Why Countries Are Fiscally Decentralizing," *Journal of Public Economics*, 89, 7: 1157–89.

Augenstein, Daniel. 2008. "A European Culture of Religious Tolerance," EUI Law Working Paper No. 4. January.

Bańkowski, Zenon and Emilios Christodoulidis. 1998. "The European Union as an Essentially Contested Project," *European Law Journal*, 4, 4: 341–54.

Barni, Monica and Guus Extra, eds. 2008. *Mapping Linguistic Diversity in Multicultural Contexts*. Berlin and New York: Mouton de Gruyter.

Bar-tal, Daniel and Ervin Staub. 1997. "Patriotism: Its Scope and Meaning," in Daniel Bar-Tal and Ervin Staub, eds., *Patriotism in the Lives of Individuals and Nations*. Chicago: Nelson-Hall, 1–19.

Bartolini, Stephano. 2005. *Restructuring Europe: Centre Formation, System Building and Political Restructuring*. Oxford, UK: Oxford University Press.

Barzini, Luigi. 1983. *The Impossible Europeans*. London: Weidenfeld and Nicholson.

Baumann, Gerd. 1996. *Contesting Culture: Discourses of Identity in Multi-ethnic London*. Cambridge, UK: Cambridge University Press.

Beck, Nathaniel and Jonathan Katz. 1995. "What to Do (And Not to Do) with Time-Series Cross Section Data," *American Political Science Review*, 89, 3: 634–48.

1996. "Nuisance versus Substance: Specifying and Estimating Time-Series-Cross-Section Models," *Political Analysis*, 6, 1: 1–36.

2001. "Throwing Out the Baby with the Bath Water: A Comment on Green, Kim, and Yoon," *International Organization*, 55, 2: 487–95.

Béland, Daniel and André Lecours. 2005. "The Politics of Territorial Solidarity: Nationalism and Social Policy Reform in Canada, the United Kingdom, and Belgium," *Comparative Political Studies*, 38, 6: 676–703.

Bell, Mark. 1998. *EU Antidiscrimination Policy: From Equal Opportunities between Women and Men to Combating Racism*. Brussels: European Parliament Directorate General for Research.

2002. "Beyond European Labour Law? Reflections on the EU Racial Equality Directive," *European Law Journal*, 8, 3: 384–99.

Benedictus, Leo. 2005. "Almost Every Race, Colour, Nation and Religion on Earth," *The Guardian*, January 21. http://www.guardian.co.uk/uk/2005/jan/21/britishidentity1.

Berezin, Mabel. 2003. "Territory, Emotion, and Identity: Spatial Recalibration in a New Europe," in Mabel Berezin and Martin Schain, eds., *Europe without Borders: Remapping Territory, Citizenship, and Identity in a Transnational Age*. Baltimore, MD: Johns Hopkins University Press, 1–32.

2009. *Illiberal Politics in Neoliberal Times: Culture, Security and Populism in the New Europe*. New York: Cambridge University Press.

Berezin, Mabel and Martin Schain. 2003. "Preface," in Mabel Berezin and Martin Schain, eds., *Europe without Borders: Remapping Territory, Citizenship, and Identity in a Transnational Age*. Baltimore, MD: Johns Hopkins University Press, vii-xii.

Berger, Peter, Grace Davie, and Effie Fokas. 2008. *Religious America, Secular Europe?* Burlington, VT: Ashgate.

Berman, Paul. 2007. "Who's Afraid of Tariq Ramadan? The Islamist, the Journalist, and the Defense of Liberalism," *The New Republic*, June 4: 37–63.

2010. *The Flight of the Intellectuals*. Brooklyn, NY: Melville House.

Berry, J. W., U. Kim, S. Power, M. Young, and M. Bujaki. 1989. "Acculturation Attitudes in Plural Societies," *Applied Psychology: An International Review*, 38, 2: 185–206.

Betz, Hans-Georg. 1994. *Radical Right Populism in Western Europe*. New York: St. Martin's Press.

Bjørklund, Tor, and Jørgen Goul Andersen. 2002. "Anti-Immigration Parties in Denmark and Norway: The Progress Parties and the Danish People's Party," in

Martin Schain, Aristide Zolberg, and Patrick Hossay, eds., *Shadows over Europe: The Development and Impact of the Extreme Right in Western Europe*. New York: Palgrave, 107–36.

Black, Ian. 2000. "Austrian Leader Asks for a Chance," *The Guardian*, March 9.

Bleich, Erik. 2003. *Race Politics in Britain and France: Ideas and Policymaking since the 1960s*. New York: Cambridge University Press.

Bohle, Dorothee and Béla Greskovits. 2007. "Neoliberalism, Embedded Neoliberalism and Neocorporatism: Towards Transnational Capitalism in Central-Eastern Europe," *West European Politics*, 30, 3: 443–66.

2012. *Capitalist Diversity on Europe's Periphery*. Cornell, NY: Cornell University Press.

Bolfikova, Eva and Miroslav Frankovsky. 1997. "Inter-generational Differences in Identification with 'Macro' Societal Units," *Sociologia*, 29, 1: 55–68.

Bolton, Patrick and Gerard Roland. 1997. "The Breakup of Nations: A Political Economy Analysis," *Quarterly Journal of Economics*, 112, 4: 1057–90.

Bolton, Patrick, Gerard Roland, and Enrico Spolaore. 1996. "Economic Theories of the Breakup and Integration of Nations," *European Economic Review*, 40, 3–5: 697–705.

Bowen, John R. 2004. "Pluralism and Normativity in French Islamic Reasoning," in Robert W. Hefner, ed., *Remaking Muslim Politics: Pluralism, Contestation, Democratization*. Princeton, NJ: Princeton University Press, 326–46.

Bowler, Shaun and David M. Farrell. 1993. "Legislator Shirking and Voter Monitoring: Impacts of European Parliament Electoral Systems upon Legislator-Voter Relationships," *Journal of Common Market Studies*, 31, 1: 45–69.

Brancati, Dawn. 2006. "Decentralization: Fueling or Dampening the Fames of Ethnic Conflict and Secessionism," *International Organization*, 60, 3: 651–85.

2008. "The Origins and Strength of Regional Parties," *British Journal of Political Science*, 38, 1: 135–59.

Braun, Daniela. 2008. "Mannheim Documentation of the Results of the European Elections, 1979 to 2004." http://www.mzcs.uni-mannheim.de/projekte/euro_elections/, accessed September 18, 2008.

Breuilly, John. 1993. *Nationalism and the State*. 2nd edition. Manchester, UK: Manchester University Press.

Brewer, Marilynn B. 1991. "The Social Self: On Being the Same and Different at the Same Time," *Personality and Social Psychology Bulletin*, 17, 5: 475–82.

2000. "Superordinate Goals vs. Superordinate Identity as Bases of Cooperation," in Dora Capozza and Rupert Brown, eds., *Social Identity Processes*. London: Sage Publications, 117–32.

Brinegar, Adam P. and Seth K. Jolly. 2004. "Integration: Using the Eurobarometer to Measure Support," in John G. Geer, ed., *Public Opinion and Polling around the World*. Santa Barbara, CA: ABC-CLIO, 497–503.

2005. "Location, Location, Location: National Contextual Factors and Public Support for European Integration," *European Union Politics*, 6, 2: 155–180.

Brinegar, Adam P., Seth K. Jolly, and Herbert Kitschelt. 2004. "Varieties of Capitalism and Political Divides over European Integration," in Gary Marks and Marco R. Steenbergen, eds., *European Integration and Political Conflict*. New York: Cambridge University Press, 62–92.

Bromley, Catherine, John Curtice, and Lisa Given. 2007. *Attitudes to Discrimination in Scotland: 2006*. Edinburgh: Scottish Centre for Social Research.

Brown, Alice, David McCrone, and Lindsay Patterson. 1999. *The Scottish Electorate: The 1997 General Election and Beyond*. New York: St. Martin's Press.

Brown, Rupert. 2000. "Social Identity Theory: Past Achievements, Current Problems and Future Challenges," *European Journal of Social Psychology*, 30, 6: 745–78.

Brubaker, Rogers. 1992. *Citizenship and Nationhood in France and Germany*. Cambridge, MA: Harvard University Press.

  1996. *Nationalism Reframed: Nationhood and the National Question in the New Europe*. Cambridge, UK: Cambridge University Press.

  2001. "The Return of Assimilation? Changing Perspectives on Immigration, and its Sequels in France, Germany, and the United States," *Ethnic and Racial Studies*, 24, 4: 531–48.

  2004. *Ethnicity without Groups*. Cambridge, MA: Harvard University Press.

Brubaker, Rogers and Frederick Cooper. 2000. "Beyond 'Identity'," *Theory and Society*, 29, 1: 1–47.

Bruter, Michael. 2004. "Civic and Cultural Components of a European Identity: A Pilot Model of Measurement of Citizens' Levels of European Identity," in Richard K. Herrmann, Thomas Risse, and Marilyn B. Brewer, eds., *Transnational Identities: Becoming European in the EU*. Lanham, MD: Rowman and Littlefield, 186–213.

  2005. *Citizens of Europe? The Emergence of a Mass European Identity*. New York: Palgrave.

Buruma, Ian. 2007. "Tariq Ramadan Has an Identity Issue," *The New York Times Magazine*, February 4, http://www.nytimes.com/2007/02/04/magazine/04ramadan.t.html?pagewanted=all.

Bush, H. W. 1989. "The End of the Cold War and the Victory of Freedom and Democracy Unleashing the Force of Freedom," Mainz, West Germany, accessed at: http://www.rjgeib.com/biography/europe/prague/freedom.html.

Caeiro, Alexandre. 2003. "The European Council for Fatwa and Research," paper presented at the Fourth Mediterranean Social and Political Research Meeting, Florence and Montecatini Terme, March 19–23.

  2004. "The Social Construction of Shari a: Bank Interest, Home Purchase, and Islamic Norms in the West," *Die Welt des Islams*, 44, 3: 351–75.

Caporaso, James A. and Min-hyung Kim. 2009. "The Dual Nature of European Identity: Subjective Awareness and Coherence," *Journal of European Public Policy*, 16, 1: 19–42.

Carey, Sean. 2002. "Undivided Loyalties. Is National Identity an Obstacle to European Integration?" *European Union Politics*, 3, 4: 387–413.

Carey, Sean and Mathew Lebo. 2001. "Europe but not Europeans: The Impact of National Identity on Public Support for European Union," paper presented at the 29th Joint Sessions of the European Consortium for Political Research, April 6–11, Grenoble.

Casanova, José. 2004. "Religion, European Secular Identities, and European Integration," Eurozine.com, http://www.eurozine.com/pdf/2004-07-29-casanova-en.pdf.

Casella, Alessandra and Jonathan S. Feinstein. 2002. "Public Goods in Trade: On the Formation of Markets and Jurisdictions," *International Economic Review*, 43, 2: 437–61.

Cassidy, Clare and Karen Trew. 1998. "Identities in Northern Ireland: A Multidimensional Approach," *Journal of Social Issues*, 54, 4: 725–40.

Castano, Emanuela. 2004. "European Identity: A Social-Psychological Perspective," in Richard K. Herrmann, Thomas Risse, and Marilyn B. Brewer, eds., *Transnational Identities: Becoming European in the EU* . Lanham, MD: Rowman and Littlefield, 40–58.

Castells, Manuel. 2002. "The Construction of European Identity," statement prepared for the European Presidency of the European Union. http://chet.org.za/files/CASTELLS%202004%20European%20Identity.pdf.

Castiglione, Dario. 2009. "Political Identity in a Community of Strangers," in Jeffrey T. Checkel and Peter J. Katzenstein, eds., *European Identity*. New York: Cambridge University Press, 29–51.

Castles, Francis G. 1999. "Decentralization and the Post-War Economy," *European Journal of Political Research*, 36, 1: 27–53.

Cerutti, Furio. 2003. "A Political Identity of the Europeans?" *Thesis 11*, 72, 1: 26–45.

Chari, Raj S., Suvi Iltanen, and Sylvia Kritzinger, 2004. "Examining and Explaining the Northern League's 'U-Turn' from Europe," *Government and Opposition*, 39, 4: 423–50.

Checkel, Jeffery T. and Peter J. Katzenstein, eds. 2009. *European Identity*. New York: Cambridge University Press.

Chopin, Isabelle. 1999a. "The Starting Line: A Harmonized Approach to the Fight against Racism and to Promote Equal Treatment," *European Journal of Migration and Law*, 1, 1: 111–29.

1999b. "Campaigning Against Racism and Xenophobia: From a Legislative Perspective at European Level," European Network against Racism, November.

Chyssochoou, Xenia. 2000a. "Memberships in a Superordinate Level: Re-thinking European Union as a Multi-National Society," *Journal of Community and Applied Psychology*, 10, 5: 403–20.

Chryssochoou, Xenia. 2000b. "Multicultural Societies: Making Sense of New Environments and Identity," *Journal of Community and Applied Psychology*, 10, 5: 343–54.

2003. "Studying Identity in Social Psychology: Some Thoughts on the Definition of Identity and its Relation to Action," *Language and Politics*, 2, 2: 225–42.

Ciciora, Alice. 2009. "Integrating Islam in Ireland." Senior Honors Thesis, Department of Political Science, University of Notre Dame, Notre Dame, IN.

Cinnirella, Marco. 1996. "A Social Identity Perspective on European Integration," in Glynis Breakwell and Evanthia Lyons, eds., *Changing European Identities: Social Psychological Analyses of Social Change*. Oxford, UK: Butterworth-Heinemann, 253–74.

1997. "Towards a European Identity? Interactions between the National and European Social Identities Manifested by University Students in Britain and Italy," *British Journal of Social Psychology*, 36, 1: 19–31.

1998. "Manipulating Stereotype Rating Tasks: Understanding Questionnaire Context Effects on Measures of Attitudes, Social Identity and Stereotypes," *Journal of Community and Applied Social Psychology*, 8, 5: 345–62.

2001. "Forever the Reluctant Europeans?" *The Psychologist*, 14, 7: 344–5.

Cinpoes, Radu. 2008. "Thematic Articles: National Identity and European Identity," *Journal of Identity and Migration Studies*, 2, 1: 3–14.

Citrin, Jack and John Sides. 2004a. "Can Europe Exist Without Europeans? Problems of Identity in a Multinational Community," in Margaret Hermann, ed., *Advances in Political Psychology*. Oxford: Elsevier Ltd., 41–69.

Citrin, Jack and John Sides. 2004b. "More than Nationals: How Identity Choice Matters in the New Europe," in Richard K. Herrmann, Thomas Risse, and Marilynn Brewer, eds., *Transnational Identities: Becoming European in the EU*. Lanham, MD: Rowman and Littlefield, 161–85.

Citrin, Jack and John Sides. 2008. "Immigration and the Imagined Community in Europe and the United States," *Political Studies*, 56, 3: 33–56.

Citrin, Jack, Cara Wong, and Brian Duff. 2001. "The Meaning of American National Identity: Patterns of Ethnic Conflict and Consensus," in Richard D. Ashmore, Lee Jussim, and David Wilder, eds., *Social Identity, Intergroup Conflict, and Conflict Resolution*. New York: Oxford University Press, 71–100.

Citrin, Jack and Matthew Wright. 2008. "The Collision between National Identity and Multiculturalism in Mass Publics," paper presented at the annual meeting of the Midwest Political Science Association, Chicago.

Condor, Susan. 2001. "Nations and Nationalisms: Particular Cases and Impossible Myths," *British Journal of Social Psychology*, 40, 2: 177–81.

Council of the European Union, the. 2000. "Racial Equality Directive," http://eur-lex. europa.eu/LexUriServ/LexUriServ.do?uri=CELEX:32000L0043:en:HTML.

Cox, Gary W. 1997. *Making Votes Count*. New York: Cambridge University Press.

Crepaz, Markus. 2006. "If You Are My Brother, I May Give you a Dime! Public Opinion on Multiculturalism, Trust, and the Welfare State," in Keith Banting and Will Kymlicka, eds., *Multiculturalism and the Welfare State: Recognition and Redistribution in Contemporary Democracies*. New York: Oxford University Press, 92–117.

Crisp, Richard J. and Miles Hewstone. 2000. "Multiple Categorization and Social Identity," in Dora Capozza and Rupert Brown, eds., *Social Identity Processes*. London: Sage, 149–66.

Csergo, Zsuzsa and James M. Goldgeier. 2004. "Nationalist Strategies and European Integration," *Perspective on Politics*, 2, 1: 21–37.

Czaja, Ronald and Johnny Blair. 1996. *Designing Surveys*. Thousand Oaks, CA: Pine Forge Press.

Da Silva, Milton M. 1975. "Modernization and Ethnic Conflict: The Case of the Basques," *Comparative Politics*, 7, 2: 227–51.

Dalton, Russell. 2008. *Citizen Politics* 5th edition. Washington, DC: Congressional Quarterly Press.

Dandoy, Regis and Giulia Sandri. 2008. "I programmi elettorali dei partiti regionalisti d'Europa. Analisi comparata del contenuto dei programmi elettorali dei partiti regionalisti," *Quaderni dell'Ossevatorio Elettorale*, 59, 2: 63–94.

Danish Ministry of Refugee, Immigration and Integration Affairs. 2010. *Statistical Overview of Integration: Population, Education, and Employment*. Copenhagen: http://www.nyidanmark.dk/NR/rdonlyres/373D7D82-3F91-4873-A3F0-1731A37DD18D/0/statistical_overview_of_integration_2010.pdf.

Dardanelli, Paolo. 2001. "The Europeanisation of Regionalisation: European Integration and Public Support for Self-Government in Scotland 1979/1997," *Queen's Papers on Europeanisation*, 5: 1–35.

    2005a. *Between Two Unions. Europeanisation and Scottish Devolution*. New York: Manchester University Press.

    2005b. "Democratic Deficit or the Europeanisation of Secession? Explaining the Devolution Referendums in Scotland," *Political Studies*, 53, 2: 320–42.

Deutsche Presse-Agentur. 2000. "Get Working on Anti-Discrimination Package, Says EU Executive," March 13.

De Vries, Catherine E. and Erica Edwards. 2009. "Taking Europe to Its Extremes: Extremist Parties and Public Euroskepticism," *Party Politics*, 15, 1: 5–28.

De Winter, Lieven. 1998. "Conclusion: A Comparative Analysis of the Electoral, Office and Policy Success of Ethnoregionalist Parties," in Lieven De Winter and Huri Türsan, eds., *Regionalist Parties in Western Europe*. New York: Routledge, 204–47.

2002. "Ethnoregionalist Parties and European Integration at the 1999 European Elections," in Pascal Perrineau, Gérard Grunberg, and Colette Ysmal, eds., *Europe at the Polls: The European Elections of 1999*. Basingstoke, UK: Palgrave, 130–45.

De Winter, Lieven and Margarita Gómez-Reino Cachafeiro. 2002. "European Integration and Ethnoregionalist Parties," *Party Politics*, 8, 4: 483–503.

De Winter, Lieven and Margarita Gómez-Reino. 2009. "Le vote européen des partis regionalists," *Revue Internationale de Politique Comparée*, 16, 4: 637–52.

De Winter, Lieven, Margarita Gómez-Reino, and Peter Lynch, eds. 2006a. *Autonomist Parties in Europe: Identity Politics and the Revival of the Territorial Cleavage*, Vol. 1. Barcelona: Institut de Ciències Polítiques i Socials.

De Winter, Lieven, Margarita Gómez-Reino, and Peter Lynch. 2006b. "Introduction: Autonomist Parties in European Politics," in Lieven De Winter, Margarita Gómez-Reino, and Peter Lynch, eds., *Autonomist Parties in Europe: Identity Politics and the Revival of the Territorial Cleavage* Vol. 1. Barcelona: Institut de Ciències Polítiques i Socials, 11–30.

De Winter, Lieven and Huri Türsan, eds. 1998. *Regionalist Parties in Western Europe*. New York: Routledge.

Delanty, Gerard. 1995. *Inventing Europe: Idea, Identity, Reality*. New York: St. Martin's Press.

Delanty, Gerard and Chris Rumford. 2005. *Rethinking Europe: Social Theory and the Implications of Europeanization*. New York: Routledge.

Demertzis, Vais. 2008. "The European Social Model(s) and the Self-Image of Europe," in Furio Cerutti and Sonia Lucarelli, eds., *The Search for a European Identity: Values, Policies and Legitimacy of the European Union*. New York: Routledge, 125–41.

Denver, David. 2002. "Voting in the 1997 Scottish and Welsh Devolution Referendums: Information, Interests and Opinions," *European Journal of Political Research*, 41, 6: 827–43.

Deutsch, Franziska. 2006. "Legitimacy and Identity in the European Union: Empirical Findings from the Old Member States," in Ireneusz Pawel Karolewski and Viktoria Kaina, eds., *European Identity: Theoretical Perspectives and Empirical Insights*. Berlin: Lit Verlag, 149–78.

Díez Medrano, Juan. 2003. *Framing Europe: Attitudes to European Integration in Germany, Spain, and the United Kingdom*. Princeton, NJ: Princeton University Press.

2008. "Europeanization and the Emergence of a European Society," IBEI Working Papers 12. Barcelona: CIDOB Edicions.

Donaghey, Jimmy and Paul Teague. 2006. "The Free Movement of Workers and Social Europe: Maintaining the European Ideal," *Journal of Industrial Relations*, 37, 6: 652–66.

Duchesne, Sophie. 2008. "Waiting for a European Identity … Reflections on the Process of Identification with Europe," *Perspectives on European Politics and Society*, 9, 4: 397–410.

Duchesne, Sophie and André-Paul Frognier. 1995. "Is There a European Identity?" in Oskar Niedermayer and Richard Sinnot, eds., *Public Opinion and Internationalized Governance Vol. 2, Beliefs in Government*. New York: Oxford University Press.

2008. "National and European Identifications: A Dual Relationship," unpublished paper: http://oxpo.politics.ox.ac.uk/materials/D-F_Publication-National-European_Identifications.pdf.

Durkheim, Émile. 1982. *The Rules of Sociological Method*. New York: Simon and Shuster.

Duverger, Maurice. 1954. *Political Parties: Their Organization and Activity in the Modern State*. London: Methuen.

Easterly, William and Ross Levine. 1997. "Africa's Growth Tragedy: Policies and Ethnic Divisions," *Quarterly Journal of Economics*, 112, 4: 1203–50.

Easton, David. 1965. *A Framework for Political Analysis*. Englewood Cliffs, NJ: Prentice Hall.

Economist. 2010. August 9, 34.

2012. February 25, 83.

Edensor, Tim. 1997. "Reading Braveheart: Representing and Contesting Scottish Identity," *Scottish Affairs*, 21, autumn: 135–58.

Eichenberg, Richard and Russell Dalton. 1993. "Europeans and the European Community: The Dynamics of Public Support for European Integration," *International Organization*, 47, 4: 507–34.

Elias, Anwen. 2008. "From Euro-enthusiasm to Euro-scepticism? A Re-evaluation of Minority Nationalist Party Attitudes towards European Integration," *Regional and Federal Studies*, 18, 5: 557–81.

Emerson, Rupert. 1960. *From Empire to Nation*. Cambridge, MA: Harvard University Press.

Erk, Jan. 2010. "Is Nationalism Left or Right? Critical Junctures in Québécois Nationalism," *Nations and Nationalism*, 16, 3: 423–41.

Eurobarometer. 1992. *Report No. 37, Public Opinion in the European Union*. Brussels: Commission of the European Communities.

1999. *Report No. 51, Public Opinion in the European Union*. Brussels: Commission of the European Communities.

2000a. *Report No. 52, Public Opinion in the European Union*. Brussels: Commission of the European Communities.

2000b. *Report No. 54.1, Public Opinion in the European Union*. Brussels: Commission of the European Communities.

2001. *Report No. 54, Public Opinion in the European Union*. Brussels: Commission of the European Communities.

2003. *Report No. 60.1, Public Opinion in the European Union*. Brussels: Commission of the European Communities.

2004. *Report No. 62, Public Opinion in the European Union*. Brussels: Commission of the European Communities.

2005a. *Report No. 63.4, Public Opinion in the European Union*. Brussels: Commission of the European Communities.

2005b. *Report No. 64.2, Public Opinion in the European Union.* Brussels: Commission of the European Communities.

2006. *Report No. 65.2, Public Opinion in the European Union.* Brussels: Commission of the European Communities.

2008. *Report No. 68, Public Opinion in the European Union.* Brussels: Commission of the European Communities.

2011a. *Report 73.3, Public Opinion in the European Union.* Brussels: Commission of the European Communities.

2011b. *Report No. 76, Public Opinion in the European Union.* Brussels: Commission of the European Communities.

2011c. *New Europeans.* Brussels: Commission of the European Communities.

European Commission. 1997. *The European Institutions in the Fight against Racism: Selected Texts.* Brussels: Commission of the European Communities.

2004. "Green Paper: Equality and Non-discrimination in an Enlarged European Union," Brussels: Commission of the European Communities. http://eur-lex. europa.eu/smartapi/cgi/sga_doc?smartapi!celexplus!prod!DocNumber&lg=en&ty pe_doc=COMfinal&an_doc=2004&nu_doc=379.

2005. "Social Values, Science and Technology," Brussels: Special Eurobarometer 225/ Wave 63.1.

2006. "Europeans and Their Languages," Brussels: Special Eurobarometer 243/ Wave 64.3.

2008. "The 2009 European Elections," Brussels: Special Eurobarometer 299/ Wave 69.2.

2010. "Geographical and Labour Market Mobility," Brussels: Special Eurobarometer 337/Wave 72.5.3.

2011. http://ec.europa.eu/news/employment/090922_en.htm.

European Parliament. 1991. "Report of the Committee of Inquiry on Racism and Xenophobia." Luxembourg: European Parliament. http://aei.pitt.edu/3128/1/3128. pdf.

European Union Agency for Fundamental Rights. 2010. *The Impact of the Racial Equality Directive: Views of Trade unions and Employers in the European Union.* Conference edition, March, http://fra.europa.eu/fraWebsite/attachments/Racial-equality-directive_conf-ed_en.pdf.

Eurostat.2011."MigrationandMigrantPopulationStatistics,"http://epp.eurostat.ec.europa. eu/statistics_explained/index.php/Migration_and_migrant_population_statistics.

Evans, Geoffrey. 1996. *The State of the Union: Attitudes towards Europe: British Social Attitudes, 12th report.* London: Sage.

Extra, Guus and Durk Gorter. 2008. "The Constellation of Languages in Europe: An Inclusive Approach," in Guus Extra and Durk Gorter, eds., *Multilingual Europe: Facts and Policies.* Berlin: Mouton de Gruyter, 3–60.

Fabbrini, Sergio. 2007. *Compound Democracies.* New York: Oxford University Press.

Favell, Adrian. 2008. *Eurostars and Eurocities: Free Movement and Mobility in an Integrating Europe.* Malden, MA: Blackwell.

Feather, Norman T. 1993. "Devaluing Achievement within Culture: Measuring the Cultural Cringe," *Australian Journal of Psychology,* 45, 3: 182–8.

1994. "Values, National Identification and Favouritism towards the In-Group," *British Journal of Social Psychology,* 33, 4: 467–76.

Fedorowich, Kent. 1999. "Reconstruction and Resettlement: The Politicization of Irish Migration to Australia and Canada 1919–29," *English Historical Review*, 114, 459: 1143–78.

Feldmann, Magnus. 2006. "Emerging Varieties of Capitalism in Transition Countries: Industrial Wage Bargaining in Estonia and Slovenia," *Comparative Political Studies*, 39, 7: 829–54.

Fernández-Huertas Moraga, Jésus and Ada Ferrer-i-Carbonell. 2007. "Immigration in Catalonia," unpublished paper, http://www.iae.csic.es/specialMaterial/a8263153727sp5537.pdf.

Fetzer, Joel S. and J. Christopher Soper. 2005. *Muslims and the State in Britain, France, and Germany*. New York: Cambridge University Press.

Finlay, Richard. 2005. "Scotland and the Monarchy in the Twentieth Century," in W. L. Miller, ed., *Proceedings of the British Academy 128: Anglo-Scottish Relations since 1900*. Oxford: Oxford University Press, 62–75.

Fishman, Robert M. and Anthony M. Messina, eds. 2006. *The Year of the Euro: The Cultural, Political and Social Import of Europe's Common Currency*. Notre Dame, IN: University of Notre Dame Press.

Fligstein, Neil. 2008. *Euroclash: The EU, European Identity, and the Future of Europe*. New York: Oxford University Press.

2009. "Who are the Europeans and How Does this Matter for Politics?" in Jeffery T. Checkel and Peter J. Katzenstein, eds., *European Identity*. New York: Cambridge University Press, 132–66.

Fligstein, Neil, Alina Polyakova, and Wayne Sandholtz. 2012. "European Integration, Nationalism and European Identity," *Journal of Common Market Studies*, 50, 1: 106–22.

Follesdal, Andreas. 2002. "Constructing a European Civic Society: Vaccination for Trust in a Fair, Multi-Level Europe," *Studies in East European Thought*, 54, 4: 303–24.

Foner, Nancy. 2005. *In a New Land*. New York: New York University Press.

Fourest, Caroline. 2007 [2004]. *Brother Tariq: The Double-Speak of Tariq Ramadan*. Translated by Ioana Wieder and John Atherton. New York: Encounter Books.

Frampton, Martin. 2005. "Sinn Féin and the European Arena: 'Ourselves Alone' or 'Critical Engagement'?" *Irish Studies in International Affairs*, 16, 1: 235–53.

Fuss, Daniel and Marita Grosser. 2006. "What Makes Young Europeans Feel European? Results from a Cross-Cultural Research Project," in Ireneusz Pawel Karolewski and Viktoria Kaina, eds., *European Identity: Theoretical Perspectives and Empirical Insights*. Berlin: Lit Verlag, 209–41.

Gabel, Matthew. 1998a. "Public Support for European Integration: An Empirical Test of Five Theories," *Journal of Politics*, 60, 2: 333–54.

Gabel, Matthew J. 1998b. *Interests and Integration: Market Liberalization, Public Opinion, and European Union*. Ann Arbor: University of Michigan Press.

Gabel, Matthew J. and Christopher J. Anderson. 2002. "The Structure of Citizen Attitudes and the European Political Space," *Comparative Political Studies*, 35, 8: 893–913.

Gabel, Matthew J. and Simon Hix. 2002. "Defining the EU Political Space," *Comparative Political Studies*, 35, 8: 924–64.

Gabel, Matthew and Kenneth Scheve. 2007a. "Estimating the Effect of Elite Communications on Public Opinion Using Instrumental Variables," *American Journal of Political Science*, 51, 4: 1013–28.

2007b. "Mixed Messages. Party Dissent and Mass Opinion on European Integration," *European Union Politics*, 8, 1: 37–59.

Gallup. 2009. *The Gallup Coexist Index 2009: A Global Study of Interfaith Relations.* Washington, DC: Gallup Poll Consulting University Press.

Gamberale, Carlo. 1997. "European Citizenship and Political Identity," *Space and Polity*, 1, 1: 37–59.

Geddes, Andrew. 2003. *The Politics of Migration and Immigration in Europe.* New York: Sage.

Geddes, Andrew and Virginie Guiraudon. 2004. "Britain, France, and EU Anti-Discrimination Policy: The Emergence of an EU Policy Paradigm," *West European Politics*, 27, 2: 334–55.

Geertz, Clifford. 1968. *Islam Observed: Religious Development in Morocco and Indonesia.* New Haven, CT: Yale University Press.

Gellner, Ernest. 1983. *Nations and Nationalism.* Ithaca, NY: Cornell University Press.

Gelman, Andrew. 2005. "The Secret Weapon." *Statistical Modeling, Statistical Inference, and Social Science"* blog. http://www.stat.columbia.edu/~cook/movabletype/archives/2005/03/thesecretweap.html.

Gerring, John and Strom C. Thacker. 2008. *A Centripetal Theory of Democratic Governance.* New York: Cambridge University Press.

Ghuman, Paul A. Singh. 2003. *Double Loyalties: South Asian Adolescents in the West.* Cardiff: University of Wales Press.

Gilroy, Paul. 1987. *There Ain't No Black in the Union Jack: The Cultural Politics of Race and Nation.* London: Hutchinson.

Givens, Terri E. 2005. *Voting Radical Right in Western Europe.* New York: Cambridge University Press.

Givens, Terri E. and Luedtke, Adam. 2004. "The Politics of European Union Immigration Policy: Institutions, Salience, and Harmonization," *Policy Studies Journal*, 32, 1: 145–65.

Gómez-Reino, Margarita. 2006. "The Galician BNG from Outcast to Success," in Peter Lynch, Margarita Gómez-Reino, and Lieven de Winter, eds., *Autonomist Parties in Europe: Identity Politics and the Revival of the Territorial Cleavage.* Barcelona: ICPS.

Gómez-Reino Cachafeiro, Margarita. 2002. *Ethnicity and Nationalism in Italian Politics: Inventing the Padania – Lega Nord and the Northern Question.* Farnham Surrey, UK: Ashgate.

2011. "Bloque Nacionalista Galego," in Anwen Elias and Filippo Tronconi, eds., *From Protest to Power. Autonomist Parties and the Challenges of Representation.* Vienna, Austria: Braumüller, 125–46.

Gómez-Reino, Margarita, Lieven De Winter, and Peter Lynch, eds. 2006. *Autonomist Parties in Europe: Identity Politics and the Revival of the Territorial Cleavage.* Barcelona: Institut de Ciencies Polítiques i Socials.

Gómez-Reino, Margarita, Iván Llamazares, and Luis Ramiro. 2008. "Euroscepticism in Spain?" in Paul Taggart and Aleks Szczerbiack. eds., *Opposing Europe? The Comparative Party Politics of Euroscepticism, Vol. 1: Case Studies and Country Surveys.* Oxford, UK: Oxford University Press, 134–51.

Goodhart, David. 2004. "Too Diverse?" *Prospect*, February: 30–37.

Gould, Andrew C. 2009. "Muslim Elites and Ideologies in Portugal and Spain," *West European Politics*, 32, 1: 55–76.

Gourevitch, Peter Alexis. 1979. "The Reemergence of 'Peripheral Nationalisms': Some Comparative Speculations on the Spatial Distribution of Political Leadership and Economic Growth," *Comparative Studies in Society and History*, 21, 3: 303–22.

Green, David Michael. 2007. *The Europeans: Political Identity in an Emerging Polity*. London: Lynne Rienner.

Group of Intellectuals for Intercultural Dialogue. 2008. *A Rewarding Challenge: How the Multiplicity of Languages could Strengthen Europe*. Brussels: European Commission.

Guibernau, Montserrat. 1996. *Nationalisms: The Nation State and Nationalism in the Twentieth Century*. Cambridge: Polity.

   2000. "Spain: Catalonia and the Basque Country," *Parliamentary Affairs*, 53, 1: 55–68.

Guibernau, Montserrat. 2007. *The Identity of Nations*. Cambridge: Polity.

   2011. "Prospects for a European Identity," *International Journal of Politics, Culture and Society*, 24, 1: 31–43.

Guild, Elspeth. 2000. "European Developments: The EC Directive on Race Discrimination: Surprises, Possibilities and Limitations," *Industrial Law Journal*, 29, 4: 416–42.

Haas, Ernst B. 1964. *Beyond the Nation-State*. Berkeley: University of California Press.

   2004. *The Uniting of Europe: Political, Social, and Economic Forces, 1950–1957*. Notre Dame, IN: University of Notre Dame Press.

Habermas, Jürgen. 1995. "Remarks on Dieter Grimm's 'Does Europe Need a Constitution?'" *European Law Journal*, 1, 3: 303–7.

   2007. *The Divided West*. Cambridge: Polity.

Habermas, Jürgen and Jacques Derrida. 2005 [2003]. "February 15, or, What Binds Europeans Together: Plea for a Common Foreign Policy, Beginning in Core Europe," in Daniel Levy, Max Pensky, and John Torpey, eds., *Old Europe, New Europe, Core Europe: Transatlantic Relations After the Iraq War*. London: Verso, 3–13.

Haesly, Richard. 2001. "Euroskeptics, Europhiles and Instrumental Europeans: European Attachments in Scotland and Wales," *European Union Politics*, 2, 1: 81–102.

Hanson, Stephen E. 2003. "From Culture to Ideology in Comparative Politics," *Comparative Politics*, 35, 3: 355–76.

Hardt-Mautner, Gerlinde. 1995. "How Does One become a Good European?: The British Press and European Integration," *Discourse & Society*, 6, 2: 177–205.

Harris, 2007. "Harris Poll Global Omnibus," *Pan Euro*, December, 17.

Harvie, Christopher and Peter Jones. 2000. *The Road to Home Rule*. Edinburgh: Polygon.

Hearn, Jonathan. 2000. *Claiming Scotland: National Identity and Liberal Culture*. Edinburgh: Polygon.

Hedetoft, Ulf. 1993. "National Identity and Mentalities of War in 3 EC Countries," *Journal of Peace Research*, 30, 3: 281–300.

Hefner, Robert W. 2005. "Introduction: Modernity and the Remaking of Muslim Politics," in Robert W. Heffner, ed., *Remaking Muslim Politics: Pluralism, Contestation, Democratization*. Princeton, NJ: Princeton University Press, 2–36.

Heller, William B. 2002. "Regional Parties and National Politics in Europe," *Comparative Political Studies*, 35, 6: 657–85.

Hemingway, Ernest. 1988. *A Farewell to Arms*. First Scribner/Macmillan Hudson River Edition. New York: Charles Scribner's Sons.

Henderson, Ailsa. 1999. "Political Constructions of National Identity in Scotland and Quebec," *Scottish Affairs*, 29, autumn: 121–38.

Hepburn, Eve. 2007. "The New Politics of Autonomy: Territorial Strategies and the Uses of European Integration by Political Parties in Scotland, Bavaria, and Sardinia 1979–2005," Ph.D. thesis. Florence, Italy: European University Institute.

    2008. "The Rise and Fall of a 'Europe of Regions,'" *Regional and Federal Studies*, 18, 5: 537–55.

Herald. 2003a. "Swinney Attacks 'Racist' Labour Policies," September 8: 11.

    2003b. "SNP Fails to Split Coalition over Asylum Seekers Stuck in (Detention) Regime," September 12: 7.

    2003c. "Evicted Asylum Seekers Denied Final Appeal: Lack of Access a Disgrace, SNP Claims," October 10: 10.

Herrmann, Richard K. and Marilyn B. Brewer. 2004. "Identities and Institutions: Becoming European in the EU," in Richard K. Herrmann, Thomas Risse, and Marilyn B. Brewer, eds., *Transnational Identities: Becoming European in the EU*. Lanham, MD: Rowman and Littlefield, 1–24.

Hewstone, Miles. 1986. *Understanding Attitudes to the European Community: A Social Psychological Study in Four Member States*. New York: Cambridge University Press.

Hewstone, Miles, Mir R. Islam, and Charles M. Judd. 1993. "Models of Crossed Categorization and Intergroup Relations," *Journal of Personality and Social Psychology*, 64, 5: 779–93.

Hix, Simon and Jan Niessen. 1997. *Reconsidering European Migration Policies: The 1996 IGC and the Reform of the Maastricht Treaty*. Washington, DC/Brussels: Migration Policy Group.

Hobsbawm, Eric and Terence Ranger, eds. 1992. *The Invention of Tradition*. Cambridge: Cambridge University Press.

Hofman, J. E. 1988. "Social Identity and Intergroup Conflict: An Israeli View," in Wolfgang Stroebe, ed., *The Social Psychology of Intergroup Conflict*. New York: Springer, 89–102.

Hollinger, David. 2006. *Post-Ethnic America*. New York: Basic Books.

Holmes, Douglas. 2009. "Experimental Identities (after Maastricht)," in Jeffrey T. Checkel and Peter J. Katzenstein, eds., *European Identity*. New York: Cambridge University Press, 52–80.

Hooghe, Liesbet, Ryan Bakker, Anna Brigevich, Catherine de Vries, Erica Edwards, Gary Marks, Jan Rovny, Marco Steenbergen, and Milada Vachudova. 2010. "Reliability and Validity if Measuring Party Positions: The Chapel Hill Expert Surveys of 2002 and 2006," *European Journal of Political Research*, 42, 4: 684–703.

Hooghe, Liesbet and Gary Marks. 2001. *Multi-Level Governance and European Integration*. Lanham, MD: Rowman and Littlefield.

    2004a. "Does Identity or Economic Rationality Drive Public Opinion on European Integration?" *PS: Political Science and Politics*, 37, 3: 415–20.

    2004b. "European Integration and Democratic Competition," *Fredriech Ebert Stiftung*: 1–8.

2005. "Calculation, Community and Cues Public: Opinion on European Integration," *European Union Politics*, 6, 4: 419–43.

2006. "Europe's Blues: Theoretical Soul-Searching after the Rejection of the European Constitution," *PS*, April: 247–50.

2007. "Sources of Euroscepticism," *Acta Politica*, 42, 2: 119–27.

2008. "European Union?" *West European Politics*, 31, 1–2: 108–29.

2009. "A Postfunctionalist Theory of European Integration: From Permissive Consensus to Constraining Dissensus," *British Journal of Political Science*, 39, 1: 1–23.

Hooghe, Liesbet, Gary Marks, and Arjan Schakel. 2008. "Regional Authority in 42 Democracies, 1950–2006: A Measure and Five Hypotheses," *Regional and Federal Studies*, 18, 2–3: 111–302.

Hopkins, Nick and Steve Reicher. 1996. "The Construction of Social Categories and the Processes of Social Change: Arguing about National Identities," in Glynis M. Breakwell and Evanthia Lyons, eds., *Changing European Identities: Social Psychological Analyses of Social Change*. Oxford: Butterworth-Heinemann, 69–94.

Hopkins, Nick and Steve D. Reicher. 1997. "Constructing the Nation and Collective Mobilisation: A Case Study of Politicians' Arguments about the Meaning of Scottishness," in Cedric C. Barfoot, ed., *Beyond Pug's Tour: National and Ethnic Stereotyping in Theory and Literary Practice*. Amsterdam: Rodopi, 5–36.

Hoppe, Marcus. 2007. "The Europeanization of Nationalist Parties? Evidence from Scotland, Wales and Padania," in Ireneusz Paweł Karolewski and Andrzej Marcin Suszycki, eds., *Nationalism and European Integration: The Need for New Theoretical and Empirical Insights*. New York: Continuum, 67–84.

Hornsey, Matthew J. and Michael A. Hogg. 2000. "Assimilation and Diversity: An Integrative Model of Subgroup Relations," *Personality and Social Psychology Review*, 4, 2: 143–56.

Horowitz, Donald. 1985. *Ethnic Groups in Conflict*. Berkeley: University of California Press.

Huntington, Samuel P. 1996. *The Clash of Civilizations and the Remaking of World Order*. New York: Simon and Schuster.

Hussain, Asifa and William Miller. 2004. "How and Why Islamophobia is Tied to English Nationalism but Not to Scottish Nationalism," *Ethnic Studies Review*, 27, 1: 78–101.

2006. *Multicultural Nationalism: Islamophobia, Anglophobia and Devolution*. Oxford: Oxford University Press.

Hutnik, Nimmi. 1985. "Aspects of Identity in a Multi-Ethnic Society," *New Community*, 12, 2: 298–309.

1986. "Patterns of Ethnic-Minority Identification and Modes of Social Adaptation," *Ethnic and Racial Studies*, 9, 2: 150–67.

International Social Survey Program (ISSP). 2003. "National Identity II," http://www.jdsurvey.net/jds/jdsurveyAnalisis.jsp?ES_COL=127&Idioma=I&SeccionCol=02&ESID=396.

Instituto Nacional Estadística. 2009. "Notas de prensa." http://www.ine.es/prensa/np551.pdf.

Institut national de la statistique et des études économiques. 2009. "Étrangers en 2009: comparaisons régionales," http://www.insee.fr/fr/themes/tableau.asp?reg_id=99&ref_id=t_0405R.

Ireland, Patrick. 2004. *Becoming Europe: Immigration, Integration, and the Welfare State*. Pittsburgh, PA: University of Pittsburgh Press.

Ivarsflaten, Elisabeth. 2005. "Threatened by Diversity: Why Restrictive Asylum and Immigration Policies Appeal to Western Europeans," *Journal of Elections, Public Opinion and Parties*, 15, 1: 21–45.

Jacobs, Dirk and Robert Maier. 1998. "European Identity: Construct, Fact and Fiction," unpublished paper, http://users.belgacom.net/jacobs/europa.pdf.

Jacobson, Jessica. 1997. "Perceptions of Britishness," *Nations and Nationalism*, 3, 2: 181–99.

Jenkins, Brian and Spyros A. Sofos. 1996. *Nation and Identity in Contemporary Europe*. London: Routledge.

Jensen, Christian and Jae-Jae Spoon. 2008. "Thinking Locally, Acting Supranationally: Niche Party Behaviour in the European Parliament," paper prepared for the Annual Meeting of the Midwest Political Science Association, Chicago.

Johansson, Karl Magnus. 2005. "Regulating Europarties: Cross-Party Coalitions Capitalizing on Incomplete Contracts," *Party Politics*, 11, 5: 515–34.

Jolly, Seth K. 2006. "A Europe of Regions? Regional Integration, Sub-National Mobilization and the Optimal Size of States," Ph.D. thesis. Durham, NC: Duke University.

2007. "The Europhile Fringe? Regionalist Party Support for European Integration," *European Union Politics*, 8, 1: 109–30.

Joppke, Christian. 1999. *Immigration and the Nation-State: The United States, Germany, and Great Britain*. Oxford: Oxford University Press.

2004. "The Retreat of Multiculturalism in the Liberal State: Theory and Policy," *British Journal of Sociology*, 55, 2: 237–57.

Jowell, Roger, Anthony F. Heath, and John K. Curtice. 1998. *Scottish and Welsh Referendum Studies, 1997*. Colchester, Essex: UK Data Archive.

Kaina, Viktoria, and Ireneusz Pawel Karolewski. 2009. "EU Governance and European Identity," *Living Reviews in European Governance*, 4, 2: 5–41.

Kaiser, Wolfram and Peter Starie, eds. 2005. *Transnational European Union: Towards a Common Political Space*. London: Routledge.

Kantner, Cathleen. 2006. "Collective Identity as Shared Ethical Understanding: The Case of the Emerging European Identity," *European Journal of Social Theory*, 9, 4: 501–23.

Karolewski, Ireneusz Pawel. 2006. "Citizenship and Collective Identity in Europe," in Ireneusz Pawel Karolewski and Viktoria Kaina, eds., *European Identity: Theoretical Perspectives and Empirical Insights*. Berlin: Lit Verlag, 209–42.

2010a. *Citizenship and Collective Identity in Europe*. London: Routledge.

2010b. "European Nationalism and European Identity," in Ireneusz Pawel Karolewski and Andrzej Marcin Suszycki, eds., *Multiplicity of Nationalism in Contemporary Europe*. Lanham, MD: Lexington Books, 59–80.

Kasekamp, Andres. 2003. "Extreme-Right Parties in Contemporary Estonia," *Patterns of Prejudice*, 37, 4: 401–414.

Katzenstein, Peter J. 2006. "Multiple Modernities as Limits to Secular Europeanization?" in Timothy A. Byrnes and Peter J. Katzenstein, eds., *Religion in an Expanding Europe*. New York: Cambridge University Press, 1–33.

Katzenstein, Peter J. and Jeffery T. Checkel. 2009. "Conclusion: European Identity in Context," in Jeffery T. Checkel and Peter J. Katzenstein, eds., *European Identity*. New York: Cambridge University Press, 213–27.

Keating, Michael. 1998. *The New Regionalism in Western Europe: Territorial Restructuring and Political Change.* Cheltenham, UK: Edward Elgar.

Keating, Michael and Liesbet Hooghe. 2006. "Bypassing the Nation-State: Regions and the EU Process," in Jeremy Richardson, ed., *European Union: Power and Policy Making.* London: Routledge, 239–56.

Kellas, James. 1998. *The Politics of Nationalism and Ethnicity* 2nd edition. Basingstoke, UK: Macmillan.

Kelman, Herbert C. 1997. "Nationalism, Patriotism, and National Identity: Social-Psychological Dimensions," in Daniel Bar-Tal and Ervin Staub, eds., *Patriotism in the Lives of Individuals and Nations.* Chicago: Nelson-Hall, 165–89.

Kitschelt, Herbert. 2007. "Growth and Persistence of the Radical Right in Postindustrial Democracies: Advances and Challenges in Comparative Research," *West European Politics*, 30, 5: 1176–1206.

Klausen, Jytte. 2005. *The Islamic Challenge: Politics and Religion in Western Europe.* New York: Oxford University Press.

Kopecky, Petr and Cas Mudde. 2002. "The Two Sides of Euroscepticism: Party Positions on European Integration in East Central Europe," *European Union Politics*, 3, 3: 297–326.

Kostakopoulou, Theodora. 2001. *Citizenship, Identity and Immigration in the European Union.* Manchester, UK: Manchester University Press.

Kousser, Thad. 2004. "Retrospective Voting and Strategic Behavior in European Parliament Elections," *Electoral Studies*, 23, 1: 1–21.

Kuru, Ahmet T. 2009. *Secularism and State Policies toward Religion: The United States, France, and Turkey.* New York: Cambridge University Press.

Kuru, Zeynep Akbulut and Ahmet T. Kuru. 2008. "A political Interpretation of Islam: Said Nursi's Faith-Based Activism in Comparison with Political Islamism and Sufism," *Islam and Christian–Muslim Relations*, 19, 1: 99–111.

Kurzman, Charles. 1998. *Liberal Islam: A Sourcebook.* New York: Oxford University Press.

Kymlicka, Will. 2001a. "Immigrant Integration and Minority Nationalism," in Michael Keating and John McGarry, eds., *Minority Nationalism and the Changing International Order.* Oxford: Oxford University Press, 61–83.

2001b. *Politics in the Vernacular: Nationalism, Multiculturalism and Citizenship.* Oxford: Oxford University Press.

Laffan, Brigid. 1996. "The Politics of Identity and Political Order in Europe," *Journal of Common Market Studies*, 34, 1: 81–102.

Laffan, Brigid, Rory O'Donnell, and Michael Smith. 2000. *Europe's Experimental Union: Rethinking Integration.* London: Routledge.

Lago, Ignacio. 2004. "La coordinación electoral del nacionalismo gallego," *Revista Internacional de Sociología*, 62, 39: 35–61.

Laible, Janet. 2000. "Nationalism and a Critique of European Integration: Questions from the Flemish Parties," in Michael Keating and John McGarry, eds., *Minority Nationalism and the Changing International Order.* New York: Oxford University Press, 223–45.

Laitin, David. 2008. *Nations, States, and Violence.* Oxford: Oxford University Press.

Laitin, David D. 2002. "Culture and National Identity: The 'East' and European Integration," *West European Politics*, 25, 2: 55–80.

2003. "The Game Theory of Language Regimes," *International Political Science Review*, 14, 3: 227–39.

Lane, Jan-Erik and Svante Ersson. 1999. *Politics and Society in Western Europe.* London: Sage.

Laurence, Jonathan. 2005. "State-Islam Relations and the Integration of Muslims in France," *French Politics, Culture and Society*, 23, 1: 36–63.

2006. "Managing Transnational Islam: Muslims and the State in Western Europe," in Craig A. Parsons and Timothy M. Smeeding, eds., *Immigration and the Transformation of Europe.* New York: Cambridge University Press, 253–75.

Lehning, Percy B. 2001. "European Citizenship: Towards a European Identity?" *Law and Philosophy*, 20, 3: 239–82.

Leith, Murray. 2006. "Nationalism and National Identity in Scottish Politics," Glasgow: Doctoral Thesis in Glasgow University Library.

Leslie, Peter M. 1989. "Ethnonationalism in a Federal State," in Joseph R. Rudolph and Robert J. Thompson, eds., *Ethnoterritorial Politics, Policy and the Western World.* Boulder, CO: Lynne Rienner, 45–90.

Lewis, Miranda. 2006. *Warm Welcome? Understanding Public Attitudes to Asylum Seekers in Scotland.* London: Institute for Public Policy Research, http://www.ippr.org/ecomm/files/warm_welcome.pdf.

Liang, Christina Schori, ed. 2007. *Europe for the Europeans: The Foreign and Security Policy of the Populist Radical Right.* Farnham Surrey, UK: Ashgate.

Lijphart, Arend. 1994. *Electoral Systems and Party Systems: A Study of Twenty-Seven Democracies 1945–90.* Oxford: Oxford University Press.

1999. *Patterns of Democracy: Government Forms and Performance in Thirty-Six Countries.* New Haven, CT: Yale University Press.

Linz, Juan J. 1973. "Early State-Building and Late Peripheral Nationalisms against the State: The Case of Spain," in Samuel Eisenstadt and Stein Rokkan, eds., *In Building States and Nations*, Beverly Hills, CA: Sage Publications, 39–116.

Lindstrom, Nicole. 2011. "Service Liberalization in the Enlarged European Union: A Race to the Bottom or the Emergence of Transnational Conflict?," *Journal of Common Market Studies*, Vol. 10, No. 5 (November 2010): 1307–1327.

Lipset, Seymour M. and Stein Rokkan. 1967. *Party Systems and Voter Alignments: Cross National Perspectives.* New York: The Free Press.

Llamazares, Iván, Margarita Gómez-Reino, and Luis Ramiro. 2008. "Euroscepticism and Political Parties in Spain," in Paul Taggart and Aleks Szczerbiak, eds., *Opposing Europe? The Comparative Party Politics of Euroscepticism.* Oxford: Oxford University Press, 134–51.

Llamazares, Ivan and Gary Marks. 1999. "Gobernación de múltiples niveles, movilización regional e identidades subestatales en la Unión Europea," in Ivan Llamazares and Fernando Reinares, eds., *Aspectos Políticos y Sociales de la Integración Europea.* Valencia, Spain: Tirant lo Blanch, 159–77.

Loewenthal, Kate M. 1995. *An Introduction to Psychological Tests and Scales.* London: UCL Press.

Lubbers, Marcel and Peer Scheepers. 2005. "Political vs. Instrumental Euro-scepticism: Mapping Scepticism in European Countries and Regions," *European Union Politics*, 6, 2: 223–42.

Lutz, Wolfgang, Sylvia Kritzinger, and Vegard Skirbekk. 2006. "The Demography of Growing European Identity," *Science*, 314, October: 425.

Lynch, Peter. 1996. *Minority Nationalism and European Integration.* Cardiff: University of Wales Press.

2006. "The Scottish Nationalist Party: The Long Road from Marginality to Blackmail and Coalition Potential," in Lieven De Winter, Margarita Gómez-Reino, and Peter Lynch, eds., *Autonomist Parties in Europe: Identity Politics and the Revival of the Territorial Cleavage*, Vol. 1. Barcelona: Institut de Ciències Polítiques i Socials, 229–51.

Lynch, Peter and Lieven De Winter. 2008. "The Shrinking Political Space of Minority Nationalist Parties in an Enlarged Europe of the Regions," *Regional and Federal Studies*, 18, 5: 583–606.

Lyons, Evanthia. 1996. "Coping with Social Change: Processes of Social Memory in the Reconstruction of Identities," in Glynis Breakwell and Evanthia Lyons, eds., *Changing European Identities: Social Psychological Analyses of Social Change*. Oxford: Butterworth-Heinemann, 31–40.

Madeley, John T. S. 2009. "Unequally Yoked: The Antinomies of Church–State Separation in Europe and the USA," *European Political Science*, 8, 3: 273–88.

Mahendran, Kesi and Iain McIver. 2007. "Attitudes towards the European Union and the Challenges in Communication 'Europe': Building a Bridge between Europe and its Citizens, Evidence Paper Two," Edinburgh: Scottish Executive Social Research, Finance and Central Services Department, http://www.scotland.gov.uk/Resource/Doc/163772/0044574.pdf.

Mandaville, Peter. 2005. "Sufis and Salafis: The Political Discourse of Transnational Islam," in Robert W. Hefner, ed., *Remaking Muslim Politics: Pluralism, Contestation, Democratization*. Princeton, NJ: Princeton University Press, 302–25.

Mair, Peter and Cas Mudde. 1998. "The Party Family and its Study," *Annual Review of Political Science*, 1: 211–29.

Mannheim Eurobarometer Trend File. 1970–2002. http://www.icpsr.umich.edu/icpsrweb/ICPSR/studies/4357.

March, Andrew F. 2007. "Reading Tariq Ramadan: Political Liberalism, Islam, and 'Overlapping Consensus'," *Ethics & International Affairs*, 21, 4: 399–413.

Marks, Gary. 2004. "European Integration and Political Conflict," in Gary Marks and Marco R. Steenbergen, eds., *European Integration and Political Conflict*. New York: Cambridge University Press.

Marks, Gary, Liesbet Hooghe, and Ryan Bakker. 2007. "Cross-Validating Data on Party Positions on European Integration," *Electoral Studies*, 26, 1: 23–38.

Marks, Gary, Liesbet Hooghe, Moira Nelson, and Erica Edwards. 2006. "Party Competition and European Integration in the East and West," *Comparative Political Studies*, 39, 2: 155–75.

Marks, Gary and Marco Steenbergen, eds. 2004. *European Integration and Political Conflict*. New York: Cambridge University Press.

Marks, Gary and Carole Wilson. 2000. "The Past in the Present: A Cleavage Theory of Party Positions on European Integration," *British Journal of Political Science*, 30, 3: 433–59.

Marks, Gary, Carole J. Wilson, and Leonard Ray. 2002. "National Political Parties and European Integration," *American Journal of Political Science*, 46, 3: 585–94.

Marsh, Michael. 1998. "Testing the Second-Order Election Model after Four European Elections," *British Journal of Political Science*, 28, 4: 591–607.

Marson, Karin. 2001. "Social Belief Structures and Identity Related Threats as Predictors of Organisational Identification, Mental Health and Work Related Attitudes," unpublished Ph.D. thesis, Psychology Department, Royal Holloway, University of London.

Martínez Herrera, Enric. 2002. "From Nation Building to Building Identification with Political Communities: Consequences of Political Decentralization in Spain, the Basque Country, Catalonia and Galicia 1978–2001," *European Journal of Political Research*, 41, 4: 421–53.

McConnell, Jack. 2003. "Speech at City Challenge Conference," Edinburgh. February 25. Reported at length in *Scotsman* February, 26, 9.

McCrone, David and Frank Bechhofer. 2008. "National Identity and Social Inclusion," *Ethnic and Racial Studies*, 31, 7: 1245–66.

McCrone, David, Alice Brown, Paula Surridge, and Katerina Thomson. 1999. *British Election Study: Scottish Election Survey, 1997*. London: Social and Community Planning Research [producer], 1998. Colchester, England: ESRC data archive/Ann Arbor, MI: Inter-University Consortium for Political and Social Research.

McCrone, David and Bethan Lewis. 1999. "The Scottish and Welsh Referendum Campaigns," in Bridget Taylor and Katarina Thomson, eds., *Scotland and Wales: Nations Again?* Cardiff: University of Wales Press, 17–40.

McCrone, David, Robert Stewart, Richard Kiely, and Frank Bechhofer. 1998. "Who are We? Problematising National Identity," *Sociological Review*, 46, 4: 629–52.

McLaren, Lauren. 2007. "Explaining Mass-Level Euroscepticism: Identity, Interests, and Institutional Distrust," *Acta Politica*, 42, 2–3: 233–51.

McLaren, Lauren M. 2002. "Public Support for the European Union: Cost/Benefit Analysis or Perceived Cultural Threat," *Journal of Politics*, 64, 2: 463–75.

Meardi, Guglielmo. 2000. "Trojan Horse for the Americanization of Europe? Polish Industrial Relations towards the EU," *European Journal of Industrial Relations*, 8, 1: 77–99.

Meguid, Bonnie M. 2005. "Competition between Unequals: The Role of Mainstream Party Strategy in Niche Party Success," *American Political Science Review*, 99, 3: 347–59.

  2008. *Party Competition between Unequals: Strategies and Electoral Fortunes in Western Europe*. New York: Cambridge University Press.

  2009. "Institutional Change as Strategy: The Role of Decentralization in Party Competition," unpublished manuscript, University of Rochester, http://www.rochester.edu/college/faculty/bmeguid/Meguid_Inst_Change_as_Strategy_2008.pdf.

Meinhof, Ulrike Hanna. 2004. "Europe Viewed from Below: Agents, Victims, and the Threat of the Other," in Richard K. Herrmann, Thomas Risse, and Marilyn B. Brewer, eds., *Transnational Identities: Becoming European in the EU*. Lanham, MD: Rowman and Littlefield, 214–46.

Mencinger, Jože. 2002. "Narodna zavest izpari, ko je treba kaj plačati," *Delo*, November 8.

  2006. "Privatization in Slovenia," unpublished paper, http://www.pf.uni-lj.si/media/mencinger.privatization.pdf.

Menéndez-Alarcón, Antonio V. 1995. "National Identities Confronting European Integration," *International Journal of Politics, Culture and Society*, 8, 4: 543–62.

Messina, Anthony M. 2006. "Why Doesn't the Dog Bite? Extreme Right Parties and 'Euro' Skepticism within the European Union," in Robert F. Fishman and Anthony M. Messina, eds., *The Year of the Euro: The Cultural, Social, and Political Import of Europe's Common Currency*. Notre Dame, IN: University of Notre Dame Press, 131–60.

2007. *The Logics and Politics of Post–WWII Migration to Western Europe*. New York: Cambridge University Press.

Messina, Anthony M. and Luis R. Fraga. 1992. "Introduction," in Anthony M. Messina, Luis R. Fraga, Laurie A. Rhodebeck, and Frederick D. Wright, eds., *Ethnic and Racial Minorities in Advanced Industrial Democracies*. New York: Greenwood Press, 1–16.

Miles, Robert and Anne Dunlop. 1986. "The Racialisation of Politics in Britain: Why Scotland is Different," *Patterns of Prejudice*, 20, 1: 23–32.

Miller, William L. 2008. "The Death of Unionism?" in T. M. Devine, ed., *Scotland and Union 1707–2007*. Edinburgh: Edinburgh University Press, 91–108.

Miller, William L. and Jack A. Brand. 1981. *Scottish Election Study, 1979*. Colchester, Essex: UK Data Archive.

Minkenberg, Michael. 2007. "Between Tradition and Transition: The Central European Radical Right and the New European Order," in Christina Schori Liang, ed., *Europe for the Europeans: The Foreign and Security Policy of the Populist Radical Right*. Hampshire, UK: Ashgate, 261–81.

Mitchell, James. 1996. *Strategies for Self-Government: The Campaigns for a Scottish Parliament*. Edinburgh: Polygon.

Mitchell, James, David Denver, Charles Pattie, and Hugh Bochel. 1998. "The 1997 Devolution Referendum in Scotland," *Parliamentary Affairs*, 51, 2: 166–81.

Modood, Tariq. 2000. "The Place of Muslims in the Secular Multiculturalism of Great Britain," *Social Compass*, 47, 1: 41–55.

2005. *Multicultural Politics: Racism, Ethnicity, and Muslims in Britain*. Minneapolis: University of Minnesota Press.

Modood, Tariq and Pnina Werbner, eds. 1997. *The Politics of Multiculturalism in the New Europe: Racism, Identity and Community*. London: Zed.

Money, Jeannette. 1999. "Defining Immigration Policy: Inventory, Quantitative Referents, and Empirical Regularities," paper presented at the Annual Meetings of the American Political Science Association, Atlanta, GA, September 2–5.

Mudde, Cas. 2000. *The Ideology of the Extreme Right*. Manchester, UK: Manchester University Press.

Mudde, Cas, ed. 2005. *Racist Extremist in Central and Eastern Europe*. New York: Routledge.

Mudde, Cas. 2007. *Populist Radical Right Wing Parties in Europe*. New York: Cambridge University Press.

2012. "The Comparative Study of Party-Based Euroscepticism: The Sussex versus the North Carolina School," *East European Politics*, 28, 2: 193–202.

Müller-Rommel, Ferdinand. 1998. "Ethnoregionalist Parties in Western Europe: Theoretical Considerations and Framework of Analysis," in Lieven De Winter and Huri Türsan, eds., *Regionalist Parties in Western Europe*. London: Routledge, 17–27.

Mummendey, Amélie, Andreas Klink, and Rupert J. Brown. 2001. "Nationalism and Patriotism: National Identification and Out-Group Rejection," *British Journal of Social Psychology*, 40, 2: 159–72.

Mummendey, Amélie and Michael Wenzel. 1999. "Social Discrimination and Tolerance in Intergroup Relations: Reactions to Intergroup Difference," *Personality and Social Psychology Review*, 3, 2: 158–74.

National Centre for Social Research. 2004. *Scottish Social Attitudes Survey, 2001.* Colchester, Essex: UK Data Archive.

Nesdale, D. and A. S. Mak. 2000. "Immigrant Acculturation Attitudes and Host Country Identification," *Journal of Community & Applied Social Psychology,* 10, 6: 403–95.

Netjes, Catherine E. and Erica E. Edwards. 2009. "Taking Europe to Its Extremes: Extremist Parties and Public Euroscepticism," *Party Politics,* 15, 1: 5–28.

Newhouse, Joseph. 1997. "Europe's Rising Regionalism," *Foreign Affairs,* 76, 1: 67–84.

Newman, Saul. 1997. "Ideological Trends among Ethnoregional Parties in Industrial Democracies," *Nationalism and Ethnic Politics,* 3, 1: 28–60.

News from Spain. 2007. "Foreigners Outnumber Spanish Citizens in 15 Towns in the Valencian Region," http://news-spain.euroresidentes.com/2007_05_01_archive. html.

Niessen, Jan. 2000. "The Amsterdam Treaty and NGO Responses," *European Journal of Migration and Law,* 2, 2: 203–14.

2003. "Making the Law Work: The Enforcement and Implementation of Anti-Discrimination Legislation," *European Journal of Migration and Law,* 5: 249–57.

Nugent, Neill. 2003. *The Government and Politics of the European Union* 5th edition. Durham, NC: Duke University Press.

2006. *The Government and Politics of the European Union* 6th edition. Durham, NC: Duke University Press.

Núñez, Xosé-Manoel. 2002. "History and Collective Memories of Migration in a Land of Migrants: The Case of Iberian Galicia," *History and Memory,* 14, 1–2: 229–58.

Ordeshook, Peter C. and Olga V. Shvetsova. 1994. "Ethnic Heterogeneity, District Magnitude and the Number of Parties," *American Journal of Political Science,* 38, 1: 100–23.

Ottolenghi, Emanuele. 2005. "Can Europe Do Away with Nationalism?" Washington, DC: American Enterprise Institute for Public Policy Research. May-June.

Outlaw, Iain. 2005. "British Election Data by Constituency," http://www.psr.keele. ac.uk/area/uk/outlaw/sheetindex.htm.

Pan, Christoph and Beate Sibyelle Pfeil. 2003. *National Minorities in Europe.* Vienna: Wilhelm Braumüller.

Paquin, Stéphane. 2002. "Globalization, European Integration and the Rise of Neo-nationalism in Scotland," *Nationalism and Ethnic Politics,* 8, 1: 55–80.

Parekh, Bhikhu. 2000. *Rethinking Multiculturalism: Cultural Diversity and Political Theory.* Basingstoke, UK: Macmillan.

Paterson, Lindsay, Alice Brown, John Curtis, and Kerstin Hinds. 2001. *New Scotland, New Politics?* Edinburgh: Polygon.

Petithomme, Mathieu. 2008. "Is There a European Identity? National Attitudes and Social Identification toward the European Union," *Journal of Identity and Migration Studies,* 2, 1: 15–36.

Phinney, Jean S., G. Horenczyk, Karmela Liebkind, and Paul Vedder. 2001. "Ethnic Identity, Immigration, and Well-Being: An Interactional Perspective," *Journal of Social Issues,* 57, 3: 493–510.

Pinxten, Rik, Marijke Cornelis, and Robert A. Rubinstein. 2007. "European Identity: Diversity in Union," *International Journal of Public Administration,* 30, 6–7: 687–98.

Pittock, Murray G. H. 2001. *Scottish Nationality*. New York: Palgrave.

Porter, Brian. 2000. *When Nationalism Began to Hate: Imagining Modern Politics in Nineteenth-Century Poland*. New York: Oxford University Press.

Powell, G. Bingham. 2000. *Elections as Instruments of Democracy*. New Haven, CT: Yale University Press.

Price, Marie and Lisa Benton-Short. 2007. "Immigrants and World Cities: From the Hyper-diverse to the Bypassed," *GeoJournal*, 68, 2–3: 103–17.

Pulzer, Peter, ed. 1988. *The Rise of Political Anti-Semitism in Germany and Austria*. Cambridge, MA: Harvard University Press.

Putnam, Robert D. 2007. "*E Pluribus Unum*: Diversity and Community in the Twenty-First Century," *Scandinavian Political Studies*, 30, 2: 137–74.

Quaglia, Lucia. 2003. "Euroscepticism in Italy and Centre-Right and Right Wing Politics," SEI Working Paper No. 60, 1–28.

Rae, Douglas. 1971. *The Political Consequences of Electoral Laws*. New Haven, CT: Yale University Press.

Raig, Ivar. 2003. "Time for Closer Transatlantic Cooperation," *EU Observer*, February 5.

Ramadan, Tariq. 1999. *To Be a European Muslim*. Leicester, UK: Islamic Foundation.

Raunio, Tapio. 2006. "The Svenska Folkpartiet: The Gradual Decline of a Language Party," in Lieven De Winter, Margarita Gómez Reino Cachafeiro, and Peter Lynch, eds., *Regionalist Parties in Western Europe*, Barcelona, Spain: ICPS, 123–39.

Ray, Leonard. 1999. "Measuring Party Orientations towards European Integration: Results from an Expert Survey," *European Journal of Political Research*, 36, 2: 283–306.

  2004. "Don't Rock the Boat: Expectations, Fears, and Opposition to EU-level Policy-Making," in Gary Marks and Marco R. Steenbergen, eds., *European Integration and Political Conflict*. New York: Cambridge University Press, 51–61.

Recchi, Ettore. 2008. "Cross-State Mobility in the EU: Trends, Puzzles and Consequences," *European Societies*, 10, 2: 301–34.

Reicher, Stephen and Nick Hopkins. 2001. *Self and Nation*. London: Sage.

Reif, Karlheinz and Hermann Schmitt. 1980. "Nine Second-Order National Elections: A Conceptual Framework for the Analysis of European Election Results," *European Journal of Political Research*, 8, 1: 3–44.

Renan, Ernest. 1882. "Qu'est-ce qu'une nation?" Conference held in the Sorbonne, March 11.

Risse, Thomas. 2004. "European Institutions and Identity Change: What Have We Learned?" in Richard K. Hermann, Thomas Risse, and Marilyn B. Brewer, eds., *Transnational Identities: Becoming European in the EU*. Lanham, MD: Rowman and Littlefield, 247–71.

  2005. "Neofunctionalism, European Identity, and the Puzzles of European Integration," *Journal of European Public Policy*, 12, 2: 291–309.

  2010. *A Community of Europeans? Transnational Identities and Public Spheres*. Ithaca, NY: Cornell University Press.

Robyn, Richard, ed. 2005. *The Changing Face of European Identity*. London: Routledge.

Roccas, Sonia and Marilynn B. Brewer. 2002. "Social Identity Complexity," *Personality and Social Psychology Review*, 6, 2: 88–106.

Rokkan, Stein and Derek Urwin, eds. 1982. *The Politics of Territorial Identity*. London: Sage.

Ros, Maria, Carmen Huici, and Angel Gómez. 2000. "Comparative Identity, Category Salience and Intergroup Relations," in Dora Capozza and Rupert Brown, eds., *Social Identity Processes*. London: Sage, 81–95.

Rosie, Michael and Ross Bond. 2006. "Routes into Scottishness," in Catherine Bromley, John Curtice, David McCrone, Alison Park, and Anthony John Parker, eds., *Has Devolution Delivered?* Edinburgh: Edinburgh University Press, 141–58.

Roter, Petra and Zlatko Žabič. 2004. "'New' and 'Old Europe' in the Context of the Iraq War and its Implications for European Security," *Perspectives on European Politics and Society*, 5: 517–42.

Rutland, Adam and Marco Cinnirella. 2000. "Context Effects on Scottish National and European Self-Categorization: The Importance of Category Accessibility, Fragility and Relations," *British Journal of Social Psychology*, 39, 4: 495–519.

Ruzza, Carlo. 2006. "The Northern League," in Lieven De Winter, Margarita Gómez-Reino, and Peter Lynch, eds., *Autonomist Parties in Europe: Identity Politics and the Revival of the Territorial Cleavage*. Barcelona: ICPS Publications.

Ruzza, Carlo, and Emanuela Bozzini. 2008. "Organized Civil Society and European Governance: Routes of Contestation," *European Political Science*, 7, 3: 296–303.

Salazar, Jose Miguel. 1998. "Social Identity and National Identity," in Stephen Worchel, J. Francisco Morales, Dario Paez, and Jean-Claude Deschamps, eds., *Social Identity: International Perspectives*. London: Sage, 114–23.

Salmond, Alex. 1997. *Hansard*. July 30, 1997: Column 396.

Samuel, Raphael. 1989. "Exciting to be British," in Raphael Samuel, ed., *Patriotism: The Making and Unmaking of British National Identity*. London: Routledge, xviii-lxvii.

Sanchez-Mazas, Margarita. 1996. "Intergroup Attitudes, Levels of Identification and Social Change," in Glynis Breakwell and Evanthia Lyons, eds., *Changing European Identities: Social Psychological Analyses of Social Change*. Oxford: Butterworth-Heinemann, 329–48.

Santer, Jacques. 1995. "Citation from Keynote Address to the World Telecommunications Forum 1995 Opening Ceremony," March 10.

Sartori, Giovanni. 1976. *Parties and Party Systems: A Framework for Analysis*. New York: Cambridge University Press.

Sassen, Saskia. 2001. *The Global City: New York, London, Tokyo*. Princeton, NJ: Princeton University Press.

Schain, Martin. 2006. "The Extreme-Right and Immigration Policy-Making: Measuring Direct and Indirect Effects," *West European Politics*, 29, 2: 270–89.

Schain, Martin A. 2008. *The Politics of Immigration in France, Britain, and the United States*. New York: Palgrave.

Schain, Martin, Aristide Zolberg, and Patrick Hossay, eds. 2002. *Shadows over Europe: The Development and Impact of the Extreme Right in Western Europe*. New York: Palgrave.

Scharpf, Fritz W. 1999. *Governing in Europe: Effective and Democratic?* New York: Oxford University Press.

2009. "Legitimacy in the Multilevel European Polity," *European Political Science Review*, 1, 2: 173–204.

Scheuer, Angelika. 1999. "A Political Community?" in Hermann Schmitt and Jacques Thomassen, eds., *Political Representation and Legitimacy in the European Union.* Oxford: Oxford University Press, 25–47.

Schlesinger, Philip. 1987. "On National Identity: Some Conceptions and Misconceptions Criticized," *Social Science Information*, 26, 2: 219–64.

Schmitt, Hermann and Evi Scholz. 2005. *Mannheim Eurobarometer Trend File, 1970–2002.* Mannheim, Germany: Mannheimer Zentrum fur Europaische Sozialforschung and Zentrum fur Umfragen, Methoden und Analysen [producers]. Cologne, Germany: Zentralarchiv fur Empirische Sozialforschung/ Ann Arbor, MI: Inter-university Consortium for Political and Social Research [distributors].

Scotsman. 2002. Signed article by John Swinney, SNP leader. "Patron Saint Should Promote Scotland," November 19.

Scottish Parliament. 1999. *Debate.* September 6.

Seiler, Daniel L. 1980. *Parties et Familles Politiques.* Paris: Presses Universitaires de France.

Sellers, Robert M., Mia A. Smith, J. Nicole Shelton, Stephanie A. J. Rowley, and Tabbye M. Chavous. 1998. "Multidimensional Model of Racial Identity: A Reconceptualization of African American Racial Identity," *Personality and Social Psychology Review*, 2, 1: 18–36.

Sen, Amartya. 2000. "Other People," *The New Republic*, December 18: 23.

Sendich, Munir and Emil Payin. 1994. *The New Russian Diaspora: Russian Minorities in the Former Soviet Republics.* Armonk, NY: Sharpe.

Shils, Edward. 1995. "Nation, Nationality, Nationalism and Civil Society," *Nations and Nationalism*, 1, 1: 93–118.

  1997. *The Virtue of Civility.* Indianapolis, IN: Liberty Fund.

Shore, Cris. 2000. *Building Europe: The Cultural Politics of European Integration.* New York: Routledge.

Sides, John and Jack Citrin. 2007. "European Opinion about Immigration: The Role of Identities, Interests and Information," *British Journal of Political Science*, 37, 3: 477–504.

Skov, Henrik. 2005. "No! to EU: Debate in Estonia," manila.djh.dk/Euestonia/stories.

Slovenian Public Relations and Media Office. 2006. "Development Minister Resigns after Just Three Months," www.uvi.si/eng/slovenia/publications/slovenia-news/3047/3048.

Small, Stephen and John Solomos. 2006. "Race, Immigration and Politics in Britain," *International Journal of Comparative Sociology*, 47, 3–4: 235–57.

Smith, Anthony D. 1991. *National Identity.* Reno: University of Nevada Press.

  1992. "National Identity and the Idea of European Unity," *International Affairs*, 68, 1: 55–76.

  1995. *Nations and Nationalism in a Global Era.* Cambridge, MA: Basil Blackwell.

Sniderman, Paul M. and Louk Hagendoorn. 2007. *When Ways of Life Collide.* Princeton, NJ: Princeton University Press.

Sniderman, Paul M., Louk Hagendoorn, and Markus Prior. 2004. "Predisposing Factors and Situational Triggers: Exclusionary Reactions to Immigrant Minorities," *American Political Science Review*, 98, 1: 35–49.

Sniderman, Paul M., Pierangelo Peri, Rui J. P. De Figueiredo, Jr., and Thomas Piazza. 2000. *The Outsider: Prejudice and Politics in Italy.* Princeton, NJ: Princeton University Press.

Soysal, Yasemin N. 2000. "Citizenship and Identity: Living in Diasporas in Post-War Europe?" *Ethnic and Racial Studies*, 23, 1: 1–15.

Spinelli, Barbara. 2005. "The End of Europe," in Daniel Levy, Max Pensky, and John Torpey, eds., *Old Europe, New Europe, Core Europe: Transatlantic Relations After the Iraq War*. London: Verso, 47–52.

Statistics Austria. 2007. "Migration," http://www.statistik.at/web_en/statistics/population/migration/index.html.

Staunton, Denis. 2000. "Haider Sparks off Fresh Controversy by Accusing Turks of Refusing to Integrate: Austria's New Government is Snubbed at Lisbon Meeting," *Irish Times*, February 15.

Steenbergen, Marco R., Erica E. Edwards, and Catherine E. De Vries. 2007. "Who's Cueing Whom? Mass-Elite Linkages and the Future of European Integration," *European Union Politics*, 8, 1: 13–35.

Steenbergen, Marco R. and Bradford S. Jones. 2002. "Modeling Multilevel Data Structures," *American Journal of Political Science*, 46, 1: 218–37.

Steenbergen, Marco R. and Gary Marks. 2007. "Evaluating Expert Surveys," *European Journal of Political Research*, 46, 3: 347–66.

Stojaspal, Jan. 2004. "Want Lower Taxes: Go East," *Time*, 11 July.

Stryker, Sheldon and Richard Serpe. 1994. "Identity Salience and Psychological Centrality: Equivalent, Overlapping or Complementary Concepts?" *Social Psychology Quarterly*, 57, 1: 16–35.

Surridge, Paula and David McCrone. 1999. "The 1997 Scottish Referendum Vote," in Bridget Taylor and Katarina Thomson, eds., *Scotland and Wales: Nations Again?* Cardiff: University of Wales Press, 41–64.

Swenden, Wilfried and Bart Maddens, eds. 2009. *Territorial Party Politics in Western Europe*. Basingstoke, UK: Palgrave.

Swidler, Ann. 1986. "Culture in Action: Symbols and Strategies," *American Sociological Review*, 51, 2: 273–86.

Swyngedouw, Marc, Koen Abts, and Maarten Van Craen. 2007. "Our Own People First in a Europe of Peoples: The International Policy of the Vlaams Blok," in Christina Schori Liang, ed., *Europe for the Europeans: The Foreign and Security Policy of the Populist Radical Right*. Hampshire, UK: Ashgate, 81–10.

Szczerbiak, Aleks and Paul Taggart, eds. 2008. *Opposing Europe? The Comparative Party Politics of Euroscepticism*. Oxford: Oxford University Press.

Taggart, Paul. 1998. "A Touchstone of Dissent: Euroscepticism in Contemporary Western European Party Systems," *European Journal of Political Research*, 33, 3: 363–88.

Tajfel, Henri. 1981. *Social Identity and Intergroup Behavior*. New York: Cambridge University Press.

Taras, Ray. 2009. *Europe Old and New: Transnationalism, Belonging, Xenophobia*. Lanham, MD: Rowman and Littlefield.

Tarchi, Marco. 2007. "Recalcitrant Allies: The Conflicting Foreign Policy Agenda of the Alleanza Nazionale and the Lega Nord," in Christina Schori Liang, ed., *Europe for the Europeans: The Foreign and Security Policy of the Populist Radical Right*. Hampshire, UK: Ashgate, 187–208.

Taylor, Bridget, John Curtice, and Katarina Thomson. 1999. "Introduction and Conclusions," in Bridget Taylor and Katarina Thomson, eds., *Scotland and Wales: Nations Again?* Cardiff: University of Wales Press, xxiii–xlii.

Tiesler, Nina Clara. 2009. Religião e pertença em discursos europeus: conceitos e agentes muçulmanos." *Análise Social*, 44, 190: 17–42.

Thiel, Markus. 2012. *The Limits of Transnationalism: Collective Identities and EU Integration*. New York: Palgrave.

Thomassen, Jacques. 2006. "European Citizenship and Identity," unpublished paper, http://www.ees-homepage.net/papers/lisbon/thomassen.pdf.

Thurner, Paul W. and Martin Binder. 2008. "European Union Transgovernmental Networks: The Emergence of a New Political Space beyond the Nation-State?" *European Journal of Political Research*, 48, 1: 80–106.

Tilly, Charles. 1975. "Reflections on the History of European State-Making," in Charles Tilly, ed., *The Formation of National States in Western Europe*. Princeton, NJ: Princeton University Press, 3–83.

Tizard, Barbara and Ann Phoenix. 1993. *Black, White or Mixed Race? Race and Racism in the Lives of Young People of Mixed Parentage*. London: Routledge.

Tronconi, Filippo. 2006. "Ethnic Identity and Party Competition: An Analysis of the Electoral Performance of Ethnoregionalist Parties in Western Europe," *World Political Science Review*, 2, 2, 137–63.

Turner, John, Michael Hogg, Penelope Oakes, Steven Reicher, and Margaret Wetherell. 1987. *Rediscovering the Social Group: A Self-Categorization Theory*. New York: Blackwell.

Türsan, Huri. 1998. "Introduction: Ethnoregionalist Parties as Ethnic Entrepreneurs," in Lieven De Winter and Huri Türsan, eds., *Regionalist Parties in Western Europe*. New York: Routledge.

University of North Carolina. 2012. "Political Parties: Chapel Hill Expert Survey" (CHES DATA). http://www.unc.edu/~hooghe/data_pp.php.

Urwin, Derek. 1983. "Harbinger, Fossil or Fleabite? Regionalism and the West European Party Mosaic," in Hans Daalder and Peter Mair, eds., *Western European Party Systems: Continuity and Change*. Beverly Hills, CA: Sage, 221–56.

Vaisse, Justin. 2008. "Muslims in Europe: A Short Introduction," *Center for the United States and Europe at Brookings*. Washington, DC: Brookings Institution, http://www.euc.illinois.edu/_includes/docs/muslims%20in%20europe-brookings.pdf.

Van Atta, Sydney. 2003. "Regional Nationalist Activism and the New Politics of Europe: A Comparison of the Bloque Nacionalista Galego and Plaid Cymru," *Regional & Federal Studies*, 13, 2: 30–56.

van Hamm, Peter. 2000. "Identity beyond the State: The Case of the European Union," Copenhagen Peace Research Institute Working Papers, June, http://www.ciaonet.org/wps/vap01/.

Van Houten, Pieter. 2003. "Globalization and Demands for Regional Autonomy in Europe," in Miles A. Kahler and David Lake, eds., *Governance in a Global Economy*. Princeton, NJ: Princeton University Press, 110–35.

    2007. "Regionalist Challenges to European States: A Quantitative Assessment," *Ethnopolitics*, 6, 4: 545–68.

Van Morgan, Sydney A. 2006. "Plaid Cymru – The Party of Wales: The New Politics of Welsh Nationalism at the Dawn of the 21st Century," in Lieven de Winter, Margarita Gómez-Reino and Peter Lynch, eds., *Autonomist Parties in Europe: Identity Politics and the Revival of the Territorial Cleavage*. Barcelona: Institut de Ciencies Polítiques i Socials (ICPS), 253–83.

Vasileva, Katya. 2009. "Citizens of European Countries Account for the Majority of the Foreign Population in EU-27 in 2008," *Eurostat*, Brussels: European Commission.

Vertovec, Steven. 2007. "Super-Diversity and Its Implications," *Ethnic and Racial Studies*, 30, 6: 1024–54.

Vincent, Andrew. 1997. "Liberal Nationalism: An Irresponsible Compound?" *Political Studies*, 45, 2: 75–295.

Von Beyme, Klaus. 1986. *Los partidos políticos en las democracias occidentales.* Madrid: CIS.

Wall Street Journal. 2008. "We're Not Headed for a Depression: No, this isn't the Crisis that Kills Global Capitalism," http://online.wsj.com/article/SB122333679431409639. html.

Wallace, William. 1990. *The Transformation of Western Europe*. London: Pinter RIIA.

Wallwork, Jodi and John A. Dixon. 2004. "Foxes, Green Fields and Britishness: On the Rhetorical Construction of Place and National Identity," *British Journal of Social Psychology*, 43, 1: 21–39.

Weßels, Bernhard. 2007. "Discontent and European Identity: Three Types of Euroscepticism," *Acta Politica*, 42, 2–3: 287–306.

Whitefield, Stephen D., Milada Anna Vachudova, Marco R. Steenbergen, Robert Rohrschneider, Gary Marks, Matthew P. Loveless, and Liesbet Hooghe. 2006. "Do Expert Surveys Produce Consistent Estimates of Party Stances on European Integration? Comparing Expert Surveys in the Difficult Case of Central and Eastern Europe," *Electoral Studies*, 26, 1: 50–61.

Wikipedia. 2010. "Islam in Europe," http://en.wikipedia.org/wiki/Islam_in_Europe.

Williams, Charlotte, Neil Evans, and Paul O'Leary, eds. 2003. *A Tolerant Nation? Exploring Ethnic Diversity in Wales*. Cardiff: University of Wales Press.

Williams, Michelle Hale. 2006. *The Impact of Radical Right-Wing Parties in Western Democracies*. New York: Palgrave.

Wintle, Michael. J. 2005. "European Identity: A Threat to the Nation?" *Europe's Journal of Psychology*, 1, 2: http://ejop.psychopen.eu/article/view/363/266.

Wittman, Donald. 2000. "The Wealth and Size of Nations," *Journal of Conflict Resolution*, 44, 6: 868–84.

Woldendorp, Jaap, Hans Keman, and Ian Budge. 1998. "Party Government in 20 Democracies: An Update (1900–1995)," *European Journal of Political Research*, 33, 1: 125–64.

Wright, Michelle. 2004. *Becoming Black: Creating Identity in the African Diaspora*. Durham, NC: Duke University Press.

Yiangou, George. 2001. "Analysing the Prospects of Forging an Overarching European Collective Identity," *Studies in Ethnicity and Nationalism*, 1, 2: 37–49.

Zaller, John. 1992. *The Nature and Origins of Mass Opinion*. New York: Cambridge University Press.

Zielonka, Jan. 2004. "Challenges of EU Enlargement," *Journal of Democracy*, 15, 1: 22–35.

Index